POOR
ATLANTA

POOR ATLANTA

POVERTY, RACE, AND THE LIMITS OF SUNBELT DEVELOPMENT

LeeAnn B. Lands

THE UNIVERSITY OF GEORGIA PRESS ▪ ATHENS

© 2023 by the University of Georgia Press
Athens, Georgia 30602
www.ugapress.org
All rights reserved

Designed by Kaelin Chappell Broaddus
Set in by 10/13 Miller Text Roman by Kaelin Chappell Broaddus

Most University of Georgia Press titles are
available from popular e-book vendors.

Printed digitally

Library of Congress Cataloging-in-Publication Data

Names: Lands, LeeAnn, 1967– author.
Title: Poor Atlanta : poverty, race, and the limits of Sunbelt development
    / LeeAnn B. Lands.
Description: Athens, Georgia : University of Georgia Press, [2023] |
    Includes bibliographical references and index.
Identifiers: LCCN 2022031516 | ISBN 9780820363295 (hardback) |
    ISBN 9780820363288 (paperback) | ISBN 9780820363271 (ebook)
Subjects: LCSH: Poverty—Georgia—Atlanta—History—20th century. |
    Poor—Political activity—Georgia—Atlanta—History—20th century.
    | Economic assistance, Domestic—Georgia—Atlanta—History—
    20th century. | Atlanta (Ga.)—Economic conditions—20th century. |
    Atlanta (Ga.)—Social conditions—20th century.
Classification: LCC HC108.A75 L36 2023 | DDC 330.9758/231—dc23/
    eng/20220818
LC record available at https://lccn.loc.gov/2022031516

for Ben

CONTENTS

CONTENTS

ACKNOWLEDGMENTS

I am grateful to archivists across the country who facilitated access to collections, especially during difficult circumstances, including staff at NARA-College Park, the Library of Congress, the Stuart A. Rose Manuscript, Archives, and Rare Book Library at Emory University, the Kenan Research Center at Atlanta History Center, the Robert W. Woodruff Library Archives at Atlanta University Center, the Wisconsin Historical Society at the University of Wisconsin, Special Collections at Georgia State University, and the Hargrett Rare Book & Manuscript Library at the University of Georgia. Staff in special collections departments at Georgia State University and Stanford University helped me track down obscure photographs, and Boyd Lewis and the Atlanta History Center allowed me to use Lewis's valuable collection of Atlanta photographs. Matthew Mitchelson generously lent his enthusiasm and cartographic skills to this project. I am particularly indebted to Kennesaw State University's ILL, GIL, and other library staff, who regularly rounded up difficult-to-access periodicals, historical documents, reports, finding aids, and other materials for me.

I am profoundly grateful to Jared Samples, who granted me access to the closed collection of his father, Rev. Cadmus A. Samples, at the Wisconsin Historical Society, and Representative James F. "Jim" Martin, who granted me use of his records at the University of Georgia prior to their opening date.

Several volunteers and activists associated with Emmaus House gave their time and insights, and I could not have told this story without them. Although I collected material and interviews from the institution's founding up to the present, I regret that I could only touch on Emmaus House's earliest years (1967 to 1976) in this book. My late father-in-law, Richard Hall, connected me with Emmaus House, and the Reverends Claiborne Jones and Elizabeth Roles facilitated access to the institution's personnel and records. Several Emmaus House staff and volunteers from the 1960s and early 1970s sat for interviews, including Mimi Bodell, Silva Griggs Britt, Jeanne Brown, Johnnie Brown, Clinton Deveaux, Samuel Dimon,

Debbie Shields Erdmanczyk, Tom Erdmanczyk, Gene Ferguson, Rev. Austin Ford, Charles "Tony" Foster, Dennis Goldstein, Margaret Griggs, May Helen Johnson, Alex Kotlowitz, David Morath, Charlotta Norby, Ray Quinnelly, Patricia Royalty, Herman Shackleford, Gregg Smith, Albert "Ned" Stone, Grace Stone, Susan Taylor, Columbus Ward, and Dee Weems. Many others shared their memories and experiences with me, and they are identified at www.thepeoplestownproject.com.

I appreciate the colleagues who provided thoughtful comments on earlier papers, conference presentations, and articles that informed *Poor Atlanta*, including Thomas A. Scott, Robbie Lieberman, Jim Martin, Randall L. Patton, Kerwin C. Swint, Edward Hatfield, Brennan Collins, Rhonda Williams, and Annelise Orleck. I likewise thank the reviewers for the University of Georgia Press for their close reading, support, and recommendations.

Various programs and offices at Kennesaw State University provided funding and in-kind support to help me complete this project. They include the American Studies program, the Department of History and Philosophy, the Norman J. Radow College of Humanities and Social Sciences, and the Center for Excellence in Teaching and Learning. The Peoplestown and Emmaus House elements of this work were also financially supported by an American Studies Association Community Partnership grant. Several undergraduate and graduate students and KSU staff members assisted in the oral history and research components of this work. Many thanks to Kendall Albert, Alexandria Arnold, Dionne Blassingame, Rachel Cronin, Callie Dodd, Kaley Harper, Nancy Hill, Janet McGovern, Cherie Miller, Anna Golden, Crystal Money, Steven Satterfield, Chris Smith, Stephanie McKinnell Tomlin, and Gayle Wheeler. I am particularly indebted to Tyler Crafton-Karnes, Gwendelyn Ballew, and Annie Moye, who worked with me on multiple research projects.

I am many years out of school, but as I worked on this book, I found myself regularly recalling discussions with and insights provided by my former instructors, including Ron Bayor, Larry Keating, Mark Rose, and particularly Ray Mohl. As I completed my MA, Mohl, who had previously written on poverty, was penning and editing new historical analysis of Sunbelt development and assigning the latest Sunbelt works to his seminars. I doubt I would have broached this topic without that background.

Portions of the manuscript previously appeared in LeeAnn Lands, "Lobbying for Welfare in a Deep South State Legislature in the 1970s," *Journal of Southern History* 84 (August 2018): 653–96. The Southern Historical Association has graciously allowed me to use that material here.

ABBREVIATIONS

ACPL	Atlanta Civic and Political League
ACLU	American Civil Liberties Union
ACRC	All Citizens Registration Committee
AFDC	Aid to Families with Dependent Children
AFSCME	American Federation of State, County, and Municipal Employees
AHA	Atlanta Housing Authority
AHC	Kenan Research Center, Atlanta History Center Archives, Atlanta
ALAS	Atlanta Legal Aid Society
AME	African Methodist Episcopal
ANVL	Atlanta Negro Voters League
AUC	Robert W. Woodruff Library Archives, Atlanta University Center, Atlanta
CACUR	Citizen Advisory Committee on Urban Renewal
CAP	community action program
CCA	Committee of Concerned Agencies
CCAA	Community Council of the Atlanta Area, Inc.
CCAC	Citizens Central Advisory Council
CNAC	citizens neighborhood advisory council
CRC	Community Relations Commission
DFACS	Division of Family and Children Services
DHR	Department of Human Resources
EOA	Atlanta–Fulton County Economic Opportunity Authority; later Economic Opportunity Atlanta
EOC	Economic Opportunity Authority
ESH	Experiments in Self-Help
FDA	Food and Drug Administration
FHA	Federal Housing Administration
GLBC	Georgia Legislative Black Caucus
GPRO	Georgia Poverty Rights Organization

GSU	Georgia State University
HEW	Department of Health, Education, and Welfare
HRC	Housing Resource Committee
HUD	Department of Housing and Urban Development
KKK	Ku Klux Klan
IADA	Ivan Allen Digital Archive, Georgia Institute of Technology, Atlanta
LOC	Library of Congress, Washington, D.C.
MACS	Metropolitan Atlanta Community Services
NAACP	National Association for the Advancement of Colored People
NAHRO	National Association of Housing and Redevelopment Officials
NARA	National Archives and Records Administration, College Park, Maryland
NASH	neighborhood bounded by Northside Drive, Ashby Street, Simpson Street, and Hunter Street
NCC	Negro Citizens Committee
NWRO	National Welfare Rights Organization
OEO	Office of Economic Opportunity
PPC	Poor People's Campaign: A National Call for Moral Revival
PPN	*Poor People's Newspaper*
PRO	Poverty Rights Office
RMARBL	Stuart A. Rose Manuscript, Archives, and Rare Book Library, Emory University, Atlanta
SCLC	Southern Christian Leadership Conference
SNCC	Student Nonviolent Coordinating Committee
SRC	Southern Regional Council
TUFF	Tenants United for Fairness
USGPO	United States Government Printing Office
VCC	Vine City Council
VCV	*Vine City Voice*
VISTA	Volunteers in Service to America
WSMDC	West Side Mutual Development Committee

POOR ATLANTA

INTRODUCTION

"Atlanta: A new kind of city," ads declared in magazines throughout the country in the early 1960s.[1] It was "the commercial, industrial and financial dynamo of the Southeast," the city's chamber of commerce asserted as part of Forward Atlanta, the campaign launched in 1961 to attract business and promote "a favorable image for the city."[2] The initiative was a success. Media outlets throughout the country pitched Atlanta. Georgia's capital was "the nation's newest boom town," *Time* magazine gushed in 1962.[3] It was the only *national city* in the Southeast, stories noted. But it was "in fast company," acknowledged Edward D. Smith, president of First National Bank and chair of the booster initiative. Atlanta needed to "develop big plans, dramatic plans" to stay ahead.[4]

The city's skyline was certainly changing. The thirty-one-story Bank of Georgia building went up in the early 1960s, as did the twenty-story Georgia Power building, the twenty-story Commerce Building, and the twenty-two-story Merchandise Mart. Indeed, Atlanta seemed perpetually under construction. Workers cut new expressways through and around downtown. A rapid transit system was in the works.[5] Leaders plotted a new terminal for Atlanta's airport and considered pursuing international traffic.[6] And the city was on the market for national sports franchises. A new $18 million baseball stadium, built on urban renewal land, would open just south of downtown in 1965. The city even touted its race relations. "No major Southern city has managed to integrate its Negroes so well and so smoothly," *Time* magazine reported.[7] The city was poised to be a major metropolitan center in the nation's blossoming Sunbelt, the term coined for the states along the U.S. southern border. Known for its sunny and warm climate, the region had, since the 1960s, experienced a

TABLE 1. Atlanta poverty, families

	1959			1969			1979		
	All income levels	Number below poverty	Percent below poverty	All income levels	Number below poverty	Percent below poverty	All income levels	Number below poverty	Percent below poverty
In Atlanta city limits	120,464*	29,177†	24.2†		19,023†	15.9†	98,457‡	23,358‡	23.7‡

* = U.S. Census Bureau, Census of Population, 1960: Supplementary Reports, *Poverty Areas in the 100 Largest Metropolitan Areas* PC(S1)-54), table 1.

† = U.S. Census Bureau, Census of Population, 1970: Supplementary Reports, *Poverty Status in 1969 and 1959 of Persons and Families, for States, SMSAs, Central Cities, and Counties* (PC(S1)-105), table 8.

‡ = U.S. Census Bureau, Census of Population, 1980: Subject Reports. *Poverty Areas in Large Cities* (PC80-2-8D), table 2.

population surge and economic growth in defense, technology, tourism, oil, agriculture, and the service industries.[8] Atlanta was *on its way*.

This is a story familiar to many.[9]

Less well known is the story of those who, while Atlanta's business and political leadership pursued their urban dreams and Sunbelt fantasies, faced down Atlanta's seemingly entrenched poverty.[10] Many neighborhoods in the older, central areas of Atlanta were in decline, including Summerhill, Bedford-Pine, Vine City and Lightning, Mechanicsville, Pittsburgh, and Peoplestown. Some areas lacked adequate sewage systems, and in some sections, streets flooded regularly. Hunger persisted. Housing was overcrowded. In 1959, the year 1960 census data was gathered, 24.2 percent of Atlanta's families lived in poverty (see table 1). Many poor residents questioned the city's priorities. "There is a crisis in low rent housing in this city," residents of the near northwest neighborhood Vine City pointed out in February 1966. Yet "our city is more interested in 18 million dollar stadiums than it is in decent housing for the poor."[11] As Atlanta's leaders fashioned a new city, Atlanta's poor joined with others distressed by persistent poverty to insist that poor families' lot should improve too. Across Atlanta, poor residents and allies organized and mobilized to confront high rents, urban development programs that bulldozed neighborhoods, low pay, poor housing conditions, inconsistently delivered city services, dangerous work conditions, welfare programs and wages that left families in poverty, lack of transparency in government programs and services, and discrimination. Using a range of techniques—petitions, lawsuits, pickets, sleep-ins, walkouts, and lobbying—poor people and antipoverty activists exposed policies and practices that robbed families of opportunity.

Poor Atlanta: Poverty, Race, and the Limits of Sunbelt Development examines the history of antipoverty organizing and related work in Atlanta from 1946 to 1976, as the city shifted status from southern regional hub to Sunbelt metropolitan area bent on becoming "the world's next great city."[12] As Atlanta experienced Sunbelt growth and pursued standing as a national (then international) city, an antipoverty movement emerged that exposed and continually highlighted the city's persistent poverty and deterioration. Despite significant hurdles and threats, the movement and campaigns became more sophisticated and durable over the period of study. City leaders, who themselves had initiated their own workforce development and antipoverty program in the early 1960s, were dismayed with the disruptive tactics of some antipoverty organizers, but their desire to build a thriving city and to reduce the possibility of urban violence encouraged them to respond to poor people's demands, though not always in productive ways. As the book details, a variety of personnel contributed to antipoverty campaigns and work in this period, demonstrating that beyond poor activists, agency heads, bureaucrats, attorneys, political and business interests, labor leaders, faith leaders and congregants, white liberals, and civil rights workers at times facilitated and catalyzed antipoverty work.

Poor Atlanta joins a growing body of scholarship documenting antipoverty movements in the late twentieth century. A number of historical studies have explored particular domains of antipoverty work—welfare rights organizing, tenant movements within public housing—or examined the implementation of federal programs such as the War on Poverty in specific cities and states.[13] Such studies have revealed oppressive, coercive social service systems, as well as attempts at and methods of grassroots organizing. Several authors have explored tactics used to address welfare concerns and tenant challenges, confirming sociologists Frances Fox Piven and Richard Cloward's conclusions that disruption was a particularly useful tool for marginalized populations such as welfare mothers.[14] Collectively these case studies indicate that antipoverty movements were about more than protecting or expanding entitlement benefits or securing safe and affordable housing. Such actions promoted citizenship, democracy, and self-determination.[15] Still, while many monographs began as case studies of particular domains of antipoverty work, a number of studies reveal that there were often no hard distinctions between, say, welfare rights and tenant rights organizing; those involved saw those movements as interconnected. For example, welfare rights organizing and actions to address problems in public housing were both part of the work of mothering and family care.[16]

A number of studies have connected antipoverty work to other social justice movements, including with the Black freedom, feminist, and labor movements.[17] Antipoverty organizing was not exclusively an African American phenomenon, but such work and actions can be seen as part of the *long civil rights movement* (LCRM), a more expansive trajectory of pro-democracy actions that began in the 1930s. The LCRM continued after 1968 as a "movement of movements" informed and inspired by the classical phase of the civil rights movement.[18] Importantly, reconsideration of the civil rights movement and its most well-known leader, Martin Luther King Jr., has resulted in new studies of economic justice organizing, which included campaigns for equitable wages, a right to basic subsistence, and affordable housing.[19] In a similar vein, scholars have exposed intersections between civil rights and labor organizing.[20] And while scholars have identified how myriad campaigns expressed shared values, historians have also demonstrated how movements emerged and unfolded in unique, local circumstances. Community-specific circumstances influenced who fought poverty and why and the methods they deployed.[21]

Given other authors' findings that social justice movements tended to be interconnected and that local circumstances regularly dictated the who, when, why, and where of different campaigns and actions, I decided to examine the broad array of antipoverty actions that surfaced in a single city, in this case, Atlanta, Georgia. That is, rather than focusing on a particular domain of antipoverty organizing or the implementation of federal policies such as the War on Poverty in a particular locale, I use a historical framework to explain how a variety of antipoverty actions and work played out across Atlanta. This approach allowed me to document the various forms antipoverty organizing took, the different personnel involved, and the variety of tactics used. I could see how and when different campaigns emerged and how they did or did not interact. And I could explore how antipoverty work related to other movements. This approach also allowed me to assess geographic factors. For example, was a campaign reliant on a neighborhood network? Or did it form around a common workplace issue? This citywide framing has proved particularly revealing.

For one, the citywide frame exposes new precursors to antipoverty activism: in the 1940s and 1950s, the expansion of Black voting rights, organizing in poor neighborhoods in response to urban renewal, the actions of the (predominantly Black) civic league movement, and, in the early 1960s, the support and activities of the Student Nonviolent Coordinating Committee (SNCC) helped establish an apparatus from which later antipoverty actions could be mounted. Additionally, in the early 1960s, well-heeled Atlantans attempted to counter poverty and "dependence" and develop a stable workforce by establishing neighborhood service centers, a project that would wind up serving as the foundation for the city's community action program (CAP). As the book shows, diminishing poverty and improving workforce development was seen by city elite as a component of the larger quest for Sunbelt prominence and leaders' goal of becoming "the world's next great city."[22] These actions were antecedents to the city's War on Poverty.

Additionally, by looking at antipoverty work citywide, this study exposes the broad range of personnel involved in diminishing poverty. Although a number of historical works have sought to recover the voices of poor activists, I am concerned with the broader group of actors and groups who attempted to counter poverty.[23] As the book reveals, participants in Atlanta's antipoverty movement, particularly in its peak period from 1964 to 1976, included poor people themselves, who, in Atlanta, were disproportionately Black, as well as public interest attorneys, white liberals who pursued a variety of social causes over their lifetime, labor leaders, religious leaders and congregants, civil rights leaders and organizations, and nonprofit volunteers and staff. I also consider the activities of politicians; business leaders engaged in civic initiatives; county, city, and state agency directors; and agency board members, as it became clear that many of these personnel influenced antipoverty work. To be sure, Atlanta's business and political leaders did not seek to upend the established social order, and they would not put their power or position at risk, but they made efforts to stabilize Atlanta families and provide the education, skills development, and social services necessary to create an able workforce. By examining the actions and motivations of the larger pool of personnel and organizations responsible for antipoverty work, we better understand how poor and near-poor Atlantans were politicized, what motivated nonpoor supporters and participants, the ways in which organizations committed to and helped sustain organizing and protest movements, the modes by which expectations for economic equity and justice diffused through the larger social fabric, and how a larger, more durable antipoverty movement emerged.

The citywide frame also reveals that Black sociopolitical leadership, which included social and business elite and members of the civil rights establishment, were ambivalent about poverty and economic justice matters, in part because, as city and civil rights leaders, they had other goals that they prioritized. Consequently, in the period under study, the city's Black elite proved to be unreliable partners in antipoverty work.[24] As a result of these divisions, Black poverty activists would embrace an identity as "poor folks," break with the city's Black elite, and organize independently of the city's local civil rights establishment. This was not a lasting schism or sharp break, though; the Southern Christian Leadership Conference (SCLC), which did not tend to organize within Atlanta while its founder and leader Martin Luther King Jr. was alive, continued to develop an economic justice focus and helped lead antipoverty actions in partnership with low wage workers and public housing tenants.

A citywide frame also exposes that while some civil rights leaders and entities were ambivalent about addressing poverty, Atlanta's public sector workers leveraged their economic circumstances and the city's desires for national status to demand improved wages, better benefits, and safer working conditions. As city leaders pursued recognition as a "national" city, garbage workers in particular consistently reminded bureaucrats and elected officials that garbage workers were critical frontline workers in the city's quest to attract tourists, corporate headquarters, and new industry. Consequently, like some recent studies, *Poor Atlanta* exposes how multiple movements intersected in the 1960s and 1970s as the rights revolution unfolded.

In looking at the various strands of antipoverty organizing that took place across the city, it becomes clear that antipoverty organizing accelerated in relationship to larger Sunbelt city-building efforts. Residents, including the poor, were acutely aware of city leaders' vision to develop a bigger, better city. And they knew how such efforts had played out before: unkept promises and bulldozed neighborhoods. Thus, in actions small and large, not always well planned and not always with articulated goals, poor Atlantans and their allies responded to Sunbelt initiatives, in some cases reacting to announced city-led plans and in other cases leveraging city leaders' desires as a way of demanding improvements.

Finally, the citywide frame makes clear that while the larger public did not necessarily label or refer to this set of actions and campaigns as an *antipoverty movement*, in its peak period, antipoverty campaigns were visible and occurred with regularity. From 1964 to 1976, there was a persistent, audible critique of policies and practices that had resulted in and entrenched poverty, inequality, and urban despair. The multiple, overlapping antipoverty actions of those years involved a range of people and entities who demanded that leaders and institutions act to relieve poverty and its attendant conditions. Although this movement's peak occurred as the national economy shifted from "the affluent society" to an era of dislocation and economic stagnation in the 1970s, antipoverty organizing did not *only* reflect growing economic instability of that period; rather, those actions built on and exposed deep frustration with larger economic and social structures that failed to address poverty and that preserved (and in cases exacerbated) inequality.

Poverty in Atlanta

Atlanta certainly endured its share of poverty throughout the twentieth century. For decades, the city and state, like the South as a whole, had collected few taxes, and consequently services were thin, infrastructure de-

TABLE 2. Atlanta poverty, individuals

	1959			1969			1979		
	All income levels	Number below poverty	Percent below poverty	All income levels	Number below poverty	Percent below poverty	All income levels	Number below poverty	Percent below poverty
In Atlanta city limits	487,455*	§	26§	484,055‡	98,612‡	20.4†	409,424†	112,581†	27.5†
SMSA‡	998,788‡	235,362‡	23.6‡	1,368,826‡	160,689‡	11.7‡	1,995,687‡	243,060†	12.2†

* = 1960 data drawn from U.S. Census Bureau, *Census of Population, 1960*, vol. 1, *Characteristics of the Population, by Census Tracts*, table P-1.

† = 1970 and 1980 data drawn from U.S. Census Bureau, CPH-L-192 Poverty Status in 1969, 1979, and 1989 of Persons by Central City Status, for Standard Metropolitan Statistical Areas Having Central Cities with a 1990 population of 250,000 or more.

‡ = Persons below the poverty level in 1969 and 1959 by race, for Standard Metropolitan Statistical Areas, table 5, U.S. Census Bureau, *Census of Population, 1970: Supplementary Report, Poverty Status in 1969 and 1959 of Persons and Families, for States, SMSA's, Central Cities, and Counties*, Series PC(s-1).

§ = The 1959 census did not count individuals in poverty. The 1966 Atlanta Community Improvement report, which used data from the 1959 census, cited Atlanta's poverty rate (of individuals) as 26 percent. It is possible the report authors simply utilized the family poverty rate from that year, which was based on the number of families living on incomes below $3000/year.

TABLE 3. Persons by poverty status in 1959, 1969, and 1979 by state, U.S. South

	Percent below poverty, 1959	Percent below poverty, 1969	Percent below poverty, 1979
United States	22.1	13.7	12.4
Alabama	42.5	25.4	18.9
Arkansas	47.5	27.8	19.0
Florida	28.4	16.4	13.5
Georgia	39.0	20.7	16.6
Louisiana	39.5	26.3	18.6
Mississippi	54.5	35.4	23.9
North Carolina	40.6	20.3	14.8
South Carolina	45.4	23.9	16.6
Tennessee	39.3	21.8	16.5
Texas	31.7	18.8	14.7
Virginia	30.6	15.5	11.8

SOURCE: U.S. Census Bureau, *Persons by Poverty Status in 1959, 1969, 1979, 1989, and 1999*, CPH-L-162, https://www.census.gov/data/tables/time-series/dec/cph -series/cph-l/cph-l-162.html.

velopment was slow, and economic and social development lagged other parts of the country.[25] During the Great Depression, poverty deepened and widened. New Deal programs helped ease some of the worst conditions, and many of those programs became fixtures in American life, including old-age benefits and Aid to Dependent Children. The South remained particularly disadvantaged, and in 1959, the year 1960 census data was actually gathered, nearly half—48.4 percent—of America's poor lived in the South (see table 2).[26] Georgia was not the poorest of the Deep South states, but its families suffered; that same year, Georgia counted 39 percent of its population as below poverty (see table 3).

In fact, as journalists discovered, poverty had lingered throughout the nation, and in 1959 just over 22 percent of the United States qualified as poor.[27] To many, that poverty rate was startling. The United States had just enjoyed unprecedented economic growth and was the world's largest economy. The nation was "the affluent society," as economist John Kenneth Galbraith asserted in his 1958 best seller. In another best-selling work, *The Other America* (1962), Michael Harrington described the irony that in the United States, poverty occurred not just in isolated instances; rather, the country suffered significant poverty amidst plenty. There had been an assumption that "the basic grinding economic problems had been solved in the United States."[28] Americans were surprised to find that was not the case.

Atlanta's poverty was at least in part due to continued in-migration from rural areas. To many rural poor, Atlanta was a beacon; it attracted mill workers hoping for better and regular wages and farmworkers fleeing oppressive sharecropping relationships. Atlanta held promise for jobs and a better life. It was a transportation nexus, a processor of the region's resources, and a regional financial hub. And, in the 1940s, it joined other cities as a war production center. Jobs seemed plentiful, though wages, working hours, and benefits (if any) may not have been all that workers hoped. Newspapers and other publications regularly commented on the migrant influx, especially in war years. Into the 1950s, the mechanization of farm work continued to drive farmworkers to cities and other industrial areas.[29] Whereas Georgia was majority rural in 1950, by 1960 over half the state's population lived in urban areas.[30] In 1959, the city of Atlanta was home to about 487,000 people, and about 125,000 lived below poverty.[31]

In post–World War II Atlanta, poverty remained closely intertwined with race: African Americans suffered poverty disproportionately.[32] Whereas 12.9 percent of Atlanta's white families lived below poverty in 1959, 46.3 percent of Black families did; 65 percent of Atlanta's poor families had a Black head of household.[33] Racial disparities meant that Black families tended to be confined to areas suffering poverty too, whether the families were poor or not. Whereas just under 26 percent of white families resided in poverty areas in Atlanta in 1959, 77.4 percent of Black families lived in poor areas.[34]

The difference in poverty levels between Blacks and whites resulted from the legacy of discrimination of whites against Blacks. African Americans were excluded from particular jobs and from acquiring particular job skills. They were prevented from advancing to supervisory roles, and they were regularly paid less than whites for equivalent work. As a result, many Black individuals and families did not accrue wealth (including property) at the same rates as whites, which affected family opportunities for generations. African Americans also had fewer means of accumulating savings for retirement, as Social Security taxes were not initially collected on positions historically dominated by Blacks. Many agricultural workers, service workers, and household workers, for example, were exempted from Social Security.[35] Additionally, exclusion of Blacks from particular neighborhoods and particular schools limited job opportunities and long-term educational gains that would improve wages and class mobility. The effects of such practices were cumulative and stifled African American achievement—as compared to whites—for generations.[36]

By the late twentieth century, then, poverty was well entrenched in the South and Atlanta. It would take persistent effort to shift resources and deliver real opportunities in education, housing, and employment. In Atlanta, the impetus to address poverty drew from several sources and evolved and grew over many years.

How the Story Unfolds

As a historical work, *Poor Atlanta* is organized chronologically and thematically. Material and chapters highlight neighborhoods in which antipoverty organizing was concentrated (e.g., Vine City), issues around which people organized (e.g., neighborhood conditions, welfare, housing rights), and entities that worked to reduce poverty and produce cultural change (e.g., Georgia Poverty Rights Organization). Approached in this way, the chapters reveal campaigns, organizations, and work that surfaced over time and across the city.

Poor Atlanta begins by describing precursors to the antipoverty movements of the 1960s and 1970s, which included the expansion of voting rights and voter registration efforts in the 1940s and 1950s, the related birth and growth of Atlanta's neighborhood civic councils over that same period, organized citizen responses to urban renewal in the 1950s, and the Student Nonviolent Coordinating Committee's 1963 campaign on Atlanta's south side. These activities boosted democratic interest and action and provided infrastructure useful to later antipoverty campaigns.

Chapter 2 describes how, prior to the announcement of the federal War on Poverty and associated CAP, Atlanta's white business and civic elite built a social welfare planning apparatus to fight poverty and help cultivate a healthy and stable workforce—a workforce that would allow city builders to realize their vision of urban prominence. When the War on Poverty was announced in 1964, civic leaders saw an opportunity to dramatically expand their project into a community action agency. As was the case in cities throughout the country, local elites resisted the "maximum feasible participation" of the poor in the operation of the city's community action agency. For their part, Atlanta's Black sociopolitical elite insisted on substantive *Black* involvement in the community action agency's upper administration. In instances where poor residents were involved in community action planning, they took their duties seriously, and poor Atlantans would continue to remind officials of federal requirements for the "maximum feasible participation" of the poor.

Chapter 3 documents grassroots organizing activities in Vine City. The

Vine City neighborhood's apparent despair as well as the presence of vocal, disgruntled residents made the area attractive to outside organizations including the Southern Regional Council (SRC) and the Student Nonviolent Coordinating Committee. By 1965, frustrated that the city's CAP was not providing more support, residents cultivated a collective identity as poor people and organized to force concessions from city officials on several points. SNCC attempted to ramp up neighborhood activism through their Atlanta Project, but the organization soon succumbed to internal pressures and folded. Despite setbacks, local organizing persisted, and residents continued applying pressure through the Vine City Council (VCC). Vine City's experience was, in many ways, typical of community organizing experiments of the era. "Bread and butter" concerns remained prevalent, and activists' reach was limited to the neighborhood.

Chapter 4 describes the further development of Atlanta's community action agency, which to many appeared in disarray. Target area residents continued to assert that they were not sufficiently involved in program planning and development. Although Black sociopolitical elite had successfully landed positions on the community action agency's board of directors, they did not appear to be acting in poor families' interest. Consequently, in 1966 and 1967, leaders of civic councils representing some of Atlanta's poorer sections increasingly rejected the leadership of Black leaders and organized as the Atlanta Grass Roots Crusade. Ultimately, the CAP could not suppress residents' frustration with urban decay, high rents, segregation, and police brutality, and violence would break out in Summerhill and Boulevard in 1966 and Dixie Hills in 1967.

Chapter 5 describes the rapid acceleration of antipoverty activity in the late 1960s and early 1970s, when welfare organizing surfaced and sanitation workers struck to improve pay and conditions. Introduced to the philosophies of welfare rights by national organizers in 1967, Atlanta's welfare mothers mobilized to insist on greater transparency in social welfare operations, more robust grants, and greater courtesy and respect. Importantly, besides having a national network from which to draw ideas and inspiration, welfare clients had a growing constellation of institutions and professionals to partner with locally, including Atlanta Legal Aid Society, which shifted from service provision to reform law, and Emmaus House, which provided space and various resources for poor Atlantans and those who sought to catalyze social change. Overlapping welfare rights organizing, in 1968, city garbage workers declared a wildcat strike, partnered with the local civil rights apparatus, and insisted on a number of reforms that would help stabilize poor and near-poor public workers.

In 1970, though, garbage workers had less success. That year they struck to improve wages and benefits, and city leaders responded by stripping the union of the little strength it had. Not every antipoverty action was a victory, but by the late 1960s, antipoverty organizing in Atlanta had become multilayered, utilized multiple tactics, and was more durable.

Chapter 6 describes how poor Atlantans and other activists confronted housing challenges in public housing and with the Model Cities program. In the late 1960s and early 1970s, as welfare rights organizing grew and the sanitation workers struck, Atlanta endured a full-on housing crisis that was caused in part by the city's reluctance to replace housing demolished in slum clearance projects. Interstate construction, urban renewal, and stadium building worsened an already-tight housing market, and Atlanta leaders proclaimed ambitious housing goals that they struggled to realize, even with additional federal funding. The Model Cities program was not an antipoverty or housing program as such, but residents looked to it to address the city's low-income housing need. But leaders stumbled through Model Cities implementation, relocating tenants to substandard housing and exacerbating dissatisfaction with the city and urban development programs. Public housing offered no relief. Most public housing communities were full, and public housing had its own frustrations for tenants. In response, Model Neighborhood and public housing tenants organized. Model Neighborhood residents insisted that they be involved in program planning and that the city live up to its housing commitments. Public housing tenants formed Tenants United for Fairness (TUFF) and worked with allies to demand a tenants' bill of rights and other improvements.

In the last chapter, *Poor Atlanta* describes how, even while the direct action techniques adopted by many civil rights, welfare, labor, tenant organizations, and civic councils would continue to have potency, some goals had remained elusive, in part because some demands required a change in law. Indeed, welfare activists in particular had been regularly deflected by welfare administrators who pointed out that activists' demands could only be achieved by legislative action. In response, welfare activists augmented protest politics by mounting lobbying and public information campaigns intended to influence state-level policy affecting poor people. Welfare lobbyists were successful in their first major battle, which energized welfare activists and opened the door for future increases in monthly welfare grants.

Certainly, 1976 was not the conclusion of antipoverty organizing in Georgia's capital, but the movement shifted in the late 1970s as the decade's economic downturn reduced family incomes and government coffers, conservatism increasingly influenced national policy, and other urban problems complicated grassroots organizing. While poverty and related conditions had not been eliminated by 1976, the story of the movement's historical development, including its tactics, problems, evolution, challenges, and successes, can inform current efforts, provide context for ongoing problems and situations, and even foster hope that successes are possible.

INTRODUCTION

CHAPTER 1

Early Beginnings

On August 5, 1963, just over one week after Atlanta Mayor Ivan Allen Jr. testified in support of a federal public accommodations bill, 250 south Atlantans demonstrated at Atlanta's city hall and presented a thirteen-page set of grievances to Allen and city officials.[1] The neighborhoods south of downtown were not uniformly poor, but there were sections of poverty amid middle- and working-class homes. Some areas showed obvious neglect. Residents suffered lax housing code enforcement, problems with sewer systems, slow street maintenance, and inconsistent garbage collection. There were few medical services, parks, or recreational programs in the area. South Atlantans had complained about poor conditions and service issues before. To residents, well-off African Americans were partially to blame. "The wealthy Negro politicians clearly do not care about our needs," they said, "because they do not share our hardships." The August 1963 statement declared that they would no longer accept "evasion and delay" from city hall. They expected a positive response within two weeks. "We will no longer be ignored," they insisted.[2] The 1963 demonstration and formal set of demands resulted from long-simmering frustrations, but also a growing sense of power and self-efficacy among Atlanta's poorest residents.

From 1945 to 1963, three phenomena combined to raise poor Atlantans' expectations that Atlanta's urban regime would finally act on poor residents' complaints and neighborhood needs. First, challenges to voting laws in the mid-twentieth century allowed formerly disenfranchised Black Georgians an opportunity to influence policy decisions that affected their lives. In the 1940s and 1950s, Atlantans launched voter registration efforts and founded neighborhood-based civic organizations—

usually called civic councils or civic leagues—to a degree they had not previously. Such organizations promoted voting and action for social and political change that would potentially result in material improvements in residents' local communities. Second, those raised expectations encouraged residents to confront the worst effects of urban renewal, the federal program intended to eliminate slums and encourage carefully planned urban development. In Atlanta, as elsewhere, urban renewal activities had initially been used to bulldoze aging and dilapidated predominantly Black neighborhoods without providing sufficient replacement housing. However, the National Housing Act of 1954 set an important precedent in that it required citizen participation in the planning of government programs. Consequently Atlantans' expectations that the city would facilitate citizen participation in urban policy making grew further. Finally, in the early 1960s, the Student Nonviolent Coordinating Committee, which had been leading a local effort to racially desegregate public accommodations, sought to leverage the growing civic council movement by helping the South Atlanta Civic League organize and mobilize to improve local conditions. In this way, civic councils, the federal requirement for citizen participation in urban renewal planning, and SNCC's 1963 efforts to mobilize South Atlantans laid important groundwork for a larger antipoverty movement in the mid- and late-1960s.

Atlanta was awash in contradictions in the postwar 1940s and 1950s. It was a city on the move, and a city marked by poverty. As World War II was concluding, a September 1945 *Saturday Evening Post* piece was less than enthusiastic about Georgia's capital. Atlanta's downtown was "less attractive than Birmingham's" and "one of the easiest places in metropolitan America to get lost."[3] But by 1953, change was evident. That year another *Post* story explained that for many businesses, Atlanta was the place to be. The city hosted corporate leaders considering the Gate City for branch offices or national headquarters, and leaders pitched the city to federal officials planning to open regional units. Atlanta had no debt, and it was bulking up its infrastructure. The airport was one of the busiest in the country. The city boasted Coca-Cola and a growing Delta Airlines.[4] To Mayor William Hartsfield, Atlanta was the Showcase City of the South.[5] Still, the mayor and corporate and civic leaders dreamed of an even bigger and more significant city. But urban greatness would be a challenge given Atlanta's deficiencies.

The Geography of Poverty

After the devastation of the Civil War, Atlanta was forced to rebuild, and residents and leaders reconstituted the city's nexus of railroads, railroad shops, warehouses, textile mills, and manufacturers. Rural families fled poverty wages, debt, and backbreaking work as farm laborers and populated Atlanta's alleys and lowlands, hastily constructing shotgun houses and small duplexes or boarding at rooming houses. Over time, pockets of poverty became fixtures near the city's industrial sites and railroad shops.

Atlanta's poorest areas included central city neighborhoods such as the Old Fourth Ward (which included Buttermilk Bottom and Bedford-Pine), Techwood, Vine City and Lightning, Mechanicsville, Summerhill, Peoplestown, and Pittsburgh (see figs. 1 and 2).[6] Poverty in these areas could be severe. In 1959, one of the census tracts encompassing Vine City and Lightning, F0026, counted just under 60 percent of its population as poor. Census tract F0042, which encompassed a portion of West End, was 49 percent poor. The eastern section of Peoplestown counted 49 percent of its population as below the poverty line.[7] Atlanta's first comprehensive study of poverty and neighborhood blight described these sections as having varying degrees of economic dependency (reliance on government programs), high juvenile arrest rates, low health (which included high infant mortality), high levels of clearance and dislocation, low levels of education, high density, and high levels of divorce, separation, or single parenthood. Poor areas were usually marked by physical blight, which in Atlanta meant substandard structures, usually of two stories or fewer, and most (68 percent) were two units or fewer (see fig. 3).[8]

In the late 1950s and early 1960s, Atlanta's poor usually lived in one of three types of areas: readily identifiable clusters of what observers often referred to as slum housing; in individual homes or small swaths of housing scattered among working-class and lower-middle-class communities; or public housing communities. Clusters of slum housing included, for example, Buttermilk Bottom, to the city's northeast; Cabbagetown, to the city's southeast; and Lightning, to the city's west. Lightning abutted the industrial enterprises along Atlanta's railroad and near manufacturers, warehouses, trades, and such that surfaced on Marietta, Peters, and West Mitchell Streets. The neighborhood included the city's only crematory, and the section had a reputation for bootlegging and prostitution.[9] Buttermilk Bottom, just outside Atlanta's central business district to the northeast, housed hundreds of Black families in apartments, single-

FIGURE 1. Atlanta's lowest-income neighborhoods as documented for the city's Community Improvement Program, 1959. Although the study was published in 1966, it relied on 1959 U.S. census data for its income statistics. The lowest-income neighborhoods included English Avenue, Techwood, Vine City (and the adjacent Lightning), Mechanicsville, Summerhill, Peoplestown, and Pittsburgh. Based on Community Council of the Atlanta Area, Inc., "Social Report on Neighborhood Analysis: Atlanta Community Improvement Program," Atlanta, 1966. Created by Matt Mitchelson, 2021.

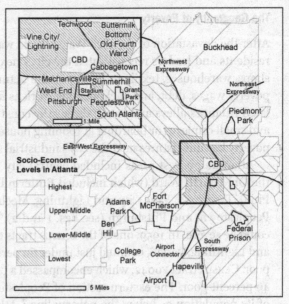

FIGURE 2. Atlanta in relationship to Georgia. Created by Matt Mitchelson, 2021.

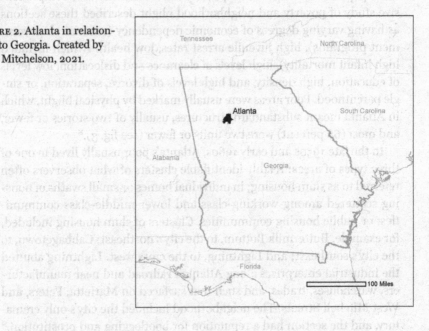

FIGURE 3. Housing just north of West End and the future site of the public housing community, John Hope Homes, c. 1940. Courtesy Atlanta Housing Authority Photographs, Kenan Research Center at the Atlanta History Center.

family homes, and duplexes (see fig. 4). While some streets in the section were paved, unpaved alleys and lanes ran behind many streets, increasing the neighborhood's density. Phoenix Alley, for example, between Piedmont and Butler, included eight small duplex units.[10] In a 1973 interview, former resident R. B. Jackson recalled the area as "very poorly built." Houses "didn't have good roofs," and, as a result, "it rained on the inside of them." Most "had toilets on the outside," and "some didn't have toilets at all."[11] In Cabbagetown, in the shadows of the Fulton Bag and Cotton Mill, cookie-cutter duplexes and single-family structures lined Reinhardt and Fenwick Streets and housed white working-class and poor residents.[12]

Poor families also lived in small clusters of housing within neighborhoods of working- and middle-class districts. Southeast Atlanta, for example, counted more than half its male workers as skilled, and the population was generally middle income. However, a high concentration of poverty could be found in Plunketown, in the southern-most reaches of Atlanta, next to the southern expressway.[13] There were no sewers in the neighborhood, few of the homes had water service, and, according to a 1966 Community Improvement Program report, the houses were "essentially shacks."[14] The average resident had not completed high school. Men tended to work in construction and industry, and the women were usually employed as domestics or in unskilled positions.[15]

FIGURE 4. Homes in Bedford Pine, c. 1971. Courtesy Bedford-Pine Neighborhood Photograph Collection, Kenan Research Center at the Atlanta History Center.

Atlanta's public housing communities, where rent subsidies helped reduce poverty to some degree, were also home to poor families.[16] Up to the 1950s, public housing had been built just outside the central business district. The first public housing complex in the nation, Techwood Homes, opened in 1936 just northwest of downtown.[17] Composed of two- and three-story apartments and townhomes in what architectural historians called a "modified Georgian" style, the community provided 604 units ranging from one to five rooms.[18] In this early wave of public housing construction, the new complexes often replaced districts of overcrowded, deteriorated housing. In Techwood's case, the new concrete units were built upon the twenty-plus acres formerly known as Techwood Flats. The Flats had no storm sewer, and journalists noted that the neighborhood flooded during every sudden rain. In at least one instance, the *Atlanta Constitution* reported, "firemen were summoned to rescue marooned families."[19]

In sum, in the late 1950s and early 1960s poor families could be found throughout much of central Atlanta—south, east, and west—either in neighborhoods of concentrated poverty, scattered among other working- and middle-class neighborhoods, or in public housing. Poor families rarely lived on Atlanta's north side. At one time zoned as "white" and still with large minimum lot sizes, poor families found few places to live in the wealthier confines of Buckhead and neighborhoods to the city's north. In 1959, of the city of Atlanta's 109 census tracts, 52 counted over 20 percent of families as living in poverty; 30 tracts had over 40 percent of families living in poverty.[20] Atlanta may have been an up-and-coming city, but it was home to many individuals and families who struggled to get by.

Political Power and the Black Establishment

In the 1940s and 1950s, Atlanta's poorer residents, particularly the city's Black poor, lacked the power necessary to influence urban development decisions that would directly benefit them. African Americans in the Jim Crow era were specifically barred from voting and suffered other discrimination, which meant they had limited residential options and suffered underfunded schools and health-care facilities. Those Black Georgians who could vote largely continued the historical trend of voting Republican—the party of Lincoln and "freedom"—though that was beginning to change as the Democratic Party considered new civil rights initiatives in the 1940s. But while Blacks were 34.6 percent of Atlanta's population in 1940 (34.7 percent of Georgia's), whites suppressed Black voting.[21] In 1945, Blacks represented only 4 percent of Atlanta's registered voters.[22] In particular, Georgia's poll tax stifled Black voter registration. The Democratic Party, acting as a private organization, limited "membership" to whites, and thus the "white primary" determined the final outcome of most elections. Not all whites could participate, though; poll taxes also dampened the registration of poor whites. Because access to the ballot was constrained, and the threat of violence loomed large for African Americans, poor families' voices were limited through much of the twentieth century. Despite these challenges, political and social expectations and norms would begin shifting in the 1940s.

Black voting power increased considerably in the 1940s and 1950s. Ellis Arnall, elected governor mid–World War II in 1943, broadened the franchise and eliminated the poll tax, potentially allowing thousands of poor and near-poor Georgians, Black and white, to vote.[23] African American organizations such as the National Association for the Advancement of Colored People (NAACP), the Atlanta Civic and Political League (ACPL), the *Atlanta Daily World*, and the All Citizens Registration Committee (ACRC) combined efforts with Black ministers to get out the vote in key 1940s elections. The *Smith* v. *Allright* (1944) and *King* v. *Chapman* (1946) court rulings eliminated the white primary, again opening up the opportunity for thousands to vote.[24]

But even while voter registration drives increased the raw number of Black voters in the late 1940s and early 1950s, other factors acted to dilute Black electoral strength in Atlanta.[25] In particular, Atlanta's 1952 Plan of Improvement strengthened white voting power. In that action, Atlanta annexed an additional eighty-one square miles, promising to increase government efficiency by reducing city-county service overlap. Because the annexed area included well-off, white suburban communities such as Buckhead, the plan brought more white voters into the city. To be sure, the Plan of Improvement was not *only* about maintaining a white majority city, but it did counter, at least to some degree, growing Black political power.[26]

Despite actions that had the effect of reducing Black voting strength, Black voting leagues worked to grow the Black vote, and leaders of those political organizations and the candidates they promoted grew in stature in Atlanta's Black community. As historian Alton Hornsby Jr. explains, by the end of the 1953 elections, it was clear that the Atlanta Negro Voters League (ANVL) was "a force to be reckoned with in city politics."[27] League leader John Wesley Dobbs and attorney A. T. Walden used bloc voting to ensure that candidates supported by the ANVL won in most races.[28] The league's work, for example, resulted in the election of Dr. Rufus E. Clement to the Atlanta Board of Education, the first Black since Reconstruction to hold elected office in Atlanta.[29]

The new board of education member and the political operatives became recognized members of Atlanta's Black establishment, the professional and social elite that led the Black community and worked with white political and business leaders to govern the city. Rufus Clement, president of Atlanta University, one of Atlanta's historically black colleges, was described by historian Isabel Wilkerson as the "tight-buttoned scion of the southern bourgeoisie" and a "distinguished accommodationist." He was typical of the "old guard" in Atlanta Black politics in that he would be uncomfortable with the sit-ins and direct action techniques of Atlanta's student-led civil rights movement from 1960 to 1961.[30] John Wesley Dobbs, an Atlanta native, had attended Morehouse College, another of Atlanta's historically Black colleges, and worked professionally as a railway mail clerk. He was committed to civic and fraternal affairs and was named Grand Master of the socially and politically important Prince Hall Masons beginning in 1932. A. T. Walden graduated from Atlanta

University and Michigan Law School, served in World War I, and then returned to Atlanta to practice law. He founded the Black Gate City Bar Association and served as counsel for a number of Atlanta's larger Black-owned companies. Like other Black community leaders, he devoted considerable time to political, fraternal, and philanthropic pursuits, including the Butler Street YMCA (a social and political center within Atlanta's Black community), the Atlanta NAACP, and the Atlanta Urban League. Like some other Black Atlantans, Walden made the shift from Republican to Democrat in the 1940s as the Democrats came to endorse civil rights. By 1957, as historian Alton Hornsby explains, Walden had become "a genuine political 'boss'—the single most influential politician in the New South."[31]

As leaders who created political power and benefited from it as Blacks increasingly made headway in the South's sociopolitical system in the 1940s and 1950, these men would later come to be seen as an older generation of leaders, traditional in their approach to civil rights as well as relations with Atlanta's white power structure. As they pursued these efforts, political leadership worked closely with neighborhood leaders to seed neighborhood-based civic leagues.

Voting Power to Civic Leagues

Citizens throughout Atlanta, including those in working-class, poor, and mixed-income neighborhoods, were increasingly politicized as voting rights expanded, in part because voting resulted in neighborhood improvements. Civic leagues became venues to voice such desires and work toward change. Such efforts were particularly evident in south Atlanta, though leagues were active throughout central Atlanta.[32]

Formed in 1951, the South Atlanta Civic League quickly attracted members from nearby communities, including Highpoint Apartments, Carver Homes, and Joyland Park.[33] South Atlanta (colloquially known as Brownsville in the late 1800s and early 1900s) was home to historically Black Clark University and Gammon Theological Seminary until the institutions moved to the west side in the 1940s, and single-family homes emerged along the mix of paved and unpaved streets south of the schools. The 452-unit Highpoint Apartments opened in 1950 in part to address the housing demand of the Black middle class.[34] Joyland Park, which broke ground in the 1920s, initially housed farmers, farmhands, and laborers, but by the 1950s the development was home to janitors, warehouse workers, drivers, domestic servants, and other unskilled and semiskilled workers.[35] The 990-unit Carver Community Apartments opened in 1953 across from Highpoint Apartments. The first public housing to be built since the conclusion of World War II, Carver prioritized veterans for the one- to four-bedroom units.[36] Drawing membership from these growing neighborhoods, by summer 1951 the South Atlanta Civic League counted over one hundred paid memberships.[37]

It is challenging to parse out the demographics and average household income of the individual neighborhoods that made up the South Atlanta Civic League—census tract lines do not align cleanly with neighborhood boundaries—but U.S. data from 1960 reveals that the tract encompassing Carver Homes and the neighborhood South Atlanta, F-55B, was 95 percent African American, with 58 percent of families living below $3,000 annually—the federally defined poverty threshold for that time.[38] The abutting neighborhoods of Highpoint, Joyland Park, and Lakewood Heights (F-67) were collectively about 43 percent Black, with 24 percent of families qualifying as poor.[39] Atlanta city planning maps indicate that Highpoint and Joyland Park were predominantly African American, while areas around Lakewood Park were predominantly white.[40] While slightly less than the city's poverty rate of 26.6 percent, the proportion of poor families in the area was high.[41]

Civic leagues allowed residents to keep up-to-date on neighborhood plans, but they also were organizations through which neighborhood power could be leveraged. In March 1955, for example, Atlanta street engineer Roy Nixon detailed street-paving plans for areas within and abutting Joyland Park, and in March 1955 the league arranged a meeting with alderman Charlie Leftwich "concerning the problems of the area."[42] Faced with distant voting sites, the league lobbied for a new precinct.[43] After precinct 1 was established in fall 1955 (which included Highpoint Apartments, the Joyland subdivision, and Carver Community Apartments), the league pledged to strengthen the nascent voting district by registering two thousand new voters.[44] *Atlanta Daily World* writer Thaddeus Stokes described the September 1956 meeting as having an "enthusiastic audience," and the three hundred attendees were treated to a vigorous debate between state representative candidates.[45] The league also lobbied for service improvements. League president L. D. Simon explained to *Atlanta Daily World* readers that the South Atlanta Civic League committee had "made a strong appeal" to Alderman Leftwich about acquiring land for a park.[46] South Atlanta's political activity paid off, at least to some extent. Leftwich returned to a league meeting in 1958 to announce that the southside would soon have a new park off Pryor Road within the Joyland subdivision.[47]

In these ways, through the 1950s, south Atlantans worked to create and maintain a political infrastructure that responded to local needs. Importantly, city officials acknowledged and worked with that structure: political candidates spoke at league meetings, and officials such as Leftwich used the structure to reach area residents. To some degree, the civic leagues augmented the Black establishment's working relationship with the city's white business and political elite.

By the 1950s, Atlanta's Black sociopolitical elite and white business and political leaders had established a system whereby Black leaders negotiated social and political needs through civil discourse and exchange, an approach both sides preferred over protest and other high visibility tactics. Protests—whether pickets or sit-ins or similar—were risky in an era when violence against Blacks, including instances of police brutality, continued to be a real threat. Further, Atlanta's Black business and social leadership shared similar business and economic outlooks to Atlanta's white business elite; violence was bad for business whether you were Black or white. Instead, Black sociopolitical elite pursued negotiated settlements with more pragmatic politicians such as Mayor William Hartsfield. Members of this community power structure believed the approach allowed the city to avoid racial confrontation that wracked other southern cities and interfered with progressive southerners' economic development goals.[48]

The civic councils furthered the Black community's work to improve services and secure other needs. Through the 1940s and 1950s, the Black community's list of desires and needs was lengthy. Few African Americans served as first responders—police and firefighters—or as doctors and nurses. Black families sought improved access to jobs, particularly jobs paying good wages, but also positions in the upper echelons of government.[49] In particular, African Americans sought more safe and affordable housing. As Robert A. Thompson Jr., head of Atlanta's Urban League pointed out at the 1947 federal Joint Committee on Housing's Atlanta hearings, Atlanta's formal and informal practice of racial zoning had created an "artificial" shortage of land on which housing intended for Blacks could be developed. Blacks comprised "a third of [Atlanta's] total population" and lived on "slightly more than one-fifth of the land."[50] African American families were also disproportionately burdened by poor housing conditions. In 1939, 71.6 percent of Black-occupied units qualified as substandard, and there had been "relatively little change" in the conditions of houses for Black families since 1940. In 1947, 57 percent of Black-occupied units lacked private bathing facilities.[51] The private housing market was not responding to the need. Of the 11,065 units proposed as of June 1947, 90 percent were intended for white residents.[52] While poor housing conditions affected much of the African American community, the heaviest burden no doubt fell on poor Blacks.

Atlanta's practice of negotiating settlements between white and Black political and business elite had helped meet some housing needs for Black Atlantans of all income levels. For example, on the city's west side, Black desires for better housing led to challenging face-offs in West End and Mozley Park in the 1940s and 1950s. There, as historian Kevin Kruse explains, white resistance to Black "encroachment" on white neighborhoods shifted over time. Initially, Black interest in white neighborhoods was met with violent, confrontational activities of fringe groups such as the Ku Klux Klan and the Columbians. Later, white resident-led "protective associations" attempted to fend off potential Black residents. Such associations eventually opted to negotiate racial transition of neighborhoods through face-to-face meetings.[53] In 1952, Mayor William Hartsfield institutionalized this approach by forming the West Side Mutual Development Committee (WSMDC), a biracial body charged with investigating rumors of neighborhood racial change and mediating racial transitions. Hartsfield named three recognized leaders to represent Atlanta's Black community on the WSMDC: builder Walter Aiken, Realtist T. M. Alexander, and attorney A. T. Walden. The white representatives drew from the Southwest Citizens Association, which had previously handled negotiations over the racial transition of Mozley Park. Using a concept of "neighborhood integrity," the WSMDC investigated complaints about changing neighborhood demographics and determined if neighborhoods should remain mono-racial (white). If neighborhoods lacked sufficient "integrity," the WSMDC helped neighborhoods navigate racial transition.[54] This approach pleased Hartsfield and other Black and white elite who, again, sought to avoid racial violence that scarred many southern cities of the era.

Positions on the WSMDC further solidified Aiken, Alexander, and Walden's status in the Black sociopolitical power structure. Walden's status has already been discussed, and Alexander and Aiken had equally impressive credentials. Walter "Chief" Aiken was born to a prominent Black Republican and "black political boss" Henry Rucker, and Aiken made his name and fortune as a builder and real estate developer. Aiken also gained notoriety as a football coach and athletic director for Clark University, one of Atlanta's historically Black colleges. T. M. Alexander, a Morehouse College graduate, launched his own insurance brokerage company, Alexander & Company, and invested in and developed real estate as the Alexander-Callaway Realty Company. He served as president of Atlanta's NAACP in the mid-1940s, and at other times he chaired the board at the Butler Street YMCA and led the Empire Real Estate Board. As chief negotiators in determining housing turnover that benefited the Black community, Aiken, Walden, and Alexander helped expand Black housing opportunity and influenced the city's racial geography.

Thus, by the time Atlanta opted to participate in the urban renewal components of the 1954 Federal Housing Act, two notable phenomena were evident. First, voting and civic leagues had emerged in Black neighborhoods, including poor and mixed-income areas, and many residents had been politicized and educated in rudimentary aspects of local democracy. Second, Atlanta's Black sociopolitical power structure had become accustomed to influencing the future development of Black housing in the Gate City, at least as much as they could within the constraints of white power. In particular, Black sociopolitical elite used negotiated settlements with white leadership to achieve their goals. Because urban renewal fell right on the heels of the work of the WSMDC, the Black establishment would help navigate the racial shoals of urban renewal as well, though poor and working-class Atlantans would grow frustrated with these tactics and lack of progress.

Urban Renewal

William Hartsfield and downtown Atlanta business leaders looked forward to the funding that 1950s federal housing bills promised. As vice president and then president of the American Municipal Association and mayor of the South's leading city, Hartsfield lobbied President Dwight D. Eisenhower and other federal officials on the need for a stronger federal-urban relationship.[55] Hartsfield himself hoped a robust urban renewal program would help check the "blight" that marred the South's capital and ease the housing crisis that had the potential to spark racial violence.[56] As Hartsfield's biographer Harold Martin notes, Hartsfield knew violence would be instigated by *whites* unhappy with racial integration. "Negroes have been taught since they were born to avoid incidents 365 days a year," Hartsfield observed.[57] More housing for the city's Black community would help alleviate long-festering complaints regularly cited by the city's Black elite, and federal housing programs had the potential to deliver on that goal.

Federal housing support was hardly new in the 1950s, but the Housing Act of 1954 promised improvements over the 1949 act. Certainly, the 1949 act was significant. It expanded the federal government's role in mortgage insurance and enlarged the public housing program. And Title 1 provided federal financing for slum clearance programs associated with urban redevelopment projects. However, the 1949 legislation had emphasized total demolition and rebuilding of neighborhoods, which often resulted in the breaking up of communities as families were dispersed across the city.[58] The 1954 law differed in that it promoted the preservation and revitalization of neighborhoods. Demolition was to be used "surgically," and, at least in theory, residents could remain living in or return to a neighborhood. Importantly, the 1954 law also differed from the 1949 act in that it required "citizen participation" in the planning and implementation of government programs.[59]

Modes by which citizens would participate in urban renewal planning were to be outlined in an applicant city's "workable plan," the name given to the report outlining a city's approach to renewal. That being said, the community participation requirement remained ill-defined and open to interpretation. Citizen participation could mean citizens were informed and knowledgeable of professionally led renewal efforts, or it could mean citizens were fully involved in deliberative processes.[60] In this period of urban renewal, citizen participation was, in many ways, an experiment. When Atlanta began cobbling together its urban renewal program in 1956, the city's leadership operationalized the 1954 citizen participation requirement by involving well-recognized middle-class and elite community leaders.

Atlanta's program reflected both white downtown business leaders' wish to boost and expand the downtown business district by eliminating surrounding slums and Black elites' desire for more Black housing and improvement around the historically Black colleges and universities on the city's west. As plans matured, white business and political elites sought to use federal urban renewal funds to protect downtown's boundaries from undesirable land use, which, in their view, included Black neighborhoods. They moved to buffer the central business district with expressways, and, when possible, move Black and poor families to more remote locations at the city's edge. Still, whites negotiated with Black leadership, and by the end of the decade, Atlanta's leaders were identifying the principal neighborhoods for urban renewal and project boundaries, decisions that were made with white business *and* Black sociopolitical leadership.[61] Interest groups, planners, and city officials initially agreed on three neighborhoods for urban renewal: Washington-Rawson, Butler Street (Buttermilk Bottom), and what was referred to as University Center, the neighborhoods abutting the city's historically Black colleges.[62]

As the city neared completing a draft proposal for the city's urban renewal program, leaders planned the launch of a citizens advisory committee, a body intended to satisfy the federal requirement for citizen participation. That city-sanctioned group would spearhead a public information campaign about, in the *Atlanta Constitution*'s words, "perhaps the biggest thing the city has ever undertaken."[63] Thus, by the time the city considered facilitating citizen participation, major decisions regarding urban renewal had already been made. White business and Black sociopolitical leaders had identified which neighborhoods would be cleared and rehabilitated, and they had begun discussing how resident displacement would be handled.

The city-sanctioned, nine-member Citizen Advisory Committee on Urban Renewal (CACUR) counted bank executives, building trades representatives, and business leaders among its members, including three Black professionals: E. L. Simon Jr.; Q. V. Williamson; and Harry V. Richardson.[64] The Black professionals appointed to the CACUR reflected Hartsfield's by-then established relationship with Black elite. E. L. Simon Jr., a second-generation student of and graduate of Clark College, served at the time as agency director at one of America's most powerful Black financial institutions, Atlanta Life Insurance Company.[65] Q. V. Williamson, arguably the city's most prominent Realtist, was president of the city's Black real estate professional organization, the Empire Real Estate Board, and a leader in the Atlanta Negro Voting League.[66] Harry V. Richardson, a Harvard graduate and former chaplain at Tuskegee, was founding president of Gammon Theological Seminary.[67] Formed as it was after the identification of urban renewal sites was largely complete and some hearings had already been held, CACUR was less a device to ensure citizen involvement in planning and more of a body to, as the *Atlanta Constitution* described, "assist in popularizing" the urban renewal program.[68] Residents of neighborhoods affected by urban renewal were not invited to participate. Accustomed to self-organizing, residents of Atlanta's poor and mixed-income neighborhoods began taking action.

Localities Committees

Observing that urban renewal was proceeding apace, Black ministers with congregations in and near the proposed renewal areas took it upon themselves to organize their own citizens committees—"localities committees"—to make residents aware of urban renewal proposals and how they would affect neighborhoods. Rev. William Holmes Borders (Wheat Street Baptist), Rev. Emory R. Searcy (Mt. Zion Second Baptist), Rev. Harold I. Bearden (Big Bethel AME [African Methodist Episcopal]), and Rev. John A. Middleton (Allen Temple AME) led the Butler Street contingent. Rev. E. W. McMillan (Warren Memorial Methodist) and Rev. A. Franklin Fisher (West Hunter Baptist) led the west side. Bishop W. R. Wilkes (AME) chaired a combined committee that would come to be known as the Negro Citizens Committee on Urban Renewal (hereafter Negro Citizens Committee or NCC).[69] As urban renewal proceeded, then, two "citizens committees" were in operation, the city-sanctioned CACUR and the Negro Citizens Committee.

Absent substantive information about how urban renewal would directly affect their neighborhoods, the Negro Citizens Committee set about studying the likely impact of the proposed urban renewal programs. Over their three-week investigation, the committee realized that more than 75 percent of the people affected by the renewal program were people of color. The committee speculated that urban renewal would result in "mass moving" of 15,000 to 20,000 families, which amounted to 75,000 to 100,000 people. "Nothing in the history of the city of Atlanta in the last hundred years" had more implications for Atlanta's Black community, the *Atlanta Daily World* asserted.[70] It was alarming news indeed. Whole communities would be uprooted, and little information was reaching residents. The CACUR may have included Black representatives, but those members did not initially consult with or take into consideration the input of poor and near-poor residents who stood to be displaced by urban renewal. The Negro Citizens Committee would enter that vacuum and attempt to address urban renewal's worst aspects, or at least inform residents of what was coming.

The Negro Citizens Committee carefully read the federal requirements and prepared a "bill of particulars" in which they detailed how Atlanta failed to meet the spirit of the 1954 housing act. Families affected by urban renewal were not provided sufficient information, the committee asserted. The federally required citizens committee (the CACUR) had been formed late and lacked appropriate representation from communities affected by urban renewal—the poor. The statement framed lack of representation of the poor as a racial representation issue. Specifically, 80 percent of areas affected by urban renewal projects were African American, but Blacks accounted for only three of the nine members. That number was not adequate, given that "80% of the total program as now proposed will affect Negroes."[71] Citizens affected by the program still had little knowledge of it. To date, no satisfactory program had been developed to relocate displaced families. It was unclear what role the CACUR was supposed to play. Urban renewal would diminish the area in which Blacks could live in Atlanta. The proposed remote relocation sites lacked water and sewage facilities, transportation, accessibility to employment, and shopping, religious, and educational facilities. What's more, the worst slums were not being identified for renewal. Instead, the neighborhoods surrounding Atlanta University Center and Butler Street had been prioritized. More attention and resources should be spent on the city's worst slums such as Lightning and Vine City on the city's near northwest side, or Buttermilk Bottom, which abutted the Butler Street renewal area.[72]

A month later, concern over the relocation of affected families became particularly acute when the city aldermen admitted publicly that ten thousand Black families would be displaced by urban renewal and highway construction. When asked how displaced families would be housed, the aldermen responded that the city would utilize a combination of existing public housing, which turned over about five hundred families a year; additional public housing; existing "standard" housing; multifamily housing subsidized under title 221 of the federal housing act; and new housing from private sources. T. M. Alexander was hardly satisfied with the CACUR's assurances. He pointed out that Black families already faced spatial constraints, even without the clearance associated with urban renewal. What's more, Alexander stated, the city was already losing around three thousand housing units a year "from dilapidation, expressway clearance and commercial reuse."[73] The city's plans seemed an insufficient response when the Black housing market was already tight and spatially limited. And while Alexander did not comment specifically on the availability of low-cost housing, it was not at all clear if city officials had identified relocation housing that would actually fit the budgets of Atlanta's poor and near poor.

By midsummer, Negro Citizens Committee leaders Bishop William R. Wilkes and Rev. William Holmes Borders had had enough. At a series of talks sponsored by the Black Atlanta Business and Professional Association, the leaders charged the urban renewal program with perpetuating discrimination and segregation. The association had developed tentative plans to purchase and develop land made available through urban renewal—a proposal that would have assisted only a small portion of families affected by urban renewal—but association representatives were getting no response from the city. Borders also expressed frustration with Mayor Hartsfield, who he felt had glossed over the concerns of the Black community.[74]

Black frustration over urban renewal was palpable at the April 1959 Atlanta hearings for the U.S. Commission on Civil Rights, a federal body charged to collect information about whether citizens were being deprived of their civil rights. An outgrowth of the early activities in the southern civil rights movement, the commission held hearings throughout the nation on voting rights, education, and housing.[75] The Atlanta hearing revealed that Atlanta's leadership held divergent views of Atlanta's housing situation. Mayor Hartsfield and others expounded on the "successes" of the WSMDC, the group that mediated racially transitioning neighborhoods. Williamson and Borders were the exceptions. They were forthright about ongoing resentment over white tactics to limit Black housing opportunity.[76] In a tense exchange with questioners, Williamson asserted that Atlanta's white leadership had turned a blind eye to twelve bombings of homes that were intended to incite racial terror and halt racial transition in Atlanta neighborhoods. To Williamson, white officials allowed white violence against Blacks by not pressing harder for investigations and the arrests of those responsible.[77] To some Black leaders, not enough was being done to address African American housing needs.

As plans for urban renewal proceeded, relocation of displaced families remained a sticky issue. Although city planners initially made attempts to move displaced families near their current communities, established white residents throughout the city blocked proposals that would bring poor families or people of color in closer proximity.[78] The Fourth Ward Zoning Committee was particularly active in preventing nearby construction of new housing for the Black and poor residents. In spring 1958, ward residents rejected a proposal for federally subsidized single-family homes at Gilbert and Brown Mill Roads.[79] In another case, white fourth-ward residents opposed new housing on the site of the former Egleston Children's Hospital in near-northeast Atlanta. Confident the site would be approved for new housing, the Atlanta Housing Authority purchased the fourteen-acre property on Forrest Road NE, where the city planned to erect a privately built, 350-unit, $3.5 million low-rent housing project intended for Black occupancy. Close to the Butler Street urban renewal site, the new housing would allow displaced residents to remain within established social networks and employment centers. To supporters of the building site, the use of the property for Black housing would help alleviate the shortage of Black housing in the city, and it would continue Atlanta leadership's preferred practice of planning where whites and Blacks would be housed, a practice that they contended encouraged stable real estate markets and reduced interracial friction. But vocal white residents in the lower fourth ward opposed what they saw as Black impingement on white areas. The zoning committee deadlocked over whether to rezone the site to allow for new housing. When the decision went to the city aldermen, they voted against the site, 11 to 3.[80]

The defeat of the Egleston site worried city leaders who feared that ongoing rejection of private building initiatives would force the city to use more public housing to deal with displacement associated with urban renewal. What's more, pressure for more Black housing could force the racial integration of public housing, a point that received more publicity after the Egleston housing site suffered defeat.[81] To reduce the likelihood of lawsuits or federal intervention that would allow Blacks to apply for units in white public housing communities, officials would need to increase the number of public housing units for Blacks, but clearly Atlanta's white residents would resist such housing near their established neighborhoods. In the meantime, federal officials increased pressure on Atlanta leaders by withholding federal funds.

In December 1959 the federal Public Housing Administration informed the Atlanta Housing Authority that federal funds for two housing projects were being held until the Egleston property had been appropriately rezoned. The threat was significant: federal funding covered two-thirds of urban renewal project costs. City officials and other observers feared that the city's entire urban renewal program would fall apart if Atlanta could not secure suitable, acceptable public housing sites.[82] Atlanta's urban renewal program could stall permanently if the issue was not resolved. With urban renewal funding under threat, by February 1960, the proposal for the Egleston site was being reconsidered, only to be rejected one month later. Instead, the 650-unit proposal in Atlanta's northwest—Field Road near Bankhead highway, distant from established white neighborhoods—was approved.[83]

In this way, urban renewal planning proceeded apace with little regard for the interests of the thousands of Atlanta poor who would be displaced. CACUR, which was not structured to represent the interests of displaced residents, was consumed by debates over relocation sites. The Negro Citizens Committee, which organized in response to problems with urban renewal implementation, better represented communities affected by displacement when compared to the CACUR. Members of the Negro Citizens Committee familiarized themselves with the federal legislation and leveraged federal requirements in an attempt to secure better outcomes for the Black community at large, which included poor Blacks. But, having organized well after urban-renewal wheels were in motion and lacking the power of city sanction, the committee could not substantively influence the white or Black power structures. As political scientist Clarence Stone points out, the neighborhood-based groups could only "react to plans that were already fully developed."[84] Indeed, requests for neighborhood-based planning were effectively ignored by the city's aldermen. Even when city officials attempted to respond to residents' desires to relocate in or near their original housing location, white opposition to low-income, Black-occupied housing prevented that from happening.

That being said, the Negro Citizens Committee acted upon the stated federal requirements that citizens be involved in urban renewal planning. They specifically deployed citizen participation language, insisted that it be followed, and raised expectations for authentic resident involvement in city building efforts that directly affected residents. Still, the 1950s urban renewal events revealed areas in which the Black and poor residents needed to assert more political power: Atlanta's poor were allocated housing not in areas that provided necessary resources—such as employment or transportation—but where white residents determined the Black poor were least likely to impact whites and white property values.

The 1950s disagreements over urban renewal expose how Atlanta's Black power structure attempted to manage Black housing and political issues related to urban renewal. Atlanta's Black sociopolitical elite, which included financial and real estate interests and figures involved in promoting and managing political participation, continued their practice of negotiating settlements with Atlanta's white business elite and the mayor. Neighborhood leadership, which included the pastors of the many Black churches that served as worship and social centers of long-established neighborhoods, as well as neighborhood residents themselves, were left out of these deals.

Poor families' prospects under Atlanta's urban renewal program would only grow worse in the early 1960s. The second largest urban renewal program in the nation (after Philadelphia's), Atlanta's program was managed by city aldermen and gave little consideration to families displaced.[85] And some poor neighborhoods, such as Vine City, were, in the *Atlanta Constitution*'s words, "too far gone" for the city to bother with enforcing code compliance, and owners were given exemptions, causing further deterioration of housing and neighborhood conditions.[86] Atlanta's disregard for code compliance ultimately caught the attention of federal officials. In 1963, the Housing and Home Finance Agency rebuked the city for failing to comply with requirements of the "workable program," which mandated that cities maintain and enforce a housing code.[87] Consequently, the city revamped its urban renewal and housing code administration.[88] The reality was that Atlanta continued to struggle to get its housing situation under control. The city had not effectively documented displacement: unless displaced families moved into public housing, they were not tracked, so it was not clear if families relocated to standard housing. And no data had been regularly gathered to track housing decline or improvements. Worse, the *Atlanta Constitution* concluded, "The problem is too big for any existing combination of federal and local programs."[89]

While the city struggled to effectively implement urban renewal and get on top of its housing problem, the context in which urban renewal took place was quickly changing. Residents of Atlanta's poorest neighborhoods were at a substantial power disadvantage in the late 1950s, but in the early 1960s, in Atlanta and elsewhere, grassroots organizations, students, and civil rights organizations were questioning existing power structures and methods by which the Black and white establishments advanced their interests. And when the Student Nonviolent Coordinating Committee (SNCC) looked to expand civil rights organizing beyond the quest for open accommodations, it could build on the neighborhood-based organizing started by the civic leagues and citizens' attempts to force change in urban renewal.

SNCC and the South Atlanta Civic Leagues

In 1963, Rev. C. D. Colbert—barber, pastor, and president of the Georgia Avenue/Pryor Street Civic League—led members of SNCC on an informal tour of south Atlanta. According to one field report, the students found conditions typical of an urban ghetto: "Streets were unpaved, and piles of trash and garbage littered the yards and streets; decrepit homes rested on shaky pillars, and underneath [those] homes streams of water from a recent rainfall created swamps—breeding grounds for insects and disease." To Debbie Amis, Plunketown in south Atlanta was "as rural as the smallest hamlet in Mississippi." It had "wooden shacks, no street paving or sewage." To the students, conditions in Atlanta's poorest neighborhoods were bleak.[90]

Prior to the tour, SNCC had been working with other Atlanta students to desegregate public accommodations. Beginning in 1960, Atlanta's Black students, and particularly the students at Atlanta's cluster of historically Black colleges, allied with SNCC and launched direct action campaigns to gain equal access to restaurants, dressing rooms, and schools. Such campaigns occurred in fits and starts as agreements were made and broken between business owners, the city, and Black leaders.[91] While the old guard civil rights leaders, which included some of the Black sociopolitical elite, preferred using established cooperative means—negotiated settlements—to meet civil rights goals, the students regularly opted for disruptive actions such as pickets and sit-ins.[92]

To SNCC, it was the existing network of civic leagues and neighborhood councils that set Atlanta's central city neighborhoods apart from other cities' "ghettoes." The leagues had "considerable political sophistication" and had been pressing for neighborhood improvements for some time. According to one SNCC field report, league leadership was well developed and "relatively militant." That being said, the leagues had been attempting to increase services and improve infrastructure through what SNCC referred to as "the usual gradualistic methods" of letters and petitions to city officials. While league members had actively registered complaints and demands with the city, SNCC felt none of those approaches had been effective.[93] SNCC member Judy Walborn wondered, "Why had 60,000 people, among which there were 10,000 registered voters, not been able to move political and economic forces of Atlanta to respond to their needs and desires?"[94]

While south Atlanta's civic leagues had been promoting voter registration and hosting political candidate events for years, SNCC contended that the average resident did not vote in their own interests. Moreover, when southside residents did vote, they "generally voted as they were advised by a small group of wealthy Negroes from the West side—Negroes who neither understood nor [were] vitally concerned about problems of the south side." SNCC was referring to Atlanta's Black sociopolitical elite, members of which occupied the neighborhoods surrounding the Black colleges to the west of downtown. To SNCC, Black elites failed to sufficiently address conditions that produced multigenerational poverty. To achieve visible results, southside residents "and not the wealthy Negro minority" must "control the votes of the 10,000 registered voters of the south side."[95] Southside residents needed to mobilize in support of their own civic leaders. What's more, they needed to better utilize direct action to make their needs known.

In the summer of 1963, SNCC staff began working with established neighborhood civic leagues to identify and address concrete desires of south Atlanta residents. Consistent with SNCC's belief in the effectiveness of direct action, the group planned a march on city hall for that August. Once at city hall, residents would demand measurable progress on a variety of unmet needs that ranged from deficient city services to lack of employment opportunities. To mobilize residents, the coalition of neighborhood civic leagues held ten mass meetings that summer. SNCC supported the effort by creating and distributing handbills and using their sound truck to announce meetings. At the mass meetings, students discussed and attempted to build enthusiasm for the march, but otherwise they encouraged local residents to take the lead and control the agenda. Throughout the summer, students and civic leaders also promoted voter registration, hoping that they would be prepared to deliver ten thousand votes for or against Mayor Ivan Allen Jr. in the 1964 election.[96] Door-to-door contact also helped workers identify residents' concerns and raise local awareness of the neighborhood civic organizations. As Walborn explained, over time local residents "became considerably more experienced" and "more and more militant" in demanding that their needs be addressed.[97]

On August 5, 1963, the South Atlanta Civic League held a march and picketed city hall, where they formally submitted their lengthy list of grievances to the mayor and city officials. "We will no longer remain the Forgotten Communities of Atlanta," residents insisted (see fig. 5).[98] The report indicted not just city officials, who had routinely discriminated against Blacks in employment, housing, and services, but Atlanta's Black leadership. The statement sharply critiqued the Black sociopolitical elite who had failed to represent or even understand the needs of Atlanta's Black poor.[99] The civic league expected the city to report on progress in addressing the complaints by August 19.[100]

About 250 people reportedly participated in the march on city hall, but at least some SNCC members were disappointed in the turnout.[101] According to one self-assessment, the march had "been structured from the top down" and "imposed upon the people," rather than "resulting naturally and spontaneously from weeks and weeks of contact work by stu-

FIGURE 5. South Atlanta residents march to city hall to deliver neighborhood griev-ances to Mayor Ivan Allen Jr., 1963. Photo by Noel Davis. Courtesy *Atlanta Journal-Constitution* Photographs collection, Special Collections & Archives, Georgia State University Library, Atlanta, Ga.

dents and leaders in the community."[102] Local civic league leadership lacked rank-and-file neighborhood support. Community-building work had been neglected in favor of mass meetings.[103] Nonetheless, the south-side civic leagues kept pressuring city hall.

After receiving a "far from satisfactory" response to the grievance re-port from Mayor Ivan Allen Jr., the civic leagues promised that "protest measures" would continue. Thus far, responses from some departments to their complaints had been inaccurate and incomplete.[104] "Our organi-zation will not be content with evasion, delay, or only partial satisfaction of our grievances," the leaders insisted. South Atlantans were expanding their organization and the scope of their activities, they warned. The city should provide the south side with "*continuous* and *adequate* service."[105]

The South Atlanta Civic League's response suggests that members were determined and organized, but SNCC members felt they had to "prod" local residents to pressure the mayor's office the day his response was due. Going forward, they doubted that league members would do the door-to-door contact required in that era of movement building. In the end, an August 1963 SNCC field report concluded, "It is questionable whether or not the present leaders of the south Atlanta civic league are capable of becoming really effective leaders in their communities."[106] But while SNCC fieldworkers may not have been satisfied with the march's success, SNCC leadership was sufficiently convinced of South Atlanta's potential to commit staff to the area that fall.

In August 1963, SNCC assigned two workers to southeast Atlanta, workers who would partner with neighborhood leadership to increase voter registration and follow up on the grievances filed with the city. "A Proposal for a Voter Education Project in Southeast Atlanta" recommended organizing a massive registration drive that would, besides expanding the voter rolls, "politically activat[e] all citizens in the area."[107] In the resulting campaign, "Operation Dragnet," teams of fifteen to twenty-five teens and adults canvased one area each week, asking those who had not yet registered to vote to commit to a specific day and time to be taken to the courthouse to register.[108] As had been the case in previous canvasing, SNCC sought to commit local residents to an ongoing civic-political structure that could be mobilized for a variety of social and political ends.

In October 1963, SNCC worker Debbie Amis still gave the south Atlanta project a mixed review. On the positive side, membership in the civic leagues had increased, and the August march had forced the city government to be "more amenable to pressure from the south side leaders."[109] Specifically, the city had appointed three crossing guards at schools that had not previously had them, had accelerated the construction of a park in Peoplestown, had hired two Black garbage truck drivers, had improved sewage infrastructure at Primrose Circle (a notoriously dilapidated section of Peoplestown), and had completed work at Joyland and Poole Creek parks. Moreover, local residents had become more sophisticated in their use of the press, and many were attending public meetings. But voter registration and civic league membership remained a challenge. One civic league had failed to grow, another had internal tensions, and many residents were still unaware of the civic leagues.[110] Although residents recognized the need to continue applying pressure to the mayor's office, they hesitated to participate in actions other than letter writing and negotiations. There remained plenty of room for improvement, SNCC concluded.

Amis also leveled other revealing criticisms. To her, the local civil rights movement ignored the concerns of the poor and working class. Moreover, Amis charged, the student movement tended to follow what she described as the "conservative" leadership that made up the Atlanta Summit Leadership Conference (hereafter Summit), a coalition of Atlanta civil rights organizations that had organized in October to pursue public accommodations.[111] In Amis's mind, those identifying with Atlanta's civil rights movement failed to reckon with "the people"; that is, they failed to bring Atlanta's local community into the movement. "Despite the super-saturation of civil rights groups in Atlanta," Amis asserted, rank-and-file residents had not been asked to state their views on civil rights. "The movement has all but snubbed and neglected the people who have to live with whatever changes that are made," Amis said.[112] To Amis, SNCC and the movement could play a greater role, for example, by demanding more from the local urban renewal program.[113] Despite these criticism, Atlanta's SNCC workers would prioritize the Open City movement over poverty and related conditions beginning in fall 1963.[114]

Direct action protests for public accommodations renewed in 1963 when a coalition of Atlanta organizations came together to launch the Open City campaign.[115] A massive multi-organization march was held on December 15.[116] During December 1963 and January 1964, students sat in at Toddle House and participated in SNCC's national campaign against Dobbs House, the parent company. Protests spread to multiple Krystal restaurants, the Atlanta airport, and other public venues.[117] To expose segregated schools and the conditions at Black schools, SNCC persuaded more than a hundred high school students to "play hooky for freedom" and occupy Mayor Ivan Allen Jr.'s office.[118] As direct action spread, white resistance grew more flagrant. In February, a Georgian Hotel manager brandished a gun at protestors, and at Harry's steakhouse, SNCC worker Debbie Amis was twice burned with a cattle prod.[119]

As the public's attention turned to the Open City actions, the southside civic leagues continued organizing, absent SNCC. Residents returned to the plodding work of holding meetings and organizing voter registration drives. But while the civic leagues provided a structure by which residents could meet to discuss area and neighborhood needs, lack of visible, public demands—perhaps lack of disruption—from Atlanta's poor and working class resulted in the status quo: continued neglect of southside neighborhoods. The Open City drive so eclipsed SNCC's south Atlanta organizing that when SNCC launched an "Atlanta Project" in northwest Atlanta two years later, its staff initially displayed no awareness of the 1963 south Atlanta work.[120] Nonetheless, organizing infrastructure had been established that would later be deployed by residents fighting poverty and related conditions.

In mid-twentieth century Atlanta, expanded voting rolls allowed African Americans to make greater demands of Atlanta's power structure. The Black community built on those gains, building voting strength through neighborhood-based civic councils. Using these structures, residents pushed for greater access to polls, but also more parks, better street lighting, and more consistent city services. But as a tool, such councils were limited, in part because they relied on traditional forms of entreaty—polite letters, requests, and petitions—that were easily or selectively ignored by Atlanta's political elite.

Urban renewal, too, increased Black and poor Atlantans' desire and ability to force social change. While Atlanta's white and Black power structure moved ahead with plans to clear acres of poor and working-class homes to allow for urban redevelopment, residents deployed new expectations for "citizen participation." To be sure, the federal Housing and Home Finance Agency was not clear on what constituted citizen participation, and they did not enforce the requirement, but Atlanta's Black and poor became aware of and tried to deploy the regulation to their advantage. When the city failed to involve residents in urban renewal planning, local congregational leaders took matters into their own hands, formed localities committees, investigated the likely impact of the federally funded program, and reported on their findings. Subsequent CACUR meetings were, in the *Atlanta Daily World*'s characterization, "explosive."[121]

When SNCC sought new projects in 1963, members were pleased to see a working civic council apparatus in South Atlanta. Residents were, to some degree, organized, which meant they potentially could be mobilized. SNCC still saw areas for improvement, though. The area's poor seemed inclined to listen to the city's Black sociopolitical elite and follow the traditional civil rights establishment. SNCC was frustrated with that group; they did not actively address issues of importance to the city's average Black resident, who was poor, lived in marginal neighborhood conditions, lacked adequate health care, suffered hunger periodically if not regularly, and lacked educational and job opportunities. SNCC committed to the area for the next year, working with residents to consider organizing tactics and strategies and helping residents appeal to the city. SNCC would return to its public accommodations work in late 1963, though, leaving south Atlanta residents to build their own movement.

While Atlanta's white political and business establishment had not aggressively acted upon poor Atlantans' needs, or even sought to identify what residents thought those needs were, city leaders were aware of poverty's impact on the human condition and how poverty limited the city's potential for business and industrial growth. As the next chapter outlines, sociopolitical elite had their own vision of how poverty should be tackled.

CHAPTER 2

Economic Opportunity Atlanta

To many in the early 1960s, Atlanta was thriving. It certainly offered promise to rural Georgians. They had been finding their way to Atlanta for decades, crowding into ageing neighborhoods such as South Atlanta, Mechanicsville, Pittsburgh, and Vine City, hoping for better wages and a more stable life. To Atlanta's city builders, many of those in-migrants presented a challenge. To be sure, the city needed workers, but the rural arrivals tended to be unskilled and poorly educated.

To realize the Atlanta Chamber of Commerce's Forward Atlanta goal of luring new industry and business to the city, Atlanta needed an able work force, and that meant diminishing the city's social problems. That was a tall order, former Oglethorpe University president and Woodruff Foundation adviser Philip Weltner explained to Atlanta's young business and social leaders in 1960. Atlanta had social problems disproportional to the city's size. It had more economically dependent people, a greater number of functionally illiterate people, a higher infant mortality rate, and a higher school dropout rate. At least 30 percent of the population was unemployed or underemployed.[1] To fix the situation, the city needed to improve its social services, which were in a sorry state. One city study found that many of the city's lowest income citizens were not even aware of the services that were available, which included general assistance, educational programs, health-care facilities, and child care. Still, those offices had challenges. The agencies that did exist neither communicated with each other nor coordinated aid. Some discriminated against Black clients. Others operated passively, not advertising benefits. Atlanta had to do a better job of linking economic development with social welfare.

Such was the thinking of the new generation of white, progressive businessmen—contemporaries of Atlanta Mayor Ivan Allen Jr.—who promoted Atlanta's growth and development in the 1950s and 1960s. Together, in 1960, the group established a citywide social planning apparatus, the Community Council of the Atlanta Area (CCAA), to provide technical assistance to human service agencies and identify gaps in planning, human, and welfare services. Almost immediately after forming, the CCAA launched a pilot neighborhood service center program that positioned a variety of social services in reach of Atlanta's most needy. But despite healthy start-up funding, the project was difficult to sustain. To Atlanta's luck, President Lyndon B. Johnson would announce his War on Poverty in 1964. The Economic Opportunity Act would allow CCAA not just to continue the pilot but to scale up the neighborhood service centers project. Thus, when Atlanta's leaders proposed a substantial community action program (CAP), they outlined a project designed entirely by the city's power structure. Subsequently, city leaders would clash with federal officials committed to the "maximum feasible participation of the poor" in program design and implementation as well as Atlanta Black sociopolitical elite who sought greater involvement of African Americans in program leadership. Of course, the War on Poverty was intended to address *poverty*, and drawing on their growing expectations to be involved in decisions that affected their lives, poor families, too, demanded that the community action agency meet its promises.

Cities such as Atlanta benefited from the positive aspects of growth in the mid-twentieth century as well as visionary leadership. Mayor William B. Hartsfield (1937–41, 1942–62) identified funding for industry and tourists and built an airport that promised to lure them, and the city had incorporated 118 square miles of suburban land, bringing a hundred thousand residents into the city and enlarging its tax base. Modern interstates traversed the city, and new skyscrapers were emerging in downtown. Still, Atlanta had suffered the urban decay that plagued many cities in the years following World War II: declining infrastructure, overcrowded and ageing housing, abandonment, high poverty, and lack of suitable mass transit. The city continued to attract displaced agricultural workers who often had few job opportunities and rudimentary reading and writing skills. Mayors Hartsfield and Ivan Allen Jr. (1962–70) first turned to the state for help in confronting urban decline, but they were continually disappointed. Rural power brokers regularly voted down financial support of Atlanta and other Georgia cities.

Atlanta did benefit from the work of a new generation of business leaders who were committed to enhancing civic life. This narrative of a socially conscious business class has long been associated with Atlanta's fifty-second mayor, Ivan Allen Jr. As Allen recalled in his memoir, when William Hartsfield was likely serving his last term as mayor, Allen wondered who could fill Hartsfield's shoes. Who would lead Atlanta into the next era? He realized that his lifelong friends were the city's emerging leaders. They were a close-knit group. "Almost all of us had been born and raised within a mile or two of each other," Allen penned. "We had gone to the same schools, to the same churches, to the same golf courses, to the same summer camps."[2] Less has been written about the individual members of Allen's social set, but like Allen, they were committed to advancing the city, its commerce, and its civic institutions. They included G. Arthur Howell Jr., a Princeton graduate, attorney, and founding partner of Atlanta's Alston & Bird law firm; W. C. "Billy" Wardlaw Jr., a Georgia Tech graduate, financier, and son of one of the original Coca-Cola investors; James M. "Jimmy" Sibley, a Princeton graduate and attorney with King & Spalding; and others equally as devoted to the South's Gate City.

The Community Council of the Atlanta Area

As active board members for the CCAA, Atlanta's business and social elite advised on welfare planning and research, though none of the board members were social welfare specialists.[3] The CCAA founders thought the organization needed men of power and standing if they were to attract the funds necessary to implement ambitious social planning programs. An early history of the CCAA explains that eighteen of the forty-eight board members formed "an advisory council of city fathers" who possessed "widespread influence and prestige."[4] Jimmy Sibley reemphasized the point in a 1962 letter to his father, John A. Sibley, who then served as president of the Trust Company of Georgia. The CCAA needed more than money, the younger Sibley explained. It also needed "the sympathetic understanding and active support" of people such as John Sibley, men who were "the elder statesmen of the community."[5] Toward that end, CCAA also benefited from the backing of Atlanta's preeminent elder statesman and philanthropist, Robert Woodruff, retired head of the Coca-Cola empire.

In forming the CCAA, Atlanta reflected a recent turn toward social service planning, a practice that emerged in the mid-twentieth century as city leaders and social service professionals sought to coordinate efforts across growing cities and proliferating agencies. To that time, social service planning had traditionally fallen under the purview of local community chests, entities that primarily raised money for social services. After World War II, many city leaders saw the value in creating separate planning agencies, and in 1960, Metropolitan Atlanta Community Services (MACS) spun off the CCAA and tasked it with coordinating agency efforts and providing research services.[6]

The formation of the CCAA coincided with the final work of the Fulton County Advisory Council on Illegitimacy and Adoption, which had been investigating Atlanta's social problems. Chaired by Philip Weltner, that committee was less concerned with the performance of individual agencies and more attentive to broader social issues.[7] Weltner himself was particularly concerned with dependency, or overreliance on government services. Dependency was a key social issue, Weltner felt, a condition that led to unemployment, illegitimate births, hopelessness, crime, and the neglect, mistreatment and abandonment of children. The country had been "living with this problem and not licking it," Weltner would later assert.[8] Social services, including health services, job training, and job placement, needed to be concentrated and positioned within reach of what were referred to as "multi-problem families."[9] Toward this end and drawing on the experience of the Greater St. Paul Community Chest and Council, the advisory council recommended that resources be delivered through neighborhood centers, which would make them more accessible to families. Weltner's position on the advisory council and the board of CCAA, as well as his role advising Robert Woodruff, ensured the CCAA was charged with implementing the committee's neighborhood center proposal. With Weltner's encouragement, the Woodruff Foundation provided CCAA with five years of funding to implement a pilot project to establish neighborhood service centers.[10]

Launched in 1961, the CCAA pilot opened offices in two neighborhoods, one predominantly Black, in Vine City, and one predominantly white, in West End.[11] Located in southwest Atlanta, West End was a mixed-income neighborhood, but some of its lower-income families suffered poverty. One pocket of low-income residents—largely unskilled laborers who did not complete high school—lived across from the state farmer's market (then on Lee Street). West End included the Joel Chandler Harris public housing community, which housed whites. Another pocket of low-income residents lived just south of West End in the area known as Bush Mountain. Much of Bush Mountain's housing was substandard, some streets were unpaved, and workers tended to be unskilled.[12] Vine City, in near northwest Atlanta, was majority poor, and about half of households were headed by women, though there were a number of middle-income families in the area. The housing stock was mixed. Some sections consisted of sound, middle-class housing. Others contained neglected and dilapidated rental housing. The neighborhood was also the site of the 677-unit John J. Eagan Homes, built for Black families in the 1940s. In 1960, Vine City was nearly 100 percent Black. West End was predominantly—over 90 percent—white.

By summer 1961, CCAA had hired two supervisors to manage the centers, and staffing was underway.[13] City agencies were asked to loan social service staff to the two centers. Because West End residents were most concerned about unemployment, CCAA secured a counselor from the State Employment Office to provide job counseling services, and they partnered with the Children's Center of Metropolitan Atlanta, Inc., to deliver day care services. By July 1961, the social service professionals operating in the West End center included a public welfare worker, public health nurse, and caseworkers from Child Service Association, Family Service Society, and Big Brothers Association of Atlanta. For the Vine City program, the staff included a public welfare worker, a child welfare worker, a public health nurse, and caseworkers from Red Cross, Family Service Society, and Bethlehem Community Center.[14] Additionally, because of the shortage of professional social workers in Atlanta, the CCAA started training local residents to serve as social work assistants, a program intended to boost local employment and extend the reach of the center and other agencies.[15] By spring 1962, the two centers were providing intensive casework to forty to fifty families.[16]

With the launch of its neighborhood service centers, Atlanta joined a number of cities experimenting with social programs to diminish delinquency and poverty. While Atlanta's program authors pointed to St. Paul as its program's inspiration, New York's program may have been the most widely known. In 1960, New York established "Interdepartmental Service Centers" to bring comprehensive social services in closer reach to multi-problem families. Later, Mobilization for Youth would operate from such neighborhood outlets.[17] At the time, these centers were very much experiments. In 1964, the report "Youth in the Ghetto: A Study of the Consequences of Powerlessness" noted that it was too soon to tell the effects of the Interdepartmental Service Centers.[18]

In Atlanta, the neighborhood project soon grew expensive and difficult to manage. The market for social work professionals was tight, and social services were costly, all the more so when delivered in concentrated fashion. In an early 1962 study, CCAA's neighborhood committee estimated that the continued operation of the two neighborhood centers would amount to $150,000, about two-thirds of which was the cost of borrowed personnel.[19] The centers operated with a "shell staff," one report explained. All but one social service worker was part-time, and it was difficult to use part-time staff effectively. The demand for services exceeded staffing, and there was need for more research on area conditions as well as program evaluation. As Philip Alston Jr., chair of the CCAA neighborhood committee, explained to the CCAA executive committee, "We need people to do our job. Absent people, we need money with which to employ people." CCAA board members were frustrated. "Without people or money our Committee should be dissolved," Alston concluded.[20]

By summer 1962, the CCAA was considering cutting the neighborhood center project—at least as the program existed then—to balance its budget.[21] By that fall, the program was still struggling. An October 1962 report indicated that the CCAA considered the program successful, but that "it was not feasible to reproduce these methods without hiring staff."[22] However, CCAA could not simply eliminate the neighborhood project; it had accepted five years of foundation funding earmarked for that purpose. CCAA opted to revamp the neighborhood project as it reconsidered CCAA's overall structure.

Complicating matters, CCAA itself needed reorganization. It had operated for some time under the guidance of the directors and various committees, and an external review of the agency highlighted its "unusual" structure of operating without an executive director. Board member R. L. "Trot" Foreman, who had retired from the insurance industry a few years prior and spent two decades supporting MACS and its predecessor organizations, had stepped in as acting director in June 1961. But the next summer, the CCAA's reorganization committee recommended the hiring of a permanent executive director.[23] The CCAA board initially disagreed about the type of professional to fill that role, but members ultimately decided to invest in a social services professional rather than a business specialist.[24] The new leader would further develop CCAA and inherit an ambitious, if underresourced, neighborhood experiment.

Michigander, World War II veteran, and social work professional Duane Beck had quite the task when he took over as executive director in early 1963. In Beck's recollection, at the time he joined CCAA, Atlanta had a high proportion of "economically dependent people," high infant mortality and high school dropout rates, and high underemployment and unemployment. The city had little technical training available and poor housing conditions. "Social programs were pretty feeble," Beck recalled, and the public welfare system "showed an unusual disregard for the condition of poor people."[25] Racial discrimination exacerbated problems. Segregation was still enforced, and Beck immediately partnered with the Atlanta Urban League to try to raise wages for Black social service workers. To Beck, social services lagged other "systems" in Atlanta. To ensure a healthy workforce, and to be a thriving commercial city, the social service infrastructure needed to be brought to parity.[26]

Parity would be difficult to achieve, though, given the few resources devoted to social welfare and workforce development. As Beck explained to CCAA directors, Atlanta's CCAA was a small operation compared to those elsewhere. Atlanta devoted 5.2 staff members to core CCAA work for which other councils averaged 41.4. What's more, Atlanta spent $0.0367 per person, and other councils spent $0.13. "Atlanta expects 1 person to do the planning that similar communities expect from 8 people," Beck summarized.[27] While city leaders recognized Atlanta's social service and workforce development needs, they put few resources toward planning efforts or services, at least in comparison to cities elsewhere.

With Beck at the CCAA helm, the agency revamped the neighborhood project, and CCAA leaders opted to concentrate their attention on the predominantly white-serving West End neighborhood, dropping the predominantly Black-serving Vine City component.[28] The CCAA launched a search for a "highly competent and technically skilled staff person" to direct the program, hiring Dave Beecher in August 1963.[29] Beecher, a white Savannah native who held a master's degree in social work from Ohio State University, had worked with CCAA as a planner in 1961 before leaving to join a private firm in Marquette, Michigan.[30] This go-round Beecher would work with West End families to manage and mitigate social issues.[31] Beecher had little time to show results: funding for the neighborhood experiment would expire in 1965, and the CCAA would once again be forced to revamp the project or dredge up additional monies. But it was not long before a new funding source presented itself: the federal government.

The War on Poverty

In January 1964, U.S. Representative Charles Weltner (fifth district), a liberal Democrat and son of Philip Weltner, alerted Atlanta's leadership to federal plans for a "war on want." Only two weeks after President Lyndon B. Johnson had announced the War on Poverty in his State of the

Union address, the younger Weltner explained what little was known about Johnson's proposal to the West End Rotary Club. Atlanta should be one of the first cities to benefit from Johnson's new program, Weltner asserted. It was an obvious candidate for funding for a number of reasons. Atlanta was a federal "sub-capital." It was prosperous but still had pockets of poverty and high rural in-migration. And it had an established body coordinating efforts of local social service agencies: the CCAA. The Johnson administration would be looking for "original thinking" and programs that would break the cycle of poverty.[32] To the leadership of Atlanta and CCAA, CCAA's neighborhood service centers project fit the bill.

Lyndon B. Johnson was particularly interested in serving the South, his home region and the poorest section of the country, and he looked to southern leadership to help smooth passage of his economic opportunity bill. Conservative southern Democrats were in positions of power as heads of key committees, and their persistent opposition to entitlement programs and government spending meant they might nix Johnson's ambitious plans. That being said, the region clearly stood to benefit from the War on Poverty's proposed programs, and not only did Georgia's leadership gladly welcome federal funds, but Phil Landrum (D-Ga.), who hailed from rural north Georgia, agreed to shepherd the War on Poverty bill through the House. Landrum was a reliably conservative southern Democrat and critic of the heavy hand of federalism, and Johnson thought his conservative credentials might dampen attacks from Congress and assure wary southerners that the federal initiative was worthwhile.[33]

Many did not expect Landrum to accept Johnson's invitation.[34] But, at least in public circles, many southern conservatives described the War on Poverty as a way of diminishing "welfarism" by putting people to work. The War on Poverty would make "taxpayers rather than tax eaters" out of welfare recipients, Landrum told the southeast conference of the American Public Welfare Association.[35] Additionally, Landrum's district would directly benefit from the Economic Opportunity Act, and conservative southern Democrats had a long history of accepting federal largesse that did not interfere with existing power structures, disturb low-wage labor markets, or challenge racial norms. In this case, Landrum was willing to pave the way for the legislation.[36]

Nonetheless, the economic opportunity bill was seen by many white southerners as potentially benefiting Blacks and troubling the racial power structure, and thus it would meet stiff resistance. Alabama senator Lister Hill, who Johnson had hoped would steer the bill through Senate, knew the electoral danger of aligning too closely with national Democrats who pressed for civil rights, and he declined Johnson's invitation. Hill's concerns were warranted, as segregationists actively fought integrationist goals in War on Poverty congressional committee meetings and hearings. For their part, Republicans regularly attempted to undermine southern support of the bill by pointing out how it would be used to differentially benefit Blacks.[37] In Senate debates, a number of southern conservatives responded as expected and complained about the racial implications of the bill. Strom Thurmond (D-S.C.) insisted the bill was another measure to impose racial integration on the South and described the bill as "pregnant with racial overtones."[38] Southerners beat back an attempt to appoint integrationist Adam Yarmolinsky as deputy director of the Office of Economic Opportunity (OEO).[39] Other southerners, though, proved willing to compromise, including Georgia's elected officials.

Although Georgia's congressional leaders were willing to negotiate, they insisted that states have final approval of CAPs. Georgia senators Richard Russell and Herman Talmadge sought a provision allowing a governor to veto the federal funding of any CAP opposed by elected officials. Russell was the most powerful member of the senate and controlled the southern caucus. He had been a staunch opponent of civil rights legislation and had only conceded to a weakened version of a civil rights bill.[40] Talmadge, a states' rights proponent and ardent segregationist who had supported programs for the rural poor, was confident such a gubernatorial veto of proposed CAPs would never be used, as many southern states needed and wanted federal monies. Rather, Talmadge explained, the amendment signaled to southern constituents that their leaders had protected states' rights.[41] Thus, despite southern concern about federal overreach, Georgia's congressional leadership played a key role in implementing the federal War on Poverty bill and ensured that local and state officials maintained some level of control over community-based programs.

As the Economic Opportunity Act wound its way through federal committees, Atlanta mayor Ivan Allen Jr. called together the CCAA, the Division of Family and Children Services, and city and county leadership to develop a community action proposal.[42] Within two weeks of Georgia legislator Phil Landrum's introduction of the bill to the House of Representatives, a CCAA newsletter explained the economic opportunity bill to members, concluding that "our experimental effort in West End has put Atlanta in a good position to participate in the Federal program." CCAA leadership had already initiated conversations with Congress, they reported, and Atlanta's tentative proposals had been "received with unusual interest."[43] By the end of June 1964, CCAA representatives had held a handful of meetings with federal staff, including War on Poverty head Sargent Shriver and AFL-CIO official and soon-to-be CAP director Jack Conway.[44]

The mayor's task force sketched out its proposal based on the bills circulating that spring and summer. At that point, Title II, the CAP, was "written in vague language," CCAA explained. Some $315 million would be available to communities for grants to develop their own antipoverty programs, and it appeared that "the type of programs developed at the local level depends largely upon the local community." The community action agencies could "be conducted, administered, or coordinated by public or private, non-profit agencies."[45] In the vision of federal program authors, these entities would be bottom-up ventures that would provide meaningful opportunities for everyday people to identify problems and fashion solutions—"maximum feasible participation of the poor."[46] CCAA understood that the success of a community action project would depend on buy-in from the local community, though it is unclear if Atlanta understood that to mean the direct involvement of affected populations or the participation of service agencies and social service personnel.[47] In summer 1964, few guidelines defined terms for early applicants, and Atlanta's leadership felt confident in proposing a ratcheted-up program of neighborhood centers that would be managed through a central office, its community action agency.

Mayor Allen dispatched task force members to New Haven and Boston to observe programs similar to what Atlanta was considering: New Haven's Community Progress, Inc. and Action for Boston Community Development, both private nonprofit corporations funded by the Ford Foundation's Gray Areas program.[48] Indeed, the problems Atlanta's leaders hoped to solve sounded very much like the issues the Ford Foundation sought to address when it announced the Gray Areas program in 1961 and subsequently funded experiments in New Haven, Boston, and three other cities.[49] At that time, the Ford Foundation's Paul Ylvisaker hoped to improve federal urban renewal, which he asserted had "only aggravated the social distress it was supposed, ultimately, to relieve."[50] The Gray Areas program was intended to speed the assimilation of new arrivals to the urban economy and improve the capacity of urban institutions to support urban populations.[51] In New Haven's model, a corporation provided comprehensive services across sectors and promoted social planning. Poor residents participated via neighborhood organizations, and community workers who "spoke the language" of the neighborhood helped bridge the divide between residents and service agencies.[52] That being said, citizen leadership was hardly a priority with those programs, and Gray Areas adopted, as historian Alice O'Connor phrased it, an "unapologetically top-down approach."[53] So, while Atlanta's neighborhood program was based on the St. Paul model, it and the New Haven and Boston programs shared commonalities, and all had drawn on recent thinking about structural and economic influences on social behavior.[54]

Indeed, the Gray Areas program served as a prototype for the federal CAP, though newer ideas about enabling local communities also came to influence the program. A number of federal staff embraced a community action ethos that sought to empower the disempowered and arm that group to build sustainable institutions. Not everyone embraced the idea of involving the poor at the highest level of decision-making, but as historian Joshua Zeitz points out, some of the younger members of Johnson's War on Poverty think tank considered community action to be "revolutionary activity." In their view, CAPs could challenge local institutions that were, in Zeitz's words, "fundamentally hostile to the aspirations of poor people."[55]

Atlanta's planning group decided to launch an independent nonprofit corporation as its community action agency, one that would enhance the city's urban renewal efforts by providing mechanisms for "social rehabilitation."[56] Allen asked the group to flesh out the details quickly. "We need to do this so that upon passage of the bill, we can swing right into action," explained the mayor.[57] By the end of the month, the CCAA was confident enough to assert that, if the Economic Opportunity Act passed, "Atlanta may be one of the first cities in the country to implement the Community Action Program."[58]

Atlanta–Fulton County Economic Opportunity Authority (EOA)

In August 1964, the city and county approved the formation of the Atlanta–Fulton County Economic Opportunity Authority (EOA), the entity that would implement the city's CAP, and began staffing the agency.[59] Atlanta mayor Ivan Allen Jr. and Fulton County Commission chair Harold McCart recruited Boisfeuillet "Bo" Jones to serve as chair of the board of the new authority. In many ways, Jones was a strategic choice. Formerly a college professor and vice president for health services at Atlanta's private Emory University, Jones spent the early 1960s in the Kennedy and Johnson administrations working as special assistant to the secretary of the Department of Health, Education, and Welfare. There he developed relationships that would help Atlanta secure federal funding. In particular, he was friends with Sargent Shriver, the former head of the Peace Corps, who was tasked by Johnson to lead the War on Poverty.[60] In 1963, Jones returned to Atlanta to run the Emily and Ernest Woodruff Foundation, the private charitable organization then directed by retired Coca-Cola visionary Robert W. Woodruff and the primary body funding the CCAA. Woodruff initially opposed the idea of Jones chairing the EOA while leading the foundation, but apparently later he agreed, perhaps because the EOA reflected and had the potential to help realize CCAA's social service planning goals.[61] As chair of the EOA, Jones capitalized on his D.C. connections. Bruce Wedge, regional director of urban renewal, sent notes to the assistant commissioner for urban planning and community development for the Housing and Home Finance Agency, Frederick Hayes, and the associate director of the federal CAP, Sanford Kravitz, indicating that "Bo Jones called me. . . . wants Atlanta to be #1. He will have a program in by the end of the week."[62]

In Atlanta, Jones went to work identifying other personnel willing and able to quickly build the city's antipoverty infrastructure.[63] Jones immediately tapped Charles O. Emmerich to serve as executive director of the new agency. A highly respected administrator, Emmerich had recently been defeated in his bid to continue as DeKalb County commissioner. Emmerich's top aide, Dan Sweat, would serve as second in command.[64] To Atlanta's business and political elite, the possibilities of the War on Poverty to improve social, economic, and labor conditions warranted the appointment of powerful and competent men to run the programs.

The EOA community action proposal was, for all intents and purposes, an expansion of CCAA's neighborhood center demonstration project. As the community action grant application outlined, the centers were intended to "provide a comprehensive array of services including homemaker, legal, family counseling, day care, employment, education [and] family planning."[65] With federal support, the EOA would build on the West End concept and open twelve new neighborhood centers in the poorest areas of Atlanta.[66]

To Atlanta's proposal authors, the neighborhood service center was not just a way to expand existing services, an approach discouraged by War on Poverty staff. Rather, the dispersal of services was pitched as an innovation in social service delivery. And the social services literature of the era bears that out. As Thomas Walz explained in a 1969 *Public Welfare* article, neighborhood service centers were seen as a possible remedy for key weaknesses in social welfare. In particular, neighborhood-based centers would counter the inaccessibility of social services. They would put social services in easy reach of those who most needed them and create coherence out of an otherwise fragmented array of social services. By facilitating geographic access and coordinating agency efforts, such centers would increase efficiencies and diminish bureaucracy, thus enlarging the client base and reducing poverty.[67] To further enhance service delivery, Atlanta's leaders planned to train social service aides utilizing what Walz referred to as the *indigenous nonprofessional*. Centers would hire residents of targeted neighborhoods as aides who would perform outreach and help alleviate the shortage of social work professionals.[68] To the program's authors, service centers offered multiple remedies to what had been seemingly intransigent problems.

Indeed, there was much to commend Atlanta's program. It offered expanded and easier access to social services, involved the poor in program delivery, and proactively sought out those who would benefit from social services. Innovation notwithstanding, to many local observers, at the point Atlanta submitted its community action application to Washington—November 16, 1964—Atlanta's War on Poverty had yet to substantively involve local Black leadership, a significant oversight given the still-active and vocal civil rights movement in what was, as Mayor William Hartsfield famously phrased it, "the city too busy to hate."[69]

Black Leadership

"As you know, a very large percentage of the population of Atlanta and Fulton County are Negro citizens," leaders of the Summit penned to Mayor Allen and Fulton County Commission chair McCart. "Unfortunately, a disproportionate number of these are persons who are in need of services that may be offered by [EOA]."[70] Formed in 1963 to collectively work toward "complete integration," the Summit represented Atlanta's major civil rights organizations.[71] Black involvement in Atlanta's War on Poverty planning had thus far been inadequate, the writers asserted. "We are sure that you share our belief that citizens should be planned with instead of for," they continued, echoing the War on Poverty's emphasis on citizen participation.[72] The Atlanta NAACP reinforced those concerns in a November 1964 telegram to Sargent Shriver. "We fear a paternalistic superficial and unworkable program," C. Miles Smith, president of the local chapter stated. They requested "an opportunity to react to the plan before final approval."[73]

Those raising the alarm over lack of Black presence in War on Poverty programming were established Black leaders long involved in promoting civil rights and increasing Black political power in Atlanta and in general. Summit cochair "emeritus" A. T. Walden (discussed in chapter 1), was arguably the leader of Atlanta's Black political establishment at the time. Most recently, when the student movement began using sit-ins to increase Black access to Atlanta restaurants and other facilities, Walden led negotiations with white politicians and business leaders.[74] Summit cochair Clarence D. Coleman, a rising star in the urban league movement, directed the southern regional office of the National Urban League.[75] Summit cochair and pastor of the large and influential Friendship Baptist Church, Samuel W. Williams worked on behalf of the Atlanta NAACP, serving as president in 1959 and 1960.[76] Williams saw the value of selective use of protest and direct action and, while associated with the NAACP, helped launch the local Southern Christian Leadership Conference. To Atlanta's establishment civil rights leadership (members of Atlanta's Black sociopolitical elite), African Americans were disproportionately affected by poverty and therefore deserved a greater presence in War on Poverty planning and administration.

Although the Summit and NAACP insisted on more Black involvement in launching the local War on Poverty, African Americans (and Black elite in particular) *were* involved in program planning at its earliest stages. Rufus Clement (introduced in chapter 1) served on CCAA's board as it developed its neighborhood centers pilot. Clement and Robert A. Thompson Jr. both served on the mayor's task force that initially proposed the EOA and recommended that Atlanta pursue Economic Opportunity Act monies. Thompson had worked as Atlanta Urban League's associate director of housing and was appointed executive director in 1960. In those positions, Thompson had helped develop new housing opportunities for working- and middle-class African Americans. In 1964, Thompson had taken a leave of absence from his duties at Atlanta Urban League to serve as assistant to the regional administrator of the Housing and Home Finance Agency in Atlanta.[77] Jesse Hill Jr., actuary for Atlanta Life Insurance, and W. R. Cochrane, secretary of the politically important Butler Street YMCA, had hosted a breakfast meeting in September 1964 at Paschal's restaurant to discuss the new antipoverty program with community leaders, and both were subsequently appointed to the board of the EOA.[78] Indeed, federal program inspectors would point out in an EOA assessment a year later that Blacks appointed to the EOA board represented Atlanta's "Negro power structure."[79] But while the Black elite were represented on the CCAA and in War on Poverty planning meetings, the Summit, Atlanta NAACP, and Atlanta Urban League insisted on substantive Black involvement in program design. By 1964, Atlanta's Black elite were well practiced in challenging Atlanta's white business and political elite, having used their increased voting strength to, for example, demand civil rights concessions from Mayor William Hartsfield.[80]

EOA board chair Bo Jones learned the extent of the Summit's dissatisfaction with Black presence in War on Poverty planning when he was in Washington, D.C., in support of Atlanta's application. There, the OEO's Jack Conway showed Jones a November 16, 1964, telegram from Samuel Williams expressing concern about the limited Black participation in designing Atlanta's community action agency. When Jones returned to Atlanta, he immediately arranged for meetings with Summit cochairs Williams and Coleman. There he "raised cain," as he later explained to federal inspections division interviewers.[81] Jones was frustrated that concerns about EOA had not been first brought to him. Complaining to Washington without first raising the issue with local authorities was "very poor procedure," Jones wrote to Conway with a copy to Williams, Coleman, and Hill.[82] But while Jones may have been irritated, the complaint worked: he increased involvement of the city's established Black leadership in Atlanta's community action agency.

A November 21, 1964, meeting between EOA and Summit leaders resulted in an "informal understanding" on several points: the EOA Board of Directors would be enlarged to allow for wider representation; employment and contracts would be awarded based on merit; a technical advisory committee and community participation committee would be established; and proportional employment of Blacks would be considered. Informal understandings in hand, the Summit telegrammed the federal OEO to alert them that "many serious objection[s were] informally resolved."[83] While the informal agreement appeared ambiguous, the Summit's telegram suggests that EOA agreed to the Summit's central demand: increased Black presence in EOA planning. On November 23, 1964, Atlanta received notification that it had been awarded $1.08 million, the fifth largest of twelve grants made to U.S. cities.[84] Atlanta's Black establishment would not rest easy, though. They would continue to keep tabs on EOA to ensure the agency lived up to its commitment.

As large as the grant was, it was only a partial award; OEO set special restrictions on Atlanta, withholding $900,000 until EOA demonstrated that there was a high degree of resident participation in Atlanta's CAP.[85] The federal office was insisting that Atlanta adhere to the requirement for the maximum feasible participation of the poor. But concerns about resident participation would have to wait, as the Summit and its supporters would soon articulate a more specific demand: the presence of African Americans in EOA's administrative ranks, in authentic, decision-making positions.

A week after the Summit had brokered an informal understanding with EOA leadership, the Summit voted to insist that a qualified Black be appointed as associate director of EOA.[86] To white leadership, the demand had simply arrived too late: Charlie Emmerich had already been busy building the War on Poverty apparatus, and the Summit's proposal to appoint an African American as associate director did not square with those plans. But after further negotiation with the Summit, Jones and Emmerich ultimately agreed that EOA would have two associate directors, one in charge of agency coordination and program implementation and one in charge of administration—"the business end of the operation," as Samuel Williams stated it in a letter summarizing the decision.[87] The letter did not identify the race of particular positions, nor did it specify the individuals who would serve in specific roles, but race was considered in subsequent appointments. Dan Sweat, Emmerich's original white choice as associate director, would serve as associate director for administration. Tilman C. Cothran, a Black professor of sociology at Atlanta University, was appointed associate director for agency resources. The director of neighborhood services—a position to which white CCAA neighborhood program head Dave Beecher had already been appointed—would communicate through the appropriate associate director, depending on whether the concern was business or programmatic. Sam Williams's summarizing the agreement suggests that the Summit was satisfied with the outcome of the negotiations.[88]

To some extent, the agreement and subsequent appointment of an African American to associate director appears an accomplishment. But as the OEO inspections division pointed out in a later report, Black appointments to EOA administration had been made after much of the administrative apparatus had already been established. And whites, with little consultation with the Black community, had made those appointments.[89] In sum, with the exception of Rufus Clement's membership on CCAA as the neighborhood program pilot was launched, Blacks had been afforded little input into the neighborhood project that CCAA developed and on which the EOA proposal was based. Generally speaking, African Americans had been an afterthought and, as the Summit had noted, were planned *for*, not *with*. But under pressure and constant scrutiny by Atlanta's civil rights establishment, EOA's racial demographics did begin to change.

As executive director, Emmerich continued to appoint Blacks to leadership positions in EOA. In February 1965, *Jet* magazine reported that "prominent negroes" were "liberally sprinkled" throughout EOA's top management. Besides Tilman Cothran, those leaders included William Fowlkes, who had served as managing editor of the Black-owned and Black-focused *Atlanta Daily World* for the twenty years prior to joining EOA, and who would direct the NASH-Washington Neighborhood Service Center; YMCA aide Harold Barrett, who would serve as assistant to Fowlkes; businessman John H. Calhoun, hired as a special consultant who would help coordinate community participation; and Frankie Adams, an Atlanta University School of Social Work professor hired to coordinate community development and training programs.[90] Additionally, by June 1965, Blacks had greater representation on the EOA Board of Directors. Besides Jesse Hill and real estate developer William L. Calloway, who had replaced W. R. Cochrane, EOA had added two additional Black board members, Martin Luther King Sr., pastor of Ebenezer Baptist Church, and Mrs. W. H. (Lucy) Aiken, wife of successful Black builder and Realtist W. H. Aiken.[91] Like Hill, Calloway, and Cochrane, King and Aiken were members of Atlanta's Black political establishment. Thus, Atlanta's Black sociopolitical elite were increasingly in positions to direct the new antipoverty infrastructure and were benefiting from it.

Nonetheless, Black presence in policy-making positions continued to concern Atlanta's Black community. By August 1965, Black civil rights leaders felt Associate Director Tilman Cothran's duties had shifted, resulting in less responsibility than Summit originally intended. It was understood, Sam Williams explained to federal staff, that Cothran would be the associate director in charge of program development and thus in charge of the program's neighborhood centers.[92] Instead, Dave Beecher served as a de facto associate director in charge of the community centers.[93] In a Washington, D.C., meeting with Jack Gonzales, Cothran complained about Bo Jones "reneging on an agreement made with the Atlanta negro community."[94] In Cothran's view, his position had been gradually downgraded, and the director of the neighborhood service centers was going around him. As Cothran outlined to an interviewer for the War on Poverty's inspections division, Dave Beecher, who was white, "found it difficult to work under a Negro" and bypassed Cothran to answer directly to Emmerich or Sweat. According to Cothran, Emmerich preferred Cothran to work on program development, research, and evaluation, not program implementation.[95] To federal program reviewers, the Cothran-Beecher conflict was primarily one of personality and not racial, but that conclusion did little to ease tensions.[96]

Atlanta's Black and white sociopolitical elite and the city's poor had different goals for EOA. To Atlanta's white power structure, EOA was an opportunity to bring its social systems to "parity" with other urban improvements—to enhance the city's workforces and better position Atlanta to become a national city. To the Black establishment, the CAP was also an opportunity to bring Black influence to bear on public policy, which would ultimately increase Black opportunity and ensure racial equity. Poor Atlantans wanted EOA to diminish and mitigate *poverty*.

Involving the Poor

While civil rights leaders insisted on proportional numbers of Blacks in EOA administration and planning, there were few demands—from any group—for direct involvement of the poor, at least initially. To some degree, it is not surprising that establishment leaders, Black or white, did not insist on consulting the poor in EOA planning. In the early 1960s, poverty was largely attributed to personal failings. If a person was poor, the thinking went, the person lacked appropriate skills, education, or work values. Once those deficiencies were eliminated, poverty would be alleviated. It followed that if poor people lacked the values, skills, or education to remedy their particular plight, it seemed unlikely they would have the inclination, knowledge, or skills to help plan the largest antipoverty program the city had ever experienced. Rather, the educated professional, who better knew the path to professional success, was the appropriate person to design an antipoverty program.[97] The Black and white administrators at the helm of EOA and on the board of directors appeared confident that they could address the major causes of poverty. Substantial involvement of the poor in program planning made little sense to political leaders and business professionals.

To be sure, Atlanta was aware of the War on Poverty requirement to involve the poor in program development; its November 1964 "Summary of the Application" pointed out the requirement for resident participation and indicated that the use of neighborhood aides was one mode by which the poor contributed to EOA programming.[98] But it was only in February 1965 that federal officials provided specific guidance on the directive requiring "maximum feasible participation" of the poor in the planning and implementation of CAPs.[99] Atlanta had begun assembling its community action agency in early 1964, launched the authority over the summer, and submitted its application in November, well before guidelines were penned. Not surprisingly, its professional elite—paternalistic—assumptions were built into program administration, and "maximum feasible participation" hardly meant that Atlanta's poor would have seats at the board of directors' table. In March 1965, when EOA responded to OEO's requirement that Atlanta demonstrate a "high degree of resident participation" to receive the award balance of $900,000, EOA established a multilayered citizen participation structure that reduced the likelihood that poor residents would be elected to the highest, decision-making level.[100]

EOA organized a "city-wide citizens' participation committee," a group that, on paper, was intended to allow resident input across the larger set of EOA programs. Begun as EOA opened its first five neighborhood centers, the committee started with eleven members but soon grew to forty.[101] As Bo Jones explained in an interview with OEO's inspections division, "The poor are supposed to be involved in the decision-making process on a lower level than the Board of Directors. . . . If you wish professional leadership in a democratic program, this is what you want."[102] Input and recommendations from Atlanta's poor were supposed to flow *up* to the board. Records are not available for the early citywide citizen participation committee or the initial board, but subsequent events suggest that poor residents had little influence over, for example, the location of EOA's first service centers, a matter that could severely impact EOA's effectiveness.

"We cannot understand why the first [neighborhood center] should begin in what is predominantly a middle class Negro neighborhood," *Atlanta Inquirer* editor Bill Strong wrote in the February 27, 1965, issue of the Black-focused newspaper, referring to NASH-Washington, the larger area encompassing Vine City and Booker T. Washington High School. Strong acknowledged that the NASH-Washington neighborhoods had impoverished sections, including Vine City, but "certainly none of the vast expanses of abject poverty common in the Southeast and Northeast section" of Atlanta.[103] At least they could have put the center in easier access to the area's poor residents. The Price Neighborhood Center, as it was called, was located within the middle-income section of the neighborhood, and the worst pockets of poverty were blocks away. The War on Poverty's inspections office echoed Strong's assessment. "To get to the Price Neighborhood Center from the center city, one goes through a depressing slum area . . . and past a public housing project. Then one enters a pleasant neighborhood with lawns, trees, and well kept frame houses. *That* is where the Price Neighborhood Center is," the report explained.[104] There had been some local and site committee desire to have the center at Beulah Baptist Church in Vine City, but those plans fell through over disagreements about renovations, and EOA administrators had been in a rush to set up the center before a visiting congressional delegation arrived. The final location was "not the best one," John Calhoun conceded in an interview with the OEO's inspections division.[105] Months later, many poor residents remained unaware of the NASH-Washington center. As former SNCC member and state representative–elect Julian Bond explained to *Atlanta Constitution* reporters, a number of the needy "[didn't] even know [it was] there."[106]

Thus, in its first year, EOA struggled to implement a citizens' participation and board infrastructure that could adequately gather and act upon insights of EOA's target group, Atlanta's poor. Consequently, the first service centers were implemented without adequate consideration and, as a result, were not in easy reach of the city's poorest residents. Attempts to establish neighborhood service centers would continue to meet challenges.

Commitment

With few models on which to draw and a massive infrastructure to design and build, EOA's implementation of neighborhood service centers was indeed slow going, in part because of attention to citizen involvement. Residents and EOA staff were in something of a catch-22. They wanted centers established quickly *and* authentic citizen involvement, which took time. The process by which the northwest center was established illustrates both residents' commitment to the promise of the War on Poverty and the challenges of citizen-led institution building in mid-1960s Atlanta.

EOA community development coordinator John Calhoun worked with local civic leaders to alert residents about the EOA program and to form neighborhood advisory councils and site committees.[107] Calhoun brought various talents and experience to his job. A founder of the Atlanta Negro Voters League and active member of the local NAACP, Calhoun was committed to grassroots political activity and organizing. (He would later help develop Atlanta's neighborhood planning units, the mechanism by which neighborhood residents would have input in city decision-making.) Calhoun pursued EOA organizing with zeal.

Calhoun called on well-known local leaders Rev. Cadmus Samples and Ortelus Shelmon of the Scott's Crossing Civic League to help implement and inform northwest Atlanta residents about EOA. As revered local leaders and early settlers of the far northwest neighborhoods, fifty-seven-year-old Shelmon and thirty-nine-year-old Samples were sound choices. Shelmon had arrived in Atlanta in 1923 from rural Georgia, where his parents had farmed. He had worked at a variety of jobs at established Atlanta institutions, including Whittier Mills, Atlantic Steel, and Southern Railway. After moving to Scott's Crossing, a settlement abutting the rail yards northwest of downtown, he joined and became a deacon at what was then known as Springfield Baptist Church.[108] As Shelmon recalled, in its early years, Scott's Crossing had no water system or streets and only three trails for wagons and buggies. He and local residents worked through their Scott's Crossing Civic League to make various improvements. They established Sweat Road (now Perry Boulevard) from Hollywood Road to Marietta Street, founded the Rosenwald-supported W. J. Scott School, and at times challenged police brutality and school segregation.[109] Rev. Cadmus Samples, a generation younger than Shelmon, was equally committed to Atlanta's northwest area. A graduate of Morris Brown College and Turner Theological Seminary, Samples was an ordained AME minister who founded the Wilkes Chapel AME Church just east of Scott's Crossing. Like Shelmon, Samples regularly committed time to civic and political projects.[110]

Together Shelmon and Samples mustered a network of church and civic leaders who provided the backbone of local support and advice for the proposed northwest neighborhood service center. They solicited names of lay leaders to serve as advisers and asked if congregations would be willing to serve as day care facilities or recreation centers. "The program needs the full cooperation of the churches in the area, to reach all the people in this war on poverty," Shelmon and Samples explained in a letter to area congregations.[111]

Community aides went house to house in Atlanta's hot summer sun, interviewing families as to their needs and explaining EOA and what the neighborhood centers would do. Then they arranged neighborhood block meetings to disseminate information about EOA and the neighborhood service centers. While the legwork was intense and time-consuming, the approach was necessary given low literacy rates and lack of telephones and transportation in Atlanta's poorest areas. Calhoun, Shelmon, and Samples divided Atlanta's northwest into sixteen sections and arranged for house meetings of ten to fifteen residents, sometimes holding two meetings a night. "These meetings are being held to acquaint small groups in the community with the Economic Opportunity Authority Program," Shelmon wrote on an invitation listing five different homes, dates, and times at which meetings would be held.[112] Few records of those discussions survive, but if the July 23, 1965, gathering was typical, the meetings were largely attended by women living in the immediate area of the host.[113] Then, in August, Shelmon and Samples worked with local high school principal Arthur Richardson and civic leaders Robert Dobbs, Mary Sanford, and Roy Sawyer to hold larger gatherings to discuss site selection and set up a temporary advisory committee for the neighborhood center.[114] Not surprisingly, some—including John Calhoun—grew impatient with the slow pace of organizing. When Calhoun suggested holding a community-wide forum before block meetings were complete, Shelmon admonished him to be patient and to finish the process that they had laid out.[115]

Northwest residents eager to become neighborhood aides likewise grew frustrated with EOA's deliberate pace. The thirty new aide positions were highly desirable: they were close to home, did not require physical labor, had low barriers to entry, and promised training. Anticipating the opening of the northwest neighborhood service center, Shelmon and Samples made EOA aware of potential employees and encouraged residents to apply to EOA. But the slow opening of centers meant the delayed hiring of aides. As Shelmon explained to the northwest center's newly appointed director, Dave Powell, applicants were growing tired of waiting. Applicants continued to attend community organizing meetings and remained committed to the EOA effort, but "so much time has passed they have become somewhat skeptical." Shelmon appended a list of twenty-four residents who had applied, all but one of whom were women.[116] Likely Shelmon's appeal had been mailed before Samples received Frankie Adams's entreaty that the gentlemen hold off on referring any more applicants. "You are aware that only a total of 30 individuals can be placed in a center as aides. . . . [T]here are several applications now pending and individuals become disturbed, as you know, when they cannot be employed."[117] Eager to work with the new EOA, northwest residents filled out applications, attended community meetings, hosted information sessions, and volunteered their congregations to host social services, such as child care. The centers were, in many ways, a community effort. They promised jobs and support, and northwest residents were anxious for new opportunities.

Concerns about EOA were, in fact, piling up. In an EOA survey intended to identify poverty-related problems that EOA was designed to address, Shelmon and Samples spoke for the Scott's Crossing residents in identifying several issues with EOA itself. There was a "lack of communication of program and progress" to the Citizen Advisory Committee "and to people who live in the target area." The center director needed to "listen to the Advisory Committee and carry out their wishes to get full community participation." Residents felt the center should hire a more diverse pool of people. "No age limit such as being too old, too short, too fat, too black or too white should be held against the applicant," Shelmon and Samples conveyed.[118] To many target area residents, EOA remained distant from poor people and their struggles.

Seeking to build a thriving "national" city, Atlanta's white civic elite cobbled together a social planning apparatus, the CCAA, that they hoped would ensure a stable, reliable, and capable workforce. In this way, white elite demonstrated an ongoing commitment to a civic welfare state. They used CCAA to experiment with building what they hoped to be a durable apparatus that would improve Atlantans' lives and opportunity.

In practice, social planning was costly and time-consuming, and CCAA board members struggled to sustain their neighborhood service centers project. The CCAA founders were fortunate that the Kennedy and Johnson administrations proposed an ambitious War on Poverty, and Mayor Ivan Allen Jr.'s staff and network helped attract federal attention and secure significant monies from the newly launched program. To the CCAA, there was much to commend the neighborhood service centers idea. They hoped to assess program outcomes, ease access to services, and utilize "indigenous" aides who would simultaneously learn new skill sets and facilitate relationships with residents of the poor neighborhoods that the programs served. The social and political power the CCAA board wielded ensured that the program and practices evolved into the city's new community action agency, Economic Opportunity Atlanta, Inc. (EOA), as the agency was renamed in the summer of 1965.

Atlanta's Black sociopolitical elite had additional goals for the city's new agency. They saw the War on Poverty as a chance to expand African Americans' roles in local policy making. Black establishment members insisted that white EOA administrators hire Black professionals in leadership positions that would have impact on the Black community. Black influence in shaping EOA arrived late, however. By the time African Americans were involved in any substantial program implementation, the white business and political power structure had launched a neighborhood service center project that, in their minds, utilized the latest social welfare innovations.

Tensions and negotiations between the white and Black establishment over management of EOA meant that the "maximum feasible participation of the poor" in the design and implementation of Atlanta's CAP went almost ignored in 1964 and 1965. To be sure, many neighborhood service centers drew on the input of area residents as the institutions and their associated programs were planned, as was the case with the Northwest Service Center. Other centers, such as NASH-Washington, continued to be, in the words of a War on Poverty inspection report, a "middle class Negro operation."[119] In those cases, poor Atlantans had little input about jobs, training, or other services designed to benefit them. When EOA signaled its intent to enforce its citizen participation provision by withholding $900,000, administrators crafted a hierarchical structure by which input would, in theory, flow up from the "grassroots" to the board. Residents remained frustrated that they had little real influence, and War on Poverty inspectors would continue to criticize the agency throughout the late 1960s.

Despite early challenges, many poor Atlantans embraced community-based planning and clearly welcomed the promises of the War on Poverty. In the northwest, for example, so many residents sought out jobs as neighborhood aides that local leaders were asked to temper their recruitment activities. Still, by the end of fall 1965, it was not clear to many of Atlanta's poor if Atlanta's community action agency would have any real value to them. Consequently, many of Atlanta's poor would organize outside EOA structures and insist on access to local political regimes.

CHAPTER 3

Vine City

The Civil Rights Act of 1964 "meant nothing to the average Vine City resident," J. Otis Cochran told colleagues in January 1965, and Lyndon Johnson's War on Poverty was not "bettering houses, jobs, streets, nor increasing welfare benefits."[1] The Morehouse College student thought a new project—Experiments in Self-Help—might jumpstart change by organizing local residents to address problems *they* cared about. A Vine City resident himself, Cochran was inspired by the civil rights movement and community organizing praxis and was compelled by neighborhood conditions and personal experiences. As a Black teenager growing up in Vine City, he had seen the dehumanizing aspects of such things as segregated streetcars and "whites only" signage. As the civil rights movement unfolded on the west side of Atlanta and revealed itself on television, in newspapers, and in day-to-day conversations, the teen tried to insert himself into the scene. He made sure to be in places where he might run into and exchange a few words with Martin Luther King Jr., who had moved to one of the nicer streets in Vine City after leaving Montgomery in 1960, and as high schoolers, Cochran and his friend James Zeke Bond tried to slip into Student Nonviolent Coordinating Committee events. Race was closely intertwined with poverty, Cochran knew, but maybe the tactics of community organizing, which he had learned about in his college classes, might help beat back poverty and urban decay. He was not alone in thinking Vine City would be an ideal site in which to experiment in antipoverty organizing.

Vine City, was, in the 1960s, simultaneously neglected by the city and the object of interest of community organizers and some civil rights groups. On paper, it was a mixed-income neighborhood, but the streets and sections in which poor families resided were particularly bereft. As was the case in south Atlanta, residents had made polite entreaties to the city to improve trash collection, street conditions, and sewer and water service, but those efforts had largely failed. Experiments in Self Help, the Vine City Improvement Association, and the Vine City Council would eventually emerge as residents struggled to organize and force landlords, the city, and others to live up to their obligations. At the same time, SNCC saw in Vine City an opportunity to experiment with urban organizing, and they established the Atlanta Project in the neighborhood in 1966. SNCC's philosophy was evolving, though, and its anti-Vietnam activities distracted the organization from its community organizing commitments. Communities throughout the South faced similar challenges as they sought to organize and take advantage of the War on Poverty's CAP. Consequently, the Southern Regional Council (SRC) opted to document and assess Vine City's experience, thinking the events might be instructive for others. Eventually, as occurred in south Atlanta, "outside" organizers would leave Vine City, and residents would continue the challenging work of mustering resources and prodding local government.

Many families in the twenty-four-block Vine City neighborhood just northwest of Atlanta's downtown certainly struggled.[2] Some 53 percent of families lived below the poverty level. About 1,300 households had deteriorated or dilapidated plumbing, and many homes shared or had no bathrooms. Housing stock was a mix of single-family homes and small apartment complexes. Most residents—approximately 80 percent—were tenants, and in 1959, the neighborhood was nearly 100 percent Black. In part due to the lack of low-income housing available elsewhere in the city, many Vine City residents had lived in the neighborhood all their lives. Services were lacking. Sewers on Magnolia, Delbridge, and Walnut Streets in particular backed up during rain, and residents endured standing water until city workers arrived to clear the stoppage. City trash pickup was irregular, which meant that rubbish collected on area streets and contributed to drainage issues.[3] Poor conditions were exacerbated by exploitative landlords who charged high rents, failed to keep up and improve their properties, and were quick to evict. Robert Lee Edwards explained that his apartment on Markham Street had holes in walls and window sashes that let in wind and cold. Windows and the bathtub leaked, and roaches and rats were common.[4] Grocers charged high prices.[5] In the mid-1960s, as cities across the United States suffered riots and forms of civil disorder, Atlanta leaders worried that Vine City was a tinderbox, that it had the potential to break into violence with any provocation.

Experiments in Self-Help

By 1965, Otis Cochran was ready to act. Armed with community organizing theory and frustrated with discrimination and entrenched poverty, the Morehouse freshman and his friends created Experiments in Self-Help (ESH). As Cochran described the project, people would start an "experiment" in their own neighborhood, such as nearby Mechanicsville or Washington Park. Different experiments would take up different issues—housing, recreation, or whatever was of interest to residents. It was "self-help" in that the "experimenters" would partner with neighborhood residents and support the projects the neighborhood wanted to pursue. In short, ESH intended to foster neighborhood-based, resident-led organizing for positive social change.

Ambitious and willing to draw on his growing social network, Cochran arranged a meeting with colleagues and friends in January 1965 to discuss launching ESH in his neighborhood, Vine City.[6] The group of six saw an opportunity to organize Vine City residents and force the city to make improvements. The historical record is not entirely clear on who was involved in this early work, but an SRC report described the group as consisting of five people, along with Cochran, the only Vine City resident. White SRC field worker Al Ulmer, who documented the project for SRC, was likely present. Historian Kathryn Nasstrom indicates that white liberal Frances Pauley, director of the Georgia Council on Human Relations (GCHR), attended.[7] White liberal Eliza Paschall, whose manuscript archives contain Vine City materials, may well have been at the table.[8] Other attendees may have included Cochran's university professors, such as white Spelman College professor Marcia L. Halvorsen, who introduced Cochran to community organizing philosophy and literature.[9]

To Cochran and his human relations colleagues, existing programs that sought to help a few individuals eliminate their personal shortcomings were an insufficient response to central Atlanta's widespread poverty. Residents needed to be mobilized to do something about the "*conditions* that caused personal shortcomings*," as a SRC report framed it.[10] Residents needed the power to influence change. But how could the group foster political consciousness among neighborhood residents and a desire to act collectively? Could residents retool power structures in a way that produced positive outcomes for Vine City? The group debated different approaches, including Saul Alinsky's methods, which took advantage of discontent, promoted the creation of broad coalitions, and embraced agitation.[11] Could existing church and social groups be mobilized toward those ends?[12]

How to organize and mobilize communities was a burning question in 1965 and 1966 as local groups sought to bring about social change or to take advantage of the War on Poverty's community action program. Indeed, as War on Poverty–inspired community action agencies proliferated across the nation and South, SRC's field organizer Al Ulmer responded to a number of inquiries from people and organizations hoping to learn how to organize and mobilize communities. One year into the War on Poverty and well into the modern Black freedom movement, community organizing practices had yet to be adequately studied and documented and certainly were not widely disseminated. Responding to a query from Sherie Hallerook at Allen University in Columbia, South Carolina, Ulmer wrote, "Materials detailing such things as tactical steps and techniques to follow in community organization are not available, at least I don't have any of them."[13] In a January 1966 letter to Robert Valder at the Alabama Council on Human Relations, Ulmer explained, "The problem in having a workshop in community organization is that almost everyone has a different opinion about what it is." Valder was seeking other potential speakers, but Ulmer indicated that there were few to suggest in the deep South: "Resource people in [community organizing] are going to be difficult to find. There is a man in Jacksonville, another in New Orleans, maybe one from here—all doing different things."[14] William "Bill" Beardske at Haverford College wrote Ulmer that he'd had little luck finding material on urban organizing. "Even the [Students for a Democratic Society] people have trouble," he pointed out.[15] Nationwide, organizations and organizers struggled to assemble a discrete and effective community organizing praxis.

Frustrated with lack of knowledge in this area just as the federal War on Poverty sought to fund local community action organizations, the SRC opted to document, analyze, and disseminate organizational strategies and tactics. Ulmer thought the experiences of Vine City's ESH might be useful to those seeking to organize community action programs as part of the War on Poverty, or others who sought to mobilize communities for social change.[16]

"The Poor Are Beginning to Organize"

To begin Experiments in Self-Help, students from Marcia L. Halvorsen's spring 1965 freshmen sociology class at Spelman College assisted in surveying Vine City residents about "problems of most concern."[17] Helped by more than fifty college students, the group surveyed 11 percent of the approximately 1,275 families, often holding extended conversations with residents. While Cochran expected residents to identify unsafe housing and poor city services as the top items of concern, residents worried more about the safety of area children. The neighborhood lacked playgrounds, and kids played in streets, abandoned structures, or trash-filled lots. But a wide range of complaints emerged—police brutality, high rents coupled with lax building maintenance, unpaved streets, and the lack of job opportunities.[18]

Armed with residents' feedback, ESH decided to help residents establish a playground. Building a playground was a sound choice for the period and was consistent with community organizing practice for the time. The safety of children was a concern easily acted upon and, in comparison to complaints about city services and high rents, a project likely to be successful. By organizing around and delivering a safe play space, ESH could help build a sense of neighborhood cohesion and self-efficacy, a foundation from which more challenging work could be advanced.[19]

Cochran and his colleagues searched for available land for the playground. After a few failed attempts, the owner of the Big Rock Store offered the use of the store's back lot. Local college students again supplied labor, meeting each Saturday at a local AME church to organize and assign tasks. They cleared the 36-by-60-foot space and built a wall to prevent erosion. Over the course of establishing the play space, an array of community members banded together in common cause, dropping by to work in the evenings, and presumably establishing new relationships and strengthening existing ones. ESH immediately sought to capitalize on these gains by creating an advisory committee of neighborhood residents and launching new initiatives.[20]

New projects brought new challenges, which resulted in a reorganization. By April 1965 community residents had indeed developed some cohesion, at least enough to feel and express dissatisfaction when ESH acted without consulting area residents. In their enthusiasm, ESH rented the Tillman family's two-story house—the largest house in the area—for use as a community center without fully discussing the opportunity with Vine City residents and without thinking through questions about ongoing building upkeep and costs. As a result of the lack of consultation and other disagreements, the Vine City residents opted to organize themselves as the Vine City Improvement Association (VCIA). In this new structure, the original group would act in an advisory role, providing technical expertise *when asked*. Toward that end, ESH prepared a brief proposal for VCIA in which they offered to canvas the neighborhood to help organize residents, but they conceded that "the only effective work that can be done in a neighborhood will have to be done by the people who live there."[21] The VCIA did decide to keep the house as a community center, but the VCIA members—that is, the Vine City residents—would set the organization's agenda going forward.[22]

The VCIA launched in summer 1965 with a burst of enthusiasm. Flyers announced the organization's first meeting, and at least sixty people turned out to elect officers and provide input.[23] Residents began fixing up the community center and opened a library. On July 1, 1965, a street carnival was held outside the newly established center, complete with food, games, and music. Over a thousand people attended, and VCIA netted $100 for community improvements. Many people signed up to join the VCIA or committed to attend the next meeting. Building on the neighborhood's energy, the VCIA soon formed committees on housing, streets, recreation, youth, cultural activities, law enforcement, and education.[24]

The committees had several achievements over the next year, and War on Poverty monies helped the group pursue small projects. The recreation committee sent twelve residents to the Atlanta Board of Alderman meeting where they requested equipment for a new playground and asked that the city begin planning for a new neighborhood park.[25] Soon afterward, a city worker arrived to inspect the playground lot, and an attorney started title searches to identify suitable park property. A housing committee also organized to prompt city action. Committee members distributed over a thousand copies of the housing code in preparation for an open meeting and petition regarding housing conditions. Two volunteers from the War on Poverty's newly established Volunteers in Service to America (VISTA) program were secured to work at the community center, and a teen youth group started holding dances.[26]

To the SRC, these accomplishments were important not only because they resulted in direct benefit to a poor neighborhood, but also because Vine City residents, in the words of an SRC report, "discovered they did have some power to do things."[27] In this case, they could organize to secure a park and other services in a period in which Atlanta had federal funds earmarked for such spending. To the SRC, developing a sense of self-efficacy and politicization were accomplishments worth pursuing and noting.

But while the VCIA had successes and struggles through the next year, the SRC expressed concern that VCIA was "almost trapped in a self improvement cycle." That is, the VCIA was increasingly providing support to individuals confronting a flawed system, not changing structural causes of poverty and inequality. The organization delivered typing classes and offered tutoring, but as the SRC asserted, "the slum child who benefits from a preschool experience is still destined for a slum school elementary education." The individual-focused self-improvement approach could never achieve more than "helping a few people overcome the slum," SRC stated. To the SRC, community organization should be "for the purpose of obtaining power: power enough to do away with the slum."[28]

VCIA also faced challenges common to voluntary organizations. The early surge of meeting attendance quickly leveled off, and VCIA found itself relying on a core of about fifteen people, with only six or seven people attending weekly meetings. Personality differences hampered activities, and committee meetings drew attendance away from the general meetings. Money issues fueled disagreements: members argued over how money should be spent and who had a voice in such decision-making. Lack of trust and personality conflicts so plagued the organization that news coverage that named or pictured particular individuals or gave attention to particular projects sparked further discord.[29]

VCIA was so riddled by internal strife that several residents broke from the group and formed the Vine City Council, which operated alongside though occasionally in conflict with the VCIA.[30] Neither organizational practice nor tensions between members of VCIA and the Vine City Council improved substantially, and a letter from SRC's Al Ulmer to Georgia representative Julian Bond indicates that the VCIA might never stabilize. The committees were "mostly paper things but occasionally they function well," Ulmer reported.[31] Although the VCIA would continue pressing for neighborhood improvement into the fall of 1966, the Vine City Council's activities soon eclipsed those of the VCIA.[32]

Neighborhood organizing was challenging under the best of circumstances, but it was all the more so when residents endured poverty and discrimination and had consistently been denied services. Residents made sincere attempts to address trenchant neglect by the city, and although early organizing attempts did not stick, the Vine City Council would have some staying power.

The Vine City Council

"I organized this neighborhood organization," resident Helen Howard explained about the Vine City Council in an interview a few years later. "Two men and six ladies started it." It "was a hard pull," Howard noted. But Howard was referring less to internal, organizational tensions and more to the council's attempts to challenge Atlanta's governing coalition—its regime of white politicians and businessmen and Black elites that informally governed Atlanta. That coalition was little accustomed or inclined to respond to the demands of politically weak constituents such as Atlanta's Black poor. Feeling nearly powerless, Vine City residents often feared making requests of landlords and city leaders, Howard explained, and initially the Vine City Council made little progress. "First we tried to go down to city hall and tell them how bad things is and how people is suffering around here," but the city did not respond. Then the council held a press conference. "We got a lot of publicity on that," Howard asserted. With small successes, residents' confidence grew. "And so we really got brave and people started demanding their rights."[33]

The *Vine City Voice*'s September 1965 front-page story, "Simple Arithmetic," signaled the council's focus on poverty and poor neighborhood conditions. In that column, in the council's newly launched, mimeographed newsletter, council founder Helen Howard laid out a budget presumably typical of a family living in Vine City. By Howard's calculations, the family ended up losing money with only the father working. Once a domestic position for the mother was taken into account, the family broke even if "the children [went] for themselves," that is, went without adult supervision while the parents were at work. But they wound up under water again if the family paid for childcare. With the children left to look after themselves—a likely outcome for the family's children over the long run, Howard concluded—"the girl goes to Grady Hospital for maternity care," and "the boy goes to jail." To Howard, low wages threatened family stability and children's futures. Because Vine City endured concentrated poverty, families throughout the neighborhood suffered and lived in constant risk. The council sought to address these issues. "We want you to fight together with us against injustice," the council implored.[34]

Besides neighborhood residents, white community organizers Hector and Susie Black were active members of the Vine City Council, and Hector served in a leadership role. A World War II veteran and graduate of Harvard, Black had worked extensively with Quaker-related groups concerned with social justice and change, as well as with the *Catholic Worker* in New York. Interested in contributing to the civil rights movement in some way, Hector and Susie Black and their children moved to Vine City in February 1965. After making a few inquiries, Hector accepted an offer to supervise the Quaker House's tutoring program in Vine City.[35] The Blacks were committed to Vine City, and they would help mobilize residents and lead Vine City Council initiatives.

The council soon had an activist bent. At the November 1965 meeting, for example, those in attendance fretted a substantial rent increase on a recently painted home and made plans to visit and discuss the issue with Wilson Realty, the property manager.[36] But while council leaders sought to take action, they struggled to generate and maintain resident interest in the VCC.

While council leaders intended to provide compelling programs and information that had direct benefits to residents, meeting attendance was frequently slim.[37] Council leaders and early members prodded area residents to show up to meetings and help improve conditions in Vine City. Dorothy Bolden explained to *Vine City Voice* readers, "This is what the people in Vine City need today, to get together and organize ourselves so we can have a voice and express our opinions and get things done out here."[38] An October 1965 advertisement for a Vine City Baptist Church meeting was typical of the VCC's early entreaties: "Let's speak out and say what it is like to 1. Live in these houses here, 2. To have no place for our children to play, 3. To be short of money and begging the city for help," the ad demanded. And in an article for the *Vine City Voice*, Hector Black asserted, "We who live here and know these conditions have a responsibility to speak out about them."[39]

In its first few months, the Vine City Council concentrated on exposing local problems via its newsletter, the *Vine City Voice (VCV)*, as well as through programming on the local radio station WAOK. "Filth" was blamed on city officials who, according to the *VCV*, failed to clean sewers, which caused trash to back up on the streets during heavy rains.[40] Surplus food programs, which distributed excess agricultural commodities to low-income families, operated on limited schedules and from inconvenient locations.[41] Bill collectors preyed on residents.[42] Wages were too low to make ends meet.[43] Naming conditions and their causes in media outlets served multiple purposes: this helped residents identify with each other's challenges, roused emotions that could be acted upon later, and alerted property owners and city officials that residents were paying attention and planning actions.

VCC members took their discontent with housing conditions directly to landlords. When Wade Turnipseed continued to rent a leaky, lockless home at 500 Magnolia Street NW to six families, council members paid him a visit, requesting that the conditions be corrected and that the overcrowding cease. If repairs were not completed, members asserted, the council would file a complaint with the city. Turnipseed ignored the appeal, and the council petitioned the city and then publicized their discontent through local radio station WAOK and the Black-focused newspaper *Atlanta Inquirer*. City building inspectors visited the home and subsequently recommended that occupancy be limited to one family and that repairs be made within forty-five days.[44]

In another case, council members asked residents to protest on behalf of a Vine City family who had suffered an eviction notice, an unresponsive welfare office, and dilapidated housing. "SO FELLOW CITIZENS OF VINE CITY, you know it's HELL to have to live like this," the newsletter urged. "So lets picket this old run-down house, the rent agent, landlords and the land lord's homes. Let's don't wait until a half dozen people be burnt to death, because most of these houses are fire traps."[45] VCC picketed the 76 Northside Drive property, which had two upstairs apartments and no fire escape. The house itself had several holes in the floor covered by plywood, and the upstairs toilet leaked through a hole in the first floor ceiling. VCC member Doris Reed later told readers that they had demonstrated all day. "We were protesting the house being there without a fire escape," she declared. "We were protesting the general attitude taken by the rent agent." Picketers assigned to the rental property carried signs reading, "Our slumlord is a lady," and "Another Tobacco Road on N'side Drive," the latter referring to Erskine Caldwell's novel depicting poverty and the oppression of tenant farmers in the South. Those protesting in front of landlord Thenie Stovall's home toted signs reading, "How many times have you fallen through your floor?" and "Does the bathroom from upstairs leak into your kitchen?" Within two weeks, VCC had scored another victory; Stovall began making repairs on her Vine City properties.[46]

Vine City Council's actions were potentially paying dividends. Mayor Ivan Allen Jr. was spotted visiting the neighborhood to observe neighborhood conditions firsthand, and the mayor reportedly drove Sargent Shriver, head of the federal government's War on Poverty, through Vine City that same week. The mayor's office told the *Atlanta Inquirer* that he was planning a ninety-day "crash program" to clean up the area, repair streets, and enforce other regulations.[47] And in the fall of 1965—after two "long hot summers" of urban riots had captured the nation's attention—the VCC drew at least some response from city hall. Atlanta has "been stepping up city services in the Vine City area for the past several months," Mayor Allen claimed, thanking the VCC for copies they had sent of the *VCV*.[48] After receiving the *Voice*, representatives from the city's Department of Parks and Recreation reportedly toured the area with neighborhood representatives to identify potential playground sites, and the city arranged a discussion of what to do with aging housing stock and abandoned properties.[49]

In its first year, the Vine City Council had marshaled local residents to begin discussing issues of concern, launched a local newsletter, and successfully pressured city officials and private landlords to begin responding to demands for sanitary and safe housing. The group documented local conditions and made those deficiencies known to neighborhood residents, elected officials, and influential individuals, Black and white. To force action, they had utilized petitions, filed complaints, and, in one case, organized picket lines to force a response from landlords. Consequently, when Student Nonviolent Coordinating Committee workers arrived in Vine City in January 1966 to (re)launch an Atlanta project, they found an active, community-based organization that had enjoyed some recent victories.

SNCC's Atlanta Project

When SNCC situated itself in Vine City in early 1966 and pondered how to organize in southern urban environments, they suggested a more ambitious version of what VCC had already established. Authors of SNCC's Atlanta Project proposal recommended circulating a newspaper; VCC had been putting out the biweekly *Vine City Voice* for three months. SNCC recommended developing a citywide tenant rights movement; VCC was already acting in support of and on behalf of many tenants. That being said, SNCC's ambitions were much larger than VCC's. Rather than focusing on a single neighborhood, SNCC's Atlanta Project envisioned developing a new strand within their organization: an urban, antipoverty, tenants' rights movement that would liberate the poor. And on January 22, 1966, SNCC announced, "The Atlanta Project. There is one."[50]

SNCC moved in to Vine City in response to SNCC member Julian Bond's ouster from the Georgia legislature. There they hoped to shore up popular support for the SNCC communications director-turned-legislator. Bond had won the 1965 election following the reapportionment of the Georgia General Assembly's lower house. But a week later, and following SNCC's release of a statement denouncing U.S. involvement in Vietnam, three members of the Georgia Assembly petitioned the house clerk to prevent Bond from taking his position. The Georgia House then voted 184 to 12 to unseat Bond. To SNCC and others, Bond's removal was a dangerous precedent.[51]

Beyond the Bond issue, a number of SNCC leaders identified political organizing of the urban poor as a natural extension of SNCC's rural work. Formed in 1960, SNCC was launched by young people who, frustrated with the slow pace of social change, initially focused on using direct action to desegregate lunch counters and the like. SNCC soon turned to bottom-up, grassroots movement building.[52]

In Lowndes County, Alabama, for example, SNCC assisted local residents in crafting an independent political party, the Lowndes County Freedom Party. SNCC workers woke before dawn to begin their days going from house to house and farm to farm, occasionally taking meals with families. Conversations focused on bread-and-butter issues—the need for running water, access to better schools, and the like. As historian Kwame Jeffries points out, SNCC had to build the movement household by household. SNCC supplemented door-to-door recruitment by involving themselves in other social networks, visiting churches, and making themselves aware of other clubs and social venues. All the while they talked and listened to residents and invited them to attend mass meetings in hopes that residents would find common cause and begin identifying possible solutions to problems.[53]

Using the organization's rural organizing experience to launch an urban grassroots movement made sense to many in SNCC. After all, poor Black residents were being forced out of Black Belt counties and into central cities where they were "ill-housed" and "unrepresented."[54] In the position paper "The Necessity for Southern Urban Organizing," members explained that migration was "[b]lackening the major urban areas of the South," and SNCC must "move towards developing control in the power centers in all of the southern states." SNCC members discussed the possibility of a pilot project in which SNCC would work in one city as a way to "learn more about how to work in urban areas." The students envisioned a process that allowed "local people to take the lead."[55]

To some Atlanta Project workers, the situation created by Bond's ouster from the state legislature was an opportunity to shift the civil rights movement's focus "away from the federal government as [the] major agent of change" and toward local political organization. Politics at the municipal, county, and state levels would be more susceptible to democratic control, SNCC argued, and thus would be more relevant to "the ordinary citizen." In Atlanta, SNCC could leverage the successes and improve on the failures of the Mississippi Freedom Democratic Party and Alabama's Lowndes County Freedom Party. Through SNCC-facilitated workshops and direct action, the Black poor "would realize that the causes for most of their problems stem[med] from a corrupt and inept city or state government." In this way, the project would expose how governments operated and would help southern Blacks—"and especially those who are poor"—overcome the fear that many had of established political authority. As it stood, Black voting power worked "to the benefit of a small few." In Atlanta, this was especially apparent. In Atlanta, SNCC warned, "the small established Negro leadership" was working rapidly to "further its control." What's more, the challenges of organizing in urban contexts were compounded by Atlanta's image of racial tolerance. "We're dealing with a city that spends millions, building and maintaining an image of racial harmony and political moderation," proponents of SNCC's Atlanta Project pointed out.[56] While Atlanta had its challenges, it seemed the perfect site to experiment with urban community organizing.

Early Atlanta project members represented a range of experiences and viewpoints. Bill Ware, who was appointed to lead the project, had worked in Ghana in the Peace Corps and embraced a pan-Africanist perspective.[57] Spelman student Gwen Robinson supported SNCC's main office and participated in Atlanta's student movement, protesting Jim Crow practices at Lester Maddox's Pickrick Restaurant and Krystals. She joined the project after directing the Laurel, Mississippi, project where, with a mostly white staff, she established a freedom school, day care center, and library and held a successful mock voter registration campaign. Robinson stayed in Laurel for almost two years, feeling that "the local folks needed a few of us 'outsiders' to help keep the fledgling movement growing."[58] Donald Stone was a Morehouse College graduate and former postal worker.[59] Michael Simmons had worked in inner-city projects while a student at Temple University in Philadelphia.[60] From a variety of backgrounds and prepared to experiment, the Atlanta Project workers hoped to foster radical change.

Atlanta Project workers imagined a multipronged approach to developing relationships with residents in Vine City and raising their political consciousness. Besides living in the neighborhood, they would launch the *Nitty Gritty*, a newspaper that would highlight the "brutal and disgusting indignities that are inflicted daily" upon Blacks by non-Blacks.[61] A freedom radio station would spread ideas in a manner similar to the mass meetings SNCC commonly held in its rural projects. Community freedom schools would be held in the summer, and a small cooperative store would provide employment opportunities and showcase "the richness of African life and culture."[62] It was a lengthy agenda that could only be realized over time. SNCC started by simply talking to people, attempting to establish rapport with neighborhood residents.

In January 1966, and reflecting SNCC's community organizing practices, Atlanta Project workers began canvasing the Vine City neighborhood, introducing themselves to residents, identifying issues of concern, and integrating themselves into the community.[63] As part of that work, SNCC members Gwen Robinson and Barbara Simon stopped by the Vine City Council office where members were assisting a recently evicted resident. Robinson and Simon offered the SNCC truck to help the family move. Later that day, SNCC workers attended a council meeting where residents discussed how best to confront Joe Schaffer, the tenant's former landlord and owner of numerous rental homes in Vine City and surrounding neighborhoods. The council suggested picketing Schaffer's properties, and even though the VCC had successfully forced property owner Thenie Stovall to improve properties two months earlier, SNCC reported that the council "didn't know what to do" and "had not really thought the whole thing through as to how to get your point through with a picket." "As a consequence," they continued, "we made a lot of suggestions."[64]

Markham Street

The Vine City Council and SNCC planned its picket against Joe Schaffer for Sunday, January 30, 1966, but freezing temperatures led VCC and SNCC members to rethink their approach. Weather conditions were severe, and they opted to distribute blankets to area families instead. Julian Bond telegrammed Mayor Ivan Allen Jr. about the suffering in his district. "There is no justification for houses without heat," Bond insisted. He demanded that Allen utilize all available resources to deliver heat and blankets, food, and medical care to those families enduring the extreme cold.[65] But Vine City organizers were interested in more than just short-term solutions; they wanted adequate housing and affordable services, and residents began considering whether a rent strike might be necessary. As VCC member Hector Black delivered supplies, he talked to residents about the possibility of withholding rent from their landlord, Joe Schaffer, until conditions improved.

Rent strikes had become a "weapon of choice" in resident-led wars on slums, at least in the North. In the early 1960s, for example, Harlem, New York, tenants launched rent strikes that quickly spread and then lingered.[66] Such strikes exposed discrimination, exploitative landlords, and cities' lack of enforcement of housing codes. But prior to the Markham Street incidents, rent strikes had been rare in Atlanta and the urban South, in part because few laws protected families who had disputes with landlords. Going on a rent strike meant one would likely wind up homeless. Nonetheless, by early 1966 residents had seen the successes of direct action as the civil rights revolution played out on TV and in Atlanta's own student movement. Disruptive action held some promise of relief. A rent strike might bring results.

The following day, Schaffer accused Hector Black of trespassing at Schaffer's rooming house, the Markham Hotel, and Black was arrested and held for $300 bail.[67] Schaffer later explained to United Press International journalists that he had heard "several complaints from people in my houses who say these civil right people come in making all sorts of noise." Schaffer said that Hector Black was not handing out blankets: "If they were really interested in distributing blankets and helping these people, I would hire a truck and help them deliver their stuff."[68] Black was acquitted of trespassing charges (it was never proven that Markham Hotel residents had asked Black to leave), and he freely admitted to reporters that he had been organizing a rent strike.[69]

The Markham Street conditions also attracted the attention of the Southern Christian Leadership Conference, the civil rights organization founded and led by Martin Luther King Jr. The wife of the Morehouse College president, Mrs. Benjamin Mays, and King's wife, Coretta Scott King, called a meeting at West Hunter Street Baptist Church to discuss the issues. Vine City Council members attended, as did Atlanta Life Insurance Company Executive Jesse Hill and Spelman College history professor Vincent Harding (who SNCC described as "'high classed' negroes of the city"). Some in attendance were not familiar with Markham Street, so the group planned to tour the area. At the same time, Vine City Council members would picket, insisting that the landlords improve housing.[70] While Martin Luther King Jr was not at the initial meeting, he and fellow SCLC leader Ralph David Abernathy planned to attend the tour and picket.[71]

Markham Street's conditions may have attracted King and SCLC's attention, but the revered civil rights leader knew little of Atlanta's poverty, even though he had a house nearby in Vine City. When King had moved from Montgomery to Atlanta in 1960, he and his family had purchased a home on Sunset Avenue. The homes surrounding the Kings' home were comfortable and "middle class." But as was frequently the case in urban areas in the 1960s, blocks of middle-class homes were often just a backyard or stone's throw away from misery and decay, and such was the housing geography of Vine City. But while the Kings lived nearby, King's work often kept him elsewhere. In the early 1960s, King traveled frequently with the SCLC and did not organize regularly in Atlanta.

Indeed, some felt that neither King nor the SCLC did much "field work" at all, a point of tension between the SCLC and SNCC. SNCC's director Stokely Carmichael complained about the SCLC's preference for short moral crusades. In one recollection of the SCLC's arrival in Selma in 1965, Carmichael recalled thinking, "Here comes SCLC talking about mobilizing another two-week campaign." "They going to bring in cameras, the media, prominent people, politicians, rat-tat-tat, turn the place upside down, and split."[72] Despite SNCC's robust experience with grassroots work, SNCC members felt eclipsed by the SCLC. In a 1975 oral history, Julian Bond explained that "King was going around making speeches but that was about it. They didn't have anybody out in the field. They had nobody doing the things we were."[73] To some, King and the SCLC were little versed in grassroots field work and community organizing. Perhaps consequently, King knew little of the squalor of Atlanta's poorest neighborhoods.

While the SCLC may not have pursued field work to a level satisfying to SNCC, and King may not have known the particulars of Atlanta's poverty, the SCLC had been conscious of and acting on economic injustice issues. Indeed, as historians have chronicled recently, King and his colleagues had been wrestling for some time with how to adequately address systemic inequality and how to mobilize the dispossessed across race and class. Particularly attuned to the impact of job discrimination, the SCLC had founded Operation Breadbasket in 1962 to desegregate jobs and open new employment opportunities for African Americans. Initially launched in Atlanta and intended to be national in scope, Operation Breadbasket would expand more rapidly in Chicago, where, after 1966, it benefited from synergies with Chicago's open housing movement.[74]

It was in Atlanta, too, that King and SCLC's C. T. Vivian attempted to forge an alliance between civil rights organizations—specifically the SCLC—and the labor movement, a "civil rights unionism."[75] At the time, the Black female workers at Atlanta's Scripto factory were frustrated with racial discrimination, discrimination that kept them isolated in low-paying jobs while white men climbed the ladder into skilled and supervisory positions. Unable to exact adequate wage concessions from management, nearly seven hundred women walked off the job in November 1964. Black community support for the strikers was mixed—Rev. William Holmes Borders of Friendship Baptist Church, for example, did not support the strike—but the SCLC and its Operation Breadbasket aligned with the workers. King portrayed the strike as the beginning of a larger labor–civil rights project. C. T. Vivian indicated that "Atlanta will become a model project for labor unions and Civil Rights cooperation."[76] Although Scripto eventually agreed to wage increases and other concessions, and the strike concluded in January 1965, the larger vision for civil rights unionism, a lasting working alliance between civil rights and organized labor, was not immediately realized.[77]

With a growing commitment to economic issues, in January 1966 Martin Luther King Jr., Coretta Scott King, Ralph David Abernathy, and others decided to visit the Markham Street area and picket to raise awareness of the neighborhood's conditions. King's January 31st tour of Markham Street and its dilapidated homes meant national publicity for Vine City and Atlanta's decayed housing stock, and the tour and conditions were covered by *Jet* magazine, the *Chicago Defender*, and local papers. "The Nobel Laureate spent almost a half an hour in a slum tenement called the Markham Hotel," the *Chicago Defender* reported. In that rooming house, eight families shared one bathroom. Some apartments lacked electricity and gas. And there, and in the national spotlight, King confessed his ignorance of Atlanta's poverty. "I had no idea people were living in Atlanta, Georgia in such conditions," he explained to reporters.[78] While King chatted with residents, others marched with signs reading, "We demand heat and light now," and "Jail Schaffer not Black" (see fig. 6).[79] One tenant begged photographers not to include her in pictures, fearing the landlord would evict her. America's most recognized civil rights leader asked area residents if they would be willing to participate in a rent strike to protest conditions. At least some indicated that they would.[80] But while King's visit would highlight the despair in the New South's capital, it would be the Vine City Council and SNCC that would continue to do the day-to-day work of organizing residents and pickets.

Organizer Hector Black's arrest and King's Markham Street tour signaled the beginning of a protracted housing battle fought in the courts and daily on the streets of Vine City. To some degree, city officials were in a bind: they needed to enforce Atlanta's housing code to qualify for federal urban renewal funding, but doing so resulted in condemnations and

FIGURE 6. Martin Luther King Jr. and other SCLC personnel tour Markham Street as residents protest conditions, 1966. Courtesy Bill Wilson photographs, Kenan Research Center, Atlanta History Center.

fewer housing units for low-income families, a situation that led to resident protests. Additionally, Atlanta was in the spotlight and under federal scrutiny. By February 1966, Atlanta had launched its War on Poverty and community action agency, EOA, and local and federal officials expected visible progress in ameliorating poverty and slum conditions. Yet in increasingly public acts, residents were showcasing the city's inability to control deteriorating housing and highlighting landlords' exploitation of the poor. (And poor residents were exposing that racial conditions in Atlanta were not as positive as had been presented by city leaders and some media reports.)

In Vine City and the adjacent Lightning neighborhood, the city's crackdown on housing code violations accelerated housing demolition and exacerbated the housing shortage. Significant sections of those neighborhoods had been zoned industrial in 1954, and that meant that once homes were vacant, they were to be razed and the land converted to industrial use. Additionally, homes immediately judged to be uninhabitable were marked for demolition with placards, and residents were alerted to vacate. City officials pledged to assist such tenants in finding other homes and pointed to the vacant units in public housing, but as *Atlanta Constitution* journalist Bruce Galphin pointed out, the housing authority gave priority to families displaced by urban renewal, a program that did not encompass Vine City and the Markham Street area. EOA had little to offer. The agency surveyed residents as to their housing needs, but no financial aid was forthcoming for housing or services such as heat and electricity.[81] Residents needed safe housing and reliable utilities at a price they could afford, but urban renewal, public housing, and the War on Poverty could provide no immediate assistance. Absent other substantive alternatives, residents and organizers pursued a rent strike.

Distressed over evictions and further loss of housing, the "citizens of the Markham Street area" drew up a petition detailing their grievances, and they tasked a delegation to deliver and discuss it with Mayor Allen. The complaint outlined residents' experiences with unsanitary living conditions, lack of heat, broken windows, and holes in floors. Facing condemnation of homes and impending eviction, residents demanded sixty to ninety days to find new housing or "some place to go" when the houses were torn down.[82] On Friday, February 4, Willie Williams, who had emerged as a resident leader, Vine City representatives, and SNCC members met with the mayor to discuss neighborhood issues, particularly what would happen to residents whose housing was condemned, but also whether tenants should have to pay rent to landlords who did not keep their properties up to code.[83] To the residents' disappointment, Allen affirmed the right of landlords to accept rent on housing no matter the condition, and he discouraged residents from pursuing a rent strike. Faced with little hope of relief from the city, Williams organized Vine City residents, knowing they might soon mobilize.[84]

Ultimately, five families decided to pursue a rent strike. After receiving condemnation orders for their homes, the families withheld rent from Schaffer "until housing conditions are improved," a declaration that produced the expected warrant and notice of eviction.[85] The tenants would gain little from the court challenge itself, but the action set in motion a series of cases that advanced tenant and public interest law in Georgia.

Tenant Law

In early 1966, landlords could evict tenants with little cause or risk. Residents seeking to fight an eviction were required to pay a substantial cash bond, which effectively quashed any potential challenges. Consequently, poor tenants had no recourse if landlords failed to make repairs or neglected their properties. If residents withheld rent—went on a rent strike—they could be evicted. If tenants made improvements themselves, landlords commonly increased the rent, reasoning that the unit had "been improved." In these ways, in this period, what tenant law existed favored landlords.

Vine City residents turned to Howard Moore Jr., a lawyer who regularly represented SNCC, to represent them as they fought to keep their homes and ensure improvements. Only the tenth Black lawyer to join the Georgia Bar, the army veteran and Boston University graduate initially worked with attorney Donald Hollowell's office addressing a range of civil rights cases and defending activists. Significantly, Moore represented Julian Bond as he fought to keep his seat in the Georgia House.[86] Moore was committed to changing law that many saw as punishing the poor and people of color.

Moore and the Markham Street families started by charging that the cost of legal proceedings discriminated against the poor. The counter-affidavits against the evictions required an accompanying cash bond payment that amounted to about twice the family's rent for six months as well as a bond premium. Those costs were burdensome for poor tenants, Moore asserted. If the tenant lost the case, the tenant lost that money and would be subject to double rent until surrendering the premises.[87] Moore arranged for a hearing to determine if pauper's affidavits—affidavits documenting a person's inability to pay the required bond—would substitute for the required bond. SNCC circulated information about the hearing to Vine City residents, encouraging them to attend. "This hearing. . . could have widespread consequences," SNCC explained. If the pauper affidavits were accepted, it could mean that poor people could finally seek legal relief from unjust evictions.[88] At the February 10 hearing, Howard argued that in requiring that a bond be paid, tenants were being forced to pay for access to the courts. Thus, the bond was a violation of the U.S. Constitution's Fourteenth Amendment. But this particular eviction warrant was withdrawn by Schaffer when, as a show of good faith, Willie Williams paid one week's rent.[89] While helpful to Williams, the withdrawal was in some ways a disappointment, as a precedent would not be set on the use of pauper affidavits. Still, other legal opportunities would surface.

Soon thereafter, SNCC activists and Vine City residents received word that Johnny Teague, another Markham Street resident, was being evicted. SNCC hurried to 444 Markham Street and found marshals beginning to clear Teague's belongings. Teague explained to an *Atlanta Inquirer* reporter that he had been paying his rent faithfully and was not aware of any legal proceedings against him. SNCC workers Bill Ware, Ruffin Harris, and Mendy Samstein attempted to return the possessions to the house

FIGURE 7. Johnny Teague, evicted from his Vine City home, 1966. Courtesy Bob Fitch Photography Archive, Department of Special Collections, Stanford University Libraries.

and were summarily arrested.[90] Teague was eventually informed that the eviction was a mistake. But to area residents, evictions, deserved and undeserved, were a constant and immediate threat (see fig. 7).[91]

Residents' fear of evictions effectively stifled potential rent strikes. Families were concerned about losing their homes, all the more so in winter, and, as illustrated above, legal solutions seemed unreliable. Consequently, SNCC struggled to muster residents willing to challenge landlords, law enforcement, and city officials. But by early 1966, city leaders were concerned about how bad press could affect the city's reputation and access to federal funds, and they appeared more willing to settle declared and potential rent strikes. Additionally, word spread that the city would give Markham Street residents priority in public housing.[92]

However, when Johnny Teague went to investigate the Atlanta Housing Authority's offer, he arrived back home to find his house being demolished, his belongings still inside. SNCC members and neighbors salvaged what they could as demolition proceeded. It is not clear why Teague's home continued to be targeted by the city, but evidence suggests that the property's owner accepted Teague's rent payment despite the city's stated intent to demolish the dilapidated structure. Thus, Teague thought he had paid rent properly and had a home.[93] "Somebody must take the blame for violating the privacy of my house," Teague insisted, "especially when I have paid the rent on time."[94]

SNCC, the VCC, and local residents hoped to use Teague's situation to its best advantage. SNCC members moved furniture into the street to further provoke a "crisis" and then blocked garbagemen sent to clear the area. Atlanta Project's Bill Ware took the opportunity to publicly denounce the city's actions and challenge the police, who had arrived on the scene.[95] Willie Williams and Hector Black also forged ahead, announcing rent strikes in a February 18, 1966, press release and outlining myriad complaints. "The members of the Vine City Council are deeply concerned about the intolerable living conditions of many people in our area," the release opened. Homes lacked electricity, gas, and running water, and toilets went unrepaired. Residents were forced to use wood from condemned and vacated homes to heat their own homes.[96] To many, the situation was particularly galling, given that the city was investing millions of dollars to build a new baseball stadium.

The Atlanta–Fulton County Stadium had become a sore point for many poor and working-class Atlanta residents. Built on the Washington-Rawson urban renewal site as part of a package of incentives to attract a major league baseball team, the stadium was one of the measures that would purportedly make Atlanta a "national city."[97] But such stadium projects seemed to many to involve sleight of hand—it was not clear where money was coming from or where money was going. Poor residents were confident they were not reaping the project's benefits, and they were unhappy that city resources were diverted to such projects when housing and urban services were lacking. "There is a crisis in low rent housing in this city," Vine City residents pointed out. Yet, "Our city is more interested in 18 million dollar stadiums than it is in decent housing for the poor."[98]

SNCC and Markham Street residents continued to be disappointed by the courts. On Tuesday, March 1, 1966, the Fulton County Superior Court upheld the Georgia law permitting a landlord to evict tenants.[99] As Howard Moore worked through the appeals process, Markham Street residents continued to use civil disobedience and the crises created by evictions to expose housing issues and poverty (see fig. 8).

FIGURE 8. Residents protest against substandard housing on Markham Street, 1966. Courtesy Dwight Ross Jr. for *Atlanta Journal-Constitution*, Special Collections & Archives, Georgia State University Library, Atlanta, Ga.

Williams and his allies found another opportunity to bring attention to exploited tenants' plight when, on Saturday, March 6, Willie Williams and another resident were ordered evicted by the Fulton County courts.[100] Williams interfered as the sheriff cleared their homes of their belongings, and he was arrested along with SNCC photographer Dwight Williams. As tenants' beds, tables, chairs, dishes, clothes, and other belongings were piled on Markham Street, SNCC and others advocated for the tenants. At traffic intersections, SNCC members solicited bail funds and ultimately gained the release of the jailed activists.[101] Once back on Markham Street, Williams read a prepared statement. "We hereby charge the city of Atlanta with defending landlords while ruling against poor, honest citizens who protest robbery and slum-housing conditions," Williams proclaimed.[102] Then, to continue drawing attention to the ongoing housing issues, Williams set up camp on a vacant lot on Haynes and Markham (see fig. 9). Williams told the *Atlanta Inquirer* that he could move elsewhere, but that he had become interested in the people exploited by Schaffer and wanted to help rehabilitate housing in Vine City.[103]

FIGURE 9. Tenant leader Willie Williams camps out after eviction, March 8, 1966. Courtesy Marion Crowe for the *Atlanta Journal-Constitution*, Special Collections & Archives, Georgia State University Library, Atlanta, Ga.

Despite threats of snow, Williams remained camped outside, accompanied by SNCC's Donald Stone and Bill Ware. "We had settled down for a long protest," one SNCC report read. SNCC parked its sound truck a block away and played music. Periodically they dedicated tunes to Schaffer, including "You've Been Cheating." To Williams they dedicated "Too Far Gone to Turn Around." While police stopped by to question the legality of the sound truck, SNCC persisted, later moving the vehicle closer to the eviction site, playing dance music and holding forth against the city and others.[104] As the group explained to journalists, they planned to stay until the federal courts ruled on their claims.[105] Atlanta officials attempted to resolve the conflict by housing displaced residents, particularly the vocal Willie Williams. The Atlanta Housing Authority made an apartment within public housing available to Williams, even offering to waive one month's rent.[106]

The tenants' legal battle dragged on, wearing down even the most ardent supporters. The major issue remained the bond requirement for tenants filing a counter-affidavit against an eviction.[107] By the time the three-judge panel convened on March 25, Williams and his supporters would have been camped out for three weeks. Not sure whether he wanted to stay out in the elements that long, Williams suggested the strikers be moved into public housing, as long as free rent and utilities were provided for the first month. Williams also expressed a personal desire to relocate to his family's home in Albany. Atlanta Project's Bill Ware was "shocked" to hear Williams was interested in leaving the city, and he feared it meant the end of the tenant movement. SNCC supporters resigned themselves to the situation when the city removed Williams's belongings.[108] The Markham Street tenant strike faded from view.

The Vine City rent strikes of early 1966 consumed supporters' time and sapped energy. Fighting systems that benefited landlords took time, money, and fortitude and was difficult to sustain. Vine City Council shut down production of the *Vine City Voice* for six months, and the emotional wear and tear threatened to drive Williams from the city.

What's more, as events unfolded on Markham Street, the SNCC organization as a whole was in transition: it was considering its place in a global freedom struggle and debating the role of Blacks and whites within SNCC. Indeed, the Atlanta Project was a locus of the emerging Black consciousness movement. In a position paper presented to the staff nearly two years prior, in March 1964, Bill Ware and others had asserted that whites were incapable of understanding the Black experience and would be more useful organizing within white communities against white racism. Ware insisted that white participation changed the tone of meetings. Those sentiments strengthened over time.[109] The Atlanta Project's increasing commitment to Black-led organizing manifested in its Vine City work. In the summer of 1966, hoping to encourage Black residents to rely on themselves and Black allies, Atlanta Project activists began harassing white community organizer Hector Black, calling him a "white Jesus."[110] Hector and Susie Black eventually decided they had become more of a problem than a benefit to Vine City, and they moved out of Atlanta.

While the Markham Street events slowed and SNCC members became consumed by internal matters, flare-ups between tenants and landlords surfaced periodically, including with notorious landlord Joe Schaffer. On August 10, 1966, residents angered by the eviction of Ella Catherine Lampkin, retrieved the Lampkins' possessions from the curb, trucked them to Joe Schaffer's home, and dumped them in the landlord's yard. According to local newspapers, the Lampkins' home had no hot water, electricity, or working toilet. She and her husband were $26 behind in rent for their $40-a-month dwelling.[111] Residents continued to use pickets and public shaming to force landlords to maintain their properties, but policy change and enforcement were the long-term solutions to improving housing conditions for the poor.

Housing issues continued to plague residents, but Atlanta SNCC members devoted more time to anti-war organizing and the global Black freedom struggle. SNCC's framing of the U.S. Black freedom struggle in global terms resulted in a broad range of activities on the ground, and SNCC's attention shifted away from its urban project and toward anti-war, anti-draft activities and racial oppression worldwide.[112] SNCC's anti-war organizing and attention to global concerns would contribute to the Atlanta Project's demise. Cleveland Sellers, program secretary in January 1967, was tidying up loose ends in SNCC operations, managing the allocation of project cars, when he realized that the Atlanta Project was not "organizing the community"—Vine City—as he thought, but developing an anti-draft program. To Sellers, Atlanta Project director Bill Ware was commandeering resources such as cars and failing to operate the Atlanta Project programmatically. SNCC chairman Stokely Carmichael fired Ware and closed the Atlanta Project.[113]

To some degree, the events in Vine City illustrate the raw enthusiasm for community organizing that had emerged in the mid-1960s United States. Inspired by the Black freedom movement and the War on Poverty's goals of collective deliberation and maximum feasible participation of the poor, well-meaning individuals and organizations made their way to poor areas in hopes of improving Americans' lives. The reality was harsh. Little had been documented about community organizing, and residents and community organizers struggled to craft a successful approach. Still, local community-based organizations such as the VCIA were able to secure a playground for area children. While residents had some hope that the much hyped War on Poverty would bring new resources, Atlanta's local community action program had been slow to launch and offered few services to residents or activists hoping to respond to poverty and its related conditions.

Rent strikes helped expose the housing issues produced in part by rapid urban growth and poorly executed urban renewal programs. The negative effects of such urban development failures fell most heavily on the poor. Property owners took advantage of lax building regulations and subdivided existing structures or built low-cost smaller homes and apartments to accommodate rural in-migration. Schaffer himself owned at least twenty-eight rental units.[114] The tight housing market allowed landlords to charge rents that were difficult for poor families to sustain, and landlords cut their costs by avoiding making improvements or addressing maintenance issues. In some cases, as evidenced in the Teague events, landlords continued to accept rent payments from tenants when properties had been condemned, leaving tenants poorer and at risk for eviction. Tenant law favored landlords, and while attorneys such as Howard Moore were willing to challenge existing law, tenants were at substantial risk if they agreed to participate in lawsuits that ultimately failed.

Vine City's local activists would not solve the larger problems of concentrated poverty, spatial inequity, economic opportunity, and structural discrimination—nor did they attempt to. They were, as SRC had observed, focused on improving individuals' ability to cope with a flawed system. Recognizing that the War on Poverty would provide only minimal support for neighborhood improvement and could not respond to decades of housing neglect, exploitation, and decline, residents and organizers turned to disruption and, when possible, pursued legal avenues to produce immediate improvements and create enforceable law. Their rent strike against a notorious local landlord attracted news coverage beyond Atlanta and drew the attention of the city's most famous civil rights figure, Martin Luther King Jr. But it produced only limited action from city officials. It was not enough to substantially change conditions in Vine City.

Vine City organizing campaigns benefited from SNCC's Atlanta Project, but local residents were not completely dependent on such organizers. Gifted but "outsider" allies such as SNCC and Hector Black would come and go, but local leaders such as Helen Howard, Dorothy Bolden, Willie Williams, and others built relationships that helped establish lasting civic structures. Helen Howard and other local residents continued community organizing through the Vine City Foundation, for example, and Bolden went on to launch the National Domestic Workers' Union of America.

Atlanta's civil rights movement continued to have a mixed relationship with Atlanta's poorest residents. In 1963, SNCC organizers in south Atlanta had been critical of the local movement for failing to take into account the concerns of rank-and-file residents. King's reaction to poverty in Vine City and Lightning indicated that not much had changed in the three years since: there was still a sharp divide between Atlanta's haves and have-nots, including the city's Black sociopolitical elite and the Black poor. While leaders in the Black freedom movement expressed a desire for economic equality, developing a workable strategy to address pressing economic issues—hunger, safe housing—proved more challenging. SNCC's Atlanta Project tried to fill these gaps, but the bulk of SNCC's Vine City work only lasted a year.

For their part, Atlanta's leaders continued to struggle to improve Atlanta's housing situation. And EOA tried to get its footing. Already facing criticism from the city's African American leadership, the agency would soon be under fire from the city's poor, including its own employees. City leaders' nightmares were realized when violence broke out in Summerhill, Boulevard, and Dixie Hills.

CHAPTER THREE

CHAPTER 4

The Poor Folks Movement

Frustrated with declining urban conditions, wretched poverty, and what they considered to be the slow implementation and poor execution of the War on Poverty, poor Atlantans like those in Vine City created their own structures and adopted their own methods to respond to exploitative landlords and declining neighborhood conditions. Atlanta's leaders, on the other hand, were calling their War on Poverty's first year a success. The federal OEO used the announcement of Atlanta's second year of grant funding to highlight the city's achievements.

As was the case in 1965, the 1966 grant was substantial, and it included $4.3 million for the community action program.[1] Atlanta officials, including Mayor Ivan Allen Jr., EOA chair Bo Jones, director Charlie Emmerich, Dan Sweat, and board members W. L. Calloway, M. L. King Sr., and Ann Woodward flew to Washington, D.C., for the announcement. There they were joined by the state's congressional leadership, Senators Herman Talmadge and Richard Russell and Representatives Charles Weltner and James MacKay. At the event, OEO head Sargent Shriver praised Atlanta as a "shining example" of how to fight poverty.[2] The spectacle was, to some degree, intended to counter negative press about the failures of Lyndon Johnson's antipoverty initiative as well as the criticisms of mayors and governors frustrated with community action's emphasis on the "maximum feasible participation of the poor."[3] Tired of what they considered to be subsidized political activism, many city and state officials demanded veto power over proposed programs, and they pushed to expand the Hatch Act—which forbade political activities by particular government offices—to include employees of community action programs.[4]

Still, Atlanta's leaders were happy to accept the accolades. It was to the city's advantage to be in the good graces of federal leaders.

Federal officials may have waxed celebratory about Atlanta's activities and vision, but back in Atlanta, poor residents and antipoverty advocates questioned the War on Poverty's progress and accomplishments. Indeed, from September 1965 through 1967, Atlanta's "war" appeared in disarray. Despite the Community Action Program's requirements for "maximum feasible participation of the poor," target area residents felt they were not sufficiently involved in program planning, and community aides felt misled about job benefits. Poor residents were not the only ones complaining. Leaders of some of the city's major civil rights organizations felt the EOA still failed to adequately involve African Americans in directing and staffing programs that primarily served African Americans. But while mainstream civil rights leaders made a case to include African Americans in the management of EOA, they initially failed to make a case to involve *the poor*, an oversight that would taint relations with poor and working-class neighborhood leaders. In 1966 and 1967, grassroots neighborhood activists increasingly rejected the city's civil rights leadership. Forming their own organization, the Atlanta Grass Roots Crusade, neighborhood civic council leaders insisted that they could better represent the interests of poor families. It was a confusing and, to many, an exasperating period. Decades of pent-up frustration with poverty, inequity, police repression, and broken promises manifested in open rebellion in three neighborhoods that housed a number of Atlanta's poor families: Summerhill, Boulevard in the Old Fourth Ward, and Dixie Hills. At the same time, the federal War on Poverty was under attack by many congressional leaders, and Atlanta would have to do more with less money.

To Benefit Whom?

In many ways, the community aides hired by Economic Opportunity Atlanta, Atlanta's community action agency, served as the front lines in Atlanta's War on Poverty. Hired from the neighborhoods that the community action program served and poor or working class themselves, the aides comprised a significant portion of a service center workforce—about 65 percent. They were critical to the neighborhood service centers' outreach effort, and as centers opened, aides remained busy. At the South Fulton service center, for example, aides made 479 door-to-door contacts in December 1965, and aides at the Northwest/Perry Homes Center made 591. There was no minimum education requirement for the positions, and when hired, aides received eight weeks training, four in the classroom and four in the field. They were introduced to the EOA program and taught how to locate and interview people who might benefit from EOA services. Primarily filled by women, the positions were more attractive than the jobs in housekeeping, cooking, and laundry that poor women often held in southern cities. Pay ranged from $2,600 to $3,850 a year.[5] To many poor Atlantans, these were highly desirable positions.

But in fall 1965, aides realized that their jobs were not all they had hoped. Length of training, employee benefits, and opportunities for permanent employment in particular had not been effectively communicated. It was not entirely obvious who was an "employee" and who was a "trainee." The distinction mattered: as trainees, aides were not entitled to pensions. Because residents of target neighborhoods had historically been excluded from pension-benefited positions, and because many jobs held by poor residents had not qualified for Social Security old-age benefits until 1950 (if then), retirement benefits were attractive to poor families.[6] Lack of such benefits for aide positions became more galling when such benefits were offered to other employees within EOA.

EOA executive administrator Charlie Emmerich proposed adopting a pension plan for the agency's "career" employees—about one hundred staff and clerical help—at the September 1965 EOA Board of Directors meeting. To Emmerich and most board members, such benefits were necessary to attract competent EOA staff, particularly since EOA competed for a short supply of social service professionals. For their part, the EOA Board of Directors did not initially discuss whether pensions should be extended to neighborhood aides; they simply accepted the benefit plan as proposed. As professionals themselves, board members likely readily understood that pensions and other benefits would attract specialized professionals. With the exception of one labor leader, board members drew from the upper echelons of business and society.[7] No board member represented or really understood the interests of the poor, and likely they did not think about how the withholding of such benefits further reinforced racial and class divisions or solidified wealth differentials.

Board members did opt to discuss which institutions would hold pension investments, in part because some board members' employers stood to gain from where that money was held. African American board members expressed their preference that pensions be deposited in Black-owned investment firms or in investment firms in which African Americans had a significant financial interest. Black land developer W. L. Calloway, for example, recommended three specific companies for group insurance. All three involved "substantial Negro business," Calloway acknowledged, and Black board member Jesse Hill served as actuary for one.[8] The group also considered Trust Company of Georgia, where white EOA board member A. H. "Billy" Sterne served as president. As *Atlanta Constitution* journalist Wayne Kelley pointed out, at the board meeting, members had no questions about EOA programs or other matters; board members Black and white appeared more concerned with how they or their group might benefit from the larger financial decisions, and for how EOA might secure more well-trained professionals.[9]

When the EOA board voted to implement pensions for professionals but not aides, EOA aides and antipoverty advocates cried foul, forcing the board to explain their position. To the board members, aides were trainees receiving temporary benefits while they learned and practiced new skills. White board member and Atlanta school superintendent John Letson reasoned that the aide program was intended to prepare aides for regular work in the general economy. W. L. Calloway argued that putting aides in the pension program would, as the *Atlanta Constitution* phrased it, "discourage them from doing what they were being trained to do." But while board members contended that aides were temporary employees, not "career employees" with a "regular employee-employer relationship," aides had less clarity on their job status.[10] One aide said that she had been told there would be eight weeks of training, after which the aides would receive employee benefits. Another explained that as a trainee she had been required to purchase insurance. Others said that since the pension issue had arisen, they had been told training would continue for ten months, after which they would need to find employment.[11] Organized labor threw its support behind the aides. Georgia AFL-CIO's Wiley Montague, who served on the EOA board, did not think pensions should be paid from EOA funds at all, but he concluded that if pensions were offered, they should be extended to all employees. Despite the pushback, the pension program was approved by the board with no pensions for aides on Thursday, September 29, 1965. But that would not silence aides' complaints.[12]

To poor Atlantans and their advocates, the pension debate came to illustrate why poor residents should be involved at the highest level of Atlanta's community action agency, the EOA Board of Directors. Absent the experience and voice of the poor, issues of relevance to the aides (including access to benefits, for example) were not proactively addressed. Even when such issues were taken up by the board, poor people's point of view was glossed over. That fall, though, federal officials had gotten serious about requiring the "maximum feasible participation of the poor" in community action programs, despite heightened criticism of the requirement.

By fall 1965, mayors and governors were complaining that the community action program's requirement for "maximum feasible participation" had moved well beyond what they assumed was meant by the federal requirement: community meetings and polite consultations. Community action funds were being used to undermine established political regimes, the mayors and governors complained. A Syracuse University program trained residents to use Saul Alinsky–type organizing methods to challenge officials, for example, and an Albuquerque community action program organized a picket of city hall to demand improved services.[13] Despite the pressure from some mayors, governors, and congressional leaders, federal OEO officials remained committed to maximum feasible participation, and they had enforcement powers. If community action programs failed to demonstrate adequate involvement of the poor in their operation, the OEO could withhold funding until the programs met the expected standard. Still, Atlanta's white and Black establishment leaders resisted substantive involvement of the poor at the highest levels of EOA as long as they could.[14]

In EOA administrators' view, Atlanta's system allowed resident input. Each service center had a resident advisory council that met and provided feedback on center programs. However, in practice, federal inspection reports revealed, the structure allowed little authentic participation by target populations. Council members were chosen by center staff members and not democratically elected by area residents. As a federal inspector explained in one report, meetings were run by "ministers and other interested citizens" who were "more accustomed to accepting responsibility" and were "more aggressive."[15] As a result, rank-and-file residents had limited opportunity to respond. More relevant to the pension issue, there were no poor people on the EOA Board of Directors. In practice, inspectors concluded, in Atlanta, "the poor are not included in decision making on any level."[16] EOA administrators insisted that the system was sufficient, though. In a three-day visit by OEO inspectors in August 1965, board chair Bo Jones explained that the four African American members of the EOA board, in the words of the report, "adequately represented the Negro community including the poverty population."[17]

OEO inspectors saw significant room for improvement. In Atlanta's case, and as had occurred with the 1965 community action grant, OEO added special conditions to the 1966 community action grant, stipulating that Atlanta abide by regulations pertaining to the maximum feasible participation of the poor. The OEO meant business: whereas the OEO had withheld $900,000 of the 1965 community action monies, in September 1965 the federal agency docked the 1966 grant $4 million until Atlanta's agency restructured its board to include representatives from targeted groups. Atlanta had ninety days in which to implement the changes.[18]

Although there had been little public discussion within Atlanta to that date regarding EOA's failure to include members of the target population on the EOA Board of Directors, reporters in Washington, D.C., assailed Mayor Ivan Allen Jr., Bo Jones, and Charlie Emmerich about the situation when the men visited D.C. to accept the 1966 grant and promote the successes of Atlanta's War on Poverty. The Atlanta contingent continued to insist that the poor had their say in EOA programming, even if they were not on the board. Board member Ann Woodward revealed other assumptions. "This is a policy-making board and you must be able to read in order to understand all these things they send us from Washington," Woodward asserted to reporters.[19] To at least one board member, then, the poor were not up to the task of serving on a board, as such service required members to consume and act on a great deal of information.

Back in Atlanta, *Atlanta Journal–Atlanta Constitution* journalist Wayne Kelley kept up the pressure, and his news pieces may well have increased awareness of the community action program requirement and EOA's failure to meet it. In a September 26, 1965, story titled "Where Is the Voice of the Poor?" Kelley pointed out that the community action program required "involving the poor in the effort to help themselves." That, he asserted, meant including the poor "in planning, policy-making, and operation of the program." Yet poor people were not appointed to the fifteen-member board of directors, Kelley noted. The board "has no poor people."[20]

With increasing public awareness of federal CAP regulations, and OEO's willingness to enforce its rules, in October 1965 the Atlanta Summit Leadership Conference expanded its purview beyond racial inequity and insisted on the greater involvement of poor people in the administration of EOA. Specifically, they called for "broad representation including the poor on [EOA] policy-making boards and activities."[21] To that point, and consistent with the organization's stated mission, the Summit had been concerned exclusively about equitable *racial* representation on the EOA board and in the upper administration of EOA.[22] The Summit's shift was not lost on Bo Jones. Until the 5 October 1965 letter, the Summit "had not expressed concern about representation of the poor," Jones asserted to Williams.[23] It was only after federal officials—the OEO—asserted demands about democratically elected representation of the poor that the Summit insisted on greater representation of poor people. Nonetheless, Jones explained, steps were being taken to incorporate poor residents onto the board, just as the CAP required.[24]

The EOA answered OEO's demand for more robust citizen participation by assembling a cumbersome, tiered citizen advisory structure that diffused citizen interest and energy but resulted in at least some poor representation on the board of directors.[25] Cobbled together by the EOA associate director Dan Sweat over a weekend, the plan circulated among interested groups and the EOA board members in October 1965.[26] It stipulated that each service center would elect a citizens neighborhood advisory council (CNAC). The CNAC would recommend new programs, review and advise the neighborhood service center director on proposed projects, and keep the community informed on EOA programs. Four-fifths of the elected representatives were to reside in the target area and have incomes that qualified them to receive services from EOA. The other one-fifth of members would be drawn from technical, professional, or business leaders in the area and would be appointed by the center director. The CNAC would elect three of its members to serve on a Citizens Central Advisory Council (CCAC), which would advise the EOA executive administrator and the EOA Board of Directors, review programs, recommend new programs, and make the CNACs aware of EOA programs and projects. The CCAC would elect four of its members to serve as voting members on the EOA Board of Directors. Thus, in the new formulation, up to 20 percent of the EOA board would draw from the poor, and those four members would be elected by the poor.[27]

Certainly, having four representatives of Atlanta's poor on the board of EOA was an achievement. Many hoped those additions would accelerate EOA's work to mitigate poverty. But complaints about EOA were many and not easily resolved.

Neighborhood Frustrations

Following its shift to demand greater representation of the poor on the board of the EOA, the Summit decided to take the lead in documenting and channeling poor families' frustrations with EOA. Beginning in October 1965, the Summit organized townhalls and other gatherings to identify what poor residents saw as their most significant issues and challenges. Residents tallied several areas of concern. EOA was slow to establish neighborhood centers. Centers were not hiring target area residents in sufficient numbers. Poor people were not adequately consulted on board decisions. Echoing the Summit's persistent and primary complaint, there was "No Negro with authority" at EOA (see chapter 2). To be sure, Tilman Cothran held a position in upper administration—associate director of community resources—but many felt he was not allowed to practice that authority.[28]

The Summit identified a number of possible responses to the complaints: increase representation from the targeted areas on the EOA board and CNACs; require CCAC review and veto power over board actions; expand the pension program to include aides; establish clear statements of all policies and employment responsibilities, including the articulation of nondiscrimination policies; consult with residents in target areas before establishing centers; and consider employment of poor people in EOA positions.[29] The group then strategized how to achieve those goals.

The Summit saw itself as the obvious spokesbody to negotiate on behalf of the Black community *and poor people* with EOA. The overwhelming majority of low-income families in Fulton County were Black, a follow-up "Preliminary Plan" noted, and consequently African Americans had a significant stake in the success of the War on Poverty. Three "clearly different" groups needed to cooperate in order to effectively influence Atlanta's program. First, there was the "unorganized or hard-core poor" who had "unusually keen insight into the subjective aspects of the problem." Then there was the "organized poor," that is, "the neighborhood councils or civic organizations," which had a "special understanding of the hopes and aspirations of poor people" and "immediate involvement and close relationship with people of poverty." Finally, there were the civil rights leaders. According to the report, that group brought the most to the table, including professional skills, "technical know-how in the [area] of power politics," the "ability to articulate the problems of the poor," and expertise to "develop programs in the important areas of education, manpower training, health, and social services."[30] The established Summit leadership, then, would serve as liaison between the poor and Black and the EOA. The Summit would manage this particular initiative by establishing a Summit Ad Hoc Committee on Poverty, a body that operated under the Summit but that was populated largely by civic league leaders, including Rev. C. D. Colbert of the Georgia Avenue–Pryor Street Civic League, Ortelus Shelmon and Rev. Cadmus A. Samples from the Scott's Crossing area, John Hood, Clarence Ezzard, Zannie Tate of the Blandtown Civic League, and Vine City's Otis Cochran.

The Summit Ad Hoc Committee on Poverty's first communication would be to Washington, D.C., to Adam Clayton Powell Jr., the powerful chair of the House Committee on Education and Labor who had emerged as a promoter of measurable racial equity and enforceable civil rights mandates. Atlanta's CAP does "not deserve its favorable national image," members of the Summit's Ad Hoc Committee on Poverty declared in their letter. Atlanta suffered "subtle racial discrimination in policy making, in program implementation, and in personnel procedures." It developed programs *for* rather than *with* the poor. And it was "more concerned with giving the appearance of attacking poverty" than in helping poor people break the cycle of poverty. The committee attributed these problems to the EOA's refusal to involve the poor at the policy-making level. But committee members also considered the issues of race and economic status to be intertwined, and they continued to insist on the need for a qualified Black to serve as a single associate or deputy director. The ad-hoc committee wanted their grievances investigated and remedied.[31]

Next the committee attempted to address the EOA Board of Directors with an expanded set of demands. The Summit was no longer satisfied with adding four representatives of the poor to the board; the Summit's Ad Hoc Committee sought to add one for each neighborhood service center, for a total of eight. They planned to make their case at the November 17 board meeting where the board prepared to vote on adding four representatives of the poor to the board. But for reasons that are unclear, the EOA board refused to let committee members speak at the meeting.[32]

The board's refusal was "a slap in the face," Cadmus Samples asserted to the *Atlanta Inquirer*. Ad Hoc Committee cochair Ortelus Shelmon was livid. "We don't want the board to plan for us but with us," he told the news outlet.[33] On the surface perhaps, the board did not appear to be acting with belligerence, as it proceeded to vote for the new community participation schema, which resulted in four representatives of the poor on the board, and they agreed that a fixed number of aides (eleven) at each center would be eligible for pensions.[34] But the board's refusal to let the Ad Hoc Committee address the board prevented the board from hearing the group's proposal to expand poor people's representation on that body, and it exacerbated an already-fraught relationship with the Summit's Ad Hoc Committee. After the board meeting, Shelmon shot off a telegram to Sargent Shriver, demanding the resignation of the board.[35] The days for velvet glove techniques were over, Shelmon declared.[36] Despite measured gains made with EOA's board, the Ad Hoc Committee planned to meet with Frank Sloan, head of OEO's regional office in Atlanta. In the meantime, and before the Ad Hoc Committee was able to meet with Sloan, OEO announced that it was releasing Atlanta's 1966 War on Poverty funding, signaling that the board structure with four new members of the poor had been approved by federal officials.[37]

In January and February 1966, and following the diligent door-to-door work of neighborhood aides, residents elected neighbors to represent them to Atlanta's CAP, launching a process that would ultimately place representatives of the poor on the board of EOA. Residents chose block representatives, who then voted on representatives to the citizens neighborhood advisory councils (CNACs).[38] Once formed, CNACs elected members to the Citizens Central Advisory Council (CCAC), who then elected members to the EOA Board of Directors.[39]

Elections appeared straightforward enough on paper but were more challenging in practice. On the positive side, residents could usually register to vote and cast ballots for EOA advisory committees close to home. The block 13 station was established at Wilborn's Grill on Hollywood Road, for example. Wheat Street Baptist, West Hunter Baptist, and St. Stephen Baptist all served as voting sites.[40] But the voting process itself did not always go as planned. According to one report, elections in Blandtown, a neighborhood abutting the rail yards of northwest Atlanta, had been interrupted because "someone in the community had died, and when someone died, they didn't do anything."[41] Moreover, with the passage of the momentous Voting Rights Act (1965), which outlawed discriminatory voting practices such as the poll tax, voting became a new process for many. Questionable voting activity was occasionally reported. While checking on voting locations, for example, one Emory researcher observed a candidate escorting "drunks" in to vote. Despite the challenges, the neighborhood service center elections were serious business to some, and a few residents even campaigned for their seats.[42]

In April 1966, the first election series concluded, and four representatives of the poor joined EOA's board of directors: Erwin Stevens, a shipping clerk and chair of the NASH-Washington Citizens Neighborhood Advisory Council; Robert Dobbs, a staff member at Bethlehem Community Center and chair of the Northwest-Perry Homes CNAC; Mrs. A. L. Benton, a health aide and member of the Summerhill-Mechanicsville CNAC; and Mrs. Mannie Wynn, a juvenile court aide and secretary of the West End CNAC.[43] Atlanta's poor had achieved at least a partial victory: a system was in place by which the poor would be elected to the board, and four representatives of the poor had been elected to the EOA Board of Directors. What's more, mechanisms were in place that allowed resident input into local program development (through the CNACs) and the EOA (through the CCAC).

Still, challenges remained for Atlanta's poor. EOA was slow to establish centers and programs. The EOA Board of Directors could not always relate to matters of importance to the poor. Black sociopolitical leaders, including those on the EOA board, did not appear to act in poor people's interest. In the spring of 1966, leaders in Atlanta's poorest neighborhoods would reject "silk-stocking leadership" and break with the Summit.[44]

Fracture

In March 1966, a reorganization of EOA's upper administration prompted established civil rights organizations and antipoverty activists to renew demands to place African Americans in more influential positions and to insist on other administrative changes. When Mayor Ivan Allen Jr. had lured Dan Sweat to the mayor's office to use Sweat's growing skill in obtaining federal grants, EOA director Charlie Emmerich took the opportunity to formally restructure EOA administration. The highest ranked Black administrator within EOA, Tilman Cothran, was reclassified as associate administrator for program development, a job that involved reviewing programs *after implementation*. To many observers, African Americans had once again been pushed out of senior leadership roles that had allowed Black input into program development and planning.[45]

Complaints immediately surfaced. As Atlanta's NAACP pointed out, the administrative restructuring left no Black personnel in the top four leadership positions within EOA. Consequently, Blacks were not in positions to review program proposals *before* they were adopted and instituted. African Americans could exercise little power over programs that, in practice, affected target populations that were disproportionately Black. The NAACP also questioned Cothran's new position, suggesting that he was removed from his previous role because he stated his opinions freely. To the NAACP, the December 1964 informal agreement in which EOA committed to having an African American as deputy director had been violated.[46] Like the NAACP, the civic league members that made up the Summit Ad Hoc Committee on Poverty felt that Cothran's change in position "removed all pretense of having a Negro second to Mr. Emmerich in program operations."[47]

Leaders of the Atlanta Summit Leadership Conference responded to Cothran's new appointment by requesting a meeting with EOA officials, but the Summit failed to invite members of the civic leagues who had formed the backbone of the Summit's Ad Hoc Committee on Poverty.[48] Worse, this had happened before. Just one month prior, the Summit had met at Gammon Theological Seminary to discuss matters regarding racial segregation, but they had not included members of the Ad Hoc Committee on Poverty. Civic league members were incensed. If they were not involved in identifying solutions, the Summit was "just a dictatorship from the top."[49] Just as EOA was not operating with authentic participation of the poor, the Summit was not sufficiently involving grassroots members.

Georgia Avenue/Pryor Street Civic League's C. D. Colbert and Vine City's Otis Cochran called a meeting of civic leagues in March 1966, where pent-up irritations with the Summit were unleashed. Meeting attendees asserted that the Summit was interested "in preserving the Summit and not the little black people's problems." Some questioned whether the Summit truly represented "the entire Negro community." Otis Cochran criticized the Summit's statement, noting that "it was not written by us, the grass-roots leadership." Rather, it was "a move by the Summit to get the grass-roots leadership to salvage [the Summit's] bunglings." Others complained that the Summit was primarily interested in keeping Tilman Cothran in EOA's upper administration, which would help ensure that the Summit remained a powerful force. Some concluded that the civic leagues should "stop doing business with the Summit and through the Summit."[50]

Frustrated with the Summit and EOA both, civic league leaders debated forming their own organization, separate from the Summit, one that would better represent the concerns of the poor. But some were reluctant to establish yet another group. "We get hung up in organizational structure," Otis Cochran pointed out. Still, those present sought to make demands of EOA. Cochran and a group of volunteers agreed to draft a list of desires and a plan of action.[51]

The resulting resolution of March 31, 1966, insisted that qualified Blacks be considered for the six top administrative positions at EOA and that one representative from each target area served by EOA be elected to the board of directors. It also called for the resignation of all non-elected board members, as well as Executive Director Charlie Emmerich.[52] The committee forwarded the resolution to Charlie Emmerich, but in their haste, they failed to sign or reveal authorship, a situation that produced confusion and may have exacerbated tensions with EOA administration (though Emmerich still circulated the statement to board members). If the board failed to respond positively in ten days, the civic leagues pledged to ask all target area residents to withhold participation in EOA and demonstrate and picket at EOA headquarters and neighborhood centers. At the same time, Rev. Cadmus Samples called for a picket of the EOA offices, explaining to an *Atlanta Constitution* reporter that they would picket every day "until the walls come tumbling down."[53]

In response to the committee's resolution, Emmerich made the case to the EOA Board of Directors that the changes to the EOA structure had been fair to the Black community. Conceding that the administration had been reduced by one person (Dan Sweat), Emmerich emphasized that he had promoted one non-white and one white, "both highly qualified and deserving individuals." "Negroes have and continue to play an important role in all EOA's activities," Emmerich insisted. As of mid-March, four of six top positions were held by non-whites, 85 percent of constituents served by EOA were non-white, and more than 70 percent of EOA employees were non-white.[54] To Emmerich, EOA primarily served and benefited Black residents and was led by a number of Black representatives and professionals. Indeed, Emmerich may have been irritated that he had spent significant time addressing Black equity concerns only to, in his mind, have to alter course and address poor people's demands, too.

The Poor Folks Movement

Facing pushback from EOA, and despite reservations that creating a new organization would sap time and energy, in April 1966 the civic league leaders who made up the Summit's Ad Hoc Committee on Poverty rebranded their group as the Atlanta Grass Roots Crusade, "the poor folks movement." Describing themselves as an "informal organization of people from various communities of low income," in early April the group again insisted that EOA address inadequate representation of the poor on the EOA Board of Directors and lack of Black representation in EOA administrative positions. "We shall continue to use all techniques at our command to show our dissatisfaction with EOA as presently structured and constituted," they asserted.[55]

The Grass Roots asked for a meeting with the EOA Board of Directors, a request that Emmerich and Jones were willing to accommodate, if, in Bo Jones's phrasing, the Grass Roots had policy matters they wished to "discuss reasonably." But Jones also signaled that EOA likely would not agree to the Grass Roots's specific desires. "I doubt that any member of the Board of the Administrator will resign on your demand," Jones said. Reiterating his December 1965 response to Rev. Samuel Williams and the

Summit, Jones asserted, "Neither you nor anyone else in Atlanta was actively concerned about representation of the poor on the Board of Directors until the Board itself voted unanimously" to meet the OEO's requirements regarding board composition.[56] On the surface, it appeared that EOA's board chair considered the Grass Roots to be unreasonable and unwilling to adopt civil, professional norms. The Grass Roots, of course, had lost confidence that civil engagement with Atlanta's white power structure would produce any substantive gains.

The Grass Roots did not end up attending the April board meeting, but they did respond to Jones. Why was EOA resisting national CAP guidelines regarding the representation of the poor? If 85 percent of the people benefiting from EOA were African American, they asked, why weren't Blacks in 85 percent of the top administrative positions? And all Blacks and "fair minded White people" should be concerned about helping people help themselves "move out of the misery of poverty."[57] The Grass Roots met with the EOA administration the following month to discuss their demands, but EOA stood firm and offered no concessions.[58]

OEO inspectors shared the Grass Roots's frustration with Atlanta's EOA leadership. In an April 1966 letter to OEO inspector general Edgar May, inspectors Robert Martin and Al Krumlauf explained that "the difficulties" Atlanta had in meeting the CAP's "special conditions" in 1965 were still present. The only difference between the present (April 30, 1966) and the six months prior was that now "the Civil Rights groups and the grassroots representatives of the poor" were "acutely aware of" the OEO's requirement for target area participation, and they were prepared to protest if OEO did not require EOA to become more representative of the community. Furthermore, the inspectors wrote, the proposed bylaws modifications about populating the advisory committees and board "plainly do not meet either the expectations of the community or the requirements of the CAP guide." It was a "status quo proposal" that "should be rejected," Martin and Krumlauf stated.[59]

To the inspectors, Atlanta's EOA leadership was manipulative, using "crisis tactics" and personal relationships to pressure OEO. The city delayed implementing changes to address the maximum feasible participation requirement and then claimed that withholding federal funds would damage the program.[60] Such tactics had worked before. "Past experience gives EOA officials very good reason to believe that we will not hold firm on our special conditions in the face of an impending financial crisis," inspectors wrote. Martin and Krumlauf stressed the importance of Atlanta's compliance. "Atlanta has 'high visibility' in the south," they asserted.

"From Orlando to Memphis we hear, 'Why should we be representative of the community? Atlanta isn't, and you let them get away with it.'" It was not totally clear why Atlanta continued to receive special treatment, but some felt that Bo Jones's close relationship with War on Poverty officials, particularly Sargent Shriver, meant that Atlanta was given a pass when it came to meeting the CAP's most stringent rules.[61]

The Grass Roots continued to pressure the EOA Board of Directors. They visited Washington, D.C., to personally register their complaints with OEO. And in mid-May, the group reasserted its demands that all aides be covered by the pension plan, that African Americans be hired as deputy director and personnel director, and that there be increased representation of the poor on the board. This time, EOA administrators deflected the demands by suggesting they be routed through the EOA's tiered advisory structure. The Grass Roots argued against that process, insisting that it would cause confusion and further delay. "Already the vast machinery of EOA, Inc. has been set in motion to brainwash the Advisory Councils" against their "reasonable" proposals.[62]

The Grass Roots also further solidified their independence from the Summit. To the Grass Roots, "The power structure in the Negro Community has outlived its usefulness in representing itself as spokesmen for the people." In June 1966 the Grass Roots issued a news release indicating that they would sponsor their own candidates in all elections. The statement repeated the group's earlier complaints about the Summit. The Grass Roots sought "not only representation, but also participation." They felt they were being spoken for and not with. The Summit was "lukewarm" on issues that concerned poor people, "as if poor people don't exist."[63] Similar sentiment was expressed at the subsequent 31 July 1966 Grass Roots meeting. "No more silk stocking representation," the minutes stated. "We represent ourselves."[64]

Urban Violence

As civic leagues and the Summit tried to hold EOA to account in Atlanta's poorest neighborhoods, tensions remained high as residents dealt with ongoing service neglect and an overbearing police force. In particular, as *Atlanta Constitution* journalist Dick Hebert reported in June 1966, "Police are keeping a close eye on Vine City, one of Atlanta's most potentially explosive slum areas."[65] City leaders were concerned that the national wave of urban violence would spark episodes close to home. Across the United States, cities were suffering violent conflict that arose from decades of social tensions. In 1964, cities such as Rochester, New York, Philadelphia, and Chicago saw urban protests, and in 1965 the Watts neighborhood of Los Angeles endured days of destruction and public disorder.[66] When *Atlanta Constitution*'s Dick Hebert speculated about Vine City's potential to "explode," Chicago's Division Street had just burst into violence after an altercation between police and Puerto Rican Week participants.[67]

In Vine City, police canvased the neighborhood in June 1966, assuring residents that police were "their friends." That police were residents' friends was a difficult case to make to poor Black Atlantans who regularly experienced police harassment. Just that past April, Mechanicsville activist Edward Moody had been assaulted by an officer when he went to pay bond for his wife at the city jail. When Moody did not respond quickly enough to the desk officer's command, he stated the officer threatened him with a weekend in jail, grabbed him, and reportedly threatened him, "I'll teach you black bastards to move when you are told."[68] Moody was jailed and fined for disobeying an officer.[69] Assurances that the police were friends of the poor hardly salved decades of concern about inadequate city services, overcrowded housing, and lack of job and educational opportunities. Even in September, as summer waned, the *Atlanta Journal* warned, "if we don't do something about the Vine City area, it's going to blow, like Watts."[70] And unrest eventually surfaced, not in Vine City, but in Summerhill, and then in Boulevard, and then in Dixie Hills.

On Tuesday, September 6, Atlanta police shot Harold Louis Prather twice in the back as he fled patrolmen and ran toward his mother's home near Capitol and Ormond Streets in the Summerhill neighborhood just south of downtown. Police suspected Prather of auto theft, but to observers, the police response far exceeded Prather's alleged crime. As Prather was ambulanced to a local hospital, crowds began to gather near Prather's mother's home, many vocally complaining about regular police harassment and brutality.[71] "This thing has been building up a long time," Summerhill resident Geneva Brown explained. "People have been shot around here before and nothing was done about it."[72]

SNCC chair Stokely Carmichael learned of the shooting midafternoon when a reporter from WAOK radio phoned him and encouraged him to head to the scene. There, Carmichael talked with residents, agreed to help with a protest, and promised to return to Summerhill after a scheduled SNCC Central Committee meeting. Before leaving, Carmichael told WAOK that African Americans were tired of such shootings, and that they would turn the city inside out "until these incidents have stopped."[73]

People continued to gather near Capitol and Ormond Streets through the afternoon, and the situation eventually grew violent. Projectiles flew. Cars were damaged. "The people from this area were very angry," Betty Jean McFavors explained in an affidavit.[74] Atlanta Project head Bill Ware arrived with the SNCC sound truck, and individuals used the loud speaker to give their impressions of events. Atlanta police directed Ware to remove the truck, but Ware refused and was arrested. SNCC's Bobby Walton continued the broadcast, but he, too, was arrested. The crowd moved toward the police and began rocking a patrol car. As the car pulled away, it hit a pregnant Black woman, which further angered bystanders. Rocks and bottles continued to fly. Police cordoned off the area. Mayor Ivan Allen Jr. arrived around 5 p.m. hoping to calm the crowd. He walked through the neighborhood, encouraging people to disperse and explaining that the armed police were there "to protect" residents. Then he climbed atop a police car to address the crowd, but spectators rocked the vehicle, and Allen stumbled off. Fires erupted. Police arrested those throwing objects and deployed tear gas, sending thirty to forty people to the hospital.[75]

At a meeting at Mt. Carmel Baptist Church that evening, SCLC's Hosea Williams and others pleaded for order and nonviolence, but they were soon drowned out by cries of "Black Power." SNCC field secretary Willie Ricks, known for his fiery oratory, had only just recently coined the "Black Power" phrase at the Meredith March against Fear in June 1966, the event following the shooting of civil rights activist James Meredith. In Atlanta, the rallying cry proved equally effective. Residents were tired of racial discrimination, poor neighborhood conditions, lack of jobs, and police oppression. Calls to assert power energized many. Residents were frustrated and angry, and violence resurfaced that evening. Reporters with the local WSB network were attacked, and their car turned over.[76] The entire Atlanta police force was deployed to quell the unrest. By the end of the night, fifteen people would be charged with such offenses as disorderly conduct and failure to move on.[77]

Many in Atlanta's leadership blamed SNCC and charismatic and outspoken Stokely Carmichael for sparking the Summerhill events. Vice president of the Summerhill Civic League Rev. Ray Williams accused the organization of whipping the neighborhood into a frenzy.[78] The *Atlanta Constitution* reported that SNCC "egged on" Blacks gathered in the area, and the Summit "came out strongly" against the students.[79] But others rejected the facile accusations. Organizations including the American Jewish Committee and American Council of Churches penned a letter to the mayor lamenting that "it would be tragic, indeed, if community consensus were to become arrayed against certain individuals and organizations" instead of recognizing the social conditions that brought on the events.[80] Carmichael, too, brushed off the charges and circulated a statement to that effect. Allen had neglected many of Atlanta's residents, Carmichael asserted. He had "refused to deal with the rats, roaches and unemployment in the black community."[81] To many, the Summerhill events were less a "riot" and more of a revolt against structural inequality, poverty, and overzealous policing. Nonetheless, police raided SNCC headquarters Thursday night, September 8, and arrested Carmichael.[82] He was held on $10,000 bond—$9,000 for the charge of "riot" and $1,000 for the charge of disorderly conduct. On September 13, the Fulton County Grand Jury charged Carmichael and fourteen others with violation of the state's "riot" statute.[83] In the meantime, protest surfaced elsewhere in the city.

On Saturday, September 10, violence flared in the lower fourth ward, the neighborhood straddling Boulevard just north of Baptist Hospital. That evening, a white man and his female companion had driven by a group of Black teens. Thinking that the kids had spoken disrespectfully to them, the white couple stopped, backed up, and asked the group if they had said something to those in the car. It is unclear how the teens responded, but the driver reportedly pulled out a gun and began firing toward the group. Hulet Varner Jr., sixteen, an African American, was killed, and his friend Roy Milton Wright was injured. Responding to the incident with other police, a white sergeant was shot, apparently by gunfire that had started in the surrounding neighborhood. Interracial tensions escalated when the ambulance driver picked up the white police officer but left the wounded Black victim. Violence would surface periodically for the next two days.[84]

It is not clear exactly what participants sought when they engaged in unorganized actions like those in Summerhill and Boulevard, but the National Advisory Commission on Civil Disorders, which was charged with investigating the causes of urban civil rest, gathered data on the frustrations of thousands of urban residents across the United States. In dozens of disorders, participants attacked "local symbols of white American society, authority and property." And while civil disorder launched from specific, precipitating events, violence usually was generated "out of an increasingly disturbed social atmosphere." To be sure, racial discrimination was a factor, but the commission also recognized that urban conflict resulted from myriad sources: poverty, joblessness and underemployment, class politics, inadequate education, poor recreational facilities, inadequate city services, and discriminatory consumer and credit practices. These were precisely the issues poor Atlantans and their allies had been complaining about for years.[85]

While Atlanta had been slow to improve conditions that were regularly cited as causes for civil disturbances, city officials, local leaders, residents, and activists were certainly aware of the connections between poor social conditions and urban unrest. EOA's Charlie Emmerich pointed out that riots began "the week after [EOA's] recreation programs ceased."[86] And the Grass Roots asked the mayor why he chose to strengthen anti-riot laws instead of attacking "the causes of such incidents," that is, police brutality, lack of parks and play areas, bad housing, unemployment, poor streets, undependable trash collection, and overcrowded schools.[87] But city leaders knew the root cause of urban violence. As Mayor Ivan Allen Jr. explained to building inspector William R. Wofford, the violence had been precipitated by the shooting of the two youth, but conditions that might spark violence had been present for some time.[88] Residents and city leaders knew what served as tinder for civil unrest, but it proved harder to agree on actionable solutions and to shift resources to historically underserved communities, particularly poor Black neighborhoods.

Atlanta leadership did act on the Grass Roots' suggestion to form a community relations body to help "avoid the disturbances" that had emerged in other cities, and now Atlanta. The ordinance forming the permanent human relations body called for a survey of services and facilities in Atlanta's economically depressed areas, including Blue Heaven, Bush Mountain, Cabbage Town, Mechanicville, Summerhill, Vine City, Lightning, and Scott's Crossing. The Community Relations Commission also decided to hold neighborhood-based forums to hear directly from residents. Often well attended and occasionally raucous, the meetings attracted rank-and-file residents as well as experienced neighborhood activists (see fig. 10).[89]

The first public hearings of the Community Relations Commission (CRC) repeated grievances poor and near-poor residents and people of color had been logging for years. Residents charged the city with job discrimination (which resulted in continued low wages) and complained of discrimination in real estate sales.[90] Carver Homes resident Louise Whatley detailed steep fines at public housing complexes. Parents were charged $5 when children played on the grass, she said, and repair charges seemed to rapidly escalate.[91] James Marshall Jr. explained that there was only one paved street in Lightning, no recreation areas, and the city was slow to pick up trash.[92] H. E. Phipps of the Peoplestown Civic League

FIGURE 10. Community Relations Commission public meeting, c. 1971. Courtesy Boyd Lewis photographs, Kenan Research Center at the Atlanta History Center.

had a lengthy list of improvements his neighborhood had requested for years, including the resurfacing of Haygood Avenue, a traffic light at Haygood and Capitol, and more recreational areas. Peoplestown's Martha Weems remarked that the city was able to resurface streets around the stadium, but not around their homes.[93] As writer Anne Rivers Siddons noted in an *Atlanta Magazine* piece on the CRC and its meetings, residents were tired of "the shunting aside, the endless referrals." There had been promises of aid, she wrote, "as long as some of the citizens at that meeting could remember."[94] But while the citizens and the commission could compile needs and suggest solutions, the agency that in many ways was intended to assuage those problems—EOA—faced threats.[95]

Criticism and Cutbacks

While in 1964 Lyndon Johnson enjoyed a landslide victory that allowed him to usher in major Great Society initiatives, in the months leading to the November 1966 congressional elections, Republicans took aim at Lyndon Johnson's War on Poverty specifically and social welfare spending in general.[96] Republicans contended that War on Poverty programs were being abused and mismanaged, and they proposed that OEO be dismantled.[97] In response to the bill authorizing a third year of War on Poverty funding, Republicans asserted that CAPs were "the most confused, mismanaged and ineffective" of the War on Poverty programs.[98] In Georgia's fourth district congressional race, Ben Blackburn echoed Republican rhetoric and attacked Democratic incumbent James MacKay on his support for Johnson's appropriation requests. To Blackburn and other Republicans, the War on Poverty was wasteful and a "boondoggle."[99]

Additionally, the escalating Vietnam crisis drew Johnson and other leaders' attention and an increasingly large segment of the federal budget. Johnson remained committed to fighting the spread of communism in East Asia, though, and he escalated the bombing of the region and committed more U.S. troops to the conflict. War costs would eat away at energy and resources that had previously poured into the War on Poverty.[100]

In the fall 1966 congressional session, Republicans altered War on Poverty legislation and programs any chance they could.[101] They blamed Democrats for urban conflict, suggesting that Democrats funded extremism, and they took Johnson to task for hiding the growing bombing campaign in East Asia.[102] The attack was successful: Republicans made political gains, and War on Poverty budgets were reduced. Although Johnson had originally requested $1.75 billion for War on Poverty programs for 1967, the House and Senate eventually approved $1.56 and $1.66 million, respectively.[103] In the November 1966 elections, the GOP gained forty-seven house seats and southern Democrats four, which would allow conservatives to continue to slow Great Society spending.[104] As the UPI explained, the "prospective new coalition of Republicans and Southern Democrats" was in a position to put some existing Johnson programs "on a starvation diet."[105]

Atlanta's EOA braced for a 40 percent reduction in federal funding for 1967, a cut that would force the organization to eliminate some existing programs and cancel the start of others.[106] All totaled, after Congress set OEO appropriations, Atlanta was expecting to receive $3.8 million in community action funding for 1967, a cut of $1.9 million for EOA.[107] Although recipients of federal grants always worked and hoped for supplemental budget appropriations, growing criticism from conservative congressional leaders made that less likely.[108]

Diminished EOA funding meant some summer programs were on the chopping block. Cutbacks in recreation services were particularly difficult to bear, falling so soon after the Summerhill and Boulevard disturbances, and the CRC heard about it. Accompanied by neighborhood children, Vine City organizer Otis Cochran asked that community centers be reopened. To Cochran (and others), the city's concerns were elsewhere, and again the city's new stadium was deployed to make a point about the city's spending priorities. If the city could afford a multimillion dollar stadium, Cochran said, it could find money for recreational programs that would prevent delinquency.[109]

EOA advocates had some victories in their fight to restore funding. In May 1967, just in time for summer, EOA and Atlanta's United Appeal identified about $260,000 that allowed playlots to be leased.[110] Mayor Ivan Allen Jr. told journalists that the summer 1967 program would serve two thousand children at twenty-five lots, sixteen more lots than had been funded in summer 1966.[111]

Although Atlanta had organized a community relations council specifically to help ameliorate conditions that sparked urban unrest, and although monies had been found to launch at least some summer recreation programs, social conditions could not be remedied quickly. Violence would erupt again, in part because of overzealous policing and in part because of festering neighborhood conditions.

Dixie Hills

In June 1967, the arrest of three Black teens and the shooting of a fourth Black resident in the southwest neighborhood of Dixie Hills again exposed Atlanta's problem with aggressive policing and urban decline. The events unfolded over four days. On Saturday, June 17, an exchange between a Dixie Hills Shopping Center security guard and area youth escalated into a scuffle. Police arrived and charged the three people involved with disturbing the peace.[112] Still, some saw SNCC as the catalyst of yet another disturbance, and the next day, June 18, police would arrest Stokely Carmichael on a charge of loitering.

White CRC vice chair and political operative Helen Bullard asked participants at a June 19 community meeting if they thought "Carmichael's presence [in Dixie Hills] precipitated this rioting," and residents responded with a list of complaints officials had heard many times: inadequate play lots, unpaved streets, high rents, poor maintenance and pest control by landlords, inadequate sewer systems. Requests for better services—such as street lighting—went ignored. The nearby grocery stores set prices too high, and product quality was low. What's more, EOA was doing little to address these issues, and as resident Wilkie Jordan pointed out, its counselors did "not take interest" in residents' concerns. EOA had facilitated some job placements, but wages were too low to support families. And residents complained of police brutality and harassment. "The policemen are causing disorder," resident Virginia Jackson stated flatly.[113] Stokely Carmichael and SNCC activists, it seemed, were hardly the problem.

On June 19, people gathered again at the Dixie Hills Shopping Center. Initially, only a few police units were in the area, but eventually words were exchanged, and the situation degenerated into another two days of violence.[114] Forty-six-year-old Black resident Willie B. Ross, who had been sitting on a step at his home, would die as a result. Three other residents, including a nine-year-old, were injured in police gunfire.[115] To Dixie Hills residents, police were harassing residents, not protecting them. A Wadley Street resident complained that police were patrolling residential areas too aggressively, running people off their own front porches and using profane language. Shirley Street resident Howard Watson asserted that the police had handled a female involved in the first night's arrest unprofessionally. He said that in poor neighborhoods, police get away with behavior unacceptable in high-income areas.[116]

Residents of Atlanta's poorest neighborhoods had been registering complaints about social conditions, including police brutality and harassment, for years, and tempers and patience had grown short. But as Atlanta's poor navigated urban unrest and the causes that sparked it, some political circles continued to critique and attack War on Poverty programs, programs that many felt would help mitigate the worst urban issues. EOA's challenges continued in summer 1967 when Charlie Emmerich died unexpectedly of a heart attack, renewing debates about the makeup of EOA's top administration.[117]

The years 1966 and 1967 proved challenging for Atlanta and its CAP. Despite federal requirements, there was little presence of the poor in policymaking bodies. Professionals such as Jones, Emmerich, and EOA board members did not always plainly state their assumptions when they denied poor people greater representation on and roles in EOA. Enough was said, though, to suggest that white and Black professionals felt poor families lacked the intellectual tools to address poverty and its related conditions. When pressed by the OEO to meet the required mandate, EOA leaders added as few poor members as they could get away with and then regularly deflected local appeals to add more.

Because Atlanta's poor population was disproportionately Black, local Black leadership took serious interest in the success of EOA. But as the War on Poverty progressed, Atlanta's Black leadership fractured, and battles between establishment civil rights leaders and leaders of poor neighborhoods—the Grass Roots—consumed energy and drew media attention. At a meeting to discuss Atlanta's school transfer policy, SCLC's Hosea Williams, an activist convinced of the value of disruptive tactics, publicly drew a distinction between the action-oriented Grass Roots and the more conservative civil rights leaders in the Atlanta Summit Leadership Conference. The Summit had "never gone to jail" and did not "know the problems" that rank-and-file residents experienced.[118] Tensions with the Summit only grew worse, and in 1968, Grass Roots members usurped the Summit's election process and ran their own candidates for Summit leadership, a process the establishment Summit leaders all but ignored. Ultimately, civic and neighborhood leaders organized a separate Metropolitan Atlanta Summit Leadership Conference.[119]

By the end of 1967, the political tide had turned against the federal program that at one time seemed poised to address some of the worse causes of poverty and related conditions. Nationally and within Georgia, conservative forces rebelled against what they saw as a rapidly expanding federal government and increased social welfare spending. As Atlanta journalist Wayne Kelley explained, although War on Poverty legislation had passed in 1964 with southern Democrats in support 60 to 40, by November 1967, "no one estimates Southern support at even 30 votes."[120] With federal cuts to War on Poverty funding, Atlanta would have to repair its mistakes and accelerate its war with fewer resources.

Atlanta's leaders had hoped they could avoid the urban violence that marred other cities in the mid-1960s, but ultimately residents would no longer accept neglect, slow progress, and, in the case of community-police relations, outright oppression. Residents rebelled, and although civil disorder as a method of protest was criticized, the threat of urban violence pushed city officials to proactively address urban conditions. Atlanta leaderships' vision of a national city could not be sustained by a city littered with dilapidated housing, abandoned buildings, and the poor, and urban violence would repel new businesses, residents, and tourists.

Atlanta's CAP was not all that many had hoped, but many of Atlanta's poor increasingly formed their own pressure groups to raise issues and reinforce their demands. Neighborhood and civic councils had allowed local areas to voice concerns about urban conditions, for example, and by the late 1960s poor residents were mobilizing to address social issues. In particular, organizing around welfare and workplace concerns swelled quickly beginning in 1966, catalyzed by residents hoping to realize the promise of the civil rights revolution.

CHAPTER 5

Welfare and Workplace

"Justice is on the side of the striking city workers," *Emmaus House News* proclaimed in April 1970, referring to the sanitation workers' strike that had expanded to insist on wage hikes and other benefits for many city workers. "Everyone who can is asked to turn out to help with picket lines, demonstrations, and to attend the mass meetings."[1] Elsewhere the mimeographed newsletter announced that the Reverend Andrew Young Jr. of the Southern Christian Leadership Conference (SCLC) was to speak to the local welfare rights organization. And it alerted readers that the Supreme Court had ruled that welfare checks could not be cut without a hearing. Indeed, the two-page issue, produced by the Episcopal diocese's inner-city mission Emmaus House, revealed a flurry of antipoverty work in Atlanta in spring 1970.

From 1967 to 1971, a wide range of actions to address poverty surfaced across Atlanta. Emmaus House opened in downtown Atlanta to provide support for those wanting to mitigate poverty and facilitate social change. Atlanta's welfare mothers formed a welfare rights organization and committed to protecting and expanding social welfare programs such as Aid to Families with Dependent Children (AFDC), the entitlement colloquially known as welfare. Attorneys, paralegals, and their support staff pursued changes in law that would better protect Atlanta's poor families. Some residents participated in the national Poor People's Campaign in Washington, D.C., the event conceived by Martin Luther King Jr. and the Atlanta-headquartered SCLC. Atlanta's predominantly Black, low-wage sanitation workers followed the example of Memphis and Savannah workers and protested an unresponsive local union, stagnant pay, and dangerous working conditions. They staged a wildcat strike in 1968 and walked out again in 1970. These multiple actions involved a variety of personnel—poor people, including welfare client–activists and laborers, white liberals, public interest and civil rights attorneys, religious leaders and congregants—and demonstrated an expanded awareness and interest in addressing poverty and inequality. In the spate of late 1960s antipoverty events and campaigns, Atlanta's activists and advocates would not achieve all their goals, but some victories were tallied, and activists and other antipoverty advocates continued to express confidence that some, if measured, economic justice gains could be achieved.

A Change Agent

The idea that the poor had rights had not occurred to Ethel Mae Mathews until the point was raised by National Welfare Rights Organization (NWRO) representatives who were visiting the recently opened Emmaus House. Mathews's own welfare caseworker had accused her of wanting to "make more babies and collect more money."[2] But the NWRO activists helped correct misinformation regularly told to Atlanta's AFDC clients, and they explained the program rules. AFDC recipients could campaign on behalf of welfare mothers without threat to their AFDC entitlements, for example, and they could use the monthly grants as they determined necessary. To recognize welfare as an entitlement, something clients had a right to if they met qualifications, represented a significant shift in thinking to Mathews and other mothers receiving welfare.

A meeting of welfare recipients seeking to understand their rights was just the sort of thing white Episcopal priest Rev. Austin Ford envisioned for Emmaus House, a mission of the city's Episcopal diocese that opened in 1967. Housed in Peoplestown, a predominantly Black and disproportionately poor neighborhood just south of downtown, Emmaus House was intended to work *with* residents (near and far) to mitigate inequality and face the range of economic injustices that poor and marginalized residents dealt with on a daily basis.[3] Originally from neighboring DeKalb County, Ford had demonstrated a commitment to civil rights as a seminarian at the University of the South. There, in 1952, he and other students protested the school's rejection of its first Black applicant. Later, as priest at the well-off and predominantly white St. Bartholomew's Church in Atlanta's North Druid Hills neighborhood, Ford was actively involved in the GCHR, an organization that promoted improved race relations and smooth integration of schools. When the diocese decided to initiate an inner-city project, the diocesan bishop asked Ford if he would take the lead. Ford agreed.[4]

Emmaus House offered a variety of services, such as children's after-school and summer programs and providing transportation to Atlantans visiting family members at Reidsville Prison. It eventually housed a chapel and held regular services. But Emmaus House was also intended to help fulfill the Civil Rights Act of 1964, Ford explained to Grace Stone, an early volunteer. By that Ford meant that Emmaus House would help residents exercise their rights under law.[5] Emmaus House was a "change agent," as Sister Marie, née Mimi Bodell, described it. Bodell, a white Sister of Notre Dame de Namur, began work at Emmaus House soon after the diocese bought the property.[6] Residents would lead that change, explained Gene Ferguson, a Black former SCLC field organizer who joined the Emmaus House staff in fall 1968. Residents knew the challenges of the neighborhood, discrimination, and poverty, the thinking went, and they would be part of solutions.[7] Emmaus House would support such work by providing space, staff support, and various supplies. Staff and volunteers would help meet other needs as they surfaced.

In March 1967, Emmaus House set up shop in two dilapidated houses on the northwest corner of Capitol Avenue and Haygood in the Peoplestown neighborhood just a mile and a half south of the Georgia Capitol, an area that was predominantly Black (about 78 percent in 1959) and largely poor (49 percent of Peoplestown residents lived below the poverty line in 1959). Residents there had endured a number of urban development initiatives. The expressway had taken homes from Peoplestown's western edge, and the area housed families displaced by the recently cleared Rawson-Washington urban renewal site, where Atlanta–Fulton County Stadium had been built in 1964–65.[8] Not all of Peoplestown's housing stock was in decline or in poor condition, but the building that would become Emmaus House's main office was a wreck. "It had been a sort of flophouse for alcoholics," Ford recalled. "There were signs on the doors saying 'two dollars a night.'"[9] Sister Marie joined Ford soon after the diocese bought the property, and together they worked with volunteers from St. Pius X Catholic High School to shovel debris from the two houses and clean them up. After making the properties habitable, Ford moved in.[10]

Nearly immediately after opening, in 1967, Emmaus House began operationalizing its goals by hosting organizers from the newly formed National Welfare Rights Organization (NWRO), with which Ford was familiar from his work with white liberal activist Frances Pauley on the

GCHR. The NWRO was fairly young itself when its representatives visited Emmaus House. The NWRO marked a new phase of civil rights organizing activity, one that recognized the relationship between civil rights and the daily struggle to support one's family on poverty wages and without a substantial safety net. As a *national* organization, NWRO intended to build a base among established welfare recipients who would demand improved services and leverage growing national concern about poverty and inequality. At its most ambitious, NWRO would argue for a right to basic subsistence. Importantly, the NWRO was *agile*: local affiliates could quickly respond to the needs of a given situation. That might mean cooperating and negotiating with systems and offices that controlled resources, or disruption.[11] In addition, NWRO and other pro-welfare activists hoped to stress the social welfare system. If many more people were recruited onto the welfare rolls, bringing the system to the brink of collapse, it would be obvious the system was inadequate. People would see that it needed to be replaced with a guaranteed annual income.[12] The NWRO offered Atlanta's dissatisfied welfare clients a chance to improve social welfare and their own family's long-term health and opportunity. Emmaus House facilitated this work, enabling poor mothers to connect with this new network.

To be sure, in the mid-1960s Atlantans needed improved access to social welfare services, including Aid to Families with Dependent Children, but also food and medical programs. Local welfare offices did not proactively advertise the availability of social welfare entitlements. Making matters worse, policies and requirements were seldom transparent, and families could not easily determine if they qualified for support. Welfare clients (and potential clients) had other complaints, too. Georgia had a "man in the house" law, which meant that if a client were in a relationship with an "able-bodied male," she could lose her AFDC benefits. In home visits, welfare workers would look for evidence of a male's presence, which clients considered an invasion of privacy. Georgia did not allocate AFDC to two-parent households, which discouraged mothers from marrying. Additionally, clients felt some welfare workers were disrespectful and condescending. Other social services were problematic, too. Surplus food was available on a limited schedule and from inconvenient locations, and poor families did not have ready access to transportation. Medical facilities were far away. Poorly executed social welfare services were at least in part a result of an entrenched anti-welfare culture that, while present across the United States, was particularly tenacious in the Deep South.[13]

Racial politics dogged AFDC. In the 1960s, AFDC served more and more Black families, and many white power brokers still cared little for Black interests. The specter of the lazy welfare family and the welfare mother birthing children for profit were difficult myths to dispel. As political scientist Martin Gilens has shown, media images had increasingly equated "welfare," particularly AFDC and later food stamps, with African Americans; and white Americans, as a general rule, equated Blacks with laziness. That myth certainly circulated in Georgia. Many white southerners remained convinced that without proper incentives, unskilled Black laborers would not work at all but would live off "the dole."[14] For example, when Georgia Department of Health and Human Resources head Bill Burson tried to persuade Glascock County officials to participate in a federal-state food program, Sheriff John L. English responded that if such a program were instituted, there would "just be a lot of [——] lined up there," using a racial epithet.[15] Of course, AFDC and food programs served white families as well; in 1967, one-third of Fulton County's AFDC recipients were white, and those families also endured criticism when they utilized public assistance.[16] But there can be no doubt that assumptions about welfare recipients in the 1960s were intertwined with racial stereotypes and widespread white beliefs about Black behavior. To ensure that Georgians—and particularly Black Georgians—worked, local white bureaucrats erected barriers to social welfare entitlements. Residents had to learn how to surmount or eradicate those obstacles.

Persuading mothers to challenge entrenched cultural assumptions and to assert their rights to means-tested entitlement programs—a benefit received if one met established criteria—was a significant challenge. Mothers were reluctant to even reveal their status as welfare clients. As Ethel Mae Mathews would explain to a journalist years later, at that time mothers were "skittish" about telling others they were on welfare. So when Ford personally invited welfare families in Peoplestown to Emmaus House to talk to organizers about the growing welfare rights movement, Mathews said, "I didn't even want to tell that nosy white man my name."[17] But welfare clients soon became welfare rights activists.

By October 1967, welfare client-activists elected officers for Atlanta's first welfare rights chapter.[18] Early members drew from Peoplestown and the adjacent Summerhill neighborhood, though the organization's geographic reach soon expanded.[19] The group met every two to four weeks, and early energy was spent distributing basic information about benefits and building confidence in grassroots democratic action. Writers for the

FIGURE 11. Welfare rights organization meeting, Emmaus House, c. 1975. Courtesy Boyd Lewis photographs, Kenan Research Center at the Atlanta History Center.

Emmaus House News, which initially served as the communication tool for the welfare rights organization, regularly implored readers to "be sure to say what *YOU* think" and reminded members that the welfare rights group was "YOUR organization" (see fig. 11).[20] Members learned about voting and state welfare regulations, including qualifications. The welfare rights organization also pursued mutual-aid projects, such as collecting money for an emergency utility fund.[21]

Living and working at Emmaus House anywhere from two months to two years, Emmaus House staff members included conscientious objectors who had been approved for domestic service, War on Poverty–funded VISTA volunteers, and others inspired by the civil rights movement or by religious or vocational inquiry. Susan Taylor, who had heard of Emmaus House when Austin Ford, Gene Ferguson, and Frances Pauley visited her Dalton, Georgia, church, began work at Emmaus House the summer after she graduated from high school in 1969. Dennis Goldstein pursued conscientious objector status around 1968 and, having an interest in civil rights activities in the South, visited Emmaus House and eventually joined the staff. When David Morath's application for alternative service was approved, he combed through the list of Selective

Service–approved work sites provided by the American Friends Service Committee. He wrote letters of inquiry to an estimated thirty sites and, beginning in late 1970, served on the Emmaus House staff for two years. The federal VISTA program brought more young people inclined to community development. In 1968, for example, Doug Favero joined Emmaus House as a VISTA volunteer, and part of his job included recruiting residents for the welfare rights organization and fostering relationships with area neighbors.[22] Idealistic young people continued to find their way to Atlanta's Emmaus House through the balance of the 1970s, many exploring how they could operationalize their religious convictions, support ongoing rights movements, or put their educations and skill sets to work.

The on-site staff was supplemented by volunteers from Atlanta-area congregations, including suburban housewives and young mothers, many armed with experience working in and managing other volunteer-based efforts. White Wellesley College graduate Muriel Lokey, a member of St. Luke's Episcopal Church, began volunteering with Emmaus House soon after it opened. She came to Emmaus House with years of experience serving her community. In the 1950s she worked with H.O.P.E., Inc., an Atlanta organization that sought to keep city schools open as desegregation proceeded. Lokey recruited Grace Stone to Emmaus House to help residents pick up surplus food, though Stone already knew Ford from when he was a priest at St. Bartholomew's. Deedie Weems, who helped poor families navigate social welfare applications and processes, became involved through St. Bede's Episcopal Church. In this way, as regular volunteers at a central city mission, housewives and mothers contributed to ongoing Black freedom and economic justice pursuits.[23]

Emmaus House staff and volunteers provided crucial support to the welfare rights organization. The mission property was a safe space for residents to meet, share grievances, and plot a future course. In addition, because Emmaus House staff could fundraise and solicit donations of money and equipment, the mission provided basic organizational supplies—a mimeograph machine, postage, paper, a phone—that were not readily accessible to poor families. Those resources and staffing allowed the production and dissemination of *Emmaus House News*, which announced organization meetings, elections, and agendas and outlined developments and changes in social welfare programs. Additionally, Emmaus House staff and volunteers were tasked with recruiting new members, and staff sometimes went door to door in neighborhoods and public housing communities. Emmaus House staff and volunteers also studied welfare regulations and helped AFDC clients and potential clients understand rules and the application process. They provided transportation to and from commodity distribution sites, welfare rights meetings, the Division of Family and Children Services (DFACS), and other agencies. In these ways, from 1967 on, Emmaus House was a reliable, consistent foundation for the welfare rights organization and its members.[24]

The Emmaus House work also influenced the staff, students, housewives, and congregants who served there, which was in part Ford's intent. Ford felt that people needed opportunities to bridge the city's racial divide, volunteer Grace Stone explained, and Emmaus House provided that opportunity.[25] "We were hoping to change attitudes," Mimi Bodell reflected.[26] Through surplus food delivery, Stone came to know various residents of Atlanta's central neighborhoods as well as the state of inner-city housing and families' issues with social welfare.[27] At Emmaus House, Sue Taylor was exposed to poverty and stark divides in society. Emmaus House helped guide her politics and, as she phrased it, her "way of being in the world."[28] Thus, Emmaus House provided a support structure for Atlanta's poor families, but it also helped educate and influence the thinking of members of more powerful social groups, including the white and privileged.

Ford had identified a unique antipoverty workforce, but it was a workforce that was historically contingent. Until the Vietnam War draft ended in the early 1970s, there was a cache of conscientious objectors from which Emmaus House was able to draw that would allow the mission to provide consistent support to poor families pursuing social change. Similarly, Emmaus House utilized the skills and labor of women from area congregations who often identified as mothers and housewives, but who sought meaningful work or to realize religious (or service) convictions. But this workforce would diminish in number as economic and cultural change encouraged women to move into the paid workforce and when the draft ceased in 1972.

In 1967 and early 1968, then, Emmaus House established a foundation that allowed it to cultivate economic and racial justice initiatives. It served as a home to Atlanta's first welfare rights organization, a group that would quickly grow and contribute to the NWRO's national network, and supported other social justice endeavors. As Emmaus House grew its reach in Atlanta, public interest attorneys were likewise seeking to shift and enlarge their role in civil and economic rights.

Atlanta Legal Aid Society

Atlanta may have been generating optimistic reports of the city's prosperity, observed L. Rosser Shelton, assistant general counsel of the Atlanta Legal Aid Society (ALAS) in December 1965, but "indigent citizens in large numbers" continued to call on ALAS for representation.[29] There still was widespread need for indigent legal services. To address that need, ALAS staff had started providing staff to EOA centers one day a week. The kinks were still getting worked out, but in the first six months of 1966, ALAS served 265 cases through those satellite locations.[30] Still, as the civil rights movement unfolded in Atlanta and beyond, some in the legal profession had a larger vision for what ALAS could accomplish.

Since the 1920s, Atlanta Legal Aid Society had provided the city's poor with basic legal services, but ALAS attorneys did not tend to pursue cases for the express purpose of changing laws that "operated to deprive poor people of justice," as an ALAS history phrased it.[31] ALAS had processed divorces, filed bankruptcies, pursued legitimacy claims, and addressed issues of child abandonment.[32] But the Black freedom movement, War on Poverty, and the encouragement of the Community Council of the Atlanta Area (CCAA) motivated ALAS to grow and move in new directions. In September 1965, CCAA recommended that rather than simply serving as an intermediary between the poor and institutions, ALAS should commit to "changing institutions."[33] Beginning in 1966, ALAS increasingly devoted time to reform law.[34] ALAS also added Black members and representatives of the poor to its board, a move that would help shift ALAS toward a more activist practice.[35]

Toward that end, ALAS piloted a project with EOA to hire two attorneys to represent indigent residents in criminal court—a prelude to a public defender program.[36] Until that time, poor Atlantans had been extended only the most basic legal representation: federal law allowed for the use of public defenders, but to date, neither Atlanta nor Georgia had created a formal public defender law or program.[37] Counties such as Fulton, home to most of the city of Atlanta, appointed attorneys to represent poor clients, but those attorneys were only paid for death penalty cases. Consequently, few attorneys agreed to do court-appointed work.[38] There certainly was need: of the 3,000 people Fulton County tried annually, about 60 percent qualified as indigent.[39] The attorneys for the pilot indigent program were immediately swamped with work. In the nine months the new program operated in 1967, the two attorneys and one investigator represented 419 defendants facing 527 misdemeanor charges.[40]

To handle and further encourage ALAS's expansion, in 1968 the ALAS Board of Directors approved the hiring of Michael D. Padnos. Padnos was no stranger to Atlanta or ALAS; he had inspected EOA operations on behalf of the OEO. What's more, Padnos's ethos fit ALAS's new direction. Padnos believed that legal services should challenge laws detrimental to the poor.[41]

In its new incarnation, ALAS began devoting significant time to shaping social welfare law and practice. As legal historian Kris Shepard explains, ALAS ensured that major welfare rights cases that came before the Supreme Court were implemented in Georgia.[42] In 1967, for example, ALAS built on Alabama's *King* v. *Smith* and, on behalf of Mrs. Irma Thomas, successfully challenged Georgia's "substitute father" (or "man in the house") rule, which denied welfare benefits to mothers if they were in a relationship with an able-bodied male.[43] In this way, by litigating key, precedent-setting cases, ALAS reformed practice; that is, it minimized the necessity for individual representation by pursuing rulings that could be applied simply in future cases.[44]

Thus, from 1966 on, ALAS broadened and increased its reach. It initiated reform-oriented litigation and policy making that directly influenced poor families' access to social welfare entitlements. Although ALAS was situated in Atlanta, its litigation had impact not just locally, but across Georgia and the South.[45] In this way, ALAS and other poverty lawyers served as a powerful arm in a growing Atlanta campaign to bolster social welfare programs and diminish poverty. They joined institutions such as Emmaus House and welfare client-activists in fighting structures that prevented economic opportunity and maintained or exacerbated inequality. They grew the antipoverty movement in Atlanta. Indeed, Atlanta's antipoverty activism reflected a larger (and growing) national movement, a movement that the Poor People's Campaign hoped to catalyze.

The Poor People's Campaign

"What good is it to be allowed to eat in a restaurant if you can't afford a hamburger?" Martin Luther King Jr. observed in 1968.[46] The question fused the multiple concerns that had moved to the forefront of the civil rights movement: an absence of jobs, barriers to job advancement, challenges with housing, and lack of educational opportunity. These issues plagued many Americans, no matter their race. And for African Americans, the Civil Rights Act (1964) and the Voting Rights Act (1965) had not accomplished as much as people had hoped. In response, King and the SCLC planned to launch a new phase of the rights revolution. SCLC's Poor People's Campaign, announced in January 1968, proposed to focus attention on poverty and economic justice. The campaign signaled a shift in thinking away from the emphasis on opportunity for the individual and toward the more ambitious goal of equality of life chances.[47] Americans needed an economic bill of rights, King and others thought, a guarantee of full employment, sufficient income, and safe housing. The SCLC and its partners would mobilize all of America's dispossessed, no matter their race. "There are millions of poor people in this country who have very little, or even nothing, to lose," King insisted.[48]

The Poor People's Campaign would draw attention to poverty in part by providing a spectacle. An array of poor would descend on Washington, D.C., build an encampment—Resurrection City—on the National Mall, hold marches, rallies, and sit-ins, and generally disrupt settled assumptions about economic conditions in the United States. People would meet with congressional representatives, and groups would brainstorm how best to combine forces. A march to Washington would build interest. The events would force politicians to confront the poor and their needs.[49]

The campaign sought to draw in a coalition of like-minded organizations that included organized labor but also the NWRO, though it was quickly evident that King knew little about welfare mothers' experience or goals or the NWRO's history and work.[50] After negotiation with King, NWRO agreed to participate, as long as they remained responsible for statements and policies having to do with welfare. Leaders made clear that NWRO mothers could not afford to make their point by going to jail. "We have children to take care of," New York's Beulah Sanders stated.[51] Welfare rights advocates around the country planned to converge on Washington, where they would participate in the campaign and arrange meetings on welfare with their senators and representatives.[52]

King's assassination in Memphis in April 1968 disrupted planning. King had insisted on joining the city's sanitation workers' strike, seeing it as integral to the SCLC's expanded vision of civil rights organizing.[53] And it was there that King was shot and killed on April 4. Mourning, civil unrest, and rethinking the Poor People's Campaign consumed time and energy, but the SCLC plowed ahead with their antipoverty agenda. Ralph David Abernathy took over leading the event, which was held that summer.

Just as the nation's eyes had been on Atlanta, King's home and birthplace, immediately after his assassination in Memphis, the national gaze remained fixed on Georgia's capital as the Poor People's Campaign was planned and implemented.[54] For Atlanta's part, city leaders had to decide how to handle the proposed mule train–led march of poor people that would make its way through the South and Georgia's capital on the way to Washington. Planning for that event took place only one month after King's assassination, and consequently Mayor Ivan Allen Jr. had to balance many concerns. Just as Allen ensured a civil and solemn memorial service for King, he pledged support for Atlanta's component of the Poor People's March.[55] The mayor established a committee to help coordinate details regarding the March to Washington, and he called for citywide cooperation. The head of the city's chamber of commerce would lead the coordinating committee, signaling that Allen and others understood how such events might influence people's (and corporate) views of the city.[56] Besides members of the SCLC, the committee included members of the Metropolitan Atlanta Summit Leadership Conference, the Summit splinter group composed primarily of civic league members (see chapter 4).[57]

Other Georgia politicians displayed a disregard for civil rights and the concerns of poor people. Senator Herman Talmadge poked fun of the Poor People's March when he spoke at a 450-person dinner in Washington, D.C., sponsored by the Georgia Chamber of Commerce.[58] Governor Lester Maddox maintained a regular tirade against the event. He labeled the demonstrators agitators and communists and suggested walling in the poor demonstrators once they gathered on the D.C. mall.[59]

The Poor People's March to Washington was, in many ways, the buildup planners hoped for. Starting in different towns, marchers and mule trains made their way across the countryside and joined together as they moved toward Washington, D.C. Churches and civic groups arranged for overnight housing, and busses transported the elderly and children.[60] The 150- to 250-person caravan that made its way through Atlanta originated in Mississippi (see fig. 12). It headed east through Montgomery, Alabama, where it was stopped for not having a parade permit, and then proceed through Birmingham. Coming into Atlanta, the thirteen-wagon mule train and accompanying marchers made their way to Georgia's capital along Interstate 20. Governor Lester Maddox was having none of it, though, and ordered troopers to prevent the caravan from using the interstate. Although 67 marchers were arrested, charges were subsequently dropped, and negotiations with the state allowed the mule train to move along the interstate between 3 and 7 a.m.[61] After events in Atlanta, participants made their way to Washington via train and bus.[62]

Ultimately, the events and march attracted ample attention, but the

FIGURE 12. A Poor People's Campaign mule train travels through Atlanta to Washington, D.C., 1968. This mule train originated in Mississippi. Once in Atlanta, the carts were loaded on trains for the final leg to Washington, and participants finished the trip via bus and train. Courtesy Billy Downs, *Atlanta Journal-Constitution* Photographs Collection, Special Collections & Archives, Georgia State University Library, Atlanta, Ga.

campaign failed on multiple levels. It had internal financial issues; FBI surveillance intimidated movement leaders; and managing Resurrection City consumed time and energy. Worse, perhaps, was the fact that thousands of poor Americans appealed to Congress and the American people as they were increasingly distracted by other matters.[63] Urban unrest, which accelerated in 1965 and then again after King's assassination in 1968, fed many people's concerns about crime and disorder. News on U.S. involvement in the Vietnam conflict, particularly as it unfolded in 1968, rattled Americans. The Tet Offensive led by North Vietnam signaled that despite President Johnson's assurances, the war might not end quickly and, worse, might end in defeat. American support for the conflict took a hit. War costs escalated, a fact the administration only revealed later and reluctantly. Deception about various aspects of the war shook American's confidence in the government, and war spending meant less money for ambitious social programs. What's more, aggressive deficit spending drove inflation, adding to Americans' anxiety.[64] In this way, a host of factors interfered with proponents' desires to advance social welfare and anti-poverty goals.

While the Poor People's Campaign was widely regarded as a failure, on the ground a broad set of entities and people continued to demonstrate concern for poverty and inequality, and the poor and near poor continued to demand that their concerns be addressed. In Atlanta, some of the city's most poorly paid employees—its garbage workers—insisted that the city raise wages and deliver authentic opportunities for advancement.

The 1968 Sanitation Workers Strike

Atlanta's garbage workers had a particularly challenging job. Every day, beginning in early hours, they collected, hauled off, and disposed of trash from residences and businesses. It was dangerous and dirty work. Rain, ice, and freezing temperatures often made the job more difficult. Workers suffered complaints from residents, attacks by dogs, and interactions with vermin.[65] They were rewarded with particularly low wages. As an *Atlanta Constitution* piece revealed, garbage collectors were the lowest rung in the male labor market.[66] Many were no longer willing to suffer those indignities quietly or without appropriate compensation. Mirroring actions taken by sanitation workers elsewhere and with a level of militance increasingly common among public sector workers, Atlanta's garbagemen allied with the city's civil rights apparatus and challenged the city to live up to its promised War on Poverty.

Atlanta sanitation workers' dissatisfaction with pay and work conditions had festered for some time.[67] Wage increases did come—reportedly "pick-up men" had their weekly pay increased to a range from $66.50 to $72.40 a week that past January, for example, but the increase failed to bring many workers out of poverty, and it did not ease work conditions nor improve advancement opportunities.[68] Black workers, who were pigeonholed into the lowest-paying, most undesirable positions, were particularly disgruntled. Jobs tended to be racially segregated—Black workers worked as general laborers while whites occupied most of the driver and supervisory roles—and Black workers were offered few or only token opportunities for advancement.[69]

To some degree, workers could rely on their union, the American Federation of State, County, and Municipal Employees (AFSCME), to represent their needs to the city. After 1945, AFSCME, and specifically its

District Council 14, had represented public sector employees throughout Atlanta, and smaller locals represented such groups as nonteaching staff in the city's public schools, health workers, and sanitation workers. Although the union counted Blacks and whites among its members, District Council 14 had long been led by racist whites. In practice, Black workers tended to be relegated to their own locals, white leaders tended not to heavily recruit African Americans, and the district council did not necessarily work to address Black needs. That meant the city's Black workers were forced to confront discrimination at their workplace *and* within their own union.[70]

But organized labor had its limits when it came to uplifting poor workers, especially in the South. Few laborers joined unions in the region.[71] Companies regularly harassed workers sympathetic to union goals and actively campaigned against unions.[72] Statutes often prevented dues checkoff—the practice in which workers agreed to have union dues withdrawn from their paychecks—and right-to-work laws meant that workers could not be compelled to join a union as a condition of employment. Such laws severely weakened the union movement.[73] Additionally, racial segregation and ongoing discrimination within locals limited the potential of labor organizing, dividing workers across racial lines and hindering groups from seeking collective gains.[74] That being said, many Black workers increasingly joined unions and used those organizations to address workplace and community issues. As African American employment in the public sector increased in the 1960s, public sector unions increasingly targeted the South and Black labor in their recruitment.[75] In Atlanta's case, the city had a working relationship with the locals that allowed voluntary dues checkoff, but the city did not acknowledge a role for the union in collective bargaining with workers.[76] Instead, unions worked as advocates on behalf of labor, which meant they were operating from an inherently weak position.[77] And perhaps because District Council 40 had historically not effectively represented Black labor, workers were willing to ignore the district council's decisions and directives.

In 1968, after years of poverty-level wages and dangerous working conditions, Atlanta's sanitation workers demanded that the city provide $100 a week take-home pay for the lowest-paid workers. Initially, the workers sought the support of District Council 14, but the council recommended instead a two-step raise that would ultimately reach 8.5 percent. The garbage workers rejected the recommendation, and on September 3, 1968, one hundred of Atlanta's sanitation workers walked off the job in a wildcat strike, a strike unsanctioned by their local AFSCME union. That action launched a thirteen-day campaign that would grow to other public works departments and demonstrate the possibilities of labor–civil rights unionism.[78]

Evidence of how individual laborers viewed the conflict with the city is sparse, but it is clear that the union, the SCLC, local newspapers, and others positioned the strike as primarily having to do with workers' poverty-level wages and lack of opportunity for advancement. On a radio announcement for one rally, SCLC leader Rev. T. Y. Rogers Jr. emphasized, "We are in a fight for the black community and all the poor people in Atlanta."[79] Similarly, Ralph David Abernathy asserted, "This is a fight for poor people."[80] The *Atlanta Constitution* explained that pickup crew pay started from $1.66 to $1.81 an hour (equivalent to $13.60 to $14.83 in March 2022), and the workers sought $2.50 (about $20.48 in March 2022) an hour.[81] In another story, the *Constitution* compared salaries to nationally established poverty levels and substandard annual incomes, further illustrating the challenges workers, and particularly public sector workers, faced. The city's alternative newspaper, the *Great Speckled Bird*, found the situation ironic: Atlanta promoted its poverty programs while paying its own workers poverty-level wages.[82] In other cases, workers highlighted Atlanta's ongoing city-building projects, questioning the city's priorities. At one meeting, worker Finley Holmes Jr. asked how the city could willfully devote money to build a stadium and civic center while paying its citizens poverty wages.[83] "This is 'the city too busy to hate,'" Abernathy reminded workers. In reality, the city was "too busy making money for the rich and ignoring and exploiting the poor."[84] In this way, civil rights leaders, religious leaders, labor leaders, and sanitation workers leveraged national and local concern for poverty, insisting that the city commit real resources to eliminating want and deliver a livable income.

But while several groups empathized with the strikers' grievances, District Council 14 continued to insist the strike was unsanctioned, and they offered no support. In contrast, though, AFSCME's office investigated the local circumstances and pledged "its full support of the sanitation workers," as Morton Shapiro, national president of AFSCME, told the *Atlanta Constitution*.[85] To AFSCME, the strike had the potential to strengthen the union's formal relationship with the city and ability to negotiate on behalf of public workers.[86] It also promised to further cement a working relationship between AFSCME and civil rights organizations.[87]

Absent recognition by District Council 14, garbage workers also saw the potential of allying with the city's civil rights apparatus, and they sought assistance from the SCLC. It made sense to reach out to the SCLC, which was but one of many civil rights organizations in the city, including the NAACP, SNCC, and the National Urban League. The SCLC in particular envisioned a more expansive economic agenda. As the Poor People's Campaign illustrated, the SCLC sought to form a broad-based coalition that would address wealth inequality and promote opportunity. The SCLC had been pursuing a stronger relationship with labor when King and others threw their support behind the Memphis sanitation workers' strike in early 1968. The subsequent victory for Memphis garbagemen (which followed King's assassination) would inspire hope among low-wage public sector workers in other cities, and in the following months, many public sector workers would demand wage and workplace improvements. Atlanta's garbage workers would borrow tactics from that strike, too, adopting the "I AM A MAN" declaration and signage, which one of historian Michael Honey's informants, James Robinson, translated as, they "weren't gonna take that shit no more."[88]

Still, while the idea of a local alliance between civil rights advocates and labor was not new, previous partnerships had been short-lived and did not result in long-lasting working relationships. Atlanta's experience was not unusual. Although some organized labor and civil rights organizers regularly articulated a commitment to a more expansive view of civil rights and labor—a form of "civil rights unionism"—local circumstances often drew civil rights activists to other actions, such as voter registration or sit-ins.[89] But in Atlanta, the potential for a labor–civil rights partnership remained high through the 1960s.

In the 1968 strike, workers used disruption to demand a fair wage, and workers' confidence in the power of withholding trash services increased through the week. On Wednesday about five hundred Black workers, joined by a few white workers, walked off their jobs. And by Friday, few among the permanently employed garbage crews were working. The city responded by recruiting labor from beyond Atlanta, and the city supplied large dumpsters for residents and businesses to use. SCLC's Hosea Williams called on workers to obstruct garbage trucks attempting to leave substations and incinerators, and strikers actively interfered with vehicles borrowed from other areas. Police were called in to escort the trucks, and pickets blocked the entrance to at least one incinerator.[90]

Within the local community, Black ministers addressed the sanitation workers' issues with their congregations. From the pulpit, ministers linked poverty wages to injustice and oppression. And they, along with more progressive white religious leaders, including Emmaus House's

Austin Ford, negotiated with the city as the events unfolded. Rallies were held at different churches nearly nightly, which helped maintain interest in the events and keep residents and families up-to-date on progress in negotiations.[91]

While urban leaders (in Atlanta and beyond) strongly opposed labor interference with municipal services, especially services as crucial as trash collection, the framing of the strike in terms of poverty and the fact that the events occurred in wake of King's assassination meant that even Mayor Ivan Allen Jr. tempered his response to the strike and confrontational public workers. Also, by late 1968, Allen had evinced some empathy with the needs and desires of Atlanta's poor. Consequently, while the city threatened to fire the striking garbage workers, leaders also continued to negotiate with the union, the SCLC, and ministers, signaling their willingness to meet at least some of the workers' demands.[92]

Workers grew more confrontational, even as the city increased its offers. On Monday afternoon, scores of strikers faced off with the mayor at City Hall. Allen explained that the city could offer a two-step pay raise but would only consider a three-step pay raise if the workers immediately returned to their jobs. One striker told other workers that to accept that offer would be "crazy." Another striker accused Allen of "not caring" about the garbagemen and pointed out that they could not afford the clothes, car, and food the mayor could.[93] In the meantime, trash piled up in neighborhoods and in downtown, a sorry display for a city claiming to be the showcase city of the South.

The strike expanded to other public works divisions as days passed, and demands and offers shifted as strikers, the SCLC, and ministers negotiated with the city. About 125 employees from the streets and sewers division walked off the job in support of the sanitation staff. Soon thereafter, AFSCME's Morton Shapiro announced that after the conclusion of the sanitation negotiations, AFSCME would begin addressing other public works workers' demands, suggesting that further union activity was on the horizon. Just as streets and sewer workers supported sanitation demands, sanitation workers reciprocated and pledged their support to other city workers. Importantly, sanitation workers and their representatives expanded their demands and insisted that wage concessions be granted to all 1,550 public works employees.[94]

After two weeks of evolving demands and offers, city leaders offered sanitation workers a 13 percent raise, but they appeared dead set against further concessions. Black sanitation workers seemed equally committed to their current desire for a four-step pay increase and a quicker timeline to receive top pay. (White workers had voted to accept the city's offer.) Convinced that they had achieved as much as possible, Shapiro, SCLC's Ralph D. Abernathy, and local ministers persuaded city officials to extend the raise to other public works employees. The gesture served its purpose, and sanitation workers agreed to end the strike. The thirteen-day conflict concluded.[95]

In the strike's wake, Shapiro and AFSCME as well as the mayor publicly acknowledged the contributions of the SCLC and its leadership, including Ralph D. Abernathy and Andrew Young Jr., signaling the significance of the civil rights–union alliance. "Some trade unionists have criticized me for inviting you in," Shapiro noted of the SCLC. But "next time we have a fight in Atlanta," he said, "I need your support."[96]

In addition to wage concessions, which brought authentic material improvement to many workers' lives, the final agreement brought some limited change to city-labor relations. In 1969, the city and the sanitation workers' local signed a nonbinding memorandum of understanding (MOU) that outlined rates of pay as well as policies on hours, overtime, and holidays. The city also agreed to union representation of workers in grievance processes. Although nonbinding, the MOU could be referenced in such worker grievances.[97] In this way, then, the standoff did result in material benefits and in some, if thin, infrastructure that would provide ongoing support to historically underpaid and oppressed workers. But as historian Seth LaShier points out, ultimately the MOU was nonbinding, and it provided no mechanism for bargaining between the city and the union.[98]

The conflict tallied other achievements. In particular, AFSCME committed to replacing local union leadership, which had regularly ignored the desires of Atlanta's Black public service workers. Throughout the strike, the local union leaders remained wedded to the position that the strike was not sanctioned and that the workers' demands were excessive.[99] In the aftermath of the strike, Shapiro publicly denounced the local union leaders and their unwillingness to represent the interests of the sanitation workers. Those leaders were "finished in this union," Shapiro promised.[100] Additionally, launched as it was in the wake of King's death and in a period when several groups were bringing attention to poverty, the 1968 sanitation strike raised awareness of poverty wages and dangerous working conditions.

Like prior labor campaigns and the Scripto strike, the 1968 walkout exposed the promise of a labor–civil rights partnership to address poverty-level wages, poor working conditions, and lack of advancement opportunities for the working poor and near poor, particularly Black workers. Those alliances would not last, however, and later labor–civil rights actions—including a 1970 AFSCME strike—would fare worse.

Breakdown

In 1968, sanitation workers had the empathy of many Atlantans, but by 1970, city leadership and the temper of the general public had shifted. When city workers, and particularly sanitation staff, again argued for improved pay, they lost a few of the advantages that they had previously counted, and city officials began undermining the public sector union movement. Over the course of the events, it became clear that, again, many of Atlanta's Black elite were unreliable partners in economic reform. They could not be counted on to forge a lasting partnership with labor, or to consistently press for substantive improvements in wages and benefits.

In 1970, city aldermen proceeded with yearly salary negotiations with city workers and AFSCME local 1644. Workers sought, among other things, a $6,000 minimum yearly salary, a $75 a month raise for all city workers, and improved benefits. The aldermen, having previously approved an 8.5 percent salary increase, ultimately refused the request, indicating that the city lacked the funds for a more significant raise. Newly elected mayor Sam Massell let discussions proceed at pace. But as negotiations dragged on, eventually the city contended that they could not legally raise salaries after March 31, a legal interpretation disputed by former attorney Maynard Jackson, the first Black vice mayor of Atlanta.[101] Labor's commitment to improved wages and benefits eventually produced a rift between the city (Massell and the aldermen) and the union.

While articulating very different concerns, AFSCME and Black elite both had initially counted mayor Sam Massell as an ally. Massell's 1969 election had depended on Black votes, and Black elite in particular felt confident that Massell would assemble a racially progressive administration, one that would hire African Americans into policy posts in greater numbers and initiate more contracts and investment with Black-owned businesses and institutions. Simultaneously, Massell also had pitched himself as the "people's candidate" and had argued for AFSCME support. Initially, once Massell took office, the mayor negotiated in good faith with the workers.[102] Laborers misread the new regime, thinking their wage and benefit demands were achievable, and they remained committed to their demands.

When aldermen voted against a pay increase, city workers walked off their jobs on March 17, 1970, producing a tense standoff between workers and the city.[103] The action encompassed city workers of many stripes, but in news stories, the *Atlanta Constitution* noted that the conflict particularly involved the sanitation workers. "We have been betrayed by the people we helped elect," workers complained.[104] In response to the walkout, city leaders offered a three-page resolution reminding workers of the city's past concessions and a modest wage increase that did not encompass all workers.[105] The workers rejected the offer, chanting, "Tear it up!"[106] About 2,500 workers remained on strike.[107] Tensions grew as Massell fired workers who remained on strike, letting go 1,400 public workers.[108] Worried that the situation would lead to urban unrest, the mayor put the police on a "state of emergency" and asked the governor to have 500 National Guard troops on standby.[109] Prisoners were soon recruited to pick up garbage downtown, police escorted garbage trucks, and the city began hiring replacement workers.[110]

Strikers grew more militant and disruptive as time wore on. This was in part a reaction to city concessions; in one case, the city offered a bonus that relied on perfect work attendance, an offer workers found insulting.[111] In early April, workers held a candlelight march through the city, chanting, "To hell with the city!" and "To hell with Massell!"[112] At other times, strikers marched through the city's major retail establishments, including the Sears, Roebuck & Co. on Ponce de Leon Avenue, the downtown Rich's department store, and Citizens Trust Bank. Pickets blocked city intersections at Courtland and Houston, then Marietta and Broad.[113] The actions brought attention to the strike, but not the level of understanding and empathy that had come with the 1968 action (see fig. 13).[114]

In 1970, the local community was more divided over its support of the sanitation workers than it had been in 1968. Particularly damaging to the strikers' cause were the actions and vocal opposition of prominent Black elites, including Senator Leroy Johnson, Rev. M. L. King Sr., and Alderman Q. V. Williamson.[115] That group had helped Massell win the mayoral runoff, and subsequently they counted on Massell to continue to improve Black access to white-collar positions in the city. Perhaps as a direct result, many Black elite aligned with Massell as he attempted to end the conflict. Those seeking a middle ground and expressing sympathy for garbage workers' demands included the SCLC, Emmaus House, a number of black ministers, and the *Atlanta Voice*. But support was thin: few nonworkers joined the picket lines, and the SCLC tasked few SCLC workers to the strike, though they began holding events for strikers be-

FIGURE 13. Workers march through Rich's Department Store during strike, April 18, 1970. Atlanta workers drew on the successful Memphis "I am a Man" practice. In this photograph, the I AM A MAN signs are rolled up to amplify voices. Courtesy Tom Coffin Photographs, Special Collections & Archives, Georgia State University Library, Atlanta, Ga.

ginning in early April.[116] Significantly, two months into the strike, Black vice mayor Maynard Jackson, reflecting an ongoing commitment to Atlanta's Black working-class and poor communities, would break with Massell and publicly support the striking workers.[117] The garbage workers' wages in particular were "a disgrace before God," Jackson asserted.[118]

After thirty-seven days, when the strike was settled, workers had won only limited concessions. The city promised raises that were not tied to an attendance policy, and they committed to a timely reassessment of job classifications. Workers were reinstated without prejudice, but they would not be paid for the period of the strike.[119]

More significantly, Massell and the aldermen would go on to damage AFSCME and its ability to adequately represent (or even advocate for) public sector workers, including some of the city's most poorly paid laborers. During the strike, city leaders undermined the union, tagging it as exploitative. Then, following up on actions launched midstrike, Massell and the aldermen stripped the union of the automatic dues checkoff that had helped maintain what strength the Atlanta local had.[120] The action was "obviously just one part of a secret campaign to totally destroy the union," AFSCME's Ramelle McCoy asserted.[121] In subsequent years, the local would move into trusteeship, meaning it was under the support of the larger AFSCME structure.[122] As historian Joseph McCartin has shown, Massell's action to fire and replace striking city workers marked a shift in how cities and the federal government handled labor relations in the public sector and how governments thwarted organized labor. Striker replacement "became normalized as a legitimate managerial tactic," a tactic implemented on the backs of the city's more poorly paid workers.[123]

For a decade, Black workers had partnered episodically with the city's civil rights apparatus to improve pay and working conditions for the city's most vulnerable workers. Whereas in 1968 city officials and community leaders had shown support for workers' goals, the demands made in 1970 revealed a different context. While the SCLC would become actively involved in managing the 1970s strike events and negotiations by early April, other Black elite avoided damaging their relationship with a mayor who they felt would help improve Black employment and advancement by publicly aligning with Massell or choosing a neutral path. These leaders may have had good intentions, reasoning that having African Americans in white-collar positions of power would allow them to retool and equalize hiring and other systems, thus boosting wages and benefits for all levels of workers. But for the time being, the choice to align with the mayor and aldermen left Atlanta's poor laborers with few benefits and, over time, a weakened union, and it meant Atlanta did not realize the full potential of a more robust labor–civil rights coalition. In the meantime, in other venues, welfare client-activists accelerated organizing, drawing on their national network for techniques and inspiration.

The Work Continues

As sanitation workers tried to improve wages and working conditions, welfare client-activists expanded activities to strengthen the social safety net. NWRO's practices and nationally led campaigns were templates local members could readily implement and learn from, and Atlanta's new welfare rights organization followed NWRO's playbook.[124] Embracing the national network's contention that welfare rights organizations should be led by welfare recipients themselves, Ethel Mae Mathews managed to oust the first president of the Emmaus House chapter, who was not a welfare client. Mathews was subsequently elected president. As was necessary in other cities and counties, Atlanta activists successfully acquired the AFDC regulation manual.[125] Beginning in December 1968, the Emmaus House chapter joined welfare rights groups across the nation in various campaigns, including those seeking one-time special grants. Such grants, given for specific purposes, were intended for items that monthly AFDC benefits did not cover. In this case, the Emmaus House chapter petitioned the Fulton County Welfare Department for a $100 "Christmas bonus" to help offset the expense of Christmas dinner, toys, clothes, and bills—enough money so that for a few days clients did not have to worry about "being set out in the street or having the gas and lights turned off," the members explained. The mothers said they were "trying to make it on less than $100 a month for rent, clothes, food, everything."[126] In support of the request, welfare clients picketed DFACS, the agency that managed AFDC for the bulk of Atlanta. With client-activists elsewhere, Atlanta welfare mothers signaled that they intended to fully participate in American life and that their families were entitled to a basic standard of living.

The picketers met with DFACS director Gilbert Dulaney and Fulton County Commission chair Charlie Brown, and the men's response revealed the hurdles client-activists would continue to face. Dulaney and Brown outlined the expenditures such a bonus required, concluding that not only did the county not have the money, but the law did not allow them to disperse funds for a holiday bonus. Mathews was fed up with rejection and what she considered to be thin explanations from privileged whites. "You white folks were born with silver spoons in your mouths," she asserted.[127] But, the protestors took advantage of their audience, using the opportunity to list other concerns. They complained about invasive monitoring by DFACS workers. One mother explained that social workers asked to use the bathroom and used that opportunity to see if welfare clients were hiding men.[128] In sharing such experiences, women alerted the administrators that they had expectations of privacy and respect. But in the end the director and commissioner emphasized that the activists' demands were being presented to the wrong people: the mothers needed to take their requests to their state congressional leaders, who made the laws governing how Georgia managed welfare.[129]

Welfare rights activists recognized that to achieve greater political power, they needed to grow the movement, and they devoted time to establishing other welfare rights chapters in Atlanta and beyond. Welfare rights members made the rounds at public housing communities asking about challenges with welfare and promoting welfare organizing. In spring 1969, for example, activists went door to door in Perry Homes. By July, Perry Homes residents had formed a chapter with twenty-six dues-paying members, and by fall the chapter had grown to thirty-one.[130] Also in 1969, Ethel Mae Mathews and Pinkie Stinson traveled to Augusta to help start a chapter in that city. A chapter was also formed in Savannah, and Emmaus House organizers expressed hope that they would soon be able to form a statewide coordinating committee.[131]

AFDC grant levels and procedures remained the central bread-and-butter concern, and protecting and expanding AFDC and other social safety net programs consumed much time and energy. In early 1969, for example, the U.S. Department of Health, Education, and Welfare (HEW) imposed a freeze on welfare payments—to be effective in July—which would keep grant payments at the same amount as the previous year. Welfare activists insisted on discussing the matter with Georgia state legislators at that winter's session. The activists sought an additional $4 million in the state budget appropriation, which would keep grants at the same level, despite the federal freeze. As noted by the *Atlanta Constitution*, the "predominantly negro" welfare activists had planned to speak at the hearings but were turned away. Representative James "Sloppy" Floyd claimed the women were "very rude." For their part, activists accused the legislature of discriminating against them based on race, and Mathews said Floyd had "a very hostile attitude."[132] The exchange marked the beginning of what would be years of hostile exchanges between welfare rights activists and state legislators as economic decline and an anti-welfare culture took its toll on Georgia's AFDC and other social welfare programs.

Threats to Georgia's thin social safety net seemed constant, and by summer of 1969 not only were activists confronting a federal freeze, they were dealing with a meager $2 per month cost-of-living increase for the forthcoming year. AFDC budget allowances had not been updated since the 1940s, the activists pointed out. "Why did the federal government let this happen?" members queried. "We will be going down to the Department of Health, Education and Welfare to see whether we can find out."[133] On June 27, some 185 welfare activists picketed the federal building in downtown Atlanta. Again, administrators invited leaders inside to share their concerns. According to Atlanta's alternative newspaper, the *Great Speckled Bird*, one administrator was clearly nervous, uncomfortable at having to face off with "people whose lives are conditioned by the papers which cross his desk."[134] Fifty mothers and supporters held a follow-up march on June 30—the anniversary of the founding of the National Welfare Rights Movement—at the state capitol.[135] Chanting, "What do you want? Money! When do you want it? Now!" the picketers were eventually invited in to meet with Assistant Attorney General Frank Blankenship. Echoing what the client-activists had by then heard many times, Blankenship explained that the welfare appropriations had been spent for the year, and any further grant increases would have to be approved by the legislature.[136]

No doubt the welfare administrators' response was disappointing. It pointed to the battle ahead. To increase grants, the activists could not simply shift procedures within the HEW or DFACS offices; they would have to alter the state budget and state policy. That would be difficult enough, but welfare mothers faced widespread deep cultural and racial bias, as further evidenced by Governor Lester Maddox's response when he learned of the meeting with Blankenship: the governor ejected the welfare mothers from the capitol, asserting they were dirty and lazy— in his words, "justa bunch of bums."[137] Still, welfare client-activists could rely on a growing antipoverty network to help shift law and policy.

Partners

Atlanta's welfare rights organization faced a complex bureaucracy resistant to change as well as racial and class bias, but activists did have a growing cache of expertise with which to partner, including reform-oriented attorneys at Atlanta Legal Aid Society (ALAS). Lawsuits, threats of lawsuits, and mediation would help improve welfare services, expand benefits, and diminish at least some threats to monthly AFDC grants.

ALAS sought to use *Goldberg* v. *Kelley* (1970)—a case the Columbia University's Center for Social Welfare Policy and Law had developed to try to establish a right to welfare—to potentially halt an impending AFDC grant cut.[138] In *Goldberg*, justices concluded that welfare recipients were entitled to a formal hearing before benefits could be cut, and activists insisted that the ruling be applied in Georgia.[139] The opportunity to use the ruling came in the early 1970s, when Social Security monthly stipends—which served as the principal income for many families—increased. The added income meant that families receiving both Social Security and AFDC would likely see their monthly AFDC grants reduced, a change that affected thousands of Georgia AFDC recipients. Making matters worse, those who lost their AFDC grants would also lose their Medicaid benefits.[140]

While the cutting of families from AFDC resulted from established income guidelines, activists pointed out that regulations also dictated that clients had a right to a hearing before changes were made to benefits. Welfare rights activists picketed at the state capitol, complaining that the cuts were imposed unfairly and without hearings. "We did not get a hearing" and "we did not get a notice," Ethel Mae Mathews explained to *Atlanta Constitution* reporters.[141] The state DFACS leadership entrenched and resisted holding hearings for that particular type of grant adjustment. In the wake of the *Goldberg* ruling, ALAS secured a temporary restraining order that prevented the state from removing families from welfare rolls. As a result, families would receive their regular welfare checks in April 1970 and a grant hearing before potentially having their stipend cut.[142]

For his part, the director of the Georgia Division of Family and Children Services, William H. "Bill" Burson, considered the court's requirements for hearings onerous. The department would have to pull 185,000 files to determine who faced cuts, and then hold a hearing for each client. Burson threatened to resign if the requirement stood. Attorneys for the state welfare office asked for a delayed implementation—until July 1—stating that they lacked the resources to provide hearings for all persons whose grants were terminated or reduced.[143] Emmaus House's Father Ford told circuit court judge Griffin Bell that "the financial crisis for the state is not nearly as great as the financial crisis of the recipients" if clients suffered AFDC cuts without a hearing.[144]

Georgia continued to appeal the case, and Burson did not resign, but he continued to insist that the requirement was untenable.[145] "It would break down the whole department," Burson insisted.[146] "Georgia is being called upon to do something none of the other states is being required to do."[147] As ALAS pursued its legal battle, welfare rights activists continued picketing at the state capitol. "Ain't no justice for poor folks," some signs read.[148] Ultimately, the Supreme Court upheld the order: Georgia would have to arrange hearings for clients whose AFDC grants were to be eliminated or reduced.[149]

Such legal sparring was typical of how poverty lawyers used legal procedure to protect poor families by stalling (if not preventing) harmful actions. Indeed, at national and local levels, public interest attorneys sought to force a "crisis" by using such tactics, hoping to usher in a more just and equitable system.[150] Such maneuvers required expertise and perseverance. Attorneys identified technicalities that helped clients achieve their goals (e.g., to maintain or increase monthly grants), sued toward particular ends, and pursued mediation, depending on the particular situation. At the same time, welfare client-activists continued to use direct action to maintain pressure on HEW, DFACS, and legislators, ensuring that social welfare stayed on the agenda for bureaucrats and policy makers. Battling bureaucrats was no doubt taxing. And perhaps unexpectedly, sometimes those same administrators proved to be allies.

Bill Burson and the Politics of Hunger

To be sure, Bill Burson had resisted implementing hearings in the wake of the *Goldberg* decision. But Burson was probably the most accommodating white state agency head that poor people could hope to have running Georgia's DFACS in the late 1960s. His efforts to fight child hunger illustrate how bureaucrats could positively influence antipoverty infrastructure and services.

A professional journalist who had covered the Korean conflict, Burson joined Georgia governor Herman Talmadge's staff as press secretary in the early 1950s.[151] Burson's decision to serve Talmadge surprised other journalists: Burson had a reputation for political moderation (journalist Margaret Shannon described him as having "a strong New Deal Democratic streak"), and Talmadge, a revered figure in Georgia politics, was well known for his embrace of white supremacy and defense of segregation. But Talmadge liked Burson and helped protect the bureaucrat when people questioned his political leanings or might otherwise have publicly challenged him. Burson remained in public service when Lester Maddox ascended to the governor's office, and he penned the new governor's inauguration address, a speech that at the time was considered to be "moderate" for Maddox, an inflammatory and volatile personality who insisted on an individual's right to do business—or not do business—with whomever he pleased, including Blacks. Maddox wanted Burson in his administration and considered him for various positions before he appointed him to lead the state welfare office in July 1967. As director, Burson spent much of his initial energy confronting childhood hunger.[152]

To Burson, hunger undermined human potential, and as he explained in an interview for *Atlanta Journal and Constitution Magazine*, "We're not going to do much about solving education, vocational training or health problems in this state unless we solve the hunger problem first."[153] Burson was particularly incensed that upwards of 70 Georgia counties lacked food programs.[154] Only 24 counties participated in the USDA food stamp program and 69 in the commodities food program, despite the more than 116,000 Georgians in need.[155]

In Georgia, hunger was a sizeable battle to engage. Not only was hunger itself significant, but as Burson suggested, some counties flat out refused to set up anti-hunger programs, even if such programs were heavily funded by federal offices (such as the Food and Drug Administration [FDA]).[156] Some resistance resulted from entrenched racial stereotypes, and Burson accused county officials who declined to invest in food programs with trying to "starve out" unskilled Blacks so that they would relocate to cities.[157] Many county officials blamed the high costs of food programs for their county's lack of participation, though the *Atlanta Constitution* described the administrative costs as "nominal."[158] Burson confronted these attitudes with little diplomacy. He threatened to shut down county welfare departments and invite federal intervention. For their part, local officials accused Burson and his agency of meddling in local affairs. Other state politicians tried to get Burson fired. Some tagged him a liberal. But Governor Maddox supported Burson's efforts to feed Georgians. "Three and a half years from now, I want it said that foremost among the accomplishments of the Maddox administration was that it fed the hungry."[159]

Burson's political connections and the respect he garnered from Georgia's most powerful leadership (Talmadge, then Maddox) allowed him the leeway to forcefully implement social programs that local power brokers often resisted. Maddox in particular expressed concern about the human cost poverty exacted on the state's residents. Where they could,

Burson (and Maddox) utilized programs funded by the federal government, or programs that offered other advantages to Georgia's residents and economy.

Although Bill Burson clearly had concerns about poverty, Atlanta's antipoverty activists had a mixed relationship with the state DFACS director. On one hand, Burson resisted court-ordered mandates for hearings for thousands of welfare clients. On the other hand, he remained committed to diminishing hunger throughout Georgia: by the time he resigned in May 1970 to seek elected office, Burson had helped bring food programs to all of Georgia's 159 counties.[160] Welfare rights organizers' ambivalence about Burson was evident in the *Emmaus House News*. In March, the organization detailed an early 1970 attempt to put the DFACS board in charge of DFACS. When Burson remained in control of the department, the *News* affirmed that "the right side won," and the welfare rights organization invited Burson to speak at the next welfare rights meeting.[161] The next month, though, the welfare rights organization took Burson to task. Activists were angry that Burson continued raising legal challenges regarding grant hearings. "Mr. Burson has forced more than 2900 families off the Medicaid program," activists insisted.[162]

Attempting to manage a growing agency on a slim budget, Burson made decisions that left activists angry and dissatisfied. But in an antiwelfare climate still rife with racial discrimination, the moderate bureaucrat advanced antipoverty work in Atlanta and Georgia, particularly by expanding food programs to all counties. Antipoverty work would be aided by moderate leadership at the Fulton County DFACS as well, and new tools would help expand antipoverty organizing.

New Tools

In July 1970, the five thousand Fulton County AFDC recipients received not only their monthly grant check, but also a card that read, "Please put my name on a mailing list to receive news of changes in the welfare system, and facts about my rights as a welfare recipient." Welfare clients could return the card in an enclosed envelope addressed to the National Welfare Rights Organization at Emmaus House (see fig. 14).[163] Likely some residents were surprised to receive such an invitation, as local DFACS offices had a reputation for not being forthcoming. They did not advertise their services, and regulations and procedures were not transparent.

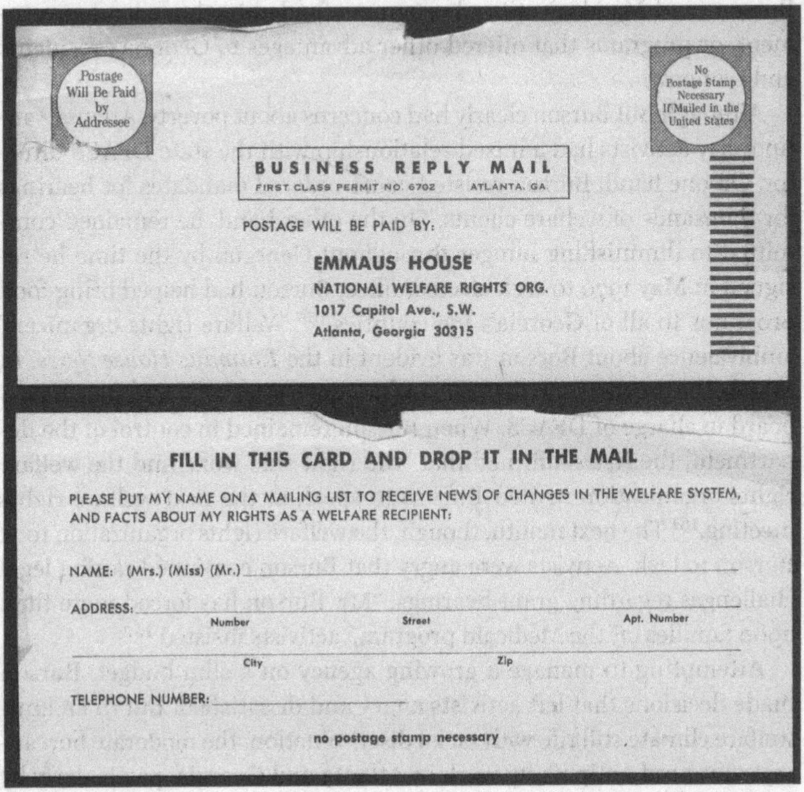

Postage
Will Be Paid
by
Addressee

No
Postage Stamp
Necessary
If Mailed in the
United States

BUSINESS REPLY MAIL
FIRST CLASS PERMIT NO. 6702   ATLANTA, GA.

POSTAGE WILL BE PAID BY:

EMMAUS HOUSE
NATIONAL WELFARE RIGHTS ORG.
1017 Capitol Ave., S.W.
Atlanta, Georgia 30315

FILL IN THIS CARD AND DROP IT IN THE MAIL

PLEASE PUT MY NAME ON A MAILING LIST TO RECEIVE NEWS OF CHANGES IN THE WELFARE SYSTEM,
AND FACTS ABOUT MY RIGHTS AS A WELFARE RECIPIENT:

NAME: (Mrs.) (Miss) (Mr.)

ADDRESS:
Number   Street   Apt. Number

City   Zip

TELEPHONE NUMBER:

no postage stamp necessary

FIGURE 14. Emmaus House produced a mail-in card regarding welfare rights and the *Poor People's Newspaper*, 1970. The card was included with welfare checks. Courtesy Frances Pauley Papers, Stuart A. Rose Manuscript, Archives, and Rare Book Library, Emory University.

The card had been arranged by Emmaus House and the welfare rights organization, and the mailing of the card to Fulton County residents was achieved after months of negotiation between Emmaus House and the state Department of Human Resources.[164] The card was included in the grant checks mailed to Fulton County AFDC clients, and director of the Fulton County DFACS Gilbert Dulaney directed caseworkers to give a card to new certified welfare recipients.[165] Those who signed up soon received the first issue of the *Poor People's Newspaper* (*PPN*), a two-page mimeographed newsletter with a header promoting welfare rights. "This is a special paper for poor people. . . . It is a paper to tell you about your rights," the first issue explained. Austin Ford thought hundreds of cards might be returned. "There were thousands," he recalled.[166]

The welfare card immediately increased demand not just for the *PPN*, but for Emmaus House's services—its information on welfare and related entitlements. The volunteers and staff were immediately overwhelmed. They plotted their next steps at the Ignatius House Jesuit Retreat Center and decided to open a new Poverty Rights Office on the Emmaus House campus. Operating from "the cottage" on the property's south end, the PRO was created specifically to assist poor Atlantans in understanding and navigating the social welfare bureaucracy. PRO was intended to house and expand on that work going forward. Muriel Lokey would manage the operation. Lokey had already been a successful recruiter, persuading scores of people to devote substantial time and energy to supporting Emmaus House and its work.[167]

PRO tackled a wide-ranging set of needs. Volunteers and staff answered questions about social welfare programs, educated clients and potential clients about entitlements, assisted in calculating budgets, helped clients request hearings, facilitated access to food services, and assisted clients in navigating the requirements of various social welfare programs. Sometimes volunteers went with clients to DFACS or other offices to ensure clear communications between the client and the agency. The office (and the *Poor People's Newspaper*) alerted clients to changes in welfare regulations as well as residents' rights to relocation assistance if they lost their home to redevelopment initiatives. They helped mediate disputes with landlords and, if necessary, secured legal assistance.[168] Moreover, the PRO worked "to see that public agencies do the job they are legally required to do." "Wherever necessary, we should *cause trouble*, on behalf of our clients," explained the PRO volunteer manual. Besides helping clients navigate the labyrinth of welfare and Social Security regulations, the PRO was committed to facilitating social change.[169]

The *Poor People's Newspaper* (*PPN*) was a critical tool in Atlanta's antipoverty movement arsenal. In disseminating strategies, tactics, and language to poor people in blocks and neighborhoods that overstretched organizations and that organizers could not always address face to face, the *PPN* extended activists' and advocates' geographic reach. The paper outlined the "new right" to a hearing before a welfare grant could be cut, and the paper explained the significance of a new wage garnishment law. Other stories highlighted welfare rights organization members and provided details of past and future welfare rights organization meetings. Information about Poverty Rights Office services was also provided. And individual victories at welfare hearings were celebrated, signaling that successes were possible.

The mail-in card, the PRO, and the *Poor People's Newspaper* proved to be powerful additions to antipoverty organizing in Atlanta. The *PPN* spread news of social service changes, welfare rights (and other) meetings, and protests. The PRO provided dedicated volunteers to assist poor families in navigating complex bureaucracies, and it alerted PRO volunteers to obstacles in welfare delivery, issues that needed to be tackled. Emmaus House and PRO workers utilized the language of laws and rights constantly, positioning poor residents as encompassed by the civil rights revolution, federal legislation, and local statutes.[170] In these ways, Emmaus House empowered residents, diminished hunger and poverty, and also sustained economic justice organizing in a critical period. Whereas the Poor People's Campaign had been widely viewed as a failure on the national level, and low-wage laborers suffered some setbacks with their union and the union's relationship to the city, in many ways Atlanta's antipoverty movement was growing.

By the end of the 1960s, antipoverty organizing was sustained by multiple groups working in different domains, though work, concerns, and personnel overlapped. Social welfare organizing expanded particularly quickly, in part because activists within that domain operated in a national network and with multiple partners. Beginning in 1967, Atlanta welfare mothers organized under the auspices of the National Welfare Rights Organization to enhance transparency in social welfare and improve benefits. A number of partners and tools catalyzed that work. Atlanta Legal Aid Services shifted to reform law and regularly pursued cases that would benefit families using federal entitlement programs. Emmaus House provided facilities and resources to poor families and people of color who sought to improve social conditions and secure newly guaranteed rights. In concrete terms, that meant Emmaus House hosted welfare rights meetings, facilitated communications through the *Poor People's Newspaper*, and provided guidance on navigating government programs via a dedicated Poverty Rights Office. Additionally, some liberal and moderate bureaucrats enabled antipoverty work. Serving as veritable gatekeepers to federal and state programs, administrators of state agencies could facilitate or interfere with access to resources, including food programs.

In 1968, low-wage laborers within the public sector contributed to the antipoverty movement in that they insisted the city live up to its commitment to the War on Poverty by raising its own workers' wages above poverty level. And when racism kept the District Council 14 from supporting workers' demands, sanitation workers turned to civil rights organizations, particularly the SCLC, for support. At that time, workers could depend on empathy from media outlets, the general public, and to some degree the mayor. Many people had been made aware of oppressive wages and working conditions suffered by the garbage workers. Others understood the irony of mounting a War on Poverty while paying workers less than a living wage.

Although workers made gains in the 1968 strike, they lost ground when they struck for higher pay in 1970, in part because city leaders had become impatient with worker demands and in part because city leaders were frustrated with the union. The city ultimately chose to undermine the union, which would have long-term effects. That the city would attempt to gut the public workers' union was not necessarily a surprise, given the context. The Sunbelt regularly circulated claims to be "business friendly," which meant they maintained anti-union statutes and laws (such as right-to-work laws) and promoted their low-wage workforce when trying to attract new business and industry.

In the late 1960s, cross-domain work was evident as Emmaus House and social welfare activists supported sanitation workers, and labor joined with civil rights organizations to promote fair wages and benefits. Activists understood that they shared concerns with other low-wage workers and poor people, and that economic structures were designed to keep their pay and entitlements in check. These understandings helped connect poor residents across the city. Poor Atlantans, whether pressing for improved social welfare benefits or a particular wage floor, insisted that they have access to the typical expectations of American families, including sufficient food, adequate shelter, regular medical care, opportunities for personal and vocational growth, and other requirements for a healthy, stable life.

In many ways Atlanta's antipoverty movement had matured by 1971. A single defeat, such as the setbacks that accompanied the 1970 sanitation workers strike, did not threaten to stall antipoverty organizing in the city. Activists could point to the development of a larger and more durable infrastructure—ALAS, Emmaus House, the Poverty Rights Office—that supplied reliable resources and person power. To be sure, the antipoverty actions of the late 1960s and early 1970s did not always produce intended outcomes: bureaucrats and elected officials regularly rejected activists' demands, and city leaders deflected laborers' requests for higher wages or more robust benefit packages. But activists counted some victories and established a foundation from which they could mount other campaigns.

CHAPTER 6

Housing Crisis

"There is a housing crisis in Atlanta," the *Poor People's Newspaper* declared in the early 1970s. The Atlanta Housing Authority, the agency operating public housing in the city, had nearly a three-year waiting list. New housing affordable to poor people was not being built. And landlords were taking advantage of the tight housing market, subdividing properties, raising rent, and keeping their costs low by avoiding repairs and upkeep. The federal government was little help, the *Poor People's Newspaper* asserted. Government programs simply tore down dilapidated housing, leaving less housing than before. The situation had to be remedied. "Let your voice be heard," the newspaper urged.[1]

Atlanta certainly needed to address its housing issues if city leaders hoped to realize their goal of becoming a national city. Mayor Ivan Allen Jr. knew that, and in 1966 he prioritized the building of low-income housing. To many, the newly created federal Model Cities program would help meet that goal. While not solely focused on the production of housing, the program was seen by leaders and residents alike as a mode by which new housing might be built and older housing improved. But after a promising start, Model Cities soon foundered, failing to deliver on housing goals. Public housing provided little relief to the pressing housing need. Communities remained at capacity, and the housing authority resisted desegregation, installed obstacles to admission, and struggled to effectively manage its communities. Residents complained of vermin, slow response to maintenance requests, disrespectful staff, unfair fines, and the lack of a grievance procedure. In response, many poor residents took cues from tenant movements across the nation, utilized welfare rights networks close to home, and organized. And then they mobilized.

From 1966 to 1971, overlapping the city's welfare rights movement and the 1968 and 1970 sanitation workers' strikes, poor Atlantans and their allies mounted housing campaigns around two issues in particular: going problems with public housing and challenges that emerged in the implementation of the federal Model Cities program.

Years of housing demolition and commercial and government building had taken its toll on the availability of housing affordable to Atlanta's poor and working-class families. From 1958 to 1968, some 75,000 people had been forced to move as a result of urban renewal, expressway construction, housing code enforcement, and public housing eviction. Between 1960 and 1965, 5,000 homes were demolished for housing code enforcement, and more than 8,000 homes were eliminated over the decade in urban renewal projects. Research Atlanta estimated that 22,545 low-income units were lost between 1960 and 1970.[2] For various reasons, low-income housing units were not quickly replaced, and as a result, families doubled up, the housing market tightened, and rents increased.

Atlanta needed to act quickly and decisively to address these issues. Overcrowding, poor housing conditions, and high rents contributed to urban unrest in the 1960s, and city leadership wanted to prevent any further civil disturbances.[3] National journalists pitching Atlanta as a "hot" city were also regularly revealing the city's flaws, including its 17,000 homes "unfit for human habitation."[4] In 1966, Mayor Ivan Allen Jr. organized a meeting, the Mayor's Conference on Housing, to brainstorm solutions to Atlanta's housing shortage. Held in November 1966, the gathering attracted four hundred people. Allen acknowledged the shortage and its causes, and he called for a "crash low-income housing program" that would put housing "within reach of citizens on the lower rungs of the economic ladder." To meet this need, he announced a new Housing Resource Committee (HRC) that would spearhead providing 9,800 housing units by the end of 1968, and 16,800 units total over five years.[5] The federal Demonstration Cities and Metropolitan Development Act of 1966 promised to help meet Allen's housing targets.

Model Cities

Model Cities, as the federal program was colloquially known, provided grants for demonstration projects to solve or substantially alleviate social, physical, and economic problems in hard-core impoverished neighborhoods in America's cities. According to local newspapers, Model Cities would be the "most comprehensive improvement program ever attempted."[6] Model Cities differed from previous federal programs in that it was intended to concentrate a variety of programmatic and material resources on the target areas. Monies could be used for new housing and renovation, but also social services such as education and vocational training, health care, and counseling. As was the case with War on Poverty CAPs, Model Cities expected residents of targeted programs to be involved in program planning and implementation.[7] It also was a sizeable program. Model Cities was envisioned to cost $12 million for planning and $2.3 billion over six years.[8]

The program reflected the reformist impulse of the Kennedy and Johnson administrations. Urban renewal, focused as it was on physical infrastructure, had failed to substantially improve urban conditions, and cities had devolved into "crisis" in the 1960s. By mid-decade, many planners and urban observers were persuaded that physical improvements needed to be accompanied by social services and infrastructure that would connect urban families to jobs and other resources.[9]

The Model Cities idea met stiff resistance from Congress, however. As proposed, the program was expensive, and a number of congressional leaders were reluctant to fund the endeavor. Some House and Senate members resented not being involved in the initial drafting. Some sought private, nongovernmental solutions to employment and housing issues. Others rejected the creation of what they saw as duplicative or competing bureaucracies. Southern legislators largely opposed the proposal, and they particularly disliked the closely aligned rent supplement program and accompanying efforts to racially integrate public housing. The need to attract southern support forced the bill's editors to, as former Department of Housing and Urban Development official Charles Haar reflected, "muffle the integration issue," and language referencing the desegregation of housing was eventually excised.[10] Despite these challenges, widespread fear of continued urban unrest helped ensure the passage of Model Cities.[11] After substantial revision and compromise, the program was signed into law in November 1966 and handed over to the newly created Department of Housing and Urban Development (HUD) for implementation. City leaders throughout the United States hoped a substantial appropriation would come in 1967—mayors insisted that bold solutions required robust financial support—but Congress continued to choke program appropriations.[12] Compromise was the result. Congress ultimately reduced the authorization from the proposed $2.3 billion over five years to $900 million over the first two years, and $24 million was allocated for initial planning.[13]

In Atlanta, officials worked to distinguish Model Cities from previous initiatives, in part because so many Atlantans—and particularly people of color and the poor—had had bad experiences with earlier urban infrastructure projects. To many Atlantans, urban renewal primarily served to displace residents, demolish homes, and increase overcrowding. Although the War on Poverty's CAP initially held out some promise to improve city services, Atlanta had struggled to effectively design and implement mechanisms for citizen involvement. Model Cities was not solely about housing, but given Atlanta's housing deficiencies, many associated the program with housing improvement specifically rather than the provision of social and educational services. Consequently, public attention regularly returned to housing goals when Model Cities progress was discussed.[14]

Clearly Mayor Ivan Allen Jr. and Atlanta's political and bureaucratic leadership had these experiences in mind as they pitched Model Cities to residents of the central city neighborhoods leaders planned to target with the federal grant. City bureaucrats repeatedly told those attending public forums that target-area residents would be involved in Model Cities planning. In mid-February 1967, for example, city planner Collier Gladin emphasized that although community improvement reports generated by the CCAA offered some proposals, "we're going to let the residents try them on for size before making them definite."[15] And officials pledged that the disasters of urban renewal would be avoided. Rehabilitation would be promoted over demolition, for example. And in perhaps the mayor's most ill-advised statement, Allen expressed his hope that "not one family [would] have to be moved out of the neighborhood."[16] Finally, officials pointed out that Model Cities was bigger than previous programs, perhaps thinking that with a larger program, positive results would be clearly evident. The proposed target area was indeed vast: the three-thousand-acre "model neighborhood," as it was referred to in grant applications and reports, exceeded the acreage addressed by the total urban renewal program to date.[17] But in early 1967, whether Model Cities would deliver on its promises to residents remained to be seen.

Central Atlanta residents were on edge as the Model Cities proposal was rolled out. Already Mayor Allen had "beefed up" code enforcement as the city tried to alleviate slum conditions, and many saw the more stringent enforcement as a sign of what might come with Model Cities.[18] Residents complained that the city had no right to demand expensive re-

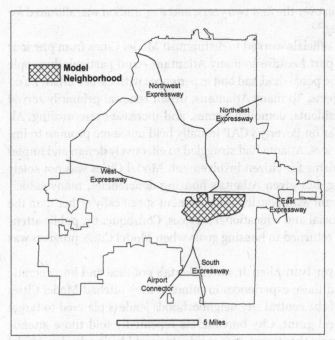

FIGURE 15. Location of Model Neighborhood, 1967.
Created by Matt Mitchelson, 2021.

pairs.[19] Others worried that they would invest in costly improvements only to have their homes demolished in later stages of the program.[20] Rumors spread that homes would be lost to new high-rise apartments and motels.[21] Many residents were uncomfortable with the unsettled details.

Counting forty-eight thousand residents, Atlanta's proposed Model Neighborhood actually encompassed six existing, central Atlanta neighborhoods: Summerhill, Adair Park, Grant Park, Peoplestown, Pittsburgh, and Mechanicsville (see fig. 15).[22] About 70 percent of those residents were Black, and as an *Atlanta Constitution* journalist observed, residents tended to be clustered by race. Four of the six neighborhoods included were "almost pure black" and two "almost lily-white." Adair Park and Grant Park were not "ghettos" like some of the other neighborhoods, the journalist noted, and were not predominantly poor. But Model Cities was not a poverty program as such, and federal Model Cities guidelines required involvement of 10 percent of the population. "It was important for Model Cities to have a representative number of whites included that were not poor to the same degree," the Model Cities director later explained.[23]

As the application detailed, the target area included some of the harshest conditions in the city. Almost half of Model Neighborhood families lived on less than $3,000 per year, 71 percent of the area's housing units were in substandard condition, and about one-third of units were thought to be overcrowded.[24] The storm sewer system was "partially obsolete and under-designed," and during heavy rainfall sewers backed up and overflowed.[25] The area contained incompatible land uses that contributed to physical blight. Many families were too poor to maintain their homes. Some sections suffered inadequate services (including poor lighting and infrequent trash collection) and remote health-care facilities. Social conditions in the area were bleak. Crime and delinquency rates were high. Many children lived in one-parent households, and school attendance and graduation rates were low.[26]

Although the model neighborhood "dramatically combined all the facets of blight and deterioration," Atlanta's public and private interests were, as the application asserted, "determined to ensure Atlanta's vital economic role as the transportation hub and capitol of the southeast." Model Cities, the proposal was saying, would help Atlanta continue its Sunbelt ascent. Atlanta was "a young, dynamic and progressive regional center," proposal writers stated. The private sector "has contributed the office buildings and high rise apartments that are transforming Atlanta's skyline." The public sector had created complementary facilities, including "the stadium and the auditorium-cultural center complex."[27] Model Cities would help complete city-building efforts.

The city acknowledged that the Model Cities program would be disruptive: some six thousand families would have to be temporarily relocated as a result of building and rehabilitation plans.[28] The relocation process would be challenging. Poor families, which included a number of elderly residents, could not afford market-rate housing, and there were few low-cost units available on the private market. Public housing provided few options: the Atlanta Housing Authority (AHA) by contract handled resident relocation services for residents displaced for urban redevelopment, urban renewal, code enforcement, and the like, and the authority struggled to identify housing opportunities for low-income families. Since taking on relocation responsibilities in 1964, the authority had successfully relocated only 50 percent of families affected by federal programs into standard housing. There was a shortage of housing in general, and a shortage of standard housing in particular.[29] To be sure, residents displaced by programs such as Model Cities had priority for public housing placement, but public housing tended to be full and had a waiting list.[30] Going into Model Cities, it was unclear how the city would improve on this record.[31]

Atlanta's Black sociopolitical elite and civil rights establishment kept a watchful eye on how the Model Cities program was being planned and administered. In its application, Atlanta had indicated that at least one executive council seat would be filled by an African American resident, but one African American out of twelve committee members hardly reflected the demographics of the city.[32] In 1959, the city counted 38 percent of its population as Black, and in 1969 that number had risen to 51 percent.[33] Because Model Cities stood to significantly impact Atlanta's African American residents, Black establishment leaders insisted on a significant, if not proportional, Black presence in Model Cities administration, just as they had with the community action agency.

Ongoing, consistent pressure from Atlanta's Black elite to appoint more African Americans to positions of power was paying off, and at least two African American candidates were in contention to lead Atlanta's Model Cities initiative. Many thought EOA's Black associate director William "Bill" Allison would be tapped to head the program, but Black Atlanta city planner Johnny C. Johnson ultimately was named director.[34] Johnson was a 1950 graduate of Morehouse College, and most of his professional experience had been in real estate.[35] One *Atlanta Constitution* piece explained that the appointment of a Black administrator had been by design; EOA had a white director, and thus, according to journalist Margaret Shannon, "it seemed both wise and fair to give the Model Cities job to a black."[36]

As soon as Atlanta was awarded its Model Cities grant, African Americans and target-area residents sought greater representation on the Model Cities Executive Board. Members of the city's Black sociopolitical elite met with Mayor Allen toward that end, and in the wake of similar demands regarding the EOA Executive Board, city officials responded quickly. They appointed two men of stature to the body, Dr. C. Miles Smith, a dentist, and Clarence Coleman, director of the southern regional office of the National Urban League.[37] At the December 1967 Model Cities Mass Convention, attendees requested that the number of Model Neighborhood residents on the executive board be increased to six, one for each of the six neighborhoods encompassed by the Model Cities program.[38] Alderman Rodney Cook and government liaison Dan Sweat persuaded city aldermen to accept the proposal, though some aldermen were reportedly reluctant to have residents outnumber elected officials.[39]

The Model Neighborhood citizen participation model in many ways mirrored EOA's citizen participation hierarchy. At Model Cities conventions, residents would elect representatives to neighborhood councils, and those councils would elect a representative to the executive board.[40] The Model Cities Mass Convention elected Lewis Peters from Mechanicsville, a Black bakery foreman and deacon of Calvary Temple Baptist Church, as cochair. Peters's neighborhood reflected the sort of issues that many Model Cities residents hoped the program would address. From 1960 to 1970, predominantly Black Mechanicsville had lost nearly half its population to housing demolition for highway building and urban renewal.

Vice chairs represented each of the six neighborhoods, and media regularly highlighted predominantly white Adair Park's choice, Calvin F. Craig, a white construction worker.[41] Craig was notable in part because he had served as the Grand Dragon of the Georgia unit of the United Klans of America, Inc. (Ku Klux Klan). But when Craig joined Model Cities, he decided not to run for reelection as Grand Dragon of the KKK. The *Atlanta Constitution* observed that, by that point, Craig had moderated his approach to race relations, and the paper quoted Craig as saying that Blacks and whites needed to sit down together and discuss their problems. While Craig reportedly drew support from some African Americans, some remained concerned that Craig's past work reflected poorly on the program.[42]

Thus, in early 1968, with a federal grant in hand, Atlanta's Model Cities plans were shaping up. The program had a director, an executive board, and a mass convention, and the neighborhoods had elected leadership. But challenges remained. Looming large was the city's history of and continuing struggle with racial segregation in housing. Some Atlantans' commitment to racial segregation threatened the mayor's ability to quell the housing crisis and answer poor residents' desires for safe and affordable housing. City leaders' (and white residents') commitment to racializing housing had, in practice, meant that Black families had fewer choices of where to live. Those restrictions would interfere with the need to temporarily (and quickly) relocate and permanently house residents.

Public Housing

Atlanta was nationally known for its public housing program, having been the first city in the nation to build government-subsidized housing in the 1930s. The city's housing authority, established in 1938 as an independent entity, managed slum clearance projects in the city, a role that entailed acquiring land and building housing.[43] The city's public housing communities provided low-cost housing to low- and middle-income families.[44] The authority's role in city housing would expand, and it would take over the rehousing of families displaced by government projects in 1964. Although the housing authority should have been a key player in identifying housing solutions in the late 1960s, its resistance to desegregation and leadership's consistent disregard for tenants meant that the authority was slow to respond to the city's housing needs.

In particular, the Atlanta Housing Authority leadership, including the board, resisted federal mandates to desegregate public housing, which meant that the authority slowed the process of rehousing families displaced by urban projects, including Model Cities.[45] Despite the July 1967 federal ruling that required public housing applicants to be housed on a first come, first served basis, Atlanta's housing authority maintained a "freedom of choice" method of housing families, an approach that gave families unlimited time to agree to an offered placement.[46] In practice, that meant that white families could continue to decline housing offers in Black communities until a unit in a white community opened up.[47] AHA missed the October 28, 1967, deadline to institute the new federal policy, and the AHA board indicated that it was delaying action until it investigated how other large cities were handling the first come, first served mandate. As the *Atlanta Constitution* explained, the AHA board members hoped that authorities would "buck HUD," thus forcing a change in the new policy.[48]

HUD responded to AHA with a compromise, and perhaps as a result, AHA continued to resist substantive racial integration. The federal office recommended that families applying for housing be required to take one of the first three choices offered or drop to the end of the waiting list. But in December, AHA continued to push back. They asked the agency to accept that sufficient integration had taken place, and to approve Atlanta's existing freedom of choice policy. In March 1968, HUD formally rejected AHA's proposal, giving the authority ninety days to refashion its tenant selection policy.[49]

Other Atlanta Housing Authority policies also complicated housing options for Atlanta's poor and working-class residents and in the process hampered relocation efforts for Model Cities. In January 1968, AHA revisited its tenant admission policy and refused to rent to women with husbands in prison and unwed mothers. Board members insisted that they were attempting to balance needs: they wanted to keep public housing safe for "decent people" while recognizing that residents were human and fallible. Under pressure from Atlantans and the Atlanta Legal Aid Society, AHA altered that policy in May 1968, but the authority maintained that if the birth of illegitimate children "reinforces a suspected shown pattern of anti-social conduct," the tenant's lease might be terminated.[50] AHA also established a city residency requirement for admission and occupation, in part out of concern that Atlanta public housing attracted rural migrants to the city.[51] For Model Cities residents, and some other residents displaced by urban rehabilitation projects, such requirements could be waived, but the fact remained that many poor had few choices with regard to housing, and certain subsets of the poor had fewer choices still.[52]

In general, tenants felt that the housing authority had little regard for tenants' opinion and little respect for them as people. By summer 1968, AHA was suffering enough criticism and tenants were so frustrated that AHA's board of directors sought to identify ways to improve the authority's image with residents. AHA board chair Edwin Sterne suggested athletic competitions and community beautification campaigns. Board member Jack Glenn asked about involving tenant leaders in authority meetings and suggested that the board visit the public housing communities as a way of engaging with residents and understanding their concerns.[53] The desire of at least some AHA board members to improve relations with public housing tenants was in contrast to AHA's existing practice. The authority had the reputation for being so resistant to involving tenants in policy- and decision-making that it was said that the administrators would not apply for HUD modernization funding (which would allow for the repair and rehabilitation of public housing) because the program required tenant participation in planning. Authority director M. B. "Robert" Satterfield denied the accusation.[54]

In these ways, from 1966 to 1968, AHA policies limited the use of public housing as an option for many poor families, including those displaced by infrastructure programs. Atlantans of color were particularly disadvantaged, as AHA continued to resist federal mandates to desegregate housing. Additionally, while public housing had been a desirable choice for potential residents in previous decades, by the 1960s residents were finding much to complain about. Model Cities challenges, too, were piling up.

"Sacrifice a Little Time"

Target-area residents felt left out of Model Cities planning practically from the get-go. In February 1968, Mechanicsville residents asserted that EOA staff had dominated and controlled the Model Neighborhood convention, which influenced voting.[55] They asked the mayor to nullify the election of Lewis Peters as mass convention cochair. A few months later, Grant Park residents complained that African American residents had no representation at a neighborhood meeting in which a vice chair had been elected.[56] Challenges continued the following year when Black Peoplestown resident and state representative Clarence Ezzard claimed irregularities in the election process and requested that the election be postponed.[57]

Whether because of frustration with flawed democratic processes or simply the lack of time to devote to civic affairs, by spring 1968, resident interest in Model Cities and meeting attendance was on the decline. In March, Mechanicsville vice chair Edward Moody pleaded with his community to "sacrifice a little time for a very important need, and attend these meetings."[58] Model Cities director Johnny Johnson reportedly was "disappointed" with the three-hundred-person turnout at the April 1968 Model Cities mass convention. New community affairs coordinator Xernona Clayton was similarly "disturbed" about lack of interest.[59] No doubt part of the challenge in maintaining resident interest was the lack of quickly visible results. Clayton sympathized, noting that "some of these people have been working with projects in the 'planning stages' for eight years."[60] "At first [residents] were all enthused," Joe Whitley, an Atlanta firefighter representing Grant Park, explained to an *Atlanta Constitution* reporter.[61] But, by September 1968, it was widely recognized that residents' willingness to commit time and effort to Model Cities planning had waned.

Although residents may not have regularly attended meetings, they were concerned about the demolition of their homes that Model Cities might bring. Sometimes they were wary of the process—residents who lived on the site of the Atlanta baseball stadium had been promised ninety days to vacate but had been given only thirty—but others simply did not want to give up their home or neighborhood.[62] In November 1968, Pittsburgh neighborhood residents considered suing the city when their homes were designated for clearance. Resident Norris Curington asked Atlanta officials to delay those plans until residents could rehabilitate their homes on their own. Residents were not unified, though;

some Pittsburgh residents recommended that demolition plans move forward.[63]

Despite the problems with Model Cities and public housing, at the December 1968 Housing Resource Committee meeting, it was announced that the city was ahead of schedule in meeting Mayor Ivan Allen Jr.'s ambitious housing goals. Just over 3,200 low- and medium-income units had been built (which targeted residents with incomes up to 80 percent of the area median income) and 6,278 were under construction. The city pointed out that the Housing Act of 1968 contained a raft of new opportunities to meet low-income housing needs.[64] The committee was enthusiastic about housing progress, but members conceded that issues remained.

In particular, middle-class and elite residents still vigorously fought the building of low-income housing nearby. The HRC acknowledged that zoning to allow more low-income housing would only come with what they called "package rezoning." In that process, officials would identify sections throughout the city for low-income housing and propose the sites as a collection. Presenting the rezoning as a package would demonstrate to aldermen and residents that *all* sections of the city would be taking on the "burden" of low-income housing.[65]

While the Housing Resource Committee reported that progress was being made on the city's housing goals, some thought Atlanta was still slow to respond to its low-income housing crisis, and that included the dean of public housing in Atlanta, Charles Palmer. Palmer, who promoted public housing as a method of stabilizing private real estate values, pointed out that if the energy and zeal "our power structure" had mobilized for the "dazzling stadium, luxury apartments and magnificent hotels and office buildings" had been mustered toward building housing for those displaced by "majestic structures," the mayor's goals for public housing would have, by that time, been very nearly reached.[66] In the meantime, frustrated public housing tenants continued to publicly expose ongoing issues with AHA, and they insisted on concrete, measurable change.

TUFF

The public housing tenant movement burst into Atlanta's consciousness in November 1968 when public housing tenants showed up to picket at the National Association of Housing and Redevelopment Officials (NAHRO) meeting at the downtown Marriott Motor Hotel.[67] As

Black tenant activist Mandy Griggs later explained in a letter to Mayor Ivan Allen Jr., the action was intended to bring to the public's attention "the deplorable conditions of life in the AHA projects."[68] Thirty picketers carried signs complaining of rats and roaches. Others accused AHA of bullying residents. Speaking for the picketers, Grady Homes resident Jean Frye told NAHRO representatives that racial segregation was still a problem in Atlanta public housing, and rent policies were unfair. Another resident pointed to issues with safety, noting that seven children had died in a creek bordering the playground at Perry Homes. Ann Brodeck pointed out that AHA lacked a grievance appeal procedure. NAHRO officials invited picketers to attend their meeting the next day too, and many returned, holding signs as Mayor Allen delivered the day's opening remarks.[69] Allen promised picketers that "their objections would be investigated.[70] After the NAHRO action, public housing tenants declared the formation of Tenants United for Fairness—TUFF.[71]

Public housing tenants organized TUFF to protest the "abusive" policies and practices of the Atlanta Housing Authority. As tenants explained in a circular distributed to four thousand public housing residents, they wanted a role in operating local housing authorities and the establishment of, as the *Atlanta Daily World* explained, "authority-wide rules governing evictions, punishments and fines."[72] The handbills repeated ALAS director Michael Padnos's earlier assertion that the AHA was an "enemy of the poor," a sentiment he expressed at an October 1968 Hungry Club forum.[73] Atlanta's Community Relations Commission stepped in to investigate tenant grievances in November 1968, holding what *Atlanta Constitution* journalist Phil Gailey labeled a "gripe-in" at Capital Homes.[74] Tenants complained of rats, issues with security deposit refunds, and an unbendable management that failed to take into account individual circumstances such as job loss or spousal abandonment.[75]

A month later, tenants followed up with the mayor, reminding him of the promise made at NAHRO and asking him to help mediate between tenants and the AHA. They demanded a tenant bill of rights and included a version drafted by the OEO-funded Housing Law Center of the Earl Warren Institute. The draft bill, which was circulating among legal aid societies in fall 1968, reflected growing interest across the country for more tenant-friendly, democratic policies in federally supported housing. The Housing Law Center offered to assist with test cases and to develop or comment on proposed housing legislation. TUFF proposed to the mayor that Atlanta be the first city to adopt the bill as a guideline.[76]

In the meantime, ALAS's Michael Padnos continued drawing attention to AHA's seeming intransigence, occasionally employing theatrics. At one meeting Padnos read an AHA letter in exaggerated Nazi German dialect, suggesting that the AHA was acting as a brutal and totalitarian regime. Padnos concluded by flinging the letter to the floor.[77] AHA's Satterfield was irked by ALAS and Padnos's performance. He wrote EOA asking that funding to ALAS be delayed until there could be an investigation into the agency. ALAS had "a disruptive influence on the housing program," Satterfield wrote, and the ALAS served "only to cause friction in the community."[78]

Still, Padnos, ALAS, and tenants generated enough concern about the AHA that a state legislative committee, which had formed in 1968 to study public housing in the state, was reconvened to investigate the AHA specifically.[79] The committee reviewed tenant complaints and ticked off a number of problematic trends: each community had been governed by different standards; tenant associations had been "stacked" with members hand-picked by the housing authority; tenant association dues were controlled by the housing authority; and increases in sliding-scale rents occurred more rapidly than decreases. The committee concluded that the complaints could not be directly addressed by legislation, but they recommended that the authority "put their house in order."[80] Specifically, they suggested that commission members' ten-year terms be shortened and that the board be enlarged.[81]

As sanitation workers had done a few months before, in February 1969, TUFF drew on the strength of the city's civil rights organizations, and particularly the SCLC, in their battle with the AHA. That month, TUFF invited civil rights organizations and human relations groups to discuss the housing authority and related tenant issues. The seventy or so persons gathered agreed to support tenants' request for a tenant bill of rights and to organize a mass meeting of tenants on public housing property. That event was designed in part to challenge the AHA's stated opposition to allowing TUFF—and its public housing tenant members—to meet at public housing communities.[82]

The following month TUFF and the SCLC held a joint meeting at Carver Homes that attracted 750 people.[83] In a follow-up letter to Mayor Allen, Michael Padnos reported that he felt safe in saying, "Every single one of these people had a specific complaint against the Atlanta Housing Authority."[84] At the meeting, SCLC's Ralph David Abernathy gave voice to the group's concerns. "We are here tonight to tell Atlanta, Georgia to STOP treating poor people in the housing projects like slaves," the civil rights leader stated. He then listed how workers and tenants at the various communities were mistreated. He complained of "slave wages," undeserved fines, and rats. If AHA did not address those issues, the SCLC and TUFF were going to "get tough with you." The AHA board needed "new blood that represented poor people," Abernathy said. Tenants deserved a tenant bill of rights and grievance panels, and AHA should recognize TUFF as the official bargaining agent for tenants.[85]

Two months later, Mayor Allen followed up with a letter to housing authority chair Edwin L. Sterne suggesting a public review of AHA's policies and procedures. By this time, spring 1969, Allen had confronted welfare rights protests, King's assassination, the Poor People's Campaign, and the 1968 sanitation workers' strike, and he had observed and absorbed societal shifts. He explained, "The demands of [TUFF are] a manifestation of one of the most profound changes in our society of the last decade." Expectations of the poor "and forgotten" had been raised. Poor families demanded "a bigger voice in the things which affect their lives," Allen noted.[86] The mayor also arranged a meeting between Dan Sweat, city director of community development John Robinson, and AHA director Satterfield.[87]

Although Allen recognized larger social changes, AHA remained difficult to deal with, in part because of its director's unwillingness to work *with* tenants. The director seemed to regularly stifle democratic impulses. In January 1969, Satterfield claimed the authority needed six months to review the proposed tenant bill of rights.[88] The authority tried to prevent TUFF from meeting on public housing property. It dragged its feet on pursuing federal funding when that funding required resident involvement in planning. It applied rules inconsistently and tried to interfere with ALAS funding because ALAS challenged AHA's management. But in April 1969, after meeting with the mayor and community development director John Robinson, AHA director Satterfield announced early retirement.[89] Satterfield's leaving, which reportedly was of his own choosing, came at a cost: the city kept him on as a consultant for the following year at a cost of $1,000 a month, an agreement that ALAS director and TUFF attorney Michael Padnos vigorously opposed.[90]

That summer Padnos continued pushing for more progressive authority leadership, appealing to the mayor to use the expiring term of board chair Edwin Sterne as an opportunity to appoint a more forward-thinking (and perhaps Black) replacement. Padnos recognized that Sterne had positive attributes: as board chair, Sterne had arranged meetings with tenants and discussed public housing challenges with ALAS. But the housing authority was still "out of touch and [lacked] sympathy with the realities of 1969," Padnos noted. "Atlanta in the 1970s needs men. . . . who can not only understand the needs and desires of poor people, but can respond to those needs positively and effectively." Realities demanded that "poor people be given a voice in managing their own lives," Padnos insisted.[91]

By summer 1969, TUFF had gained some ground. AHA board chair Edwin Sterne was talking with tenants in various communities, attempting to identify and address complaints.[92] When the Perry Homes chapter of TUFF initiated meetings with AHA in summer 1969, AHA recognized the legitimacy of the organization and agreed that the TUFF chair could take grievances to the housing manager.[93] But concessions were still granted reluctantly and after much effort. In July, TUFF continued pressuring AHA by holding a four-hundred-person rally led by SCLC's Ralph D. Abernathy.[94]

Consistent disruption produced results with the housing authority. That fall, AHA pledged that extra rent would no longer be charged to children under age twenty-one living with their parents, whether the children were working or not. A rent cap of $90 was installed. Regular pest control would be provided. Tenants would not be charged for damages to property unless the damage was done willfully by the tenant. Utility allowances would be raised. And "most important of all," according to *Emmaus House News*, grievance panels made up of tenants, elected by secret ballot, would be formed at each public housing community.[95]

Disruption paid off in actions in individual communities as well. Beginning in November 1971, for example, tenant members of the Concerned Citizens of East Lake formally requested grass, laundry facilities, and more street lights at the complex, only to be ignored by management. Residents then picketed the East Lake Meadows management offices and requested an audience with Lester Persells, who replaced M. B. Satterfield as AHA director and who continued to deflect their entreaties. Residents continued their press. "We are not going to let these agencies put poor people down any longer," Concerned Citizens of East Lake leader Eva Davis said of the situation.[96] On February 1, 1972, 285 tenants declared a rent strike. Three days later, Purcells met with the tenants and agreed to a gradual implementation of most of the twenty-six demands put forward by the tenants.[97]

In 1968, tenants in Atlanta's public housing observed the possibilities of collective action and disruption and joined forces with welfare rights activists, civil rights organizations, and labor to pursue better housing and more democratic public housing management. Results were slow to arrive in some cases—it took persistent action to force change within bureaucracies such as the Atlanta Housing Authority—but change was clearly possible. The authority director, who regularly interfered with tenant desires for property improvements, was eventually removed, and more progressive property management practices were implemented. Tenants' work was certainly not complete: activists had to stay vigilant to ensure the authority and community management lived up to their commitment to Atlanta's low-income families. Activists would continue to have to keep close watch on Model Cities, as well.

A Troubled Agency

By spring 1969, the *Atlanta Constitution* was referring to the local Model Cities agency as "troubled." That was worrisome, as city officials felt that newly elected Republican president Richard Nixon might cut supplementary funds from the program if the administration got wind of the city's struggles to implement the program.[98] Atlanta's officials had expected the city to be awarded a $7.1 million supplement intended to kickstart the city's five-year redevelopment plan.[99]

Federal support for Model Cities as a whole was in question. Lyndon Johnson had put much stock in Model Cities to help ease poverty and quiet urban tensions, but none of the 150 funded programs across the United States had advanced beyond planning stages when Johnson declined to run for another term and left office in 1968. Nixon promised a program overhaul for Model Cities, insisting on more input by private industry and a shift to a block grant approach, which would allow cities and states more flexibility in how federal money was spent. To settle the ongoing debate over who controlled programs, citizens or local officials, Nixon declared that local officials had authority.[100] Program changes and Nixon's decision to review the Model Cities program interfered with the delivery of grant funds announced in January 1969. Despite these threats to Model Cities funding, *Atlanta Constitution* reporter Alex Coffin suggested there were reasons for optimism in the Atlanta program: parks that would serve area youth might be ready by summer, and land was being acquired for housing, though construction itself was not scheduled for six months.[101]

Residents were not so optimistic. Dissatisfaction with the Model Cities citizen participation structure only seemed to grow. In January 1970, residents of Model Cities neighborhoods again challenged the methods by which their representative leadership was elected. At what the *Atlanta*

Constitution described as a "wild and name-calling" public hearing, some accused Model Cities as being managed "behind closed doors."[102] Welfare rights and housing activist Ethel Mae Mathews ticked off complaints: residents had not been sufficiently informed of the day of the meeting and election, young people had been excluded, and there were irregularities in the voting and meeting process.[103] To many, the operation of Model Cities remained opaque.

Housing continued to be a central concern for Model Neighborhood residents. In January 1970, an Emmaus House volunteer discovered that Model Cities resident Alice May Heflin and her four children had been relocated to a run-down, unheated apartment at 600 Martin Street. Some units in the twelve-apartment complex had broken windows. There was no seat on Heflin's toilet, and subfreezing temperatures had caused pipes to burst.[104] AHA suspended three staff members as the authority investigated why substandard units had been let to Model Cities families.[105] Many families grew frustrated waiting for permanent housing to be built. "The Model Cities program has not yet put up *any* housing except the three trailers at the corner of Washington and Atlanta," Emmaus House staff complained. "Is Model Cities just another Urban Removal?" they asked, deploying the term many residents used to criticize urban renewal.[106]

With problems and complaints piling up, by September 1970 the *Atlanta Constitution* was asking if Atlanta's Model Cities program was a "colossal flop." Progress was not "visible." Austin Ford observed that while the main thrust of Model Cities was to provide housing, there were "actually fewer places to live here than before."[107] In Dan Sweat's analysis, Model Cities had struggled to coordinate the different service providers and entities, and citizen participation processes required time and often brought power struggles.[108] Some blamed Model Cities director Johnny Johnson for lack of progress, suggesting that Johnson was a poor administrator, and the *Atlanta Constitution* indicated that Johnson had "battled" with Mayors Allen and Massell as well as chief of staff Dan Sweat.[109]

When it seemed to Model Cities residents that things could not get worse, they did. On October 1, 1970, the *Atlanta Constitution* revealed that 150 mobile homes were sitting unused in a field south of downtown. Part of a fleet of 200 units purchased to serve as temporary shelter for Model Cities residents, the installation of mobile homes had stalled as appropriate land was acquired or prepared. At least one area originally identified for the mobile homes had been opposed by surrounding neighborhoods.[110] Besides the fact that the mobile homes sat unused, *Atlanta*

Constitution reporters critiqued the cost of the units, which, with installation, amounted to just over $1.5 million. The reporters contended that higher-quality units could be purchased and installed from a local dealer at lower cost.[111] Under increased public scrutiny and attention from Mayor Sam Massell, city aldermen finally approved the placement and use of 129 mobile homes, but that action did little to satisfy residents.[112]

On Monday, November 9, 1970, fifty residents expressed their deep frustration with the program's four years of housing inactivity by "sleeping in" at the Model Cities headquarters. Attendees insisted, "We demand that you make the Model Cities program a program to help people instead of what it is now, a program to clear land." Protestors accused Model Cities administrators of enjoying "plush chairs," "plush desks," and "fat paychecks" while poor Atlantans endured "shanty shacks." Model Cities money should go toward housing—permanent housing and temporary relocation housing—instead of salaries for staff members, protestors insisted. "Yes, housing. That's what we want," Ethel Mae Mathews explained. "If we don't get it, we're going to take over your housing" (see fig. 16).[113] After twenty-six hours and pledges from the Model Cities director and Mayor Massell to eliminate red tape and take quicker action for better housing, protesters declared victory and abandoned their sleep-in. Massell promised to open 108 mobile homes immediately and complete construction on 500 permanent homes within a year. As the *Atlanta Constitution* pointed out, the pledge was significant in part because in the four years since the program began and the eighteen months since the program had been funded, no new or permanent housing had been built in the Model Cities neighborhoods.[114]

Soon, though, Johnson and the Model Cities Executive Board were back-pedaling, "clarifying" that their pledge was meant to be a commitment to *begin* construction on housing units. At a Model Cities Executive Board meeting in November 1970, Johnny Johnson explained that in early 1971, construction would launch on 300 to 400 units in the Summerhill neighborhood, and soon thereafter construction would begin on 100 to 200 units in the Pittsburgh neighborhood. Thus, within a year, 500 units would be underway. Summerhill representative Mattie Ansley wasn't buying it. The "wool's being pulled over our eyes," she asserted. Protesters booed executive board members, and Ethel Mae Mathews explained that residents were "disgusted and disappointed." They had been misled. Another sleep-in was promised if action to build housing was not soon taken.[115]

FIGURE 16. Activists protest at Model Cities offices, 1970. Courtesy Boyd Lewis photographs, Kenan Research Center at the Atlanta History Center.

Faced with setback after setback, in 1971 Model Cities residents pursued legal action to force housing to be built. Attorney Archer D. Smith III filed suit on behalf of nine Model Cities residents against AHA, the City of Atlanta, and the U.S. Department of Housing and Urban Development, charging that the three entities had violated the 1970 Uniform Relocation and Real Property Acquisition Act, which required that residents displaced by government action be given relocation advantages and priorities. The suit asked that no additional property be acquired in the Model Cities area until housing affordable to displaced residents was built on already cleared land.[116]

Indeed, relocation assistance for displaced Model Cities residents appeared to be a low priority for the Atlanta Housing Authority. In May 1971, thirty mobile homes still sat unused, and the *Atlanta Constitution* reported that some Model Cities families were still being relocated to substandard housing—from "squalor to squalor" as journalist Duane Riner phrased it.[117] Still, despite sleep-ins, public protests, and lawsuits, goals for the production of new, permanent housing under the Model Cities program continued to be missed. An Emory University evaluation indicated that with regard to Model Cities' housing goals, the program had produced "minor achievements and major frustrations."[118] A Georgia State University study indicated that, as a result, residents were "very angry and hostile."[119] By that time, Model Cities had such a bad reputation that some agencies concealed their relationship to it.[120] Model Cities director Johnny Johnson pointed to the Federal Housing Administration (FHA) as the bottleneck in redevelopment, an accusation FHA brushed off.[121] Johnson defended Model Cities programs in a "chronology of events" assembled for FHA and the HUD regional office, a document the *Atlanta Constitution* described as an "elaborate rationalization."[122] The *Atlanta Constitution* concluded, "In Atlanta, after more than two years and $14 million," the Model Cities program was "a colossal failure."[123]

In August 1971, Atlanta finally saw ground break for the first new Model Cities–funded housing at Azalea Gardens in Peoplestown at the corner of Tuskegee and Connally Streets. The $600,000 complex was financed under FHA 236 and sponsored by Mt. Nebo Baptist church. Of the thirty-five air-conditioned units, 40 percent were reserved for residents receiving public assistance (20 percent for those receiving public housing, 20 percent for those receiving rent subsidies).[124] Despite the planned gala ribbon cutting in late May 1972, not all units were ready for occupancy; two buildings still needed work. Six weeks later, Azalea Gardens still had no occupants as the complex had yet to meet building requirements. No one was prepared take responsibility for the delay. Model Cities blamed the sponsoring church, Mt. Nebo. The church blamed the contractor, Bankhead West. And the contractor blamed local Model Cities requirements.[125]

As Azalea Homes opened, Model Cities seemed destined for federal elimination. If Nixon were reelected in 1972, Dan Sweat predicted, he would "cut out every evidence of Great Society programs." HUD officials predicted an earlier demise, noting that HUD secretary George Romney planned to aggregate a number of grant programs into "community development." If that were the case, Atlanta's aldermen would have to decide how to prioritize spending, and Sweat acknowledged that history would "probably accord Model Cities as a failure here and nationwide."[126]

The Model Cities program certainly disappointed residents in Atlanta. The city's 1972 application for Model Cities supplemental funds indicated that there had been few physical improvements in the Model Neighborhood. Street conditions and sanitation "remain[ed] substantially the same." In a sample of Model Neighborhood structures, 59 percent displayed "unapproved and inadequate refuse storage," and 21 percent of sampled structures had "exterior signs of rat infestation."[127] Staff pointed fingers at the "lack of funds with which to alleviate present problems," specifically a "limited city budget for operations and equipment." But staff also blamed residents, whose "attitudes of indifference and unsanitary habits" also contributed. The city had expressed high aspirations for the production of housing units in its original application: Model Cities would build 6,000 standard units, 4,821 of which would replace dilapidated structures. A 1973 evaluation report indicated that only 42 new housing units had been completed since the program launched, 307 were still under construction, and just over 1,000 had been rehabilitated or repaired. Model Cities had "made little impact on the problems of inadequate housing," an *Atlanta Constitution* journalist concluded.[128] In retrospect, city planner Collier Gladin indicated that the program had been "oversold locally and nationally."[129]

The Model Cities experience would only contribute to poor Atlantans' cynicism about the benefits of urban development initiatives and promises of neighborhood improvement. To be sure, Atlanta's leaders had learned lessons from their implementation of other government programs. After challenges setting up its community action agency, for example, the city designed citizen participation structures for Model Cities from the get-go, though many issues surfaced during implementation. Citizen participation would eventually wane, but residents still expected the city to deliver on its promises.

In housing as in welfare rights and labor conflicts, antipoverty activists often felt they had to create near-crisis conditions to force a response that favored Atlanta's poorest citizens. Indeed, disruption continued to be a useful tactic in part because public protests, interference in operations, and rent strikes captured the attention of the media, politicians, and housing management and put in doubt Atlanta leaders' declarations that Atlanta could be the world's next great city and "the place to be in the South."[130] While administrators, managers, and city officials grew impatient with such tactics, those actions produced results. In housing, such tactics paid off. The mayor tasked city staff to deal with tenant demands, a problematic public housing administrator stepped down, AHA commission members took greater interest in tenant issues, and by the end of 1972, each community had a tenant-based grievance committee. In the case of Model Cities, disruption had less clear results, though resident action clearly exposed Atlanta's ineffectiveness in implementing the ambitious program and the city's challenges providing shelter for the city's poor and near poor. But although disruptive tactics could prompt action, in some cases some systems (some *problems*) could not be moved without policy change, and poor Atlantans would have to figure out how to do that work.

From 1966 to 1971, coalition building across various antipoverty domains benefited antipoverty organizing. Coalition building was possible because activists identified similar challenges and problems. Welfare rights activists recognized the same oppressive structures in housing that they experienced in social welfare delivery. Inequitable workplace practices resembled issues that surfaced in housing. While activists may have had a primary identity as civic council leaders or welfare rights members, individuals and groups saw how their interests intersected, and thus different groups worked together to improve families' day-to-day lives. Geography, too, facilitated coalition building in this period. Many welfare rights activists lived in public housing and organized by public housing community.[131] Many civic council members and sanitation workers lived in the Model Neighborhood. Geographic proximity facilitated organizing. Tenants frustrated with housing, welfare, or wages could easily meet, communicate, organize, and mobilize. Emmaus House and its tools—the *Poor People's Newspaper*, meeting space, transportation—facilitated and encouraged organizing across domains. Thus, from 1966 to 1971, antipoverty organizing in Atlanta accelerated, became more robust in that organizing and campaigns took place in different domains (housing, welfare rights, labor issues), and developed a more substantial apparatus. Nevertheless, it had become evident that Atlanta's antipoverty movement still lacked the ability to influence legislation, and many antipoverty activists felt it was singularly important to change laws that limited opportunity for poor people.

CHAPTER 7

Lobbying for Welfare

Atlanta's welfare rights activists could tick off many achievements since they had started organizing in 1967. They had secured copies of the state AFDC regulations. They had distributed information about the new *Poor People's Newspaper* to every AFDC client in Fulton County, which resulted in hundreds of subscribers. Many welfare mothers who had demanded fair hearings had won their challenges. Clients felt more confident in asking questions about AFDC budgets and grants. But clients' demands also had been deflected many times by county administrators and state officials. DFACS head Gilbert Dulaney had told welfare mothers that Fulton County had no money for special grants, nor could it legally distribute them. State assistant attorney general Frank Blankenship had explained to activists that the state could not increase AFDC monthly grants without new legislation. Although several politicians and government bureaucrats were sympathetic to poor families' plight and even engaged in or facilitated antipoverty work, Atlanta's poor families could not easily turn their measured or ambitious goals into legislation and policy. Legislation mattered, as states had substantial latitude in setting enrollment qualifications and regulations for AFDC and other social welfare entitlements.

The Georgia Poverty Rights Organization (GPRO) formed in the mid-1970s specifically to do that work—to amplify traditional direct action protest tactics and translate the desires of poor families and their allies into legislation and practice. Lobbying would *complement* ongoing direct action campaigns and the litigation strategies of poverty lawyers. Legislative change was particularly critical in mid-1970s Georgia: not only was the economy foundering, but in 1975 state legislators had installed a $32 cap on average monthly AFDC grants, a regulation that would result in grant *cuts* for some families. Thus, as inflation and unemployment grew in the 1970s, Atlanta's and Georgia's poor were forced to survive on less. What's more, with such a cap in place, AFDC grants could not be increased.[1]

A specific set of factors converged in mid-1970s Georgia to encourage Atlanta's antipoverty activists to persistently lobby state officials and agencies regarding AFDC and allow the organization to successfully eliminate the $32 ceiling on average monthly AFDC grants. For one, Georgia's part-time legislative structure and thin legislative apparatus meant that legislators lacked resources to fully investigate all the complex issues that came before them and prepare appropriate legislation. Consequently, legislators benefited from the expertise and services provided by lobbyists. But several other factors came into play. Atlanta had been, since 1967, home to active welfare rights organizations that could be quickly mobilized to promote or defeat proposed legislation. Black voting power had grown since the Voting Rights Act of 1965, and that power could potentially be leveraged on social welfare issues. Relatedly, the governor and a significant faction of the state legislature reflected a new racial liberalism, a shift on which the GPRO and welfare rights activists could capitalize. Growing Black voting power also had resulted in more Black elected officials in the General Assembly, a group that had organized as the Georgia Legislative Black Caucus (GLBC). These Black lawmakers could apply pressure within the General Assembly and hinder legislation that would negatively affect the poor. Finally, government bureaucrats in health and human services sometimes pursued goals similar to those of GPRO, and thus they were potential partners in expanding social welfare legislation. This particular collection of circumstances created opportunities for liberal, pro-welfare advocates that, in most cases, had not existed ten years earlier. Indeed, GPRO would successfully eliminate the $32 cap and establish a firm foundation for future antipoverty work. Thus, while welfare client-activists' national network, the NWRO, struggled in the early 1970s and eventually shuttered, Atlanta's welfare rights movement, with its network of activists and variety of tactics, remained active and continued to achieve victories.

In the 1970s, the needs of Atlanta's and Georgia's poor, particularly the Black poor, remained significant. To be sure, Great Society and other federal programs had helped diminish poverty nationally and in the state.

In Georgia, the percentage of persons living below the federal poverty line dropped from 39 percent in 1959 to 20.7 percent in 1969 (see table 1). Still, African Americans remained disproportionately at risk; according to a 1973 antipoverty report, nearly one of every two Black Georgians lived below the poverty line, compared to one in nine white Georgians.[2] Although the War on Poverty had reduced poverty, as the 1970s progressed, inflation and unemployment cut into those economic gains, and many turned to AFDC to make ends meet. In February 1973, the U.S. Department of Health, Education, and Welfare (HEW) announced that Georgia had added some 3,500 families to its AFDC rolls, the third highest increase in the nation.[3]

A family's eligibility for AFDC was determined by income level in comparison to the state's *standard of need*. As Georgia Department of Human Resources head Thomas M. "Jim" Parham explained to state legislators in early 1976, that standard often had a weak relationship to the actual cost of living. In the most recent federally mandated adjustment to the standard of need in 1971, Georgia had established its standard as $227 per month for a family of four—two-thirds of the poverty level and about $1,396 in 2017 dollars.[4] States were not required to meet 100 percent of the standard of need, and Georgia's AFDC benefits met 70.2 percent of the standard in 1974.[5] That is, AFDC helped Georgia families, but it did not bring families out of poverty.

It was in this context that a marked increase in AFDC applications ignited a new round of heated debates about the state's role in supporting poor single mothers and their children. In April 1975, Georgia officials announced that the state's spending on AFDC had tipped over the $32 average-per-person cap that the General Assembly had quietly inserted into budget legislation in January 1975. At that time, legislators had sought to limit welfare expenditures to the dollar amount at which the federal government provided matching funds. That is, when the average per-person grant exceeded $32, Georgia was responsible for additional dollars spent. In practice, this meant that welfare payments were readjusted every quarter as the Department of Human Resources received reports on expenditures.[6]

On the surface, the $32 cap appears to have been yet another tactic in a long line of measures that states—and particularly southern states—used to control AFDC enrollment and expenditures. Such measures included "man in the house" (i.e., substitute father) and suitable home rules. To control spending, Georgia and other Deep South states used a public assistance formula in lieu of the Medicaid formula to calculate average grants, a choice made because the former allowed for a lower overall financial investment by the state.[7] As state politicians tamped down on social welfare spending, conservatives at the federal level incrementally shifted social welfare to *workfare*, a set of programs authored in large part by southern politicians. Such programs were intended to favor those considered to be the "deserving poor," and states constrained spending by limiting and otherwise managing enrollment. That body of legislation included the Work Incentive program (1967), the 1971 Talmadge amendments, Supplemental Security Income (1972), and the Earned Income Tax Credit (1975).[8]

Georgia's $32 ceiling had almost immediate repercussions. When the state's economy slowed in early 1975, welfare applications increased, and costs to the state crept higher. To avoid overspending the new $32 ceiling, the Department of Human Resources (DHR) was forced to reduce monthly welfare allocations by 3 percent in May, an action that would negatively affect 63 percent of families receiving AFDC. As a result, families' monthly grants went less far: they would only meet 67 percent of the standard of need, down from 70.2 percent. Making matters worse, families dropped from AFDC would lose Medicaid coverage and would have to cover health-care costs on their own. Georgia's welfare allocations, which already failed to lift families out of poverty, were shrinking. "Now is the time for ACTION," white liberal Atlantan Frances Pauley asserted in a May 20 letter to 3,500 members of the GCHR.[9]

The Committee of Concerned Agencies

Using the GCHR network, on May 23, 1975, Pauley and Emmaus House director Austin Ford convened a meeting in Atlanta of organizations alarmed by the recent reductions in AFDC and related programs. Georgians "will not stand for our children to be sacrificed," Pauley insisted in her appeal.[10] This ad hoc Committee of Concerned Agencies (CCA), as the group identified itself, developed a lengthy to-do list. Its members would hold public demonstrations, identify ways to correct the public's misunderstandings about welfare, and pen a response to the *Atlanta Constitution*'s recent "Welfare Mess" series. Additionally, the group petitioned Governor George Busbee, Lieutenant Governor Zell Miller, and House Speaker Thomas B. "Tom" Murphy, asking that welfare payments be restored to previous levels and that no further reductions be made. As the petition explained, AFDC grants failed to raise families above poverty level. And levels of benefits had not been revised substantially since

March 1972, despite a 30 percent increase in the cost of living. Ultimately, the CCA's goals required legislative change, and those present committed to organizing a "concerted political lobby effort" at the next General Assembly, Georgia's annual legislative session held at the state capitol in downtown Atlanta.[11]

Pauley herself reflected a period in which many highly skilled women had spent their adult lives rearing children and volunteering their time in social and political endeavors. She had devoted many years to the DeKalb County League of Women Voters and Georgia League of Women Voters, where she promoted racial justice issues. In the early 1950s, Pauley had promoted Citizens Against the County Unit Amendment, a coalition opposed to efforts to install the county unit system of state representation in Georgia's constitution. And as school systems considered desegregation, with Eliza Paschall she had supported H.O.P.E., the Help Our Public Education campaign. Pauley's experience led her to be hired as executive director of the GCHR. Pauley then worked for the U.S. Department of Health, Education, and Welfare (HEW) in Mississippi, managing school desegregation efforts. By 1975 she was an experienced activist and public interest professional.[12]

Father Austin Ford also had a robust advocacy résumé. He maintained an extensive network ranging from civil rights activists to politically powerful members of the Episcopal diocese and its congregations. Additionally, he served on boards that pressed for political change and racial justice, including the Georgia chapter of the American Civil Liberties Union (ACLU) and the GCHR.

The Committee of Concerned Agencies was a markedly liberal coalition that reflected Pauley's and Ford's sociopolitical network. It included the ACLU, ALAS, the Georgia Citizens Coalition on Hunger, the NAACP, the SRC, the League of Women Voters of Atlanta, and the Martin Luther King Jr. Center, all of which were Atlanta based, though many of the organizations' members lived elsewhere in the state. Although many who attended the May 23 meeting to form the CCA were agency staff, attorneys, and bureaucrats unaccustomed to lobbying the state's political leadership, a few were well versed in influencing political processes, and as a group they sought to learn and do more.[13]

Lobbying a part-time legislature meant considerable work. In 1975 and 1976, and consistent with legislatures throughout the South, Georgia's legislators served part-time—the General Assembly was limited to forty days a year—and there were few multipurpose, much less specialized staff supporting legislative work. State-funded legislative aides helped draft bills and provided other administrative support when the General Assembly was in session, but in general, individual legislators had little dedicated administrative support or professional assistance to investigate legislative issues. Thus, in Georgia, even legislators seeking to ease poverty could offer only limited help in translating liberal desires into concrete policies. Consequently, lobbyists and interest groups could fill a gap by providing elected officials with research support and specific policy recommendations.[14]

Expanding AFDC in the mid-1970s would be a challenge. Economic decline had resulted in lean state budgets, and there were no signs the economy was on the rebound. Manufacturing was in decline. Capital spending had slowed. Unemployment was high. And the inflation rate remained high. "More and more people are being laid off the job," the *Poor People's Newspaper* reported in February 1975. "Food [prices] go up every week," Atlanta welfare rights organization president Ethel Mae Mathews observed. "Gas and light bills are out of sight."[15] Cultural opposition to means-tested entitlements such as AFDC had grown. The National Welfare Rights Organization folded in 1975, leaving local affiliates without an overarching structure or a natural network to turn to for support, advice, and ideas.[16]

On the positive side, at least some of the state's political leadership reflected a new racial liberalism. The legislature and governor's office counted few race-baiters and racial demagogues after the 1970 governor's race, though the legislature continued to be dominated by white conservative Democrats. Georgia's experience represented a larger pattern across the South as New South Democrats relied less on racial politics in their campaigns and platforms and more on promoting government efficiency and economic development. Governor George Busbee, a well-respected politician, reflected that turn. In his 1974 gubernatorial campaign against Lester Maddox, Busbee tended to avoid racially divisive language and tactics and instead highlighted his "workhorse" reputation.[17] In office, Busbee embraced long-term planning, adopted effective management practices, and accepted legislative independence. While Busbee did not court the Black vote, he welcomed Black endorsement, and African Americans overwhelmingly backed him over Maddox.[18]

Growing Black voting strength had the potential to influence legislation related to AFDC. As previously discussed, Black voting strength had grown in Atlanta since the 1940s, which allowed for the development of a politically powerful Black sociopolitical elite. By the early 1970s, Black votes mattered *statewide* as well. After the passage of the Voting Rights

Act of 1965, Black voting strength in Georgia increased significantly. In 1963 only 27 percent of Georgia's eligible Black population was registered to vote, but in 1968 that number had reached 56 percent. By then, attracted by the Democratic Party's willingness to address civil rights, Black voters had joined the Democratic ranks. Importantly, as political scientists Byron E. Shafer and Richard Johnston have noted, Black southerners joined the party as "national Democrats"; traditional southern Democrats had resisted the national party's civil rights plank.[19] By 1975, 26.6 percent of Georgia's registered voters were Black.[20]

Besides a new racial liberalism and increased Black voting strength, the CCA could also take advantage of recent growth and interest in public organizing and lobbying. Popularized by Common Cause, a "citizens lobby" formed by John Gardner in 1970 to promote transparency in government, the number of public interest groups and lobbyists mushroomed in the 1970s. Of course, consumer protection leagues and good government organizations (including the League of Women Voters) had existed before 1970, but the social justice concerns of the 1960s combined with public alarm over the Watergate scandal and the Vietnam conflict encouraged citizen-led democratic action. Such public interest groups hoped to make government more accountable, sought to protect human and natural resources from what were considered to be the excesses of business and power, and foregrounded the concerns of underserved groups.[21]

Starting out, the CCA drew on techniques used by other public interest organizations, the experiences of its members, and scholarly assessments of lobbying approaches to develop a multipronged plan to influence AFDC policy. As past president of the Georgia League of Women Voters, Pauley would have been intimately familiar with the league's system of interviewing legislators and its practices of communicating with and mobilizing its members. Additionally, evidence suggests that the CCA researched lobbying tactics. Preserved in Pauley's files is the 1958 *Annals of the American Academy of Political and Social Science* special issue "Unofficial Government: Pressure Groups and Lobbies," which includes articles on "how pressure groups operate," the use of litigation as a form of pressure group politics, and political interest groups as "policy shapers." Pauley also collected lobbying materials generated by other public interest and pressure groups, including the NAACP and the American Association of Retired Persons.[22]

At the same time, the CCA worked with like-minded organizations that used complementary approaches to bringing about social and political change. In particular, the committee drew on the strength, experience, and proximity of Atlanta's welfare rights organizations, which by the early 1970s included the chapter headquartered at Emmaus House and chapters at a number of public housing communities. Those groups could be depended upon to draw the attention of the public, media, bureaucrats, and politicians to issues related to poverty. And, as recipients of welfare, members could explain the impact of AFDC policy in authentic ways. That being said, many local and state leaders considered welfare mothers' demands an annoyance. Georgia politicians sometimes greeted the women with disdain and blocked their access to policy-making venues. In 1969, when client-activists were meeting with the assistant attorney general about welfare payments, Governor Lester Maddox summarily ejected the members from the capitol, explaining, "They have no place, these people—unclean, dirty—in the governor's office."[23] But while welfare activists did not always have an empathetic governor, the CCA could turn to another organization for visible support within the legislature.

Although Black elected officials had a greater presence in Atlanta and Georgia by the end of the twentieth century, and Black voter rolls had increased substantially, the Georgia Legislative Black Caucus had only just formally organized during the 1975 state legislative session. Admittedly, Black legislators had met, shared resources, and strategized informally for years. But in 1976, the Black Caucus still counted few members—20 of 180 House members and 2 of 56 in the Senate—and what members it did have had not yet ascended to powerful committee posts or leadership positions. Additionally, as the Southern Center for Studies in Public Policy observed in its annual Georgia legislative review, it was "difficult for the Black Caucus to establish a binding strategy or agenda"; caucus members held different political perspectives, in part because they represented the varying needs of different parts of the state.[24] The CCA and welfare rights organizations looked to the Georgia Legislative Black Caucus to fend off attacks on social welfare and support antipoverty bills as they moved through the House and Senate.[25]

The CCA launched its lobbying offensive against the $32 cap by crafting letters and circulating a petition while welfare client-activists publicly demonstrated their dissatisfaction with AFDC policies. In May, the Welfare Mothers Fight Back Committee, which was organized specifically to target the 1975 welfare cuts, marched in front of the Georgia capitol, blaming Governor George Busbee for the changes to AFDC and demanding a meeting with him. "We want Busbee!! We want Busbee!!" they chanted.[26] After some confusion about whether the governor was willing to meet with protesters, Busbee departed for a scheduled trip to New Orleans, leaving the demonstrators frustrated. Deploying allusions to the urban conflicts that had rocked America's cities in the 1960s, Phyllis Randolph, the spokesperson for the Welfare Mothers Fight Back Committee, asserted, "We don't want this [demonstration] to get out of hand, but this is going to be a long, hot summer, and the crowd is very angry."[27] By early June, welfare mothers had held four protests. At the June 4 demonstration, Busbee still refused to meet with the women, and Randolph, foreshadowing years of regular marches and public actions, promised, "We'll be back."[28]

CCA advocates and welfare mothers wanted further cuts to the state budget to be taken from programs other than those meant to reduce hunger and poverty, but in 1975, Georgia was struggling financially, and stakeholders throughout the state competed for scarce resources. When Busbee greeted Georgians on television on June 19, he told them he wanted to discuss "what may be the most crucial problem confronting your state government in the past 40 years."[29] The recession was eating into state revenues, and Busbee recommended that the General Assembly balance the budget by reducing spending in the coming year. Together, national and state economic decline, a desire to prevent overspending, a persistent anti-welfare climate, and competing policy issues did not bode well for Georgia's antipoverty lobby as it faced the summer's special legislative session, a session called specifically to address the state's financial crisis.[30]

Over the six-week special session, scores of CCA supporters mounted a defense of the state's welfare programs, attempting to correct basic misunderstandings about AFDC in hopes of preventing further reductions to monthly grants. They assembled and mailed packets with "The Facts Surrounding Georgia's AFDC Reduction" to legislators, developed a sample press release, and appealed to legislators and area newspapers. During the session, CCA members accompanied 130 children from Emmaus House's summer programs as they hand-delivered letters to legislators. Some of the letters were read on the floor of the House as the young people listened from the gallery. "Dear Members of the General Assembly," wrote nine-year-old Tammie Scruggs, "I think you should stop cutting our checks because we need food and money so we can buy our clothes."[31] But if the CCA had a network of people willing to write, speak, and demonstrate in behalf of welfare recipients and other poor families, it did not have many organizational allies lobbying at Georgia's capitol. The lobbyist register for 1976 no longer exists, but in 1975 only 8 of 346 registered lobbyists represented organizations that might have addressed poverty-related issues in conversation with legislators.[32]

Recently formed and with few powerful friends in the legislature, the CCA had only marginal success during the 1975 summer special legislative session. Legislators *did* support an increase in the fiscal year 1976 appropriation that would keep AFDC payments at their present levels. But, as Pauley told supporters, "the terrible proviso"—the $32 ceiling on average monthly grants—was retained.[33] As a result, expected increases in the AFDC rolls made it likely that AFDC payments would have to be cut again in order to keep the payment average below $32. The CCA left the summer session convinced of two things: it must make members of the Georgia General Assembly aware of the effects of the $32 AFDC ceiling, and it must educate the media and the public about the myths and realities of welfare. State leaders, in contrast, focused on reducing welfare error rates and costs.[34]

Before CCA could begin preparing for the January 1976 legislative session, a change in Department of Human Resources procedures alerted CCA members to the importance of attending not just to AFDC *policy* but also to AFDC *administration*. The state had been using an older, more complex formula to compute AFDC payments, a formula that relied on the calculation of individual need and increased the likelihood of mistakes. A proposed flat grant method of calculation was simpler and would reduce errors. But in making that change, the department would create more challenges for AFDC recipients: thousands of clients would be dropped from the welfare rolls. CCA and its allies quickly mobilized, in this case not to influence the legislation, but to modify administrative procedures that negatively affected Georgia's poor.[35]

CCA deployed fiscal, moral, and emotional appeals to persuade the board of directors for the Department of Human Resources not to implement changes that would affect so many families receiving AFDC. As Pauley pointed out in an August 20, 1975, letter, if Georgia switched to the flat grant, six thousand families would be dropped from AFDC and consequently would also lose Medicaid, most poor families' only form of medical insurance. Financially, the flat grant did not make sense, Pauley insisted, perhaps thinking that a fiscal argument would resonate with board members. "The family will go without medical care or the burden will fall back on the charity hospital with the local tax payer paying 100% of the bill instead of the 33% he now pays," Pauley asserted.[36] At the board's August meeting, welfare rights activist Ethel Mae Mathews told the board that the action was an "injustice to all of us who are poor and have to live on a fixed income." Echoing Phyllis Randolph's earlier allusion, Mathews asserted that it would be "a long, hot summer" if the reduction was implemented. Emmaus House's Father Austin Ford noted that cutting the smaller family grants would likely result in a higher average payment overall, perhaps again tipping it over the $32 cap. DHR board chair Jack Watson lamented, "We find ourselves in the desperately excruciating position of having to make choices among awful choices."[37] Ultimately, however, the board voted to switch to the flat grant. To the CCA and those it represented, the situation was distressing. AFDC payments would continue to fluctuate—likely downward—and many families would lose access to medical care, further burdening poor Georgians.[38]

The debate over the flat grant was an important lesson for antipoverty advocates. Going forward, the CCA needed to monitor not just lawmaking, but also administrative procedures, as those, too, clearly had significant effects on the group's constituents. What perhaps appeared to be small administrative issues were, in practice, substantial barriers. Significant improvements in the state's AFDC program were not possible without changes to bureaucratic processes. What's more, the CCA needed a stronger base and a more effective approach to influence Georgia's AFDC law and administration.

The Georgia Poverty Rights Organization (GPRO)

On October 11, 1975, CCA members, pastors, Black and white homemakers, social welfare agency heads, lawyers, and welfare recipients from across the state met at Emmaus House to learn more about poverty and welfare in Georgia and to formally organize to lobby at the Georgia General Assembly. Georgia Legal Services' Wayne Pressel explained how recent changes in AFDC had resulted in payment reductions and reduced rolls. Rick Bent of the Georgia Citizens Coalition on Hunger showed attendees how state revenue increased as a result of the food stamp program. At the business meeting that followed, American Civil Liberties Union attorney Gene Guerrero moved that the Georgia Poverty Rights Organization—the new name to replace the CCA—"become a statewide viable organization" and that a legislative package be drawn up.[39] The members intended to use "community organization, public information, and legislative action to obtain a decent standard of living, including medical care, for all Georgians."[40] Frances Pauley, who had retired from the Department of Health, Education, and Welfare (HEW) in 1973, was elected the volunteer director, which in practice meant that she served as executive administrator, office staff, and chief lobbyist. The GPRO operated with no paid staff.[41]

Attorney Dennis Goldstein identified tasks in preparation for the 1976 legislative session opening in January. The GPRO would compile an AFDC fact sheet for legislators. A committee would contact legislators individually just before the legislative session and then again during the session. Some GPRO members would arrange to speak at committee hearings. A statewide mailing list would be prepared, and people on the list would be asked to write their legislators concerning AFDC. At the same time, Goldstein advised, a task force should encourage Georgia's federal representatives, such as Congressman Andrew Young Jr to raise the ceiling on the AFDC matching funds from $32 to $35. It was an ambitious agenda for the three months leading up to Georgia's next General Assembly.[42]

The GPRO continued its preparations throughout the fall of 1975. At its November meeting, the group prioritized removing the $32 ceiling, raising AFDC grants to meet 100 percent of the standard of need, and ensuring that the standard of need reflected the cost of living in 1975. In a follow-up letter, the GPRO encouraged stakeholders to make appointments with their legislators and members of the appropriations committee, which handled the state's budget proposal. Delegations were advised to discuss among themselves how to best present arguments and to "practice answering questions that the men might ask."[43]

The scenarios provided by the GPRO were intended to help members educate legislators on the facts and realities of welfare in Georgia. For the question "the state is not collecting the taxes we collected last year, how can we increase the budget?" the GPRO suggested that members advise legislators to avoid cutting budget items related to basic human need. To the question "where can we get the money?" GPRO suggested that cuts be made to administration, or that raises be eliminated.[44] The GPRO also provided detailed facts that corrected common assertions about welfare abuse. To the statement "People are getting welfare who don't deserve it," the organization recommended pointing out that less than 1 percent of cases "are even suspected of fraud" and that the largest grant (which was for a family of seven or more) was $199, which the GPRO presumed the listener would judge as low. In this way, GPRO members attempted to dispel myths of welfare and encourage legislators to identify other methods of saving state money.[45]

But before GPRO could start lobbying legislators, they faced the AFDC cuts caused by the transition to the flat grant, the new method of computing AFDC grants. In early November 1975, nearly seven thousand families were dropped from the welfare rolls as Georgia transitioned away from the more complex AFDC formula. That fall and winter, AFDC families faced more cuts. Monthly checks that already failed to bring families out of poverty were further reduced and constantly in flux. It was difficult for families to keep up. And GPRO also struggled to stay on top of changes.[46]

The GPRO met regularly throughout the fall in preparation for the January 1976 General Assembly, so it is not entirely clear why the group had no representation at the November 19 board of directors meeting at which the DHR was considering another welfare payment cut for January 1976, a cut necessary to keep the average monthly welfare payment under $32. Perhaps the GPRO was not yet on the board mailing list, or perhaps the organization had not yet prioritized meeting regularly with the DHR board (which the GPRO would do from 1976 on). But this lack of representation left the GPRO, at the December board meeting, in the position of protesting an AFDC cut that had already been unanimously approved.

The December Board of Human Resources meeting was an exercise in frustration for the GPRO and other welfare advocates. Pauley appealed to the board to reconsider the November action that resulted in grant cuts. The board, director, and other DHR staff agreed that the $32 limit imposed hardship on poor people, but they also noted that raising or eliminating the $32 cap required legislative action. The DHR director had more bad news: as a result of the switch to the flat grant and the now impending January 1976 reduction, it was expected that $4.5 million of AFDC appropriations would be left unused. That is, the state's laws governing AFDC simultaneously diminished AFDC grants to the state's poor and left monies budgeted for AFDC unspent. Without legislative action to assign the unspent funds to AFDC, legislators and the governor could—and likely would—choose to spend those monies elsewhere. After these disappointments, GPRO members and their supporters rarely failed to attend the regularly scheduled DHR board meetings. The issue also reinforced the need for legislative change, which, as the GPRO knew, was unlikely to happen without legislative pressure.[47]

As had become the pattern, the Atlanta's welfare rights chapters greeted the forthcoming grant reductions and other news with public protest. On December 22, more than fifty Black women and children entered the capitol and demanded an audience with Governor Busbee. Chanting "Fed up! Fired up!" and "Busbee say cut-back, we say fight back," the group distributed GPRO-authored leaflets explaining the welfare grant reductions.[48] Later, after being denied entry to Busbee's office, the women continued their demonstration at the Fulton County welfare office.[49]

While the GPRO may have expressed dissatisfaction with board decisions and supported the public protests, the DHR director Jim Parham frequently pursued ends similar to those of the GPRO. Like the GPRO, the director sought ways to raise AFDC payments, and he hoped to jettison the $32 cap, which had proved to be an administrative burden. In November 1975 Parham complained about the structures that required frequent grant reductions. At a local Kiwanis Club luncheon, Parham called the $32 proviso "terrible" and suggested that it be eliminated.[50] He recommended that the state switch to the alternative method of calculating AFDC payments (the formula used to calculate Medicaid grants), even though the change would require a one-time payment of $17 million up front and on top of the existing AFDC budget. The advantage of adopting that formula, he explained, was that *all* state dollars spent on AFDC—not just those spent bringing the average payment to $32— would be matched by the federal government, two-to-one. Thus, at least on these specific matters, the GPRO could count on the highest-ranking DHR official to promote the GPRO's goals to the governor and to legislators, while the DHR could rely on an outside organization to lobby for policies in the best interest of the DHR and its clients.[51]

Despite significant threats, the increasingly regular cuts to welfare funding, and a need to attend to policy and bureaucratic procedures, the GPRO concluded 1975 on a hopeful note. It had formally organized and roughed out a plan to begin lobbying state politicians. It was working closely with direct action-oriented welfare rights organizations and had a statewide network willing to travel to the capital to pressure the political leadership. And at least in some areas, it experienced synergies with the DHR director. Though it was still a young organization that depended on volunteer labor, the GPRO was well positioned going into the 1976 Georgia General Assembly.

Eliminating "the Terrible Proviso"

On January 13, 1976, GPRO hosted welfare proponents from twenty-one towns across the state to lobby state legislators at the annual General Assembly. From temporary headquarters at Central Presbyterian Church, directly across the street from the capitol, members prepared to educate

FIGURE 17. Welfare rights activists march at Georgia Capitol during the annual General Assembly, 1976. Courtesy Boyd Lewis photographs, Kenan Research Center at the Atlanta History Center.

legislators and allies on a variety of issues. GPRO members planned to attend sessions of the House and Senate as well as Appropriations Committee meetings, meet with legislators and DHR director Parham, hand out leaflets, and picket. GPRO activists were reminded to tell their legislators that "we cannot stand another cut in AFDC grants," and to "ask your legislator why the general assembly talks about cost-of-living increases for other people and then cuts grants where it is most needed."[52] For the forty days of the General Assembly, GPRO members and Pauley worked nearly nonstop to respond quickly to budget proposals, amendments, disappointing votes, and legislative negotiations (see fig. 17).

Using printed materials and press releases, the GPRO provided legislators, staff, and advocates its take on Georgia's welfare spending and policies. For example, one flyer challenged rhetoric commonly deployed in welfare debates of the 1970s. "Does welfare violate American values?" the pamphlet asked. "No," was the response, "the concept of welfare stands in the greatest and proudest American tradition of helping others to help themselves."[53] Other pamphlets attempted to humanize welfare families and persuade through story. One such flyer pictured a child crouching on the ground, looking up at the camera. "The child in this picture is a welfare dependent," the text explained. Both parents were dead, and the child lived with the grandmother in a household of nine. Georgia estimated that the family needed $222 a month to live, but the state allowed a maximum grant of $199. "Could you live on these amounts?" the flyer asked the reader. "Would you ask a child to live on these amounts?"[54] In a January press release, the GPRO emphasized the "double effects" of the $32 proviso; besides limiting the benefits to "Georgia's poor children," the $32 limit resulted in surpluses of nearly $5 million in appropriations for AFDC, surpluses that could not be spent on the poor without legislative action.[55] Moreover, as they explained in letters to the Fulton County delegation, AFDC payments had not kept pace even as Georgia's per capita income had increased: Georgia had risen to thirty-third in the nation in per capita income, but the state ranked forty-sixth in average monthly AFDC grants. With these and other materials, GPRO hoped to arm sympathetic legislators, persuade ambivalent politicians, and soften the resolve of more entrenched leadership.[56]

Time, energy, and dealmaking were largely reserved for the battles over eliminating the $32 cap in the fiscal year 1977 budget.[57] As attention turned to the next year's budget, Parham launched what the *Atlanta Constitution* described as "an all-out push" to abandon the $32 limit in the fiscal year 1977 appropriations act.[58] In testimony to the joint Senate-House Appropriations Committee and in a sixteen-page report outlining the recent history of welfare funding, the DHR director carefully explained that the appropriations bill, at least as the draft stood in late January, would necessitate further cuts in monthly payments to AFDC families, perhaps beginning as early as August or September. At the same time, GPRO members lobbied committee members to eliminate the $32 payment ceiling and increase funding for AFDC. "We still may get the $32 proviso out of the new bill," Pauley told supporters in a midsession update.[59]

The ensuing legislative battle revived long-standing racial tensions and exposed party divisions over entitlements. Although electoral tides had been shifting since the 1960s, white conservative Democrats still dominated Georgia's state legislature in the mid-1970s, and generally speaking, few white southern Democrats openly favored means-based entitlement programs. They were not "entitlement liberals," and most were fiscal conservatives. Georgia Legislative Black Caucus members were more sympathetic to entitlement legislation, though they, too, were careful with state spending. Republicans were still few in number. The state Republican Party was marked by infighting in the mid-1970s, and some members even considered switching to the Democratic Party. But most were fiercely and vocally conservative. Given Republicans' staunch opposition to means-tested entitlements, their votes on welfare-related issues often aligned with those of traditional southern Democrats.[60]

While the Georgia House and Senate were both fairly described as conservative, the House reflected a more traditional southern Democratic outlook and mode of political operation, and thus it presented the most significant threat to the GPRO's goals. Even so, House Speaker Tom Murphy's conservative bent and his power to shape Georgia legislation did not mean that the GPRO's proposals had no chance of fair consideration in the Georgia General Assembly—but *anti*-AFDC proposals would likely surface. Thus, the GPRO and its allies had to devote time not just to trying to remove the $32 ceiling but also to fending off further attacks on welfare and the poor. The final days of the 1976 legislative session illustrate the range of measures Georgia conservatives took to stifle AFDC expansion and how many Georgians still associated African Americans with welfare.

As the joint House-Senate Appropriations Committee considered the fiscal year 1977 budget, Republican Robert Culp "Bob" Beckham of Augusta filed House Bill 1186, a proposal to require that Georgia AFDC recipients carry welfare identification cards and pick up welfare checks monthly, in person. Beckham contended that the proposal would prevent the "theft" of an average of five hundred AFDC checks each year, and Democrat Robert Howard of Marietta, expressing his support, asserted, "The American people are fed up with rip-offs."[61] More than that, Beckham argued, the proposal would "reverse the trend toward a welfare society," as the *Atlanta Daily World* phrased it, presumably by curtailing enrollment in AFDC. After a two-hour debate, the bill cleared the House by a vote of 126 to 28.[62]

Black Caucus members were outraged. Representative Douglas C. Dean, a Democrat from Atlanta, called a press conference on behalf of the caucus and declared the Beckham bill "the most racist piece of legislation to pass this body since I've been in the General Assembly." SCLC field worker and Georgia senator Hosea L. Williams labeled the bill "dehumanizing" and encouraged Georgians to "come to the Capitol by the thousands and let these people know how they feel about this bill!" Others pointed out the challenges the requirements would present for recipients. Benson Ham, a Democrat from Forsyth and the only white representative to speak publicly against the proposal, contended that people drawing AFDC checks did not have cars and could not afford the taxi fare necessary to pick up checks. Ham urged House leaders not to act too hastily. DHR head Parham predicted that having clients pick up checks monthly would be a "logistical nightmare." The response was so heated that the following day, the House voted to reconsider the bill.[63]

The next week, Beckham and Randy Karrh, a Democrat from Swainsboro, proposed amendments to the bill requiring that clients show themselves quarterly rather than monthly; and while some members of the legislature fought the compromise on larger principles, others undermined the proposal by focusing on the bureaucratic details. Parham stuck to his original assessment, calling the proposal an "administrative nightmare." Black Caucus members used a variety of tactics to defeat or at least delay the bill. In one emotional appeal, Black Caucus member David E. Lucas chastised his fellow representatives. "Poor people have no lobbyists! All 180 members of this House represent poor people." He noted that his colleagues had more sympathy for the poor people of Bangladesh than those "back home."[64] Bobby Lee Hill and John D. White proposed an amendment that would require doctors and dentists to apply in person for their Medicaid reimbursement checks. Anti-welfare sentiment ran high, though, and Republican Walter Davis insisted that he had "rather see 320,000 children starve to death than see one undeserving person receive a penny of welfare."[65] Ultimately, the House passed the bill requiring quarterly visits to the local welfare offices, 124 to 39.[66]

In the House-Senate conference committee, though, neither side would compromise, and the Beckham bill was dead. "Only a handful of lawmakers fought the philosophy of the bill," the *Atlanta Journal* reported, "but many objected to the mechanics, which were seen as expensive, and/or demeaning, to the poor."[67] In a 1988 oral history, Georgia senator Virginia Shapard recounted that Beckham was outraged that the bill had stalled. "He stormed out," she recalled.[68]

The Beckham bill and the associated debate made clear that conservative Democrats and Republicans would continue to deploy rhetoric associating welfare mothers with criminality and fraud and to propose legislation to curtail state investment in AFDC and other means-tested programs. In contrast, the Georgia Legislative Black Caucus, though small in membership, could and would point out the racial implications of the anti-welfare agenda, thus keeping white southern racism in the national media's eye. But Beckham's bill was out of the way, at least for 1976, and the GPRO and its allies could turn their attention back to the fiscal year 1977 appropriation bill.

The Department of Human Resources and the Georgia Poverty Rights Organization continued to work toward the elimination of the $32 cap in the fiscal year 1977 appropriation bill. Senators were unwilling to aban-

FIGURE 18. Welfare rights activists face off with Governor George Busbee over AFDC, c. 1976. Courtesy Boyd Lewis photographs, Kenan Research Center at the Atlanta History Center.

don the $32 cap outright, however (after all, responsibility for any spending above that level fell directly to the state). Instead, they proposed easing the average welfare allocation to $33. That suggested bump, along with disagreements on pay raises for state employees and contributions to health programs, guaranteed a vigorous debate in the joint conference committee.[69]

In the last week of February, as the House-Senate conference committee set about reconciling the two chambers' state budgets, Senate majority leader John R. Riley, a Democrat from Savannah and member of the joint committee, told the *Atlanta Constitution* that "the fiercest fighting would be over the ceiling on welfare payments," and indeed it was.[70] In committee discussion, Senate members defended their proposed $33 ceiling, but House conferees Joe Frank Harris, Marcus Collins, and Clarence Vaughn proved intractable. Befitting his reputation, Busbee attempted to broker a compromise: the $32 cap was the last bottleneck in passing the fiscal year 1977 budget, and as the *Atlanta Constitution* explained, Busbee "made it clear he wanted to avoid the embarrassment of having welfare recipients march on the state Capitol in protest" (see fig. 18).[71] In a closed-door meeting, the governor recommended that the committee accept the Senate's suggested AFDC reduction of $900,000, and that the House accept language "that would allow money to be spent," which meant eliminating the $32 cap. As the governor pointed out in his notes, "There would be no increase in welfare checks to anyone," a stipulation that was viewed favorably by conservative Democrats and Republicans.[72] The conference committee accepted the proposal.[73]

Despite other last-minute attempts to stall the bill, ultimately it passed, and on March 15, 1976, the *Poor People's Newspaper* proclaimed "VICTORY!" The $32 proviso had been eliminated from the fiscal year 1977 appropriations bill. The GPRO, in coalition with activists, politicians, and bureaucrats, had its first victory. To be sure, AFDC remained a contentious issue in the Georgia General Assembly for years thereafter, but as the *Poor People's Newspaper* pointed out, "AFDC mothers can breathe a little easier."[74]

While antipoverty organizing had grown more robust in Atlanta throughout the late 1960s and early 1970s, direct action activists had been regularly put off by politicians and administrators who contended that current law, regulations, or appropriation restrictions prevented them from acting on activists' demands. Activists needed people, staff, or an organization to translate their demands and desires into legislation. Consequently, activists decided to dedicate significant time and effort to lobbying legislators and bureaucrats so that appropriate changes could be made to law and administrative regulations. The Georgia Poverty Rights Organization formed to fulfill that role. Founders intended GPRO to augment, not replace, disruptive tactics, and it served that purpose.

Atlanta's antipoverty activists were well positioned to do pro-welfare lobbying, in part because, as residents of Georgia's capital, they had ready access to the state's annual forty-day General Assembly. While activists from other Georgia cities and towns participated in the assembly, they could not stay long and could not respond quickly to changes in bills, upended meeting schedules, and the like. Atlanta's activists could also relatively easily visit state offices and attend regular meetings of state boards, including the board of the Department of Health and Human Services, which governed significant elements of AFDC. GPRO learned quickly to take advantage of that proximity, and GPRO and welfare rights organization representatives would regularly attend and participate in meetings. This proximity paid dividends. GPRO and welfare rights organization members were a persistent presence at Board of Human Resources meetings and the General Assembly, which meant legislators and board members were forced to reckon with how policy and law affected poor Atlantans and poor Georgians in a way they had not heard five or ten years prior.

GPRO launched in coalition with other liberal organizations and partnered with groups that adopted complementary tactics, allowing these groups to shape arguments to their audience and apply pressure in multiple venues. Welfare client-activists disrupted meetings and the halls of government, which potentially embarrassed image-conscious state leaders such as Governor George Busbee. Black Caucus members ensured that activists were alerted to potentially damaging welfare legislation and helped stall such initiatives in the General Assembly. Emmaus House provided resources and supplemented protests and pickets with sympathetic figures such as Tammie Scruggs, alerting citizens to the real impact of anti-welfare initiatives and implying that anti-welfare forces were anti-children. It took a barrage to eliminate the $32 ceiling.

The elimination of the $32 cap on average monthly grants was a significant achievement for GPRO, as it would allow for future *increases* in AFDC grants, which meant grants might be brought up to the state's standard of need. Additionally, as the first major battle for GPRO, it signaled to antipoverty activists that legislation could successfully be changed. For the next decade-plus, the GPRO would build on this foundation and take on other significant welfare battles.[75]

CONCLUSION

By the late 1970s, Atlanta could well claim the Sunbelt city moniker. It was the urban hub and transportation nexus in a growing metropolitan area. It had a robust tourist and convention industry and sizeable service sector. It was strong in finance, insurance, and real estate, and home to state government and regional federal offices. It was the capital of a low-regulation state with a business-friendly tax structure. It claimed racial liberalism. It was warm and boasted southern hospitality.[1]

In the post–World War II era, pursuing a Sunbelt vision of urban development may have, at first glance, seemed a fruitful approach for advancing the well-being of all or most Atlantans. But poor and near-poor Atlantans and other antipoverty activists made clear that they had their own ideas about what made a city great and what needed to be improved. From 1946 to 1976, poor Atlantans and their allies insisted that leaders address poor residents' most salient concerns.

The origins of Atlanta's antipoverty movement can be found in aging Atlanta neighborhoods, where migrants—new and old arrivals—had settled and scraped by, and where city officials envisioned new civic centers and stadiums or revitalized neighborhoods that would house a Sunbelt workforce. In the 1940s and 1950s, residents of those areas used their growing voting power, civic councils, new allies such as SNCC, and federal regulations attached to urban development programs to insist on citizen participation in decisions that affected their lives. In South Atlanta, residents organized to demand neighborhood improvements and picketed for more consistent services. In the early 1960s, in the city's northwest, Vine City organizations worked with SNCC's Atlanta Project and community organizers to pressure exploitative landlords, demand better infrastructure, and build recreational spaces for area children. In the city's northeast, residents and pastors of Buttermilk Bottom and nearby areas targeted by urban renewal drew on federal mandates for citizen participation and insisted on greater involvement in those processes. Thus, well before federal leaders articulated a War on Poverty, poor individuals and families were organizing to insist that city officials invest in poor people's lives and neighborhoods too.

Atlanta's city leaders, too, were thinking about poverty in the early 1960s, but they had their own take on the problem, and their own approach. Atlanta's white political and economic elite were committed to easing poverty in that they were interested in improving the quality of the city's workforce and relieving social problems. That would directly benefit leaders' goals to become a national, and later an international, city. Toward that end, to improve human capital, business leaders used the Community Council of the Atlanta Area to experiment with a new social service delivery schema, neighborhood service centers. In this way, antipoverty work in Atlanta in the 1960s and 1970s operated in relationship to Sunbelt city-building efforts.

Atlanta's poor would deploy leaders' desires for urban status to their own ends. Activists contrasted leaders' new booster initiatives to the lack of services and infrastructure in their neighborhoods. The city talked a good game about a War on Poverty, Vine City residents, EOA neighborhood aides, and the city's sanitation workers pointed out, but the city seemed less willing to back up those promises with livable wages, substantive benefits, adequate urban infrastructure, building code enforcement, and regular and consistent city services. Frustrated from years of neglect, welfare mothers and garbage workers, children wanting playgrounds, and residents seeking streetlights marched, picketed, chanted, blocked streets, slept in program offices, marched through department stores, and put Atlanta's poverty on display, to the city and state's chagrin. By the late 1960s, then, poor and near-poor residents and various allies were regularly revealing the underbelly of "the world's next great city."

Initially, from 1946 to 1964, activism around poverty was episodic and geographically limited, but from 1964 on, antipoverty organizing became more robust in that more groups and individuals fighting poverty and related issues surfaced and interacted. Phrased another way, Atlanta's antipoverty apparatus—its constellation of people and entities—grew and became more complex over that period. From 1964 on, the apparatus included poor people who participated in antipoverty activities and their primary organizing venue (e.g., Vine City Council, TUFF, welfare rights), allies such as neighborhood-based community organizers (e.g., SNCC's Atlanta Project), organizations that provided support for people and groups seeking social change (e.g., Emmaus House), civil rights and public interest attorneys (e.g., Howard Moore, ALAS), organized labor (particularly public sector workers), some civil rights organizations (e.g., SCLC), and public interest agencies and lobbying organizations (e.g., GPRO). This apparatus grew and became more resilient in part because awareness and understanding of poverty and inequality grew over the period, and people were committing hours, months, years, or lives to promoting civil and economic rights. That desire to create change in the area of poverty and inequality can also be seen, to some degree, in the actions of DHR bureaucrats who installed food programs across Georgia or committed to better communicating social welfare resources to Atlanta's poor families. And it can be seen in the periodic work of suburban housewives and other congregants who, for example, delivered commodities to poor families. While these participants did not engage in dramatic actions, it is no exaggeration to say that the activities they pursued benefited countless poor Atlantans and poor Georgians.

Indeed, Atlanta's antipoverty movement attacked poverty and its conditions on multiple fronts and using a variety of tactics. Civic councils still used traditional forms of entreaty—letter writing and petitions—but would quickly shift to pickets and other public disruption when necessary. ALAS and other public interest attorneys used mediation and legal means to change social welfare and build tenant law. Welfare client-activists used disruption—including sleep-ins and lay-ins—to draw attention to welfare cuts and poverty-level entitlements. Tenants in public and private housing used rent strikes to confront landlord negligence and high rent. The Poverty Rights Office provided support and filled gaps, translating complex regulations for clients, assisting with applications, connecting clients to resources, and educating residents about entitlements and rights. Emmaus House facilitated a growing activist network by providing space and resources to welfare and tenant rights activists and creating tools such as the *Poor People's Newspaper*. City sanitation workers disrupted city services and public spaces to alert residents of poverty-level wages and force city action. GPRO lobbied legislators as well as public agency board members and bureaucrats to influence social welfare legislation and administrative practices. In this way, poverty was confronted in different domains and by various means, and activists gradually chipped away at harmful policies and administrative practices.

Atlanta's poor and near poor were not the only groups to benefit from antipoverty work. Atlanta's Black sociopolitical elite and civil rights establishment had long sought a greater voice in decision-making and programs affecting Black lives, and it followed that Black leaders and local civil rights leaders demanded substantial Black involvement in the staffing and upper administration of Economic Opportunity Atlanta and related endeavors. EOA did hire African Americans in large number as neighborhood aides, clerks, midlevel program managers, and center directors, and some Black professionals were appointed to the EOA Board of Directors. But for the first few years, white administrators resisted appointing African Americans to top administrative positions and initially opposed expanding Black presence on the EOA board. Persistence paid off, though. Black membership on the EOA board was eventually increased. When the city received Model Cities funding, Atlanta's leaders tapped an African American professional to lead the agency. In this way, components of the city's social service infrastructure that targeted the city's lowest income groups, including the War on Poverty and Model Cities programs, were used by groups *beyond the poor* for socioeconomic advancement.

The civil rights establishment's broader agenda meant that while Atlanta's antipoverty movement unfolded in relationship with the larger Black freedom movement, antipoverty activists and civil rights leaders were periodically in conflict. The Atlanta Summit Leadership Conference sought to speak for the interests of the city's African American community, including poor people, but poor Atlantans came to think that the Summit did not really understand poor people's concerns. Consequently, poor activists broke from the Summit and formed the Atlanta Grass Roots Crusade to specifically represent the issues of poor people. This was not a hard break, though; antipoverty activists would continue to leverage the power of civil rights organizations, including SNCC until 1967 and the SCLC, especially after it began developing economic initiatives targeting poverty and economic justice *and* devoting time to Atlanta-specific actions. Thus, in Atlanta, the civil rights movement's relationship with local antipoverty organizing was inconsistent, and some civil rights organizations such as the Summit tended to foreground antipoverty work only when it aligned well with its existing policy priorities.

Over the period covered here, 1946 to 1976, antipoverty activists and their allies scored many wins. In part this was because, especially in early stages of organizing, they sought discreet, achievable goals. Indeed, many initially had fairly reasonable requests: streetlights, a playground, regular trash pickup, a working toilet. Neighborhood organizing prompted city service improvements and the building and equipping of recreational spaces for children. Public housing tenants achieved more explicitly stated rights, including grievance procedures, and could identify several community improvements that resulted from their actions. Welfare client-activists gained access to budgets, rules, and regulations. Slum conditions in general were beginning to diminish. The $32 ceiling on average AFDC grants was eliminated, which opened the door to grant increases. Sanitation and other city workers achieved better wages and benefits. Certainly, not every program or effort was a success. But wins could be counted, and they contributed to Atlantans' well-being, stabilized many, and improved people's opportunities and life chances.

There were losses, and some were significant. In response to the 1970s sanitation strike, for example, Mayor Sam Massell weakened public sector unions by eliminating dues checkoff. In a few years, checkoff was restored, but the action undermined labor organizing and revealed city leaders' desire to seriously damage public sector organizing. As historian Joseph McCartin has shown, later political administrations, including those initially friendly to labor, would escalate the attack and embrace worker replacement strategies to deal with public sector strikes.[2] Thus, in Atlanta, as was the case across the Sunbelt, union busting and antiunion policy remained a critical regional feature. Indeed, a 1977–78 survey of southern leaders indicated that cheap labor, which was in part a product of antiunion practices and policy, continued to be "a major attraction for industry."[3] Historian James Cobb observed that by the end of the 1970s, "antiunionism had supplanted racism as the South's most respectable prejudice."[4] Boosters' commitment to antiunionism came at a cost to workers. Economists Bob Hall and Bob Williams have shown that as the U.S. South industrialized in the late twentieth century, capital gained a disproportionate share of economic improvements. To be sure, workers' salaries rose over *Poor Atlanta's* period of study, but wages did not match the value added by workers' labor. In Georgia, from 1963 to 1976, value added by workers rose 173 percent, but wages rose only 120 percent over that period. Not surprisingly, then, wealth inequality remained relatively static, even as the South benefited from Sunbelt growth.[5]

What became clearer to antipoverty activists, as antipoverty organizing unfolded over the 1960s and into the more economically unstable 1970s, was that Sunbelt growth did not benefit all Atlantans equally, poverty remained tenacious, and the U.S. economy would not continually expand (and, indeed, could still fluctuate significantly). Larger, more systemic changes to the socioeconomic system were required. Certainly, antipoverty organizing resulted in some wins. But for Atlantans, as for many Americans, any number of events—shifts in family makeup (divorce, a new child), high medical bills, a layoff—could quickly throw a family into poverty.[6] To many, a more comprehensive social safety net was necessary, one that provided adequate child and family care and that ensured regular employment, basic necessities, and shelter. Such systemic change would eliminate families' sense that they were simply living from crisis to crisis.

From 1964 on, antipoverty activists continued to devote themselves to immediate bread-and-butter concerns, but they also committed time and effort to pursuing broad-based policy change, change that potentially would strengthen and close the gaps in the nation's social safety net. In part this was done through participation in larger national networks. Almost immediately upon forming a local welfare rights organization, for example, Atlanta activists became involved in NWRO campaigns and attended national meetings. Activists brought back news and campaign ideas, updating other members at their regular chapter gatherings. But organizations such as the NWRO also argued for more ambitious, transformative goals, such as a guaranteed income. At the same time, Atlantans contributed to the SCLC's national Poor People's Campaign, where activists argued for, besides a guaranteed income, universal childcare, a living wage, and tax reform. In this way, Atlanta activists signaled and enacted their commitment not just to incremental change, but to more long-lasting economic transformation.[7]

Designing and implementing antipoverty policy change at the national level would only grow more challenging through the late 1970s. The national political culture continued to shift. Voters grew more conservative. They distrusted government. They felt many poor were undeserving of government aid. And they were tired of protest, which they increasingly associated with urban unrest. Such sentiments made it harder to repair, much less expand, the U.S. social safety net. Furthermore, political leadership was unreliable. As governor of Georgia (1971–75), Jimmy Carter regularly expressed concern for the plight of the state's poor (even arguing that southern wages should have parity with wages elsewhere) and appointed Jim Parham, a social-work-trained liberal bureaucrat to run the state's Department of Human Resources, the entity responsible for the bulk of Georgia's entitlement programs. But as president, Carter resisted extensive spending and had limited success delivering promised welfare reforms.[8] What many antipoverty activists referred to as "the war on the poor" would accelerate, and growing dissatisfaction with spending on the liberal antipoverty agenda would lead to, particularly after the election of President Ronald Reagan in 1980, "the war on the War on Poverty," an attempt to dismantle the War on Poverty infrastructure and impose work requirements for social aid.[9]

A war on the poor could be observed within Atlanta, too, even as antipoverty activism continued. As Atlanta prepared for the 1996 Olympics (an event former chamber of commerce head Sam A. Williams referred to as "the biggest economic development tool Georgia and Atlanta have ever had"), local leaders arranged Project Homeward Bound, a plan to clear the streets of homeless folks by providing one-way bus tickets out of Atlanta. Poverty would not be ameliorated or mitigated; the poor would be shunted from view. At the same time, more severe anti-panhandling laws were considered.[10] Homes of low-income and poor families were again threatened by stadium building.[11] In addition, public housing units were redeveloped for athlete housing, eliminating some five thousand housing units.[12] At the same time, in an effort to remake public housing, the Atlanta Housing Authority razed thousands of public housing units in a nationally publicized, Department of Housing and Urban Development HOPE VI–funded effort to redesign social housing, an initiative that did not effectively rehouse all displaced individuals and families.[13] Sunbelt growth and development came at a cost, and that cost was often borne by the city's poor.

Nationally, a more ambitious economic transformation, or at least a more complete and substantive safety net to stabilize poor and near poor families, has remained elusive. While poverty rates have dropped since the period described here (the poverty rate was 10.5 percent in 2019), poverty remains pervasive, and, indeed, surprising for such a wealthy nation.[14] We still rediscover poverty on a regular basis.[15] "Still Poor: 25 Million," Woodrow Ginsburg declared in the *New York Times* in 1980, "despite the economy's expansion."[16] "Poverty in America is much more widespread than has been previously acknowledged," the *New York Times* wrote in 2007, nearly thirty years later.[17] The United States was four years into an economic expansion, the paper noted, and "the percentage of Americans defined as poor was higher than at the bottom of the last recession in late 2001."[18] The nation surely had the resources to end "the destitution and deprivation" that poverty imposed, Ginsburg observed in his 1980 piece.[19] But as John Kenneth Galbraith noted in an introduction to a 1984 edition of his 1958 classic *The Affluent Society*, as Americans had become more affluent, it became easier to ignore and rationalize the plight of the poor.[20] That is, it was easier to blame the poor for being poor.

New organizing initiatives offer promise. In 2017, the Reverend William Barber, a North Carolina pastor, launched the Poor People's Campaign: A National Call for Moral Revival (PPC: NCMR) to unite poor people and their allies around shared economic injustice.[21] At the time, Barber and others were compelled by growing social and economic divisions in the United States, divisions they felt political leaders, particularly Donald Trump, were exacerbating. In response, Barber and like-minded activists spearheaded Moral Mondays, consistent acts of civil disobedience that disrupted the North Carolina legislature and its "attempt to crucify the poor, the sick, the children, the unemployed."[22] Moral Mondays grew in North Carolina and spread to other locales, signaling a widespread and growing frustration with attacks on hard-working Americans and impatience with a government that has left low-income individuals and families in constant risk of poverty.[23] In the lead-up to the 2020 election, the PPC: NCMR led a nonpartisan voter outreach effort intended to "unleash the power" of the millions of poor and low-income Americans.

To many, a war on the poor had resurfaced. Candidate and then president Donald Trump blamed the poor for their own poverty while promising to revive the economy for the middle class. Trump built his populist movement in part by making promises to Americans hurt by major economic shifts. He pledged to ease Americans' tax burden, revive manufacturing, and protect U.S. markets, which many middle-income and working-class Americans hoped would translate into jobs, job stability, and better pay and benefits. "Trumponomics"—lower taxes, reduced regulations, and enhanced trade deals—would purportedly help all Americans.[24]

Trump's policies would not help the poor, though, and many felt that Trump directly attacked and undermined low-income families. Despite the popularity of many social insurance programs, beginning in 2018, Donald Trump took aim at entitlement programs. He declared victory over poverty, insisted that the Great Society and subsequent safety nets did not work, and demanded that public assistance programs further increase work requirements.[25] Poverty was the fault of those suffering poverty, Trump implied, not low wages or loss of income, lack of jobs, insufficient entitlements, or out-of-reach medical costs.[26] In 2019, the president's proposed changes to the food stamp program would have stripped vital assistance from about one million *working* poor Americans, many of whom lived in areas with high unemployment. In another instance, the administration proposed to adjust the federal poverty line, a move that would have cut millions from entitlement programs that provided food, medical care, and energy assistance.[27] What made these moves particularly galling was that at the same time as he pushed social spending cuts, the president proposed substantial tax relief to the richest Americans.[28]

In fact, economic inequality grew over Trump's four-year presidency. America's economic middle continued to suffer, and inequality grew faster than in previous decades: the gap between highest and lowest income brackets increased by nearly 9 percent a year.[29]

The outbreak of COVID-19 in 2019 and the U.S. response to the pandemic also had significant impact on poverty. From the beginning of the pandemic to spring 2021, some 74 million Americans lost work, and the national poverty rate increased nearly 2 percent in 2020 to 11.4 percent. Significantly, that poverty rate figure counted those individuals and families who benefited from federal relief, which means that without the federal stimulus package, far more would have suffered. The lowest-income Americans were hit hardest: workers earning less than $34,000 a year accounted for 53 percent of jobs lost. Further parsing of income statistics shows that part-time workers and those employed seasonally bore the brunt of the economic crisis. The level of suffering has been and continues to be staggering: 24 million Americans have reported experiencing hunger, and 6 million have reported fear of being foreclosed on or evicted. Among the lowest-income Americans, 47 percent reported being behind on housing payments. Twenty percent of American children now live in poverty. As analysts have pointed out, the pandemic has baldly exposed the flaws of the U.S. social safety net but also the benefits that such economic safety measures can provide.[30]

Many Atlantans see the most promise in Democratic and progressive platforms, and the political tide has recently been shifting left. In 2020, Georgia voted Democratic—"turned blue"—in the presidential and senate elections. That transition was caused in part by metro Atlanta's changing demographics but also by Democratic operative Stacey Abrams's commitment to getting more African Americans to the polls and the PPC: NCMR's efforts to reach poor and low-income voters.[31] The 2020 elections experienced the highest voter turnout among poor and low-income voters in U.S. election history: 35 percent of all voters were low income, and 37.84 percent of Georgia voters were low income. The PPC: NCMR attributes that uptick in battleground states such as Georgia to its voter outreach efforts, which they assert "helped bring over 39,000 non-voters from 2016 into the 2020 elections." Poor and low-income voters are "the sleeping giant," the PPC: NCMR contends, "yet to be pulled into political action." That drive specifically engaged issues that matter to low-income individuals and families, including a living wage, health care, strengthened antipoverty programs, and systemic racism.[32]

As a candidate for president, Democrat Joe Biden promised more liberal economic measures—an American Rescue Plan—including an improved child tax credit that many point to as a form of guaranteed income.[33] The transition in the Senate—as of 2021 it is 50 percent Republican and 48 percent Democratic, with two independents who caucus with the Democrats and with the Democratic vice president serving as tiebreaker—means that progressive antipoverty measures have a chance of passing, measures that might at some point combine into a comprehensive safety net encompassing housing, health care, employment, and income.[34] It will be a long haul, as several interest groups benefit from the economic infrastructure as it stands and will continue to oppose any significant change. As of fall 2021, the administration had to cut significant programs from the original proposal, such as paid family leave and free community college. Likely, substantive change will require a coalition of interest groups and allies that pursue a range of solutions—organizations and people that address immediate crises and others that pursue systemic change. Longtime welfare rights leader Ethel Mae Mathews would likely remind Atlantans today as she did in 1972, "We have worked hard but we still have much more to do."[35]

NOTES

Introduction

1. "Atlanta," *Forum Magazine*, April 1969, 42, Ivan Allen Digital Archive (IADA), folder 15, box 4, http://allenarchive.iac.gatech.edu/items/show/1802. Also see *Atlanta Journal and Constitution*, 27 January 1963.

2. *New York Times*, 16 November 1964 and 19 June 1961, respectively. On the Forward Atlanta approach, see *Atlanta Constitution*, 19 June 1961; *Atlanta Journal and Constitution*, 27 January 1963.

3. *Time*, 17 August 1962, 20.

4. *Atlanta Constitution*, 19 June 1961.

5. *New York Times*, 8 July 1962.

6. *Atlanta Constitution*, 1 July 1968.

7. *Time*, 17 August 1962, 20. As *Time* noted in a separate story, the local *Atlanta Constitution* "was one of the first and is still one of the few Southern papers to accept the 1954 U.S. Supreme Court decision on public school integration." *Time*, 19 June 1964, 36. Later that year the *New York Times* wrote that "Atlanta today is the most liberal city in the Southeast in its attitude toward the Negro" (16 November 1964).

8. The *Sunbelt* moniker was popularized in Phillips, *Emerging Republican Majority*. Carl Abbott provides a brief overview of urbanization trends in Sunbelt development in Carl Abbott, "Urbanizing the Sunbelt," *OAH Magazine of History*, 1 October 2003, 11–16. In the 1990s, a number of scholars challenged the usefulness of the Sunbelt concept. See, for example, Mohl, *Searching for the Sunbelt*. The usefulness of the "Sunbelt" term and the significance of the region continues to be interrogated. See, for example, Nickerson and Dochuk, *Sunbelt Rising*.

9. On Atlanta's city-building and "hype" see, in particular, Frederick Allen, *Atlanta Rising*; Rutheiser, *Imagineering Atlanta*; Stone, *Regime Politics*; Stone, *Economic Growth and Neighborhood Discontent*.

10. Other scholars have touched on parts of Atlanta's antipoverty story, usually through examination of the city's Black freedom and Black power movements. See, for example, Harmon, *Beneath the Image*, 200–19; Carson, *In Struggle*; Brown-Nagin, *Courage to Dissent*, chap. 9; Tom Davies, *Mainstreaming Black Power*, 158–67; Grady-Willis, *Challenging U.S. Apartheid*, 83–113. On Atlanta's welfare rights movement, see Horowitz, "It Came from Somewhere." And on tenant organizing in Atlanta public housing as a political opportunity structure for Black residents, see Rodriguez, *Diverging Space for Deviants*.

11. "Vine City Council," press release, February 18, 1966, folder 13, box 1, Student Nonviolent Coordinating Committee Papers, Vine City Project (Atlanta), Wisconsin Historical Society.

12. On the Forward Atlanta approach, see *Atlanta Constitution*, 19 June 1961; *Atlanta Journal and Constitution*, 27 January 1963. In 1972, the Atlanta Chamber of Commerce launched its new Forward Atlanta booster campaign with the theme "Atlanta. The world's next great city." *Atlanta Constitution*, 1 October 1972.

13. Case studies of welfare rights organizing include Orleck, *Storming Caesars Palace*; Kornbluh, *Battle for Welfare Rights*. Studies of tenant organizing in public housing include Williams, *Politics of Public Housing*; Baranski, *Housing the City*. Works examining how War on Poverty programs unfolded in different cities and states include Clayson, *Freedom Is Not Enough*; Phelps, *People's War on Poverty*; Germany, *New Orleans after the Promises*; Ashmore, *Carry It On*; Korstad and Leloudis, *To Right These Wrongs*; Orleck and Hazirjian, *War on Poverty*.

14. Piven and Cloward, *Poor People's Movements*. Later historical assessments of welfare organizing demonstrate that, in practice, a number of techniques were used to effect change. See, for example, Orleck, *Storming Caesars Palace*.

15. A number of authors position welfare rights and community action organizing as part of a larger quest for citizenship rights, including Nadasen, *Welfare Warriors*; Phelps, *People's War on Poverty*; Clayson, *Freedom Is Not Enough*; Kornbluh, *Battle for Welfare Rights*; Williams, *Politics of Public Housing*.

16. Rhonda Williams in particular makes the case that tenant activists saw welfare rights, tenant rights, and other forms of antipoverty work and citizenship as interconnected. See Williams, *Politics of Public Housing*. Jessica Wilkerson makes similar points about movement overlap in Wilkerson, *To Live Here*.

17. On coalition building and the interconnectedness of movements, see K'Meyer, *Civil Rights in the Gateway*; Ashmore, *Carry It On*; Jessica Wilkerson, *To Live Here*; Pope, "Living in the Struggle."

18. In 2005 Jacquelyn Dowd Hall argued for scholars to consider a "long civil rights movement." Hall contends that the long movement began in the 1930s (i.e., prior to *Brown* v. *Board of Education*) and continued as a "movement of movements" after the passage of federal civil rights legislation in 1964 and 1965 and King's assassination in 1968. As Hall explains, the narrower and traditional story of the civil rights movement emphasized the southern struggle and the leadership of King, highlighted noneconomic objectives, and implied a movement decline. In recent years, other scholars have reperiodized the civil rights movement and documented how freedom actions played out beyond the South. Hall, "Long Civil Rights Movement," 1233–63. Sundiata Keita Cha-Jua and Clarence Lang challenged Hall's argument, noting that the "long movement" thesis "collapses periodization schemas, erases conceptual differences between waves of the [Black Liberation Movement,] and blurs regional distinctions in the African American experience" (265). Cha-Jua and Lang, "'Long Movement' as Vampire," 265–88. In subsequent years, scholars have expanded the geographic and temporal boundaries of the Black freedom struggle while continuing to demonstrate the heterogeneity and discontinuity of actions across time and space. Important works

in this vein include Sugrue, *Sweet Land of Liberty*; Lieberman and Lang, *Anticommunism*; Kruse and Tuck, *Fog of War*.

19. Historians have recently highlighted the economic dimensions of the civil rights movement. Gavin Wright, for example, outlines significant gains in income and occupational status that resulted from the civil rights movement in Wright, *Sharing the Prize*. Sylvie Laurent argues that King's promotion of economic justice continued a long line of Black radicalism. See Laurent, *King and the Other America*. Other scholars have shown that the anticommunist movement prompted Black freedom activists to retreat from the pursuit of economic equality. See Lieberman and Lang, *Anticommunism*. On King and SCLC's Poor People's Campaign, see McKnight, *Last Crusade*; Mantler, *Power to the Poor*.

20. On the relationship of civil rights organizing to labor organizing in particular, see Korstad, *Civil Rights Unionism*.

21. The local nature of Black freedom struggles is explicitly discussed in the introduction to Theoharis and Woodard, *Groundwork*. Variation among local Black freedom movements in Georgia is examined in Tuck, *Beyond Atlanta*. Other authors have revealed that antipoverty organizing, too, was profoundly local. Karen Hawkins, for example, has exposed the significant influence of "moderates" in implementing antipoverty policy in eastern North Carolina. Hawkins, *Everybody's Problem*. Los Angeles's War on Poverty was shaped by different neighborhoods' and ethnic groups' desires and goals. See Bauman, *Race and the War*. The significance of local circumstances and the variety of local outcomes of War on Poverty initiatives are also explored in Orleck and Hazirjian, *War on Poverty*.

22. Other authors have identified antipoverty work taking place prior to the 1960s, including, for example, Williams, *Politics of Public Housing*.

23. A number of works specifically seek to recover the voices and points of view of poor activists who pursued economic and social justice. See, for example, Orleck, *Storming Caesars Palace*; Nadasen, *Welfare Warriors*; Williams, *Politics of Public Housing*. Karen Hawkins has recently revealed the important role played by (nonpoor) political moderates in shifting antipoverty policy. See Hawkins, *Everybody's Problem*.

24. In this way, *Poor Atlanta* builds on points Maurice Hobson makes about class dynamics within Atlanta's Black community historically. See Hobson, *Legend of the Black Mecca*.

25. On southern shifts from an agriculture-based, regional economy toward industrialization, see Wright, *Old South, New South*. On the crusade to attract industry to the region, which included highlighting the region's low-wage, nonunion labor force, see Cobb, *Selling of the South*.

26. On the New Deal in the South, see Biles, *South and the New Deal*; Sullivan, *Days of Hope*. See U.S. Census Bureau, table 17, Historical Poverty Tables, https://www.census.gov/data/tables/time-series/demo/income-poverty/historical-poverty-people.html.

27. U.S. Census Bureau, "Incidence of Poverty for Families, by Sex and Color of Head: 1959 to 1966," table C, *Current Population Reports*, series P-60, "The Extent of

Poverty in the United States, 1959 to 1966," https://www2.census.gov/library/publications/1968/demographics/p60-54.pdf.

28. Harrington, *Other America*, 1.

29. *Atlanta Constitution*, 5 August 1945; *Atlanta Constitution*, 29 September 1959.

30. State Library of Iowa, State Data Center Program, "Urban and Rural Population for the U.S. and All States: 1900–2000," https://www.iowadatacenter.org/datatables/UnitedStates/urusstpop19002000.pdf.

31. U.S. Census Bureau, 1960 Census of Population, *Characteristics of the Population*, table P-1. The number of poor was calculated based on data in table 1.

32. This disparity was experienced across the United States. In 1959, 18.1 percent of whites lived below poverty, and 55 percent of African Americans lived below poverty. See U.S. Census Bureau, Historical Poverty Tables, "Poverty Status of People by Family Relationship, Race, and Hispanic Origin: 1959 to 2018," table 2.

33. U.S. Census Bureau, Census of Population, 1970, PC(S1)-106, Supplementary Report, *Poverty Status in 1969 and 1959 of Persons and Families, for States, SMSA's, Central Cities, and Counties: 1970 and 1960*, table 8. The census did not gauge poverty status as such in 1959, but "poverty level" was subsequently identified as having an income less than $3000 per year for a family of four.

34. U.S. Census Bureau, 1960 Census of Population, PC(S1)-54, Supplementary Report: *Poverty Areas in the 100 Largest Metropolitan Areas*, 13 November 1967, table 2. Report writers observed, "The majority of nonwhite families whose economic status placed them above the poverty level were nevertheless residing in Poverty Areas" (1).

35. On the exclusion of agricultural, service, and household workers from Social Security, see Larry DeWitt, "The Decision to Exclude Agricultural and Domestic Workers from the 1935 Society Security Act, *Social Security Bulletin* 70, no. 4 (2010).

36. On the racial wealth gap, see Shapiro, *Hidden Cost*.

Chapter 1. Early Beginnings

1. Allen's testimony is described in *New York Times*, 27 July 1963.

2. "The City Must Provide. South Atlanta: The Forgotten Community," appended to Judy Walborn, "The South Atlanta Project—SNCC, 1963," SNCC papers, reel 37.

3. *Saturday Evening Post*, 22 September 1945.

4. *Saturday Evening Post*, 31 October 1953.

5. *Atlanta Journal and Constitution*, 19 January 1958.

6. Community Council of the Atlanta Area (CCAA), *Social Report on Neighborhood Analysis: CITY of Atlanta, Georgia* (Atlanta Community Improvement Program, 1966): chart B-7, p. B-15.

7. U.S. Census Bureau, 1960 Census of Population, *Characteristics of the Population*, table P-1.

8. CCAA, *Social Report on Neighborhood Analysis: City of Atlanta, Georgia* (Atlanta Community Improvement Program, 1966): C-5

9. Porter, "Black Atlanta," 106–7.

10. Characterizations of houses numbered 173 A/B to 191 A/B, and 190 A/B were developed from Sanborn Fire Insurance Maps, Microfilm, AHC.

11. Michael Porter, private interview with Dr. R. B. Jackson, recorded 17 September 1973, as quoted in Porter, "Black Atlanta," 104.

12. Characterizations of houses at 177 to 215, 176 to 212 Rhinehardt, and 183 to 199, 182 to 206 Fenwick were developed from Sanborn Fire Insurance Maps, microfilm, AHC.

13. The spelling of Plunketown varies widely.

14. CCAA, *Social Report on Neighborhood Analysis*, B-21.

15. CCAA, *Social Report on Neighborhood Analysis*, B-21.

16. On the shifting demographics of Atlanta public housing, see Rodriguez, *Diverging Space for Deviants*, particularly chaps. 2 and 3.

17. Techwood was built before the Atlanta Housing Authority was established in 1938.

18. "Techwood Homes," GA-2257, National Park Service, Historic American Building Survey, http://lcweb2.loc.gov/master/pnp/habshaer/ga/ga0600/ga0662/data/ga0662data.pdf.

19. *Atlanta Constitution*, 16 August 1936.

20. U.S. Census Bureau, Census of Population, 1960, vol. 1, *Characteristics of the Population, by Census Tracts*, table P-1.

21. U.S. Census Bureau, Census of Population, 1940, vol. 2, Characteristics of the Population; Bayor, *Race and the Shaping*, table 1.

22. Bayor, *Race and the Shaping*, table 2.

23. For discussion of Arnall's philosophy, campaign for governorship, and commitment to broad suffrage, see Patton, "Southern Liberals and the Emergence" chap. 3. Arnall also promoted legislation to lower the voting age from twenty-one to eighteen, which also expanded the electorate. *Atlanta Constitution*, 23 December 1944; *Atlanta Constitution*, 19 January 1947; Bacote, "Negro in Atlanta Politics," 343–44.

24. Bacote, "Negro in Atlanta Politics," 345–47; Harmon, *Beneath the Image*, 18–24. On the ACPL, also see Harmon, *Beneath the Image*, 14–15. As the manager of the black bloc vote, the ANVL would go on to play a significant role in the white business-black political power coalition. Harmon, *Beneath the Image*, 59–60.

25. Hornsby, *Black Power in Dixie*, 81–82; Bayor, *Race and the Shaping of Twentieth-Century Atlanta*, 85–87.

26. Hornsby, *Black Power in Dixie*, 71–72, 85–86, 93. On Hartsfield's concerns about white suburbanization and growing black voting strength, see Bayor, *Race and the Shaping*, 85–86.

27. Hornsby, *Black Power in Dixie*, 84.

28. Hornsby, *Black Power in Dixie*, 92.

29. Isabel Wilkerson, *Warmth of Other Suns*, 258.

30. Isabel Wilkerson, *Warmth of Other Suns*, 401. Generational and philosophical divisions within Atlanta's early 1960s civil rights movement are examined in Brown-Nagin, *Courage to Dissent*, particularly chap. 6. Sam Williams had attended a July 1964 war on poverty planning meeting involving Atlanta leadership and federal administrator Frederick Hayes. *Atlanta Constitution*, 10 July 1964.

31. Hornsby, *Black Power in Dixie*, 92.

32. As historian Charles Connerly explains in his study of race and city planning in

Birmingham, Alabama, neighborhood-based civic leagues were a method regularly used by African Americans to organize to improve quality of life in neighborhoods, which included promoting street and infrastructure maintenance, public safety, and the creation and maintenance of parks and recreational areas. Civic leagues defined membership on the basis of location—usually neighborhood but sometimes by other geographies. Connerly, *"Most Segregated City in America"*, 218–19. Atlanta civic leagues are noted in *Atlanta Daily World*, 31 August 1947, 4 September 1947, 7 September 1947.

33. *Atlanta Daily World*, 20 February 1955; *Atlanta Daily World*, 26 February 1956. The civic league emerged from the previously organized South Atlanta Home Owners League. As the ADW reported, "The league has taken the lead in aiming for improvement of living conditions in the area such as water mains, street lights, gas and street signs, and members feel their aim has changed to that of a civic organization." *Atlanta Daily World*, 21 June 1953.

34. The Federal Housing Administration, which insured the loans for Highpoint Apartments, initially balked at the proposed rents, explaining that they were too high for Black occupants. *Atlanta Daily World*, 4 June 1950; Lands, *Culture of Property*, 188–89.

35. Lands, *Culture of Property*, 141. City directories for the period often include reverse indices that allow one to identify who lived at specific addresses. The name directory frequently provides occupation. Historical Atlanta city directories can be found at the Kenan Research Center at Atlanta History Center and the Woodruff Library at Emory University.

36. *Atlanta Daily World*, 18 February 1953.

37. *Atlanta Daily World*, 21 June 1955.

38. On the establishment of $3,000 as the poverty threshold for a family of four in the early 1960s, see Gordon M. Fisher, "The Development and History of the Poverty Thresholds," *Social Security Bulletin* 55 (1992).

39. U.S. Census Bureau, Census of the Population, 1960, vol. 1, Characteristics of the Population, by Census Tracts, table P-1. I included all families earning $2999 or less in the city of Atlanta (Fulton and Dekalb county portions).

40. Map of Atlanta (June 1961), ATLPM0101, Planning Atlanta City Planning Maps Collection, Georgia State University Library. This particular map, according to the map description provided by GSU, "depicts, in red, non-white areas in December 31, 1962, and, in blue, additions to the non-white areas in 1963. Areas are hand-shaded. Revised 1954; Revised 1959; Revised 1961; Revised 1963. Revised December 31, 1963."

41. I calculated the poverty rate of Atlanta families based on data from U.S. Census Bureau, Census of Population, 1960, *Characteristics of the Population, by Census Tracts*, table P-1. I included all families earning $2999 or less in the city of Atlanta (Fulton and Dekalb county portions).

42. *Atlanta Daily World*, 13 March 1955; 27 March 1955.

43. *Atlanta Daily World*, 11 November 1955; 20 November 1955.

44. *Atlanta Daily World*, 20 November 1955.

45. *Atlanta Daily World*, 7 September 1956.

46. *Atlanta Daily World*, 2 November 1958.

47. *Atlanta Daily World*, 28 February 1960.

48. Atlanta's period of negotiated settlements between Black elite and the city's white business and political leaders is described in Stone, *Regime Politics*, chap. 3. Also see Hunter, *Community Power Structure*, particularly chap. 5.

49. Clarence Bacote outlined the benefits of voting power in his testimony to the U.S. Commission on Civil Rights, *Hearings before the U.S. Commission on Civil Rights*, 576–93.

50. U.S. Congress, Joint Committee on Housing, *Hearings before the Joint Committee on Housing*, 1947, 1261.

51. U.S. Congress, Joint Committee on Housing, *Hearings before the Joint Committee on Housing*, 1263.

52. U.S. Congress, Joint Committee on Housing, *Hearings before the Joint Committee on Housing*, 1265.

53. Kruse, *White Flight*, chap. 2.

54. On Mozley Park and the formation of the West Size Mutual Development Corporation, see Bayor, *Race and the Shaping*, 60–65; Kruse, *White Flight*, chap. 2.

55. Martin, *William Berry Hartsfield*, 96–97.

56. Hartsfield regularly worked to defuse potential racial conflict. See, for example, the discussion of city bus desegregation and the integration of Atlanta schools in Martin, *William Berry Hartsfield*, 118–19, 52–54.

57. Martin, *William Berry Hartsfield*, 139.

58. "Citizen Participation in Urban Renewal," 487.

59. While citizen participation is often associated with the War on Poverty's CAPs and their requirement for the maximum feasible participation of targeted groups, Economic Opportunity Atlanta staffer Frankie Adams points to urban renewal programs as the origin of "citizen participation." Frankie Adams to Center Directors, 8 December 1965, folder 28, box 1, Frankie Adams Collection, AUC; "Dynamics of Citizen Participation," folder 27, box 1, Frankie Adams Collection, AUC. See Housing and Home Finance Agency, "The Workable Program—What It Is" (O-F-357141) (Washington, D.C.: Government Printing Office, 1955). An overview of the urban renewal components of the 1949 and 1954 acts and the relationship between the two acts is outlined in "Citizen Participation in Urban Renewal," 489–92; von Hoffman, "Lost History of Urban Renewal," 281–301.

60. Smith, "Study of the Relationship." Other cities embraced rehabilitation and citizen participation in later urban renewal efforts. See, for example, Spiers, "'Planning with People,'" 221–47; Miller and Tucker, *Changing Plans*, 48–49.

61. Holliman, "From 'Crackertown' to the 'ATL,'" 44–47. On urban renewal in Atlanta, also see Stone, *Economic Growth and Neighborhood Discontent*.

62. *Atlanta Constitution*, 5 April 1957; Stone, *Economic Growth and Neighborhood Discontent*, 61–65; *Atlanta Constitution*, 20 August 1957. On siting of Black housing near the city's edge, see Stone, *Regime Politics*, 40; Stone, *Economic Growth and Neighborhood Discontent*, 48–49; *Atlanta Constitution*, 3 November 1957; *Atlanta Daily World*, 6 February 1958.

63. *Atlanta Constitution*, 29 September 1957.

64. *Atlanta Constitution*, 18 January 1958, 20 March 1958. Mayor Hartsfield ap-

pointed architect Cecil Alexander as committee chair. *Atlanta Constitution*, 18 January 1958.

65. *Atlanta Daily World*, 3 September 1959.

66. *Atlanta Daily World*, 11 August 1985.

67. *Atlanta Daily World*, 9 June 1991. At the time of his appointment, Richardson was planning and assembling what would become Atlanta's Interdenominational Theological Center. Brown-Nagin, *Courage to Dissent*, 418.

68. *Atlanta Constitution*, 18 January 1958.

69. As ad-hoc committees, these groups sometimes were referred to by different names in the local newspapers. A follow-up mass meeting was scheduled for 8 January at Wheat Street Baptist Church. *Atlanta Daily World*, 5 January 1958, 10 April 1958.

70. *Atlanta Daily World*, 9 March 1958.

71. The Negro Citizens Committee on Urban Renewal compiled grievances into a twelve-page memo titled "The Slum Clearance and Urban Renewal Program of the City of Atlanta and its Impact on Minority Citizens." The memo is reprinted in U.S. Commission on Civil Rights, *Hearings before the U.S. Commission on Civil Rights*, 563–58, quote on 564.

72. Comments and information on the CACUR meetings are also reprised in *Atlanta Constitution*, 20 March 1958, 8 April 1958; *Atlanta Daily World*, 9 March 1958, 11 March 1958.

73. *Atlanta Daily World*, 8 May 1958.

74. *Atlanta Daily World*, 3 July 1958. "Above all," the paper concluded, "the Negro community is entitled to more information about the plans than now seems to be available." *Atlanta Daily World*, 16 October 1958.

75. Dulles, *Civil Rights Commission*, 52.

76. Dulles, *Civil Rights Commission*, 57–58.

77. U.S. Commission on Civil Rights, *Hearings before the U.S. Commission on Civil Rights*, 556–58.

78. That is, established residents did not simply reject public housing; residents rejected the proximity of the poor and Black, no matter whether their housing was public or privately funded. The resistance to the establishment of low-cost housing that, given Atlanta's demographics, would most likely be occupied by Blacks, continued a long pattern of white resistance to the proximity of Black-occupied housing. See Lands, *Culture of Property*, 85–89. Housing for displaced families usually took the form of public housing, Title 220 multifamily housing, or Title 221 single-family homes.

79. *Atlanta Constitution*, 17 April 1958, 21 April 1958. Since Title 221 housing was usually sited on land zoned R5, the committee proposed upgrading two hundred acres of property at Gilbert and Brown Mill Roads to R4, a change that would prevent the building of Title 221 housing on that land. *Atlanta Constitution*, 9 May 1958, 5 June 1958, 17 July 1958.

80. *Atlanta Daily World*, 9 December 1959, 13 December 1959; Stone, *Regime Politics*, 42–43.

81. Stone, *Economic Growth and Neighborhood Discontent*, 70.

82. *Atlanta Constitution*, 30 December 1959.

83. *Atlanta Constitution*, 23 February 1960, 8 March 1960.

84. Stone, *Economic Growth and Neighborhood Discontent*, 85. Atlanta's experience with citizen participation in urban renewal is consistent with the analysis put forward by law scholar Barlow Burke Jr. in 1971. Burke, "Threat to Citizen Participation," 754.

85. Ivan Allen Jr. acknowledged that "when the city signed these contracts with the federal government in the beginning of the urban renewal program, the Board of Aldermen had no intention of carrying them out. All they wanted was the money." As quoted in *Atlanta Constitution*, 29 July 1965.

86. *Atlanta Constitution*, 28 July 1965.

87. Atlanta adopted a housing code in 1957 in order to qualify for urban renewal funds. *Atlanta Constitution*, 28 July 1965.

88. In a reorganization of its urban renewal functions, the city moved urban renewal department head Malcolm Jones to the building inspector's office and shifted urban renewal projects and relocation services to the Atlanta Housing Authority. *Atlanta Constitution*, 28 July 1965.

89. *Atlanta Constitution*, 26 July 1965.

90. Debbie H. Amis, "Atlanta," 16 December 1963, SNCC papers, reel 42. The spelling of Plunketown varies over time and in different publications.

91. On the 1960 to 1961 Atlanta student movement, see the essays collected in Garrow, *Atlanta, Georgia*; Brown-Nagin, *Courage to Dissent*, chap. 6.

92. Hornsby, *Black Power in Dixie*, 115. Also see Harmon, *Beneath the Image*, 152–55; Lefever, *Undaunted by the Fight*, 171.

93. Judy Walborn, "The South Atlanta Project—SNCC, 1963," SNCC papers, reel 37. SNCC members also noted that they needed to identify what neighborhood residents had previously requested so they could assess if the city had responded adequately.

94. Walborn, "South Atlanta Project," SNCC papers. Also see Debbie Amis, "Atlanta," 16 December 1963, SNCC papers, reel 42.

95. Walborn, "South Atlanta Project," SNCC papers.

96. Walborn, "South Atlanta Project," SNCC papers.

97. Walborn, "South Atlanta Project," SNCC papers.

98. "The City Must Provide," SNCC papers, reel 37 (emphasis in original). Also see L. D. Simon et al. to Mayor Ivan Allen Jr., 19 August 1963, SNCC papers, reel 46.

99. " City Must Provide," SNCC papers.

100. "South Atlanta Project—Critical Analysis," 18 August 1963, SNCC papers, reel 46. (The report can also be found on reel 37.)

101. The estimated number of participants is from an internal field report. "South Atlanta Project," SNCC papers. Given that the report is lamenting the "low" turnout, there is little reason to think the number is inflated.

102. "South Atlanta Project," SNCC papers.

103. "South Atlanta Project," SNCC papers.

104. Simon et al. to Allen, 19 August 1963, SNCC papers.

105. Simon et al. to Allen, 19 August 1963, SNCC papers (emphasis in original).

106. "South Atlanta Project," SNCC papers.

107. "A Proposal for a Voter Education Project in Southeast Atlanta," SNCC papers, reel 37.

108. When it was discovered that few residents could successfully pass the registration exam, SNCC set up a VEP School. "Report from South East Atlanta," Debbie Amis to SNCC, October 1963, SNCC papers, reel 48. Also see Stone, *Regime Politics*, 31.

109. "Report from South East Atlanta," SNCC papers.

110. "Report from South East Atlanta," SNCC papers; Debbie H. Amis, "Atlanta," 16 December 1963, SNCC papers, reel 42.

111. In 1963, differences in approach between organizations were apparent, as when A. T. Walden resigned from the Summit after a "disorderly" demonstration at the Heart of Atlanta Hotel. See Stone, *Regime Politics*, 58. These frustrations continued into 1964. See Hornsby, *Black Power in Dixie*, 116. Scholarly works describing divisions within Atlanta's Black community typically focus on tensions between the "old guard" negotiators who worked with the city's white business community and the direct-action-oriented students movement. On disagreements about how to approach civil rights issues in Atlanta, see, for example, Harmon, *Beneath the Image*, 93–94; Brown-Nagin, *Courage to Dissent*, chap. 6; Lefever, *Undaunted by the Fight*, 171.

112. Amis, "Atlanta," SNCC papers.

113. Amis, "Atlanta," SNCC papers; Harmon, *Beneath the Image*, 183.

114. Harmon, *Beneath the Image*, 162–65.

115. Harmon, *Beneath the Image*, 157.

116. "3000 March in Atlanta," *Student Voice*, 16 December 1963.

117. Tuck, *Beyond Atlanta*, 115–16.

118. Harmon, *Beneath the Image*, 157. Also see Lefever, *Undaunted by the Fight*, 174.

119. "Resistance Mounts," *Student Voice*, 11 February 1964.

120. See papers related to the Atlanta Project formation in SNCC papers, reel 37.

121. *Atlanta Daily World*, 11 April 1958.

Chapter 2. Economic Opportunity Atlanta

1. "CCAA, Inc., A Short History, 1960–1973," folder 12, box 5, Community Council of the Atlanta Area Records, RMARBL (hereafter cited as CCAA Records).

2. Allen and Hemphill, *Mayor*, 30.

3. Early CCAA documents specifically stated that social welfare planning supported the needs of business and industry and also indicated the need for business and commercial support of social welfare planning. "Memorandum," folder 5, box 11, CCAA Records; Robert L. "Trot" Foreman Jr.'s son, Robert L. Foreman III, changed his name to Robert L. Foreman Jr. after his father died. See Buckhead Heritage Society interview, http://www.buckheadheritage.com/sites/default/files/Buckhead%20Heritage%20Oral%20History%20Project%2C%20Robert%20Foreman.pdf; Arthur Howell, "Report of the Chairman to the Board of Directors of the Community Council," 3 May 1962, folder 13, box 5 CCAA Records.

4. "The Community Council of the Atlanta Area," folder 9, box 1, CCAA Records.

5. "Jimmy" to John A. Sibley, 8 May 1962, folder 1, box 42, Emily and Ernest Wood-

ruff Foundation Records, RMARBL (hereafter cited as Woodruff Foundation Records). On John A. Sibley, see *Atlanta Constitution*, 8 September 1946.

6. The early history and philosophy of CCAA is described in the following: Duane Beck to Edward M. Abrams, 22 January 1973, folder 2, box 4, CCAA Records; Howell, "Report of the Chairman," CCAA Records; Duane W. Beck to Richard Block, 4 May 1965, folder 11, box 5, CCAA Records; Duane W. Beck, "Community Council of the Atlanta Area, Inc.: A Creature of the Sixties," folder 12, box 5, CCAA Records; Report of Community Council of the Atlanta Area, Inc., October 1962, folder 15, box 10, CCAA Records.

7. *Atlanta Journal and Constitution*, 31 January 1960.

8. Philip Weltner to R. W. Woodruff, 20 April 1962, folder 15, box 8, Woodruff Foundation Records.

9. Weltner originally articulated the challenge of serving multiproblem families from remote agencies in his report for the Illegitimacy and Adoption Committee for the Fulton County Welfare Department. See *Atlanta Journal and Constitution*, 31 January 1960.

10. On the Greater St. Paul Community Chest and Council, Inc., see Birt, "Family-Centered Project of St. Paul." Jimmy Sibley points out that St. Paul was used as a model in "Jimmy" to John A. Sibley, 8 May 1962, Woodruff Foundation Records. The neighborhood center project derived from the findings and recommendations of an August 1960 report generated at the behest of the Fulton County Advisory Council on Illegitimacy and Adoption and prepared by Dr. Philip Weltner. *Atlanta Journal and Constitution*, 27 November 1960, 26 March 1961, 24 September 1961. The relationship between CCAA and Weltner's work with the Public Welfare Department Committee on Illegitimacy and Adoption is articulated in an untitled document that begins, "The Atlanta Area Community Council, Inc was formed to provide Atlanta with social research and social planning," folder 11, box 5, CCAA Records.

11. *Atlanta Journal and Constitution*, 24 September 1961, 27 November 1960, 26 March 1961, 24 September 1961. "Neighborhood Program" attached to CCAA Board of Directors Suggested Agenda, 4 May 1961, folder 14, box 10, CCAA Records. The neighborhood project was originally coordinated by Thomas E. Garnett Jr. and advised by the New York social research firm Community Research Associates. Garnett would leave CCAA at the end of 1962.

12. The description of West End is based on CCAA, *Social Report on Neighborhood Analysis: City of Atlanta, Georgia* (Atlanta Community Improvement Program, 1966), B-20; and U.S. Census Bureau, Census of Population, 1960, vol. 1, *Characteristics of the Population, by Census Tracts*, table P-1.

13. Inez B. Tillison to Duane W. Beck, 25 October 1965, folder 11, box 5, CCAA Records. Also see "Oral History Interview with Estelle Clemmons, 1978 September 27," interviewed by Bernard West, Living Atlanta Oral History Collection, AHC, http://ohms.libs.uga.edu/viewer.php?cachefile=dlg/livatl/ahc-637-032-001.xml.

14. That staffing plan continued for about one year. Tillison to Beck, 25 October 1965, CCAA Records.

15. Tillison to Beck, 25 October 1965, CCAA Records; "Communique" of the CCAA, May-June 1963, folder 11, box 5, CCAA Records.

16. "Neighborhood Committee: Five Year Program Projection," attached to CCAA Budget and Policy Subcommittee Meeting March 26, 1962," folder 9, box 33, CCAA Records.

17. Mobilization for Youth received Gray Areas funding from the Ford Foundation.

18. "Youth in the Ghetto: A Study of the Consequences of Powerlessness," Harlem Youth Opportunities Unlimited, Inc., 1964. In 1966, at the U.S. Conference of Mayors, New York mayor John Lindsay would detail plans for neighborhood-based "one-stop" job centers to help address chronic unemployment. Lindsay's plans were at least in part authored by New Haven War on Poverty head Mitchell Sviridoff. *New York Times*, 13 June 1966. On Mobilization for Youth, see Carroll, *Mobilizing New York*, chaps. 1 and 2.

19. "Neighborhood Committee," CCAA Records.

20. Philip H. Alston Jr. to the members of the Executive Committee, 29 March 1962, folder 9, box 33, CCAA Records.

21. Philip Weltner to Robert Woodruff, 19 June 1962, folder 1, box 42, Woodruff Foundation Records. The CCAA board minutes discuss the use of aides to extend the work of trained professionals. See Board of Directors Minutes, 8 November 1961, folder 7, box 13, CCAA Records.

22. "Summary and Comments on 'Looking to the Future,'" 5 August 1963, folder 13, box 7, CCAA Records. Thomas E. Garnett Jr. resigned effective 31 December 1962. Tillison to Beck, 25 October 1965, CCAA Records.

23. Tillison to Beck, 25 October 1965, CCAA Records; *Atlanta Journal and Constitution*, 18 June 1961.

24. Duane W. Beck, "Community Council of the Atlanta Area, Inc.: A Creature of the Sixties," folder 12, box 5, CCAA Records.

25. Beck, "Community Council of the Atlanta Area," CCAA Records.

26. Duane W. Beck to Edward M. Abrams, 22 January 1973, folder 2, box 4, CCAA Records.

27. Duane W. Beck, "Report of the Executive Director for the Finance Committee," November 1963, folder 16, box 1, CCAA Records. Beck was referring to "Annual Statistical Summary: Community Welfare Councils: 1962" (dated October 1963), contained within the same folder.

28. It's unclear why West End was chosen over Vine City, and few details can be found regarding the Vine City pilot project.

29. Joseph F. Haas to Philip Weltner, [no date, but late 1963], folder 15, box 7, CCAA Records. The hiring of Beecher is noted in "Capsule Report to the Board of Directors," 31 July 1963, folder 16, box 10, CCAA Records.

30. *Atlanta Constitution*, 8 August 1963.

31. Untitled [1964 CCAA] report attached to Haas to Weltner, [no date, but late 1963], CCAA Records. The report indicates that "it was thought that a neighborhood which had some pride and some leadership should be selected as the pilot area." Presumably West End fit that bill, but it is not clear what, if any, other neighborhoods were considered. Duane W. Beck and Inez B. Tillison to Frank Shackleford, 26 June 1964, folder 2, box 9, CCAA. Progress on the neighborhood program as it was carried

out by the CCAA can be found in "Report to the Board of Directors: Social Planning in the Neighborhood," 20 January 1964, folder 17, box 10, CCAA Records.

32. *Atlanta Constitution*, 11 January 1964. CCAA board member James P. Furniss, a Yale graduate and a member of senior management at Citizens & Southern, was "struck by the parallel between the aims of the Community Council and those expressed by President Johnson." He planned to touch base with CCAA leadership and recommend that CCAA take an active role in managing Atlanta's involvement. James P. Furniss to Charles Weltner, 24 March 1964, folder 22, box 10, CCAA Records.

33. Biles, *Fate of Cities*, 116. Also see *Atlanta Journal and Constitution*, 22 March 1964.

34. Gillette, *Launching the War on Poverty*, 131–34.

35. *Atlanta Constitution*, 27 August 1964.

36. Landrum's commitment was aided in part by the security of his seat. The newspaper serving Landrum's district, the *Gainesville Daily Times*, supported the bill, which meant Landrum would not have to endure media criticism for supporting a liberal program, at least in his own district. Ashmore, *Carry It On*, 35.

37. Ashmore, *Carry It On*, 38.

38. Ashmore, *Carry It On*, 41.

39. Biles, *Fate of Cities*, 117.

40. Zelizer, *Fierce Urgency of Now*, 32–33.

41. Ashmore, *Carry It On*, 41–42; Zelizer, *Fierce Urgency of Now*, 140.

42. Minutes, Council Antipoverty Liaison Committee with Mayor Allen, 13 July 1964, folder 6, box 33, CCAA Records; "Special Memo to Board of Directors," 1 December 1964, folder 17, box 10, CCAA Records.

43. CCAA Newsletter, 30 March 1964, folder 3, box 106, Atlanta Urban League Papers, AUC. Also see CCAA Board of Directors meeting, 2 April 1964, folder 11, box 13, CCAA Records.

44. CCAA Board of Director Minutes, 21 May 1964, folder 11, box 13, CCAA records; CCAA Board of Director Minutes, 22 June 1964, folder 11, box 13, CCAA Records; Dudley Morris to Richard Boone, 25 July 1964, folder: Econ. Opportunity Atlanta, Inc., box 104, RG 381, OEO, Office of Operations, Migrant Division, Grant Files, 1966–71, NARA.

45. Community Council of the Atlanta Area Newsletter, 30 March 1964, folder 3, box 106, Atlanta Urban League Papers, AUC.

46. Korstad and Leloudis, *To Right These Wrongs*, 170–71.

47. Community Council of the Atlanta Area Newsletter, 30 March 1964, folder 3, box 106, Atlanta Urban League Papers, AUC.

48. See Minutes, Executive Committee, CCAA, 29 June 1964, folder 11, box 13, CCAA Records.

49. On the Ford Foundation's Gray Areas programs, see Ferguson, *Top Down*; O'Connor, "Community Action, Urban Reform," 586–625.

50. Sundquist, *Politics and Policy*, 122.

51. Halpern, *Rebuilding the Inner City*, 91–92.

52. Sundquist, *Politics and Policy*, 122–24.

53. O'Connor, *Poverty Knowledge*, 131. On the Gray Areas' adherence to Chicago School assumptions and desire for comprehensive social service reforms, see O'Connor, *Poverty Knowledge*, 131–36.

54. Conclusions from the group's observations of New Haven and Boston are outlined in Minutes, Council Antipoverty Liaison Committee with Mayor Allen, 13 July 1964, folder 6, box 33, CCAA Records.

55. Zeitz, *Building the Great Society*, 79–89, quote on 82.

56. Council Antipoverty Liaison Committee with Mayor Allen, 13 July 1964, CCAA Records; CCAA Executive Committee Minutes, 29 June 1964, folder 11, box 13, CCAA Records.

57. As quoted in *Atlanta Constitution*, 16 July 1964.

58. CCAA Communique, July 1964, folder 3, box 106, Atlanta Urban League Papers, AUC.

59. I refer to both the Atlanta–Fulton County Economic Opportunity Authority and the subsequent organization, Economic Opportunity Atlanta, which incorporated in summer 1965, as EOA. C. O. Emmerich to Sargent Shriver, 6 July 1965, folder: Econ. Opportunity Atlanta, Inc., box 104, RG 381, OEO, office of Operations, Migrant Division, Grant Files, 1966–71, NARA.

60. *New York Times*, 17 March 1964. Regarding the Jones-Shriver friendship, see Matusow, *Unraveling of America*, 255.

61. Frederick Hayes to Richard Boone, stamped 13 July 1964, folder: Econ. Opportunity Atlanta, NARA.

62. Transmittal slip, E. Bruce Wedge to Frederick O'R. Hayes and "Kravitz," 3 September 1964, folder: Econ. Opportunity Atlanta, NARA.

63. *Atlanta Constitution*, 18 August 1964.

64. Dan Sweat interview by Clifford Kuhn and Shep Barbash, 22 November 1966, Georgia Government Documentation Project, Special Collections and Archives, Georgia State University Library, Atlanta. Sweat started as head of DeKalb County's research and information department. In 1963 he agreed to serve as Emmerich's executive assistant. *Atlanta Constitution*, 13 January 1963.

65. "Highlight Memorandum: Application for Grant under Title II-A," folder "Economic Opportunity Atlanta," NARA.

66. *Atlanta Constitution*, 25 November 1964; Emory University Center for Research in Social Change, "A Comprehensive and Systematic Evaluation of the Community Action Program and Related Programs Operating in Atlanta" (Atlanta: Emory University, 1969), 17; "Highlight Memorandum: Application for Grant under Title II-A," folder "Economic Opportunity Atlanta," NARA. The twelve proposed centers included West End; NASH-Washington; Price High School; South Fulton; Peoplestown-Summerhill-Mechanicsville; Northeast; Edgewood; Northwest-Perry Homes; Northwest-Bowen Homes; Techwood; Pittsburgh; and North Fulton. The population served by each ranged from ten thousand (South Fulton) to forty thousand (NASH-Washington) residents.

67. Walz identified the Juvenile Delinquency and Control Act of 1961 as the parent of the modern neighborhood service center. Walz, "Emergence of the Neighborhood," 147–56.

68. Walz, "Emergence of the Neighborhood," 147–56.

69. WSB-TV newsfilm clip, 9 March 1960, WSB-TV newsfilm collection, reel 0919, 49:52/58:10, Walter J. Brown Media Archives and Peabody Awards Collection, University of Georgia Libraries, Athens.

70. C. D. Coleman, S. W. Williams, and A. T. Walden to Ivan Allen Jr. and Harold F. McCart, 1 September 1964, folder 2, box 24, Samuel W. Williams Collection, AUC.

71. Brown-Nagin, *Courage to Dissent*, 228–29.

72. Coleman, Williams, and Walden to Allen and McCart, 1 September 1964, AUC. Also see Robert Carey to Samuel Williams, Clarence Coleman, and George Bess, 2 September 1964, folder 9, box 25, Eliza K. Paschall Papers, RMARBL, Emory University, Atlanta (hereafter cited as Paschall Papers).

73. Telegram, 16 November 1964, folder: Atlanta-Fulton County Economic, box 104, RG381, OEO, Office of Operations, Migrant Division, Grant files, 1966–71, NARA. Robert N. Moore Jr. to files, 16 February 1965, file: Atlanta-Fulton County, box 102, RG 381, OEO, office of Operations, Migrant Division, Grant Files, 1966–71, NARA.

74. On A. T. Walden, see Brown-Nagin, *Courage to Dissent*, chaps 1, 2, and 6; Tuck, *Beyond Atlanta*, 93.

75. *Atlanta Daily World*, 14 August 1979.

76. *Atlanta Daily World*, 12 December 1962, 4 January 1963, 31 Jan 1964; *Atlanta Constitution*, 6 July 1964, 13 July 1965. On Atlanta branch leadership and national office concerns, see Brown-Nagin, *Courage to Dissent*, 334–37. Rose Marie Wells notes Williams's tenure as president as 1959 and 1960 and then from 1965 to 1967. See Wells, "Samuel Woodrow Williams," 29.

77. On Thompson's work on housing and the Atlanta Urban League, see Wiese, *Places of Their Own*, 184–88. On Thompson's 1964 appointment to HHFA, see *Atlanta Daily World*, 15 May 1964.

78. *Atlanta Inquirer*, 19 September 1964. As Jesse Hill explained to the Voices across the Color Line Oral History Project, Butler Street YMCA served as a "continuous forum of Black leadership in Atlanta," a command center and meeting site for Atlanta's Black elite, and home to the Atlanta Negro Voters League and the All Citizen Registration Committee. In early 1965, W. L. Calloway would be appointed to fulfill Cochrane's unexpired term. *Atlanta Inquirer*, 20 February 1965.

79. Ed May and Bob Clampitt to Martha McKay and Al Krumlauf, 20 September 1965, folder: CAP, Atlanta, Ga., 1965, box 19, RG 381, OEO, Inspection Division, Inspection Reports, 1964–67, NARA.

80. The evolution of Hartsfield's relationship to Atlanta's Black power structure is highlighted in episode 25 of the radio documentary *Will the Circle Be Unbroken?*

81. The inspections division was created to alert the OEO director, Sargent Shriver, of potential or emerging issues. William Haddad, the first inspector general, saw the inspections office as a way to enforce the maximum feasible participation requirement in CAPs. As quoted in Martha McKay and Al Krumlauf to Ed May and Bob Clampitt, 20 September 1965, folder: CAP, Atlanta, GA, 1965, box 19, RG 381, OEO, Inspection Division, Inspection Reports, 1964–67, NARA. Ashmore, *Carry It On*, 64–65.

82. Boisfeuillet Jones to Jack Conway, 20 November 1964, folder: Atlanta Fulton

County Economic," RG381, OEO, Office of Operations, Migrant Division, Grant files, 1966–71, NARA.

83. C. D. Coleman and S. W. Williams to Boisfeuillet Jones, 24 November 1964, folder 2, box 24, Samuel W. Williams Collection, AUC. According to the *Atlanta Inquirer*, Atlanta's EOA proposal was submitted to Washington without "any prior Negro knowledge or participation," though that was clearly not the case.

84. Crawford, *Comprehensive and Systematic Evaluation*, 17. *Atlanta Constitution*, 25 November 1964; David A. Grossman to Jack Conway, "Atlanta-Fulton County CAP—Finding and Recommendations," undated, folder: Atlanta Fulton County Economic, box 104, RG 381, OEO, office of Operations, Migrant Division, Grant Files, 1966–71, NARA; C. O. Emmerich to Sargent Shriver, 27 November 1964, folder: Atlanta Fulton County Economic, box 104, RG 381, OEO, office of Operations, Migrant Division, Grant Files, 1966–71, NARA.

85. Statement of CAP Grant, GA-CAP-306/1, folder: Atlanta-Fulton County Econ. Oppor. Authority, box 102, RG 381, OEO, Office of Operations, Migrant Division, Grant Files, 1966–71, NARA.

86. "Race Determines Employment at EOA, Inc.," folder 11, box 1, Cadmus Allen Samples Papers, WHS (hereafter cited as Samples Papers). Used with permission of the Cadmus Samples heirs.

87. Samuel W. Williams to Charles O. Emmerich, 4 December 1964, folder: Atlanta-Fulton County Economic, box 104, RG 381, OEO, office of Operations, Migrant Division, Grant Files, 1966–71, NARA.

88. C. O. Emmerich to Jack Conway, 25 January 1965, folder: Econ. Opportunity Atlanta, Inc., box 104, RG 381, OEO, office of Operations, Migrant Division, Grant Files, 1966–71, NARA; Samuel W. Williams to Charles O. Emmerich, 4 December 1964, folder: Atlanta-Fulton County Economic, box 104, RG 381, OEO, Office of Operations, Migrant Division, Grant Files, 1966–71, NARA.

89. Dan Sweat discusses his hiring as well as negotiations with Black leadership in Sweat interview by Kuhn and Barbash, 22 November 1966, Georgia Government Documentation Project; *Atlanta Inquirer*, 20 February 1965. Bo Jones comments on Black demands in his interview with inspections division personnel in McKay and Krumlauf to Way and Clampitt, 20 September 1965, NARA.

90. *Jet*, 18 February 1965. The NASH acronym referred to the neighborhood bounded by Northside Drive, Ashby Street, Simpson Street, and Hunter Street.

91. C. O. Emmerich to Sargent Shriver, 6 July 1965, folder: Atlanta-Fulton Co. Economic Opportunity Authority, box 102, RG 381, OEO, Office of Operations, Migrant Division, Grant files, 1966–71, NARA. "Community Action in Atlanta," December 1965, folder 29, box 8, EUA 10 Emory University Center for the Study of Social Change papers, MARBL. "Realtist" was a term adopted by Black real estate professionals. The term "realtor" was and is trademarked by the National Association of Realtors, a professional organization that did not, at that time, grant realty licenses to Blacks.

92. Notes of 4 August 1965 conversation, appended to Harry Miller to Bill Haddad and Bob Clampitt, 5 August 1965, folder: CAP, Atlanta, Ga., 1965, box 19, RG 381, OEO, Inspection Division, Inspection Reports, 1964–67, NARA.

93. Notes of 4 August 1965 conversation, appended to Miller to Haddad and Clampitt, 5 August 1965, NARA.

94. Ed May and Bob Clampitt to Jack Gonzales, 8 December 1965, folder: CAP, Atlanta, Ga., 1965, box 19, RG 381, OEO, Inspection Division, Inspection Reports, 1964–67, NARA.

95. This set of inspection division interviews is contained in McKay and Krumlauf to Way and Clampitt, 20 September 1965, NARA.

96. "Refunding Evaluation Visit," August 11–13, 1965, folder: CAP, Atlanta, Ga., 1965, box 19, RG 381, OEO, Inspection Division, Inspection Reports, 1964–67, NARA.

97. Eugene Patterson exposes this thinking in *Atlanta Journal and Constitution*, 5 December 1965. That being said, Atlanta's leaders, including Allen, CCAA director Duane Beck, Woodruff Foundation consultant Philip Weltner, and Coca-Cola magnate Ernest Woodruff, acknowledged that racism, and institutional racism, influenced social outcomes.

98. "Summary of the Application for a Community Action Program," 16 November 1964, folder 15, box 7, CCAA Records.

99. The requirement for "maximum feasible participation" was first made explicit in "Community Action Program Guide," section 5, part B, vol. 1, February 1965. See Crawford, *Comprehensive and Systematic Evaluation*, 21.

100. Statement of CAP Grant, GA-CAP-306/1, NARA.

101. Crawford, *Comprehensive and Systematic Evaluation*, 22. On the citywide citizens participation committee, see Dare, "Involvement of the Poor," 65.

102. McKay and Krumlauf to Way and Clampitt, 20 September 1965, NARA.

103. *Atlanta Inquirer*, 27 February 1965.

104. Emphasis in report. "Atlanta, Ga. trip report," Ben Zimmerman, 17 October 1966, folder: CAP, Atlanta, Ga., June 66–67, box 20, RG 381, Inspection Division, Inspection Reports, 1964–67, NARA.

105. John Calhoun interview attached to McKay and Krumlauf to May and Clampitt, 20 September 1965, NARA; Clifford Kuhn and Shep Barbash, 22 November 1966, Georgia Government Documentation Project, Special Collections and Archives, Georgia State University Library, Atlanta.

106. *Atlanta Constitution*, 2 August 1965.

107. The approach to communicating with target areas and setting up centers is outlined in Interview with John Calhoun, appended to McKay and Krumlauf to May and Clampitt, 20 September 1965, NARA; Interview with John Calhoun, folder 42, box 11, Emory University, Center for Research in Social Change, Director's Files, RMARBL. Also see Crawford, *Comprehensive and Systematic Evaluation*, 21.

108. The spelling of Scott's Crossing varies across historical documents; I use Scott's Crossing for consistency.

109. *Atlanta Inquirer*, 14 August 1965.

110. *Atlanta Constitution*, 10 September 1984.

111. Shelmon and Samples to "Pastors and Churches," 2 July 1965, folder 3, box 1, Samples Papers.

112. Untitled, 1 August, 1965, folder 3, box 1, Samples Papers.

113. Shelmon to John Calhoun, 26 July 1965, folder 4, box 1, Samples Papers; Shelmon and Samples to Calhoun, folder 1, box 1, Samples Papers.

114. To "Friend", 11 August 1965, folder 3, box 1, Samples Papers.

115. Ortelus Shelmon and Rev. C. A. Samples to John Calhoun, 30 July 1965, folder 1, box 1, Samples Papers.

116. Ortelus Shelmon to David Powell, 8 October 1965, box 1, folder 5, Samples Papers.

117. Frankie V. Adams to Rev. C. A. Samples, 27 September 1965, folder 1, box 1, Samples Papers.

118. Scott's Crossing Civic League and Northwest Organizations, Ortelus Shelmon, C. A. Samples to C. O. Emmerich, 11 November 1965, folder 3, box 1, Samples Papers. The Scott's Crossing complaints were echoed in an inspection office report assessing the entirety of Atlanta's program. See "Atlanta, Ga. trip report," Ben Zimmerman, 17 October 1966, NARA.

119. Summary notes of interview with Mrs. S. Christopher Stevenson, Ed May, and Bob Clampitt to Martha McKay and Al Krumlauf, 20 September 1965, folder: CAP, Atlanta, Ga., 1965, box 19, RG 381, OEO, Inspection Division, Inspection Reports, 1964–67, NARA.

Chapter 3. Vine City

1. SRC, "A City Slum: Poor People and Problems" (Atlanta: SRC, 1966), 3. The report can be found in folder 2, box 61, Paschall Papers.

2. A 1965 survey indicated that residents considered Vine City to be the area bounded by Northside Drive, Hunter Street, Sunset Avenue, and Simpson Street. See SRC, "City Slum," 1–2.

3. *Atlanta Inquirer*, 4 September 1965.

4. Affidavit of Robert Lee Edwards, SNCC papers (microfilm), reel 37.

5. "Purpose of the Atlanta Project," SNCC papers (microfilm), reel 45; SRC, "City Slum," 1–2.

6. Date was established from SRC, "City Slum."

7. Nasstrom, "'This Joint Effort,'" 31.

8. See box 65, Vine City Project, Paschall Papers, RMARBL.

9. Author interview with J. Otis Cochran, 23 August 2012.

10. SRC, "City Slum," 3.

11. Author interview with J. Otis Cochran, 23 August 2012. On Saul Alinsky and the methods used by his Industrial Areas Foundation, see Horwitt, *Let Them Call Me Rebel*.

12. SRC, "City Slum," 4.

13. [Al Ulmer] to Sherrie Hallerook, 22 October 1965, SRC papers, reel 214.

14. Ulmer to Robert Valder, 11 January 1966, SRC papers, reel 214.

15. "Bill" [William Beardske] to Al [Ulmer], 4 May 1966, SRC papers, reel 214.

16. Annual Report, Community Organizing Project, SRC papers (microfilm), reel 214; Lewis and D'Orso, *Walking with the Wind*, 399–400.

17. Marcia L. Halvorsen, "An Analysis and Interpretation of Data on the Social

Characteristics of Residents of 'Vine City,'" 15 June 1967, Project 6-8162, folder 4, box 65, Paschall Papers. Halvorsen, a white economist, joined Spelman in 1964, compelled by her interest in the civil rights movement and racial justice. "Donor Stories: Marcia L. Halvorsen," United Negro College Fund, https://uncf.org/the-latest/donor-stories -marcia-l-halvorsen. Halvorsen taught at Spelman College until 1975. Also see author interview with J. Otis Cochran, 23 August 2012.

18. Halvorsen, "Analysis and Interpretation of Data."

19. SRC, "City Slum."

20. SRC, "City Slum"; *Atlanta Constitution*, 1 July 1965; "Vine City Story," Paschall Papers; "Dear Experimenter," 28 April 1965, folder 4, box 65, Paschall Papers; author interview with J. Otis Cochran, 23 August 2012.

21. "Proposed Community Organizing Project," SRC, reel 214.

22. SRC, "City Slum"; "Dear Experimenter," 18 April 1965, Paschall Papers; author interview with J. Otis Cochran, 23 August 2012.

23. There are conflicting reports on attendance. See "Vine City Story," Paschall Papers.

24. *Atlanta Constitution*, 1 July 1965; *Atlanta Journal*, 1 July 1965; J. Otis Cochran to "Experimenters," folder 4, box 65, Paschall Papers; "Vine City Story," Paschall Papers.

25. SRC, "City Slum."

26. SRC, "City Slum." VISTA, modeled on the Peace Corps, placed volunteers in local communities so as to expand the capacity of an area or project to fight poverty. Zeitz, *Building the Great Society*, 83.

27. SRC, "City Slum," 11.

28. SRC, "City Slum," 14.

29. SRC, "City Slum," 12.

30. SRC, "City Slum"; Hector Black to Eliza Paschall, 16 September 1966, folder 4, box 65, Paschall Papers. Cochran spent the summer of 1965 in eastern Kentucky at a community-organizing summer school. When he returned, Vine City Council had been formed. Author interview with J. Otis Cochran, 23 August 2012.

31. Al Ulmer to Julian Bond, September 30, [1965], SRC, reel 214.

32. *Atlanta Inquirer*, 10 October 1965; *Atlanta Inquirer*, 8 October 1966. VCIA may have lost its energy when its energetic founder, Otis Cochran, graduated from Morehouse College (1968) to attend Yale Law School.

33. Helen Howard, as quoted in Lerner, *Black Women in White America*, 516.

34. *Vine City Voice*, 6 September 1965.

35. Black to Paschall, 16 September 1966, Paschall Papers.

36. "*Vine City Voice*, 4 December 1965.

37. SRC, "City Slum," 10.

38. *Vine City Voice*, 18 September 1965. Drawing on her experiences organizing in Vine City, Dorothy Bolden (Thomson) went on to organize the National Domestic Workers Union of America, Inc., in 1968. See Beck, "National Domestic Workers Union," 195–211.

39. *Vine City Voice*, 30 October 1965. *Atlanta Constitution*, 1 July 1965; "Vine City Story," Paschall Papers; Black to Paschall, 16 September 1966, Paschall Papers.

40. *Vine City Voice*, 6 September 1965.

41. *Vine City Voice*, 18 September 1965.

42. *Vine City Voice*, 2 October 1965.

43. *Vine City Voice*, 16 October 1965.

44. *Atlanta Inquirer*, 31 July 1965; *Atlanta Inquirer*, 28 August 1965; *Vine City Voice*, 6 September 1965.

45. *Vine City Voice*, 5 November 1965.

46. *Vine City Voice*, 12 November 1965. Also see *Vine City Voice*, 5 November 1965.

47. *Atlanta Inquirer*, 28 August 1965.

48. *Vine City Voice*, 30 October 1965.

49. *Vine City Voice*, 30 October 1965.

50. Report attached to Elisabeth to "all N.Y. Staff," 22 January 1966, SNCC papers, reel 45. The report postdates the cover letter.

51. Allen and Hemphill, *Mayor*, 181–82. Also see Grady-Willis, *Challenging U.S. Apartheid*, 80–84. In *Bond* v. *Floyd* (1966) the Supreme Court ruled that Bond had been denied his right to freedom of speech. He was subsequently seated.

52. On SNCC, see Carson, *In Struggle*; Jeffries, *Bloody Lowndes*.

53. Jeffries, *Bloody Lowndes*, 66–67.

54. Report attached to Elisabeth to "all N.Y. Staff," SNCC papers.

55. "The Necessity for Southern Urban Organizing," folder 8, box 33, Forman Papers. On SNCC's Atlanta project, also see Grady-Willis, *Challenging U.S. Apartheid*, 83–113.

56. Report attached to Elisabeth to "all N.Y. Staff," SNCC papers. Also see "Prospectus for an Atlanta Project," SNCC papers, reel 45; No title, but the typescript begins, "As a result of Julian Bond's unseating, SNCC has formed an Atlanta Project," folder 1, sc3093 Mendy Samstein Papers, Wisconsin Historical Society; Carson, *In Struggle*, 193.

57. Carson, *In Struggle*, 193.

58. Lefever, *Undaunted by the Fight* 199, also see 183–85, 97–99. On Robinson, also see Harmon, *Beneath the Image*, 197–99.

59. Perkins, "Atlanta Vine City Project," 29.

60. Perkins, "Atlanta Vine City Project," 31.

61. "Necessity for Southern Urban Organizing," Forman Papers.

62. "Necessity for Southern Urban Organizing," Forman Papers. Also see Report attached to Elisabeth to "all N.Y. Staff," SNCC papers.

63. Report attached to Elisabeth to "all N.Y. Staff," SNCC papers, reel 45.

64. Report attached to Elisabeth to "all N.Y. Staff," SNCC papers.

65. "136th District Protests Inadequate Housing," 31 January 1966, SNCC papers, reel 41.

66. *New York Times*, 28 September 1963; Lawson and Naison, *Tenant Movement in New York City*, 175–79; Mandi Jackson, "Harlem's Rent Strike," 53–79.

67. *Afro-American*, 12 February 1966. On Markham Street events, also see Lefever, *Undaunted by the Fight*.

68. *Afro-American*, 12 February 1966.

69. *Atlanta Journal*, 28 February 1966.

70. Report attached to Elisabeth to "all N.Y. Staff," 22 January 1966, part 3—Markham Street Affair, SNCC papers, reel 45.

71. Report attached to Elisabeth to "all N.Y. Staff," part 3, SNCC papers.

72. Jeffries, *Bloody Lowndes*, 59.

73. Sue Thrasher and Bob Hall interview with Julian Bond, December 1975, Southern Oral History Project, University of North Carolina.

74. Beltramini, "S.C.L.C. Operation Breadbasket," 13, 20. On Chicago's Operation Breadbasket, also see Deppe, *Operation Breadbasket*. On King and the Chicago movement, see Ralph, *Northern Protest*, 414–22; Thomas Jackson, *From Civil Rights to Human Rights*; Finley, *Chicago Freedom Movement*; Honey, *To the Promised Land*; Sugrue, *Sweet Land of Liberty*; Laurent, *King and the Other America*.

75. On "civil rights unionism," see Korstad, *Civil Rights Unionism*. Korstad provides an overview of the confluence of multiple activist streams on pages 3–11. Korstad argues that the civil rights unionism he is describing collapsed in the late 1940s and early 1950s.

76. C. T. Vivian to Affiliate Leaders, 7 December 1964, folder 17, box 299, SCLC papers, RMARBL, as quoted in LaShier, "'To Secure Improvements,'" 167.

77. *Atlanta Journal and Constitution*, 21 December 1964; LaShier, "'To Secure Improvements,'" 155–68; Honey, *To the Promised Land*, 88–94.

78. As quoted in *Atlanta Inquirer*, 5 February 1966, and *Chicago Defender (National Edition)*, 5 February 1966.

79. Signage can be read in VIS 99.235.17; VIS 99.235.01; VIS 99.235.03, Bill Wilson Photographs Collection, AHC.

80. *Chicago Defender* (national ed.), 5 February 1966; *Los Angeles Sentinel*, 10 February 1966; *Atlanta Inquirer*, 5 February 1965.

81. *Atlanta Constitution*, 2 February 1966, 3 February 1966.

82. "To Mayor Ivan Allen," SNCC papers, reel 41.

83. Report attached to Elisabeth to "all N.Y. Staff," part 3, SNCC papers; "Day-to-day account of events in Markham area," SNCC papers, reel 41; *Atlanta Constitution*, 5 February 1966.

84. Report attached to Elisabeth to "all N.Y. Staff," part 3, SNCC papers; *Atlanta Constitution*, 5 February 1966.

85. *Atlanta Constitution*, 5 February 1966.

86. Brown-Nagin, *Courage to Dissent*, 282–84.

87. As explained in *Atlanta Journal and Constitution*, 29 January 1967.

88. Press release, undated, begins "Tomorrow at 9:00 a.m. in the civil court of Judge Osgood Williams," folder 1, box 1, Student Nonviolent Coordinating Committee, Vine City Project Records, Wisconsin Historical Society, University of Wisconsin (hereafter cited as SNCC-VCP).

89. Report attached to Elisabeth to "all N.Y. Staff," part 3, SNCC papers. The SNCC report indicates that Schaffer also expected to lose the case.

90. *Atlanta Inquirer*, 12 February 1966; *Atlanta Constitution*, 10 February 1966.

91. *Atlanta Inquirer*, 19 February 1966. The following week Teague arrived home to find that the house was being demolished, his belongings inside. Report attached to Elisabeth to "all N.Y. Staff," part 3, SNCC papers.

92. Report attached to Elisabeth to "all N.Y. Staff," part 3, SNCC papers.

93. Report attached to Elisabeth to "all N.Y. Staff," part 3, SNCC papers.

94. "Statement by Mr. John Teague," SNCC papers (microfilm), reel 37.

95. Report attached to Elisabeth to "all N.Y. Staff," part 3, SNCC papers.

96. "Vine City Council," press release, February 18, 1966, box 1, folder 13, SNCC-VCP.

97. Allen himself associated the stadium with city status. See Allen and Hemphill, *Mayor*, 152.

98. "Vine City Council," press release, February 18, 1966, SNCC-VCP. On the Atlanta–Fulton County Recreation Authority—which was the stadium authority, having been reactivated in 1963—and park spending, see Keating, *Atlanta*, 98–99; Allen and Hemphill, *Mayor*, 152–60. On the reactivation of the stadium authority, see *Atlanta Constitution*, 4 June 1963.

99. *Atlanta Constitution*, 2 March 1966, 3 March 1966, 5 March 1966, 8 March 1966; *Atlanta Journal*, 3 March 1966, 5 March 1966.

100. The exact dates of the early March 1966 evictions and court actions vary slightly between the news coverage and the SNCC report.

101. Report attached to Elisabeth to "all N.Y. Staff," part 3, SNCC papers.

102. *Atlanta Constitution*, 8 March 1966.

103. *Atlanta Inquirer*, 12 March 1966.

104. Report attached to Elisabeth to "all N.Y. Staff," part 3, SNCC papers.

105. *Atlanta Journal*, 8 March 1966.

106. Report attached to Elisabeth to "all N.Y. Staff," part 3, SNCC papers.

107. *Atlanta Constitution*, 11 March 1966; *Atlanta Constitution*, 26 March 1966.

108. Report attached to Elisabeth to "all N.Y. Staff," part 3, SNCC papers.

109. On the development of a philosophy of racial separatism within SNCC, see Carson, *In Struggle*, chap. 13.

110. "White Jesus, Hector Black, Vine City, and SNCC," *Newsweek*, 25 June 1966, 29.

111. Willie Williams provided shelter for another tenant evicted that day, Ruby Tinner. Tinner had lost her dwelling when the city found her Schaffer-owned property too derelict to repair. *Atlanta Inquirer*, 13 August 1966.

112. Grady-Willis, *Challenging U.S. Apartheid*, 102–9.

113. Stokely Carmichael to William Ware, 14 February 1967, folder 9, box 33, Forman Papers; Stokely Carmichael to William Ware, 22 February 1967, folder 9, box 33, Forman Papers; Cleveland Sellers to William Ware, 3 February 1967, folder 9, box 33, Forman Papers.

114. *Shaffer* v. *Atlanta, et al.*, Book 2291, p. 269 [unclear], Civil Action, File No. B-31065, Fulton Superior Court, contained in Howard Moore Papers, folder 10, box 48, RMARBL.

Chapter 4. The Poor Folks Movement

1. Press release, OEO, 14 September 1965, folder: CAP, Atlanta, Ga., box 19, RG 381, OEO, Inspection Division, Inspection Reports, 1964–67, NARA; *Atlanta Constitution*, 14 September 1965.

2. *Atlanta Constitution*, 14 September 1965.

3. *Atlanta Constitution*, 14 September 1965; Biles, *Fate of Cities*, 148–49.

4. *New York Times*, 12 April 1965.

5. "Briefing: Neighborhood Services Organization," 31 December 1965, file: Atlanta Background, box 19, RG 381, OEO, Inspection Division, Inspection Reports, 1964–67, NARA.

6. Regularly employed farm and domestic workers were excluded from old-age benefits until the Social Security Amendments of 1950s. And even after the establishment of Social Security, many farm and domestic workers were not "regularly employed" and may not have contributed to social security. See Tamar B. Breslauer and William R. Morton, *Social Security: Major Decisions in the House and Senate since 1935*, updated 28 March 2019, Congressional Research Service, RL30920, https://fas.org/sgp/crs/misc/RL30920.pdf.

7. *Atlanta Journal and Constitution*, 26 September 1965.

8. *Atlanta Journal and Constitution*, 26 September 1965. Citizens Trust Company, Southeastern Fidelity Fire Insurance, and Atlanta Life Insurance Co. were the suggested companies.

9. *Atlanta Journal and Constitution*, 26 September 1965.

10. *Atlanta Constitution*, 30 September 1965; *Atlanta Constitution*, 4 October 1965; *Atlanta Constitution*, 7 October 1965.

11. *Atlanta Constitution*, 4 October 1965; Shrider, "Use of Indigenous Persons." Also see "Of Concern to Neighborhood Aides," in Agenda, Atlanta All-Citizens Poverty Meeting, 19 November 1965, folder 8, box 1, Samples Papers.

12. Mrs. W. H. Aiken indicated that she voted against the plan because she did not fully understand the details of the proposal. *Atlanta Constitution*, 30 September 1965.

13. Woods, *Prisoners of Hope*, 200–201; Zeitz, *Building the Great Society*, 85. On Alinsky's organizing methods, see Horwitt, *Let Them Call Me Rebel*.

14. Journalist Wayne Kelley describes the requirement for maximum feasible participation in *Atlanta Journal and Constitution*, 14 November 1965.

15. Al Krumlauf to Edgar May and Robert Clampitt, 21 September 1965, folder: CAP, Atlanta, Ga., 1965, box 19, RG 381, OEO, Inspection Division, Inspection Reports, 1964–67, NARA.

16. Martha McKay and Al Krumlauf to Ed May and Bob Clampitt, 20 September 1965, folder: CAP, Atlanta, Ga., 1965, box 19, RG 381, OEO, Inspection Division, Inspection Reports, 1964–67, NARA.

17. "Refunding Evaluation Visit," August 11–13, 1965, folder: CAP, Atlanta, Ga., 1965, box 19, RG 381, OEO, Inspection Division, Inspection Reports, 1964–67, NARA.

18. The award was originally announced in September. See press release, OEO, 14 September 1965, folder: CAP, Atlanta, Ga., 1965, box 19, RG 381, OEO, Inspection Division, Inspection Reports, 1964–67, NARA. "Special Condition—Atlanta Grant 9/65," folder: CAP, Atlanta, Ga., 1965 box 19, RG 381, OEO, Inspection Division, Inspection Reports, 1964–67, NARA. OEO also required EOA to make corresponding changes in its articles of incorporation.

19. *Atlanta Constitution*, 20 September 1965.

20. *Atlanta Journal and Constitution*, 26 September 1965. Also see *Atlanta Journal and Constitution*, 14 November 1965.

21. As quoted in Boisfeuillet Jones to Samuel Williams, 16 December 1965, folder: CAP, Atlanta, Ga., box 19, RG 381, OEO, Inspection Division, Inspection Reports, 1964–67, NARA.

22. *Atlanta Daily World*, 2 February 1964. A 5 August 1965 letter summarized the Summit's interactions with EOA to date. The summary made no reference to poverty or poor people's interests. At least in early August 1965, the Summit was not promoting the interest of the poor specifically. Harry Miller to Bill Haddad and Bob Clampitt, 5 August 1965, folder: CAP, Atlanta, Ga., 1965, box 19, RG 381 OEO, Inspection Division, Inspection Reports, 1964–67, NARA.

23. Jones to Williams, 16 December 1965, NARA. The 5 October 1965 letter was also referred to in [unknown] to Edgar May and Robert L. Martin, 13 March 1966, box 19, RG 381, OEO, Inspection Division, Inspection Reports, 1964–67, NARA.

24. Jones to Williams, 16 December 1965, NARA.

25. According to later correspondence, the EOA Board of Directors authorized the EOA chair and staff to develop a plan "that would meet the conditions concerning involvement of residents in policy making decisions of economic Opportunity Atlanta." C. O. Emmerich to Theodore M. Berry, 22 October 1965, folder: CAP, Atlanta, Ga., 1965, box 19, RG 381, OEO, Inspection Division, Inspection Reports, 1964–67, NARA.

26. In a 1996 oral history, Dan Sweat explained that he threw together this organizational structure over a weekend of beer and football. Dan Sweat interview by Cliff Kuhn and Shep Barbash, 22 November 1996, Georgia Government Documentation Project, Special Collections and Archives, Georgia State University Library, Atlanta.

27. "Citizen Involvement," folder 3, box 1, Samples Papers; Crawford, *Comprehensive and Systematic Evaluation*, 22. A copy of Atlanta's revised plan for citizen participation can be found in "Economic Opportunity Atlanta, Inc., Citizen Involvement," folder: CAP: Atlanta Background, box 19, RG 381, OEO, Inspection Division, Inspection Reports, 1964–67, NARA. *Atlanta Constitution*, 10 November 1965; *Atlanta Constitution*, 20 November 1965; Harvey Gates report, Interview with John Calhoun, 2 February 1967, folder 42, box 11, Emory Center for Research in Social Change Papers, RMARBL. The EOA approved the proposal at its November 1965 meeting.

28. "Complaints stated at Ad Hoc Committee on EOA," 23 October 1965, folder 4, box 1, Samples Papers.

29. "Agenda for Ad Hoc Committee Meeting," 26 October 1965, folder 8, box 1, Samples Papers; Ad Hoc Committee Minutes, 27 October 1965, folder 8, box 1, Samples Papers; "What the Poverty Program Needs" [draft], 26 October 1965, folder 8, box 1, Samples Papers; *Atlanta Constitution*, 20 November 1965.

30. "A Preliminary Plan of Action for the Negro Community in the War on Poverty," folder 8, box 1, Samples Papers.

31. Ad Hoc Summit Committee on Poverty et al. to the Honorable Adam Clayton Powell, 8 November 1965, folder 8, box 1, Samples Papers.

32. At the 17 November 1965 meeting of the board, W. H. Montague requested permission for the Ad Hoc Committee to address the meeting, but Anne Woodward motioned not to allow the group to address the board, and that motion carried. *Atlanta Inquirer*, 27 November 1965.

33. *Atlanta Inquirer*, 27 November 1965.

34. Boisfeuillet Jones to Dorothy Bolden, 21 June 1966, folder 3, box 1, Samples Papers.

35. *Atlanta Inquirer*, 27 November 1965.

36. *Atlanta Inquirer*, 27 November 1965.

37. *Atlanta Journal and Constitution*, 12 December 1965.

38. There were two hundred neighborhood block organizations in the twelve areas served by neighborhood service centers.. *Atlanta Journal and Constitution*, 8 January 1967.

39. Harvey Gates report, Interview with John Calhoun, 2 February 1967, RMARBL; *Atlanta Journal and Constitution*, 8 January 1967; *Atlanta Inquirer*, 3 December 1966; Economic Opportunity Atlanta, Inc., "Citizen Involvement," folder 33, box 7, Paschall Papers; *Atlanta Constitution*, 28 January 1966, 8 January 1967.

40. *Atlanta Constitution*, 4 February 1966.

41. "Joyce Montgomery's report," 15 January 1967, box 11, folder 39, Emory Center for Research in Social Change Papers, RMARBL.

42. "Joyce Montgomery's report," 15 January 1967, RMARBL.

43. *Atlanta Inquirer*, 16 April 1966.

44. As quoted in Grass Roots Crusade, minutes, 31 July 1966, folder 4, box 1, Samples Papers.

45. *Atlanta Independent*, 2 April 1966.

46. In response, the NAACP sent a letter of protest to Frank Sloan, Regional Director of EOA, with copies to Shriver, Congress, and Powell, as noted in *Atlanta Inquirer*, 2 April 1966. Also see *Atlanta Inquirer*, 26 March 1966.

47. C. A. Samples, Benny T. Smith, and Zannie Tate to "Grass Roots Leaders, SNCC, and To Whom It May Concern," 22 March 1966, folder 1, box 1, Samples Papers.

48. Ad Hoc Committee Minutes, 30 March 1966, folder 4, box 1, Samples Papers.

49. *Atlanta Constitution*, 23 February 1966. Also see *Atlanta Constitution*, 13 February 1966.

50. Ad Hoc Committee Minutes, 30 March 1966, folder 4, box 1, Samples collection.

51. Ad Hoc Committee Minutes, 30 March 1966, Samples collection. Author interview with J. Otis Cochran, 4 August 2016. Also see *Atlanta Daily World*, 1 April 1966.

52. Untitled, 31 March 1966 resolution, folder 4, box 1, Samples collection; untitled, begins "Whereas, on March 18, 1966," folder CAP: Atlanta, Ga., January-March 1966, box 19, RG381; untitled, begins "Whereas, on March 18, 1966," Atlanta Urban Leagues papers, AUC; *Atlanta Inquirer*, 2 April 1966; Boisfeuillet Jones to J. Otis Cochran, 13 April 1966, folder 3, box 1, Samples Papers; C. O. Emmerich to EOA board members, 2 April 1966, folder 11, box 107, AUL papers; *Atlanta Journal*, 1 April 1966.

53. *Atlanta Constitution*, 12 April 1966. Bernard Boutin to Sargent Shriver, 4 April 1966, "Administrative, Georgia" folder, Box 11, RG 381 Community Services Administration, OEO, NARA.

54. "A report," 2 April 1966, attached to C. O. Emmerich to EOA board members, 2 April 1966, folder 11, box 107, AUL Papers.

55. Mabel Henderson, Otis Cochran, and C. A. Samples to Board of Directors Atlanta EOA, Inc., 5 April 1966, folder 1, box 1, Samples Papers. Emmerich responded that he would forward the letter to all board members. C. O. Emmerich to C. A. Sam-

ples, 6 April 1966, folder 1, box 1, Samples Papers. Samples et al. identified their group as the Atlanta Grass Roots Crusade when they picketed EOA headquarters on Monday, 11 April 1966. *Atlanta Constitution*, 12 April 1966.

56. Boisfeuillet Jones to J. Otis Cochran, 13 April 1966, Samples Papers. Also see C. O. Emmerich to J. Otis Cochran, 12 April 1966, folder 3, box 1, Samples Papers.

57. Committee for Correspondence to Boisfeuillet Jones, 18 April 1966, folder 1, box 1, Samples Papers.

58. Jones to Bolden, 21 June 1966, Samples Papers.

59. Robert Martin and Al Krumlauf to Edgar May, 30 April 1966, folder: CAP: Atlanta, Ga., June 66–67, box 20, RG 381, NARA.

60. EOA had missed the March 1 deadline to submit a plan to meet the special conditions. Instead, they submitted in mid-April, when funds had nearly expired.

61. Martin and Krumlauf to May, 30 April 1966, NARA.

62. Benny T. Smith, J. Otis Cochran, Dorothy Bolden, and Rev. C. A. Samples to Boisfeuillet Jones, 14 May 1966, folder 4, box 1, Samples Papers.

63. Atlanta Grass Roots Crusade, "News release," 13 June 1966, folder 4, box 1, Samples Papers.

64. Grass Roots Crusade, minutes, 31 July 1966, folder 4, box 1, Samples Papers; Atlanta Grass Roots Crusade, "News release," 13 June 1966, Samples Papers; Atlanta GrassRoots Council, Proposed Constitution, 1966, folder 4, box 1, Samples Papers.

65. *Atlanta Constitution*, 24 June 1966.

66. On the urban protest of the 1960s, see Levy, *Great Uprising*.

67. *Atlanta Constitution*, 24 June 1966.

68. *Atlanta Inquirer*, 16 April 1966.

69. *Atlanta Inquirer*, 16 April 1966.

70. *Atlanta Journal*, 4 September 1966, as quoted in Grady-Willis, *Challenging U.S. Apartheid*, 115.

71. On the September 1966 events in Summerhill, see Grady-Willis, *Challenging U.S. Apartheid*, 117–28.

72. Affidavit of Geneva Brown, SNCC papers (microfilm), reel 37.

73. Carmichael v. Allen, 267 F. Supp. 985 (N.D. Ga. 1967).

74. Affidavit of Betty Jean McFavors, SNCC papers (microfilm), reel 37.

75. *Carmichael v. Allen*; *Atlanta Constitution*, 7 September 1966.

76. *Atlanta Constitution*, 7 September 1966.

77. *Carmichael v. Allen*.

78. *New York Times*, 8 September 1966.

79. *Atlanta Constitution*, 7 September 1966, 8 September 1966.

80. *Atlanta Constitution*, 10 September 1966.

81. *Carmichael v. Allen*.

82. *New York Times*, 8 September 1966; *Atlanta Constitution*, 9 September 1966; Carson, *In Struggle*, 226.

83. *Carmichael v. Allen*.

84. *Atlanta Constitution*, 11 September 1966; *Atlanta Journal and Constitution*, 11 September 1966; *Atlanta Constitution*, 12 September 1966, 13 September 1966, 14 September 1966.

85. National Advisory Commission on Civil Disorders, *Summary of Report*, 5, 6.

86. *Atlanta Journal*, 22 September 1966.

87. "Q's suggested for the Mayor," 29 September 1966, folder 4, box 1, Samples Papers.

88. Ivan Allen Jr. to William R. Wofford, 30 January 1967, document 13, folder 2, box 1, IADA, http://allenarchive.iac.gatech.edu/items/show/124.

89. "Newsletter of the Community Relations Commission: First Quarterly Progress Report," Box 7, Folder 17 (Complete Folder), IADA, http://allenarchive.iac.gatech.edu /items/show/3041. Also see *Atlanta Constitution*, 29 January 1967.

90. *Atlanta Constitution*, 17 February 1967.

91. *Atlanta Constitution*, 17 February 1967; City of Atlanta, Community Relations Commission, public hearing, 16 February 1967, folder 1, box 12, Paschall Papers.

92. Atlanta, Community Relations Commission, public hearing, 16 February 1967, Paschall Papers.

93. City of Atlanta, Community Relations Commission, Summerhill-Peoplestown Areas Meeting (Mount Carmel Baptist Church), 28 March 1967, folder 1, box 12, Paschall Papers.

94. Anne Rivers Siddons, "Seeds of Sanity," *Atlanta Magazine*, July 1967, 56. Also see "Newsletter of the Community Relations Commission: First Quarterly Progress Report," IADA.

95. "Newsletter of the Community Relations Commission: First Quarterly Progress Report," IADA.

96. *Atlanta Constitution*, 21 February 1966.

97. *Atlanta Constitution*, 29 September 1966.

98. *Atlanta Journal and Constitution*, 29 May 1966.

99. *Atlanta Constitution*, 21 February 1966, 25 October 1966.

100. Zelizer, *Fierce Urgency of Now*, 222–23. On the rising challenges of fighting communism while paying for Great Society programs, see Zeitz, *Building the Great Society*, 217–26.

101. *Atlanta Constitution*, 26 September 1966, 27 September 1966.

102. *Atlanta Constitution*, 5 October 1966; Zelizer, *Fierce Urgency of Now*, 222–23.

103. *Atlanta Constitution*, 21 October 1966.

104. *Atlanta Journal and Constitution*, 4 December 1966.

105. *Atlanta Constitution*, 10 November 1966. Also see Woods, *Prisoners of Hope*, 298–99.

106. *Atlanta Journal and Constitution*, 4 December 1966; *Atlanta Inquirer*, 19 November 1966, 31 December 1966; *Atlanta Constitution*, 31 December 1966, 16 January 1967.

107. *Atlanta Journal and Constitution*, 4 December 1966; *Atlanta Inquirer*, 10 December 1966.

108. *Atlanta Inquirer*, 3 December 1966; *Atlanta Journal and Constitution*, 12 December 1966.

109. *Atlanta Constitution*, 17 February 1967.

110. *Atlanta Constitution*, 5 May 1967.

111. *Atlanta Constitution*, 18 May 1967. The playlots were funded through the supplementary federal budget.

112. "Report on Dixie Hills Episode," 12 July 1967, Atlanta Community Relations Commission Papers, folder 20, box 2, AUC; *Atlanta Constitution*, 19 June 1967; National Advisory Commission on Civil Disorders, *Report*, 29.

113. Minutes, CRC hearing, Dixie Hills, 19 June 1967, Box 7, Folder 17 Complete Folder, IADA, http://allenarchive.iac.gatech.edu/items/show/3041.

114. *Chicago Tribune*, 20 June 1967; *Atlanta Constitution*, 20 June 1967; 21 June 1967; "Report on Dixie Hills Episode," 12 July 1967, Atlanta Community Relations Commission papers, folder 20, box 2, AUC.

115. *Atlanta Constitution*, 21 June 1967; "Report on Dixie Hills Episode," 12 July 1967, Atlanta Community Relations Commission papers, folder 20, box 2, AUC;

116. Community Relations Commission, hearing (Dixie Hills), 19 June 1967, minutes, document 33, folder 17, box 7, IADA, http://allenarchive.iac.gatech.edu/items/show/3074. On behalf of the CRC, Eliza Paschall visited Dixie Hills and held an emergency meeting at the EOA Center on Verbena Street.

117. *Atlanta Constitution*, 28 June 1967.

118. *Atlanta Constitution*, 27 September 1967. On Hosea Williams, see LaShier, "'To Secure Improvements,'" chap. 3.

119. *Atlanta Constitution*, 14 February 1968, 7 March 1968, 11 May 1968. Reverence Joseph Boone, who helped lead SCLC's Operation Breadbasket, would serve as co-chair of the MASLC. *Atlanta Constitution*, 13 September 1967.

120. *Atlanta Journal and Constitution*, 5 November 1967.

Chapter 5. Welfare and Workplace

1. *Emmaus House News*, 8 April 1970.

2. Carole Ashkinaze, "Ethel Mae Mathews Tells It Like It Is for the Welfare Mothers," *Atlanta Constitution*, 17 July 1981.

3. The diocese was also facing its own transgressions. According to Ford, it was the diocese's internal struggle with racial matters that helped launch Emmaus House. In 1963 the Episcopal Diocese's Lovett School had denied admission to Martin Luther King Jr.'s son and subsequently passed resolutions denying entry to any African American applicants. On the Lovett School and integration, see Harris, "Forcing Progress"; "The Lovett School Controversy," https://episcopalarchives.org/church-awakens/exhibits/show/escru/lovett-school; author interview with Austin Ford.

4. Author interview with Austin Ford.

5. Author interview with Grace Stone. On activities at Emmaus House in its earliest years, see author interview with Tom and Debbie Erdmanczyk; author interview with Dennis Goldstein; author interview with David Morath.

6. Author interview with Mimi Bodell.

7. Author interview with Gene Ferguson; not on the Peoplestown Project website, but in author's possession.

8. On the conditions in Peoplestown in Emmaus House's earliest years, see author interview with Dennis Goldstein; author interview with David Morath.

9. Author interview with Ford.

10. In 1959, Peoplestown was represented in census tracts F0055A and F00046. U.S. Census Bureau, *Census of Population, 1960*, vol. 1: *Characteristics of the Population, by Census Tracts*, table P-1. Stone, *Economic Growth and Neighborhood Discontent*, 54; Holliman, "From Crackertown to Model City?," 374, 81; author interview with Bodell.

11. Nadasen, *Rethinking the Welfare Rights Movement*, 29–30.

12. Nadasen, *Rethinking the Welfare Rights Movement*, 28–29; Piven and Cloward, "Weight of the Poor."

13. On challenges with AFDC and food programs, see author interview with Goldstein; author interview with Morath; author interview with Tom and Debbie Erdmanczyk.

14. *Atlanta Constitution*, 27 September 1972. While spending on social welfare programs expanded beginning in the 1960s, the most dramatic increase in AFDC spending came with the War on Poverty. See Gilens, *Why Americans Hate Welfare*, 18–21. The increase in AFDC rolls was at least in part explained by the increased mechanization of agriculture and related job displacement. Piven and Cloward, *Regulating the Poor*, 200–211. Georgia Poverty Rights Organization (GPRO) attributed the uptick in AFDC applicants to the rising unemployment rate, noting that "many AFDC recipients are unemployed maids, who are ineligible for unemployment compensation." "The facts surrounding Georgia's AFDC reduction," folder 6, box 91, Pauley papers. AFDC served disproportionately more Blacks because Blacks in the United States were disproportionately poor. Gilens, *Why Americans Hate Welfare*, 68. The *Atlanta Constitution*'s survey is discussed in "White Georgians Bitterly Resent Welfare," *Atlanta Constitution*, 27 September 1972, 10A.

15. *Atlanta Constitution*, 5 September 1967.

16. U.S. Commission on Civil Rights, *Toward Economic Opportunity in Housing*, 2.

17. Ashkinaze, "Ethel Mae Mathews Tells It"; author interview with Ford.

18. The Emmaus House welfare rights organization was founded in June 1967.

19. No membership list could be found, but addresses for various members are listed in issues of the *Emmaus House News*. See, for example, 9 October 1967, 8 November 1967.

20. *Emmaus House News*, 8 November 1967.

21. *Emmaus House News*, 8 November 1967, 28 August 1968. On the birth and actions of the welfare rights organization at Emmaus House, see author interview with Goldstein; author interview with Morath; author interview with Tom and Debbie Erdmanczyk.

22. Author interview with Goldstein; author interview with Morath; author interview with Susan Taylor; Mariangela Favero, "Alumni Profile: Learning What America Is Really About," *VISTA Source*, Summer/Fall 2001.

23. Muriel Lokey interview, Voices across the Color Line Oral History Project, AHC, 4 January 2006; author interview with Grace Stone; author interview with Deedie Weems. The Episcopal diocese served as a base from which volunteers could be mined, but Ford and the other core staff regularly pitched the cause to congregations that sought to contribute to mission and service work in some way. Former staff

and volunteers are responsible for these observations about the Emmaus House work-force. See, for example, author interview with Goldstein; author interview with Morath; author interview with Patricia Royalty; author interview with Stone.

24. On how Emmaus House staff supported the welfare rights organization specifically, see author interview with Goldstein; author interview with Morath; author interview with Tom and Debbie Erdmanczyk.

25. Author interview with Stone.

26. Author interview with Bodell.

27. Author interview with Stone.

28. Author interview with Taylor.

29. Atlanta Legal Aid Society, Inc., to Board of Directors and Advisory Committee, December Activities, 1965, folder 2, box 1, Atlanta Legal Aid Society Papers, AHC (hereafter ALAS papers).

30. Atlanta Legal Aid Society, Inc., to Board of Directors and Advisory Committee, June Activities, 1966, folder 3, box 1, ALAS papers.

31. "Atlanta Legal Aid Society History," 18–19, folder 5, box 9, ALAS papers. Also see Shepard, *Rationing Justice*, 28–31.

32. The types of cases ALAS confronted were regularly outlined in monthly summaries to the ALAS board of directors. See, for example, Atlanta Legal Aid Society, Inc., to Board of Directors and Advisory Committee, "August [1965] Activities," folder: Activities Report, 1965, box 1, ALAS papers. Shepard describes the early history of ALAS in Shepard, *Rationing Justice*, 28–30.

33. "Development and Implementation of a Comprehensive Legal Assistance Program for Indigents in Atlanta-Fulton County," as quoted in "Atlanta Legal Aid Society History," 18, ALAS papers.

34. "Atlanta Legal Aid Society History," 18–19, ALAS papers.

35. "Atlanta Legal Aid Society History," 18, ALAS papers.

36. "1967 Annual Report," folder 7, box 1, ALAS papers. That program was phased out after the county hired a new public defender in late 1967. *Atlanta Journal and Constitution*, 24 December 1967.

37. The Georgia movement may have gained greater momentum when Governor Carl Sanders publicly promoted such a program in 1964. *Atlanta Constitution*, 19 January 1966; *Atlanta Constitution*, 12 August 1964. Prison reform and various attorney groups continued to push for Georgia to create a public defender program in 1965, and a state legislative committee was established to investigate the possibility. *Atlanta Constitution*, 3 December 1965, 9 July 1965, 5 September 1965. A bill establishing a public defender program was initiated for consideration by the 1967 General Assembly. *Atlanta Constitution*, 17 December 1966.

38. *Atlanta Constitution*, 22 February 1967, 17 March 1967.

39. *Atlanta Constitution*, 24 December 1967.

40. *Atlanta Journal and Constitution*, 24 December 1967. Georgia's first public defender was sworn in to serve Fulton County in October 1967. *Atlanta Constitution*, 20 October 1967; "1967 Annual Report," ALAS papers.

41. Shepard, *Rationing Justice*, 30; "1967 Annual Report," ALAS papers.

42. Shepard, *Rationing Justice*, 45.

43. *Atlanta Constitution*, 17 June 1968, 17 July 1968, 3 October 1968. Similarly, in 1969, in *Bryson* v. *Burson*, ALAS attorneys applied *Shapiro* v. *Thompson* (1969) to end Georgia's one-year residency requirements for AFDC applicants. *Atlanta Constitution*, 24 June 1969, 1 August 1969, 5 August 1969, 23 August 1969, 31 December 1969; Shepard, *Rationing Justice*, 45.

44. "Atlanta Legal Aid Society History," 20–21, ALAS papers.

45. It is important to note that Atlanta was exceptional in its access to determined and well-armed poverty lawyers. Elsewhere in the deep South, Kris Shepard explains, "legal services attorneys were scarce." Shepard, *Rationing Justice*, 33.

46. Laurent, *King and the Other America*, 8. On the Poor People's Campaign, see McKnight, *Last Crusade*; Laurent, *King and the Other America*; Mantler, *Power to the Poor*; Fairclough, *To Redeem the Soul*, chap. 14.

47. The shift is noted by William Julius Wilson in the foreword to Laurent, *King and the Other America*, 8.

48. Laurent, *King and the Other America*, 8.

49. Honey, *To the Promised Land*, chapter 4.

50. Michael Honey describes this coalition in broad terms in Honey, *To the Promised Land*, 120.

51. Mantler, *Power to the Poor*, 105.

52. Nadasen, *Welfare Warriors*, 71–74.

53. On King and the Memphis sanitation strike, see Honey, *Going Down Jericho Road*.

54. On how Allen and Atlanta responded to King's assassination, see Allen and Hemphill, *Mayor*, 193–218.

55. Allen, *Atlanta Rising*, 158–60.

56. *Atlanta Constitution*, 7 May 1968.

57. *Atlanta Constitution*, 7 May 1968.

58. *Atlanta Constitution*, 30 April 1968.

59. *Atlanta Constitution*, 15 May 1968.

60. On the role of the mule train in the Poor People's March on Washington, see Mantler, *Power to the Poor*, 133–36; McKnight, *Last Crusade*, 94–106.

61. *Atlanta Constitution*, 15 June 1968.

62. *Atlanta Constitution*, 17 June 1968.

63. McKnight, *Last Crusade*, 9, 28, 141.

64. On the cultural significance of Vietnam and the shift in Americans' views of the conflict, see Self, *All in the Family*, chap. 2. On the relationship between the Vietnam conflict, growing frustration with Great Society programs, urban unrest, and urban policy, see Biles, *Fate of Cities*, 149.

65. *Atlanta Constitution*, 19 February 1968.

66. *Atlanta Constitution*, 10 September 1968, 11 September 1968.

67. *Atlanta Constitution*, 19 February 1968.

68. *Atlanta Constitution*, 5 September 1968; *Great Speckled Bird*, 13 September 1968.

69. On the surface, the city appeared to offer some opportunities for advancement: Black workers seeking truck-driving supervisor roles could take tests, but if

they passed, they sat indefinitely on a waiting list waiting for a position to open. *Great Speckled Bird*, 13 September 1968.

70. LaShier, "To Secure Improvements, 259, 268–75, 280.

71. Hild and Merritt, introduction to *Reconsidering Southern Labor History*, 8–9.

72. Anti-union campaigns are described in a number of labor histories, including Phillips-Fein, "Business Conservatism," 9–26; Gunn, "'Good Place to Make Money.'"

73. On the impact of dues checkoff, see Harlon Joye interview by Philip LaPorte, 9 May 2006, L2006-09, Voices of Labor Oral History Project, Special Collections Department, GSU.

74. As William Powell Jones explains, for example, the CIO financially supported civil rights efforts but retreated from organizing Black workers when white workers felt threatened by racial equity. Jones, "'Simple Truths of Democracy," 250–70.

75. LaShier, "'To Secure Improvements,'" 206–08, 213–14; Hower, "'Threshold Moment.'"

76. *Great Speckled Bird*, 13 September 1968.

77. LaShier, "'To Secure Improvements,'" 262–63.

78. LaShier, "'To Secure Improvements,'" 183–84.

79. Rev. T. Y. Rogers Jr., "Spot announcement, WAOK & WIGO," 12 September 1968, folder 24, box 286, Southern Christian Leadership Conference Papers, RMARBL (hereafter SCLC papers).

80. Ralph David Abernathy, "RDA 9-11-68," folder 11, box 341, SCLC papers.

81. *Atlanta Constitution*, 6 September 1968, 9 September 1968. Dollar calculations completed using the U.S. Bureau of Labor Statistics' Consumer Price Index Inflation Calculator, https://www.bls.gov/data/inflation_calculator.htm.

82. *Great Speckled Bird*, 13 September 1968.

83. *Atlanta Constitution*, 9 September 1968.

84. Abernathy "RDA 9-11-68," SCLC papers.

85. *Atlanta Constitution*, 6 September 1968.

86. *Atlanta Constitution*, 6 September 1968.

87. LaShier, "'To Secure Improvements,'" 303.

88. Honey, *To the Promised Land*, 146.

89. On "civil rights unionism," see Korstad, *Civil Rights Unionism*. Korstad provides an overview of the confluence of multiple activist streams on pages 3–11. Korstad argues that the civil rights unionism he is describing collapsed in the late 1940s and early 1950s.

90. *Atlanta Constitution*, 7 September 1968, 10 September 1968; LaShier, "'To Secure Improvements,'" 285.

91. *Atlanta Constitution*, 13 September 1968. Rallies are noted in *Atlanta Constitution*, 12 September 1968, and on flyers contained in folder 11, box 341, SCLC papers. Dennis Goldstein describes Emmaus House's relationship to the strike in the author's interview with Goldstein. Also see the author's interview with Ford. The list of those arrested in the 1968 strike includes Emmaus House's Ford, Goldstein, Gene Ferguson, Bob Beishlein, and Sandra Schlein, and Black ministers who had participated in urban renewal organizing covered in chapter 1, including Rev. J. D. Grier. See "People Arrested," folder 24, box 286, SCLC papers, RMARBL.

92. *Atlanta Constitution*, 12 September 1968.

93. *Atlanta Constitution*, 10 September 1968.

94. *Atlanta Constitution*, 12 September 1968.

95. LaShier, "'To Secure Improvements,'" 325–26. Notes on this final set of demands are in folder 11, box 341, SCLC papers.

96. *Atlanta Constitution*, 14 September 1968.

97. LaShier, "'To Secure Improvements,'" 331.

98. LaShier, "'To Secure Improvements,'" 332.

99. *Atlanta Constitution*, 13 September 1968.

100. *Atlanta Constitution*, 14 September 1968.

101. *Atlanta Constitution*, 17 April 1970; LaShier, "'To Secure Improvements,'" 337–38.

102. LaShier, "'To Secure Improvements,'" 335, 337.

103. LaShier, "'To Secure Improvements,'" 340.

104. *Great Speckled Bird*, 23 March 1970.

105. LaShier, "'To Secure Improvements,'" 341.

106. *Great Speckled Bird*, 23 March 1970.

107. LaShier, "'To Secure Improvements,'" 339–40.

108. *Atlanta Constitution*, 21 March 1970; LaShier, "'To Secure Improvements,'" 341–42. McCartin points out that this firing reflects a larger shift in how governments handled public sector strikes in general and sanitation worker strikes in particular. McCartin, "Fire the Hell out of Them,'" 67–91.

109. *Atlanta Constitution*, 21 March 1970.

110. *Atlanta Constitution*, 23 March 1970.

111. *Atlanta Constitution*, 8 April 1970.

112. *Atlanta Constitution*, 8 April 1970.

113. *Atlanta Constitution*, 17 April 1970.

114. Joseph A. McCartin describes the increasing militancy of public sector workers in McCartin, "Fire the Hell out of Them,'" 72.

115. LaShier, "'To Secure Improvements,'" 347, 349–54.

116. LaShier, "'To Secure Improvements,'" 353–56, 365–66. *Emmaus House News* included appeals for support of the strikers. See, for example, *Emmaus House News*, 8 April 1970; *Atlanta Constitution*, 5 April 1970.

117. Hobson, *Legend of the Black Mecca*, 59; McCartin, "Fire the Hell out of Them,'" 69–70.

118. *Atlanta Constitution*, 17 April 1970. Maurice Hobson points out that the strike was part of a growing rift between Massell and Jackson. Hobson, *Legend of the Black Mecca*, 58–59. On divisions within the Black and civil rights community over the strike, see LaShier, "'To Secure Improvements,'" 347–66.

119. *Atlanta Constitution*, 23 April 1970.

120. *Atlanta Constitution*, 4 August 1970. Garbage workers threatened to strike to reinstitute dues checkoff in 1971. *Atlanta Constitution*, 20 May 1971. Dues checkoff would be reinstated under Maynard Jackson in 1975. *Atlanta Constitution*, 14 June 1975.

121. *Atlanta Constitution*, 4 August 1970.

122. LaShier, "'To Secure Improvements,'" 347–54. Joye interview by LaPorte, 9 May 2006, GSU.

123. McCartin, "'Fire the Hell out of Them,'" 71. On businesses' anti-union campaigns in the 1970s, see Windham, *Knocking on Labor's Door*, particularly chap. 3.

124. NWRO's national network provided inspiration, talking points, and organizing tactics. Atlantans attended national meetings and kept abreast of national and other chapters' campaigns.

125. Author interview with Ford.

126. *Emmaus House News*, 18 December 1968.

127. *Atlanta Constitution*, 19 December 1968.

128. *Atlanta Constitution*, 19 December 1968.

129. *Atlanta Constitution*, 19 December 1968. The significance and range of the special grant campaigns are addressed by Nadasen, *Welfare Warriors*, 80–93. And like NWRO chapters across the country, Atlanta NWRO activists picketed for an Easter bonus and launched a local version of NWRO's Sears credit campaign. See *Atlanta Constitution*, 27 March 1969; *Great Speckled Bird*, 21 April 1969, 28 April 1969. The national Sears campaign is discussed in Nadasen, *Welfare Warriors*, 109–13.

130. *Emmaus House News*, 23 July 1969, 10 September 1969.

131. *Emmaus House News*, 28 May 1969.

132. *Atlanta Constitution*, 7 February 1969. The federal freeze and its effects in Georgia are described in *Atlanta Constitution*, 16 February 1969.

133. *Emmaus House News*, 25 June 1969. The bulk of *Emmaus House News* can be found in folder 20, box 69, Pauley papers.

134. *Great Speckled Bird*, 7 July 1969.

135. *Emmaus House News*, 9 July 1969.

136. *Atlanta Constitution*, 1 July 1969.

137. *Atlanta Constitution*, 1 July 1969. Also see *Emmaus House News*, 23 July 1969.

138. On the Center's goals for *Goldberg v. Kelley*, see Martha Davis, *Brutal Need*, 103–4.

139. *Atlanta Constitution*, 24 March 1970.

140. *Emmaus House News*, 22 April 1970; *Atlanta Constitution*, 26 March 1970.

141. *Atlanta Constitution*, 16 April 1970.

142. *Great Speckled Bird*, 13 April 1970.

143. *Atlanta Constitution*, 21 April 1970.

144. *Atlanta Constitution*, 30 April 1970.

145. *Atlanta Constitution*, 25 April 1970.

146. *Atlanta Constitution*, 29 April 1970.

147. *Atlanta Constitution*, 30 April 1970. Indeed, Burson threatened to resign three times in his three-year career as state welfare director. *Atlanta Constitution*, 6 May 1970.

148. *Atlanta Constitution*, 16 April 1970. Also see *Emmaus House News*, 22 April 1970.

149. *Atlanta Constitution*, 23 June 1970, 24 June 1970.

150. See Martha Davis, *Brutal Need*, chap. 4.

151. *Atlanta Constitution*, 28 August 1953. Talmadge served as Georgia governor from 1948 to 1955 and was elected to the U.S. Senate in 1956.

152. *Atlanta Constitution*, 17 August 1969.

153. *Atlanta Journal and Constitution Magazine*, 3 December 1967.

154. *Atlanta Constitution*, 5 September 1967.

155. Burson commissioned the hunger study soon after taking office. *Atlanta Constitution*, 3 August 1967; *Atlanta Journal and Constitution Magazine*, 3 December 1967. A total of 143,120 Georgians participated in the two food programs, as noted in *Atlanta Constitution*, 3 August 1967.

156. *Atlanta Constitution*, 26 August 1967.

157. *Atlanta Constitution*, 4 September 1967. Also see *Atlanta Constitution*, 5 March 1968.

158. *Atlanta* Constitution, 3 August 1967.

159. *Atlanta Constitution*, 14 September 1967. Also see *Atlanta Constitution*, 17 August 1969, 15 July 1968, August 1967.

160. *Atlanta Constitution*, 6 May 1970.

161. *Emmaus House News*, 11 March 1970.

162. *Emmaus House News*, 22 April 1970.

163. The 27 May 1970 newsletter indicates that the welfare rights organization received permission to mail the card "after many months of negotiation" with the State Division of Family and Children's Services. *Emmaus House News*, 27 May 1970. The 8 July 1970 Emmaus House News refers to the card being mailed that month with "your welfare check." *Emmaus House News*, 8 July 1970. Elsewhere in the newsletter, it was estimated that five thousand cards were mailed. The card can be found in folder 10, box 69, Pauley Papers.

164. Austin Ford recalled that the card was arranged with Jim Parham, but Parham was not yet appointed as DHR head. It is more likely that the mailing was negotiated with then DHR director Bill Burson.

165. *Emmaus House News*, 12 August 1970.

166. The first *Poor People's Newspaper* does not have a date or volume number. The *Poor People's Newspaper* can be found in the Muriel Lokey Papers, AHC. Author interview with Ford.

167. *Emmaus House News*, 23 September 1970. The newsletter notes the office opening "in the cottage" at Emmaus House. Author interview with Goldstein.

168. Author interview with Stone; author interview with Deedie Weems (in possession of author); author interview with Goldstein; author interview with Patricia Royalty.

169. "Relationship Between the PRO and Emmaus House," Volunteer Handbook, May 1980, folder 3, box 1, Muriel Lokey Papers, AHC.

170. "Decent Housing and Tenants' Rights under Law," *Poor People's Newspaper*, July 1972. Also see "Tenants Have Legal Rights!" *Poor People's Newspaper*, March 1974.

1. *Poor People's Newspaper*, May 1974.

2. "Atlanta's Fight against Substandard Housing: Is It Working?," Research Atlanta, October 1972, table 4; *Atlanta Constitution*, 28 July 1968.

3. See, for example, the statement issued by the Council on Human Relations of Greater Atlanta in the wake of the September 1966 Summerhill civil disturbance. "Statement Issued by Council on Human Relations of Greater Atlanta, Inc.," 8 September 1966, document 15, folder 7, box 19, IADA, http://allenarchive.iac.gatech.edu /items/show/8588. Atlanta's Model Cities application also indicated that its Model Neighborhood was selected over other areas in part because of evidence of previous unrest. See City of Atlanta, "A Model Neighborhood for Atlanta: Application to the Department of Housing and Urban Development for a Grant to Plan a Comprehensive City Demonstration Program" (1967), part 2, p. 17 (hereafter cited as "Model Neighborhood Application").

4. As quoted in Maggie Bellows, "It's News: Atlanta Is Hot," for United Press International, *Atlanta Journal and Constitution*, 23 April 1967.

5. As quoted in *Atlanta Constitution*, 16 November 1966. On the establishment of the Housing Resource Committee (HRC) and its original goals, see Housing Resources Committee, General Functions, 3 August 1967, document 4, folder 17, box 5, IADA, *http://allenarchive.iac.gatech.edu/items/show/2491*; Housing Resources Committee, minutes, 14 February 1967, document 37, folder 17, box 5, IADA, http:// allenarchive.iac.gatech.edu/items/show/2524; Housing Resources Committee, minutes, 12 December 1968, document 27, folder 2, box 5, IADA, http://allenarchive.iac .gatech.edu/items/show/1888.

6. *Atlanta Constitution*, 10 February 1967. Also see *Atlanta Constitution*, 25 January 1967, 26 January 1967.

7. Haar, *Between the Idea and the Reality*, 48.

8. Haar, *Between the Idea and the Reality*, 59.

9. Haar, *Between the Idea and the Reality*, 18–19.

10. Haar, *Between the Idea and the Reality*, 82. Outside of Congress, urban leaders fretted that Model Cities might divert funds from other grant programs. Haar, *Between the Idea and the Reality*, chap. 3.

11. Concern over 1960s civil unrest is described in Haar, *Between the Idea and the Reality*, chap. 1.

12. *Atlanta Constitution*, 3 February 1967; Haar, *Between the Idea and the Reality*, 23.

13. *Atlanta Constitution*, 10 February 1967. On the policy development of and congressional issues with Model Cities, see Woods, *Prisoners of Hope*, 256–59.

14. *Atlanta Constitution*, 19 June 1969, 30 May 1971.

15. *Atlanta Constitution*, 24 February 1967.

16. *Atlanta Constitution*, 2 February 1967.

17. *Atlanta Constitution*, 14 March 1967.

18. *Atlanta Constitution*, 28 April 1967.

19. *Atlanta Constitution*, 2 February 1967.

20. *Atlanta Constitution*, 3 February 1967.

21. *Atlanta Constitution*, 3 February 1967. Also see *Atlanta Constitution*, 20 February 1967.

22. *Atlanta Constitution*, 3 February 1967.

23. *Atlanta Constitution*, 29 June 1969.

24. "Model Neighborhood Application," part 2, pp. 3, 19–20.

25. "Model Neighborhood Application," part 2, pp. 20–21.

26. "Model Neighborhood Application," part 1, pp. 1–5.

27. "Model Neighborhood Application," part 1, p. 1.

28. *Atlanta Constitution*, 20 February 1967; "Model Neighborhood Application," part 3, p. 166.

29. On challenges with relocation, see "Model Neighborhood Application," part 3, p. 166.

30. In April 1967, the executive director of AHA reported to the housing resources executive committee that, at that time, public housing had 8,874 units "with virtually no vacancies." Housing Resources Executive Committee, minutes, 6 April 1967, document 25, folder 17, box 5, IADA, http://allenarchive.iac.gatech.edu/items/show/2512. It was noted that the waiting list for public housing was "long." *Atlanta Constitution*, 6 August 1965.

31. Malcolm D. Jones to Dan E. Sweat Jr., 6 August 1969, folder 7, box 3, IADA, http://allenarchive.iac.gatech.edu/items/show/1019; "Model Neighborhood Application," part 3, pp. 165–66.

32. *Atlanta Constitution*, 25 August 1967.

33. Bureau of Census, *Eighteenth Census* (1960), part 12, p. 51, and *Nineteenth Census* (1970), vol. 1, part 12, p. 73, as quoted in Bayor, *Race and the Shaping*, table 1, p. 7.

34. *Atlanta Constitution*, 1 December 1967, 23 January 1968.

35. *Atlanta Constitution*, 23 January 1968.

36. *Atlanta Constitution*, 29 June 1969.

37. *Atlanta Journal and Constitution*, 19 November 1967; *Atlanta Constitution*, 22 November 1967, 23 November 1967. Lack of subsequent protest suggests that Atlanta's Black leadership found these appointments adequate, or at least not worthy of further public complaint.

38. *Atlanta Constitution*, 6 December 1967, 10 December 1967. The vast majority of attendees were from Grant Park: 230 Grant Park residents attended. The next best representation was from Pittsburgh with 67 residents. *Atlanta Constitution*, 11 December 1967, 16 December 1967, 21 December 1967, 22 January 1968.

39. *Atlanta Constitution*, 16 December 1967.

40. *Atlanta Constitution*, 18 November 1967. *Atlanta Journal and Constitution*, 19 November 1967.

41. In contrast to Peoplestown, Summerhill, Pittsburgh, and Mechanicsville, Craig's Adair Park had been virtually unscathed to date by urban improvement programs. Keller, "Spatial Patterns of Involuntary Moves," 25–26.

42. *Atlanta Constitution*, 6 December 1967, 22 January 1968, 26 March 1968, 29 April 1968, 18 January 1970, 11 October 1970. Regarding Craig's shift in philosophy, see his obituary in the *New York Times*, 24 April 1998. Also see Clayton and Gulliver,

I've Been Marching All the Time, 100–109. Craig considered running for Model Cities chair in 1970 and apparently had support from some African Americans. *Atlanta Constitution*, 18 January 1970.

43. Rodriguez, *Diverging Space for Deviants*, 5, 42–44.

44. On the transition in the populations public housing served, see Rodriguez, *Diverging Space for Deviants*, particularly chaps. 2 and 3.

45. As urban studies scholar Akira Drake Rodriguez has explained, the authority had a long history of racializing space in Atlanta. Rodriguez, *Diverging Space for Deviants*, 7.

46. There had been earlier mandates to integrate housing, including John F. Kennedy's Executive Order 1106 (1962). As Katie Marages Schank points out, the AHA regularly claimed to be "in compliance" with such orders and the Civil Rights Act of 1964. But as Sam Williams noted, compliance "on paper" was not always authentic compliance. Schank, "Producing the Projects," 234–35.

47. *Atlanta Constitution*, 31 October 1967.

48. *Atlanta Constitution*, 31 October 1967.

49. *Atlanta Constitution*, 15 March 1968. On the desegregation of Atlanta's public housing see Schank, "Producing the Projects," 235–39.

50. *Atlanta Constitution*, 8 May 1968.

51. After complaints, the residency requirement was lengthened from six months to one year in June 1968. *Atlanta Constitution*, 19 June 1968.

52. For example, some residents displaced by urban renewal–type projects received waivers for this requirement. Between 1 November 1967 and 30 June 1968, some 2,903 people applied for public housing in Atlanta; 141 people were turned down because of the residency requirement. Housing Resources Committee with Zoning Committee and Planning and Development Committee, Special Meeting, minutes, 2 August 1968, document 42, folder 1, box 5, IADA, http://allenarchive.iac.gatech.edu/items/show/1846; Atlanta Constitution, 8 May 1968.

53. *Atlanta Constitution*, 3 July 1968.

54. *Atlanta Constitution*, 7 August 1968.

55. *Atlanta Daily World*, 11 February 1968, 21 February 1968.

56. *Atlanta Journal*, 20 August 1968.

57. *Atlanta Constitution*, 27 January 1969.

58. *Atlanta Daily World*, 14 March 1968.

59. *Atlanta Constitution*, 22 April 1968, 15 May 1968.

60. *Atlanta Constitution*, 24 May 1968.

61. *Atlanta Constitution*, 23 September 1968.

62. *Atlanta Constitution*, 23 September 1968.

63. *Atlanta Constitution*, 29 November 1968. There were also plans for clearance in Summerhill in 1969–70. *Atlanta Constitution*, 10 October 1968.

64. Housing Resources Committee, minutes, 12 December 1968, document 27, folder 2, box 5, IADA, http://allenarchive.iac.gatech.edu/items/show/1888.

65. Housing Resources Committee, minutes, 12 December 1968, IADA.

66. Housing Resources Committee, minutes, 12 December 1968, IADA.

67. *Atlanta Constitution*, 11 November 1968; *Atlanta Daily World*, 9 November 1968; Schank, "Producing the Projects," 241.

68. Mandy M. Griggs et al. to Mayor Ivan Allen Jr., 3 December 1968, folder 8, box 3, IADA, http://allenarchive.iac.gatech.edu/items/show/1069.

69. *Atlanta Constitution*, 9 November 1968.

70. *Atlanta Constitution*, 11 November 1968.

71. *Atlanta Daily World*, 18 November 1968; Shepard, *Rationing Justice*, 55.

72. *Atlanta Daily World*, 18 November 1968.

73. *Atlanta Constitution*, 3 October 1968.

74. *Atlanta Constitution*, 27 November 1968.

75. *Atlanta Constitution*, 27 November 1968.

76. "Housing: Public Housing: Tenants' Bill of Rights," *National Clearinghouse for Legal Services Clearinghouse Review*, September 1968, 20; Griggs et al. to Allen, 3 December 1968, IADA.

77. *Atlanta Daily World*, 1 December 1968.

78. *Atlanta Constitution*, 19 December 1968.

79. *Atlanta Daily World*, 19 December 1968.

80. *Atlanta Constitution*, 14 January 1969.

81. *Atlanta Constitution*, 14 January 1969.

82. *Atlanta Constitution*, 2 March 1969.

83. The Atlanta Housing Authority allowed use of the Carver Homes facility when it was announced that Mayor Ivan Allen Jr. and other elected officials had been invited. *Atlanta Constitution*, 2 March 1969.

84. Michael D. Padnos to Ivan Allen Jr., 6 March 1969, folder 7, box 3, IADA, http://allenarchive.iac.gatech.edu/items/show/975.

85. As quoted in "We are here tonight," [attached to Padnos to Allen, 6 March 1969], folder 7, box 3, IADA, http://allenarchive.iac.gatech.edu/items/show/976. Also see *Atlanta Constitution*, 5 March 1969.

86. Ivan Allen Jr. to Edwin L. Sterne, 6 March 1969, folder 8, box 3, IADA, http://allenarchive.iac.gatech.edu/items/show/1076.

87. Allen to Sterne, 6 March 1969, IADA.

88. Padnos to Allen, 6 March 1969, IADA.

89. *Atlanta Constitution*, 19 March 1969.

90. *Atlanta Constitution*, 30 March 1969. Associate Director Lester Persells would take over the directorship.

91. Michael D. Padnos to Ivan Allen Jr., 24 June 1969, folder 4, box 3, IADA, http://allenarchive.iac.gatech.edu/items/show/826.

92. *Atlanta Constitution*, 1 April 1969.

93. *Emmaus House News*, 25 June 1969.

94. *Atlanta Constitution*, 23 July 1969; *Emmaus House News*, 13 August 1969.

95. *Emmaus House News*, 10 September 1969.

96. *Poor People's Newspaper*, June 1972.

97. *Poor People's Newspaper*, May 1972, June 1972.

98. *Atlanta Constitution*, 7 April 1969.

99. *Atlanta Constitution*, 16 April 1969, 29 April 1969, 10 May 1969.

100. *Atlanta Constitution*, 29 April 1969, 30 April 1969.

101. *Atlanta Constitution*, 31 March 1969.

102. As quoted in *Emmaus House News*, 11 January 1970. The city ultimately threw out the original election results and ordered new elections for early March. *Emmaus House News*, 24 February 1970.

103. *Emmaus House News*, 28 January 1970.

104. *Atlanta Constitution*, 21 January 1971.

105. *Atlanta Constitution*, 25 January 1971.

106. *Emmaus House News*, 11 March 1970.

107. *Atlanta Constitution*, 27 September 1970.

108. *Atlanta Constitution*, 27 September 1970. Minutes of a December 1968 "grant review board" meeting suggest that the Model Cities agency and other city departments and agencies did not adequately communicate and cooperate. Grand Review Board minutes, 31 December 1968, document 62, folder 2, box 15, IADA, http://allenarchive.iac.gatech.edu/items/show/5605.

109. *Atlanta Constitution*, 5 October 1970. Also see Kaplan, Gans, and Kahn, *Model Cities Program*, 33–38.

110. *Atlanta Constitution*, 1 October 1970, 28 October 1970.

111. *Atlanta Constitution*, 1 October 1970, 3 October 1970.

112. *Atlanta Constitution*, 6 October 1970; *Atlanta Daily World*, 8 October 1970.

113. *Atlanta Constitution*, 10 November 1970.

114. *Atlanta Constitution*, 11 November 1970.

115. *Atlanta Constitution*, 18 November 1970.

116. *Atlanta Constitution*, 26 March 1971. The original motion was dismissed, and the attorney indicated that a new motion was to be filed. It is not clear if there was any follow-up.

117. *Atlanta Constitution*, 31 May 1971.

118. *Atlanta Constitution*, 1 June 1971.

119. *Atlanta Constitution*, 30 May 1971.

120. *Atlanta Constitution*, 30 May 1971.

121. *Atlanta Constitution*, 31 May 1971.

122. *Atlanta Constitution*, 31 May 1971.

123. *Atlanta Constitution*, 1 June 1971.

124. *Atlanta Constitution*, 20 August 1971, 23 August 1971.

125. *Atlanta Constitution*, 6 July 1972. By mid-August 1972, all units were occupied. *Atlanta Constitution*, 18 August 1972.

126. *Atlanta Constitution*, 4 June 1971.

127. Atlanta, Office of the Mayor, Atlanta Comprehensive Demonstration Program [Model Cities Application], Application to the Department of Housing and Urban Development for Supplemental Funds, September 1971, I-B-55 (hereafter cited as "Model Cities Application").

128. The proposal and 1973 evaluation are discussed in *Atlanta Constitution*, 12 October 1973.

129. *Atlanta Constitution*, 2 June 1971.

130. *Atlanta Constitution*, 1 October 1972. Also see *Atlanta Constitution*, 2 May 1970;.

131. Akira Drake Rodriguez exposes the significance of public housing in organizing various marginalized interest groups in Rodriguez, *Diverging Space for Deviants*.

Chapter 7. Lobbying for Welfare

1. Elizabeth Chief, "Need Determination in AFDC Program," *Social Security Bulletin*, 42 (September 1979): 11–21. "AFDC: The $32 Barrier," attached to Jim Parham to Members of the Georgia General Assembly, 2 February 1976, folder 16, box 32, Pauley Papers.

2. *State of Georgia Anti-Poverty Report* (Atlanta: State Economic Development Office, 1973), 12.

3. *Atlanta Constitution*, 14 February 1973.

4. Jim Parham to Members of the Georgia General Assembly, 2 February 1976, Pauley papers. The Georgia monthly standard equated to $2,724 per year in 1971; U.S. Census Bureau, *Characteristics of the Low-Income Population: 1971*. For 1971 to 2017 inflation calculations, see the U.S. Bureau of Labor Statistics' Consumer Price Index Inflation Calculator, https://data.bls.gov/data/inflation_calculator.htm.

5. Chief, "Need Determination in AFDC Program," 11, 17–19. The state's method of calculating standard of need and AFDC grants is outlined in Jim Parham to Members of the Georgia General Assembly, 2 February 1976, Pauley papers.

6. Press release, April 14, 1975, folder entitled "Welfare Grants," RCB 19219, 1975–1983, Gov. George D. Busbee, Gov. Busbee's Work Files, Georgia Archives, Morrow, Ga., hereafter cited as Busbee Work Files; *Atlanta Constitution*, 15 April 1975; [Frank Samford], "Notes on Georgia's AFDC Program," n.d., folder 2, box 48, Pauley papers.

7. Peterson and Rom, *Welfare Magnets*, 100–103. According to the Bureau of Labor Statistics' Consumer Price Index (CPI) Inflation Calculator, $227 in January 1971 equates to about $1,396.14 in July 2017. See *https://data.bls.gov/cgi-bin/cpi-calc.pl?cost1=227&year1=197101&year2=201707*. In suitable home rules, agency workers had substantial latitude in deciding what qualified as a "suitable home," and staff could decide whether a family met the qualifications for a monthly welfare grant.

8. On the construction of the workfare state, see Bertram, *Workfare State*; Mittelstadt, *From Welfare to Workfare*.

9. Frances Pauley to "Council Member," May 20, 1975, folder 6, box 91, Pauley papers.

10. Pauley to "Council Member," 20 May 1975, Pauley papers.

11. "Minutes of Meeting of Representatives of Agencies Concerned about Welfare Cuts," 23 May 1975, folder 6, box 91, Pauley papers. Also see Pauley to "Council Member," 20 May 1975, Pauley papers; "History of work on increasing benefits for AFDC-as I remember it," 1 January 1986, folder 1, box 47, Pauley papers; [Untitled and unpublished response to the "Welfare Mess" series], folder 6, box 91, Pauley papers; "Minutes of the meeting of Concerned Citizens' Groups," 3 June 1975, folder 3, box 47, Pauley papers; Petition to Governor George Busbee, Lieutenant Governor Zell Miller, Speaker of the House Thomas Murphy, 28 May 1975, folder 6, box 91, Pauley papers;

Atlanta Constitution, 31 May 1975. The "Welfare Mess" was a weeklong series of front-page articles in the *Atlanta Constitution*, 18–25 May 1975.

12. "Minutes of Meeting of Representatives of Agencies Concerned about Welfare Cuts," 23 May 1975, folder 6, box 91, Pauley Papers. On Pauley, see Murphy Davis, *Frances Pauley*; Nasstrom, *Everybody's Grandmother and Nobody's Fool*. On the fight over the county unit system of representation and its impact on the balance of power in the Georgia legislature, see Coleman, *History of Georgia*, 390–98. On the role of women and "traditional" women's organizations in confronting sociopolitical issues in this period, see Chappell, "Rethinking Women's Politics," 155–79. On women, voluntarism, and public interest work, see Ruth Mary Meyer, "Lobbying for the Public Interest," *N.C. Insight*, Fall 1980, 22–29.

13. Author interview with Austin Ford, 6 March 2009; Allison O. Adams, "Cultivating Hope," *Emory Magazine*, Fall 1995, *http://www.emory.edu/EMORY_MAGAZINE/ fall95/austinford.html*.

14. The National Conference of State Legislatures classified the practices of U.S. state legislatures on a spectrum from "professional" (full-time) to "amateur" (part-time). Here I use the term "part-time" to describe Georgia's legislature. See National Conference of State Legislatures, "Full-Time and Part-Time Legislatures," 14 June 2017, http://www.ncsl.org/research/about-state-legislatures/full-and-part-time -legislatures.aspx. Also see Pingree and McCommons, "Organization of the Georgia General Assembly," 3–27; Ryles, "Typology of Functions," 29–42.

15. *Poor People's Newspaper*, February 1975.

16. On the closing of NWRO, see Nadasen, *Rethinking the Welfare Rights Movement*, 134–36.

17. Boyd, *Georgia Democrats*, 223.

18. Boyd, *Georgia Democrats*, 222–27. Boyd, "1966 Election in Georgia," 305–40; Cobb, *South and America*, 122–23. On Georgia's adoption of modern governance practices in the late 1960s, see Main and Gryski, "George Busbee"; Bartley, "1940 to the Present," 339–407, esp. 403–7. On the 1974 Busbee-Maddox race and its significance to new racial liberalism, see Boyd, *Georgia Democrats*, 222–27.

19. Shafer and Johnston, *End of Southern Exceptionalism*, 54.

20. Shafer and Johnston, *End of Southern Exceptionalism*. Increased Black voting could produce a backlash among white voters that resulted in policy outcomes such as reduced AFDC spending. See Radcliff and Saiz, "Race, Turnout, and Public Policy," 775–94; Krueger and Mueller, "Moderating Backlash," 165–79.

21. On the significant levels of grassroots political action in the 1970s, see Foley, *Front Porch Politics*. For analysis of the strategies and tactics of pressure groups and lobbying organizations of the period, see Berry, *Lobbying for the People*.

22. "Unofficial Government: Pressure Groups and Lobbies," *Annals of the American Academy of Political and Social Science* 319 (September 1958), copy in box 93, Pauley Papers. See, especially, Turner, "How Pressure Groups Operate," 63–72.

23. *Atlanta Constitution*, 1 July 1969. *Emmaus House News*, 23 July 1969; *Atlanta Constitution*, 7 February 1969. In their classic work, *Poor People's Movements*, Piven and Cloward contend that disruption was the most effective means by which the poor could influence political power structures. On the tensions between gradualist, civil

methods of interracial political negotiation and insurgent protest politics, see Lang, *Grassroots at the Gateway*.

24. "Black Caucus," *Georgia Legislative Review 1976*, 82–83, Southern Center for Studies in Public Policy.

25. "Black Caucus," *Georgia Legislative Review 1976*; Bass and De Vries, *Transformation of Southern Politics*, 154. On the history of the GLBC, see Holmes, "Georgia Legislative Black Caucus," 768–90.

26. *Atlanta Voice*, 14 June 1975.

27. *Atlanta Constitution*, 23 May 1975.

28. *Atlanta Voice*, 14 June 1975. *Atlanta Constitution*, 20 May 1975; John E. Long et al. to Governor George Busbee, undated, folder 6, box 91, Pauley papers.

29. *Atlanta Journal Constitution*, 22 June 1975.

30. "Address by Governor George Busbee on Statewide Television, June 19, 1975," folder 14, box 64, Pauley papers. *Atlanta Journal*, 18 June 1975, 20 June 1975.

31. "Tammie Scruggs to Members of the General Assembly," undated, folder 6, box 91, Pauley papers. "The Facts Surrounding Georgia's AFDC," n.d., folder 6, box 91, Pauley papers; Welfare Mothers Fight-Back Committee, "Why Cut AFDC?," folder 6, box 91, Pauley papers; "Sample Press Release or Letter," folder 6, box 91; Elinor S. Metzger [president, Atlanta-Fulton County League of Women Voters] to "Member of the Fulton County Delegation," June 3, 1975, folder 6, box 91, Pauley papers; Frances Pauley to "_____" [form letter], July 15, 1975, folder 6, box 47, Pauley papers.

32. Lobbyist Registers, 1975 and 1977, RCB 6475, Secretary of State, Front Office, Lobbyist Registrations, Georgia Archives. See Mary Jane Stinson, "National Program—Human Resources," April 1976, folder 12-9-07, RCB 50047 Georgia League of Women Voters Records, Georgia Archives, Morrow, Ga.

33. Pauley to "_____," July 15, 1975, Pauley papers.

34. "Georgia's AFDC Reduction and What To Do about It," n.d., folder 6, box 91, Pauley papers. *Atlanta Journal and Constitution*, 29 June 1975; T. M. Jim Parham to Members, Board of Human Resources, July 23, 1975, attachment to Board of Human Resources Minutes, 23 July 1975, RCB 47062, ID 80/1/1 Human Resources—Commissioner—Board of Human Resources Minutes, 1972–1983, Georgia Archives, Morrow, Ga.

35. *Atlanta Constitution*, 24 July 1975; Busbee discussed the complexity of calculating AFDC budgets in [Governor's office] press release, 17 July 1975, exhibit C attached to Board of Human Resources minutes, 23 July 1975, RCB 47060, ID 80/1/1 ID Human Resources—Commissioner—Board of Human Resources Minutes, 1972–1983, Georgia Archives, Morrow, Ga.

36. Frances Pauley to Board of Directors of Georgia Department of Human Resources, 20 August 1975, attachment to Board of Human Resources Minutes, August 20, 1975, RCB 47060, ID 80/1/1 ID Human Resources—Commissioner—Board of Human Resources Minutes, 1972–1983, Georgia Archives, Morrow, Ga.

37. *Atlanta Constitution*, 21 August 1975.

38. Pauley to Board of Directors of Georgia Department of Human Resources, 20 August 1975, attachment to Board of Human Resources Minutes, 20 August 1975, Georgia Archives; *Atlanta Constitution*, 21 August 1975; former Georgia House of

Representatives member Jim Martin observed that loss of Medicaid benefits was of particular concern. Interview with James F. (Jim) Martin, Atlanta, Ga., 3 June 2014, in possession of author.

39. Georgia Poverty Rights Organization, minutes, 11 October 1975, clipped to 16 October 1975 Minutes, folder 3, box 32, Pauley papers.

40. Georgia Poverty Rights Organization Agenda, 8 November 1975, folder 4, box 32, Pauley papers.

41. Georgia Poverty Rights Organization, minutes, 11 October 1975, Pauley papers; Georgia Poverty Rights Organization Agenda, 8 November 1975, Pauley papers. Pauley took no salary; she met past and current definitions of a "professional" lobbyist, as opposed to a citizen communicating his or her own personal views. She was specifically tasked by an organization to lobby, was reimbursed for expenses (by Emmaus House), devoted considerable hours to the GPRO on a weekly basis throughout the year, and registered with the state as a lobbyist. Nasstrom, *Everybody's Grandmother and Nobody's Fool*, 117–34. On the founding of the GPRO, see also Frances Pauley to "Friend," 12 September 1975, "Georgia Poverty Rights Organization, 1975, 1976" folder, box 91, Pauley papers; RSVP slips for the 11 October 1975 meeting, folder 3, box 32, Pauley papers; "History of work on increasing benefits for AFDC—as I remember it," 1 January 1986, folder 1, box 47, Pauley Papers.

42. Dennis [Goldstein] to Frances Pauley, 17 September 1975, folder 14, box 32, Pauley papers; Frances Pauley to "Friend," 12 September 1975, Pauley papers.

43. Frances Pauley to "member", 17 November 1975, folder 10, box 37, Pauley papers. Georgia Poverty Rights Organization Minutes, 8 November 1975, folder 11, box 91, Pauley papers.

44. Pauley to "member," 17 November 1975, Pauley papers. By contrast, in 1978, the GPRO and its allies pitted entitlement increases against the proposed re-leafing of the "gold dome" of the Georgia Capitol. See *Atlanta Constitution*, 16 January 1978, 17 January 1978, 19 January 1978.

45. Pauley to "member", 17 November 1975, Pauley papers.

46. *Atlanta Constitution*, 8 November 1975.

47. Board of Human Resources Minutes, 19 November 1975, Georgia Archives; T. M. Jim Parham to all DHR staff, 20 November 1975, folder 14, box 32, Pauley papers; Board of Human Resources Minutes, 17 December 1975, RCB 47060; Jack H. Watson Jr. to Rev. Austin Ford, 22 December 1975, "Yearby I correspondence" folder, 1977 Legislative Papers, James F. (Jim) Martin Papers, Richard B. Russell Library for Political Research and Studies, University of Georgia Libraries, Athens, Ga.

48. *Atlanta Journal*, 23 December 1975.

49. *Atlanta Journal*, 23 December 1975; *Atlanta Constitution*, 23 December 1975.

50. *Atlanta Constitution*, 26 November 1975.

51. *Atlanta Constitution*, 26 November 1975; *Atlanta Journal and Constitution*, 30 November 1975; *Atlanta Constitution*, 21 November 1975.

52. Frances Pauley to "friend," 26 December 1975, folder 10, box 37, Pauley papers.

53. "Georgia's Welfare Recipients: Victims or Villains?" [with Pauley's handwritten notes], folder 10, box 91, Pauley papers.

54. Untitled pamphlet ["The child in this picture is a welfare dependent"], folder 10, box 91, Pauley papers.

55. "Hunger Hurts" [flyer], folder 11, box 91, Pauley papers. Press release, 13 January 1976, folder 4, box 37, Pauley Papers.

56. GPRO to Members of the General Assembly, 1975, folder 10, box 37, Pauley papers; GPRO to Members of the Fulton County Delegation of the Georgia General Assembly, 6 January 1976, folder 11, box 91, Pauley papers; Frances Pauley to DHR Board of Directors, n.d. [1975], begins "For a few days after the summer session," folder 10, box 37, Pauley papers.

57. On the supplementary 1976 budget and unsuccessful attempts to remove the $32 cap, proposed primarily by members of the Black Caucus, see T. M. Jim Parham to Jack Watson, chair, and members of the Board of Human Resources, 21 January 1976, folder 17, box 53, Pauley papers. With the $32 ceiling intact, GPRO and its allies realized, larger AFDC allocations mattered little; excess allocations, by law, could not be spent. *Atlanta Constitution*, 25 January 1976.

58. *Atlanta Constitution*, 5 February 1976.

59. Frances Pauley to "member," 28 January 1976, folder 11, box 37, Pauley papers. Jim Parham to members of the General Assembly, 2 February 1976, folder 16, box 32, Pauley papers; *Atlanta Constitution*, 9 February 1976.

60. On "entitlement liberals," see Gareth Davies, *From Opportunity to Entitlement*. Tim Boyd writes that in the early 1970s, "The Republican Party seemed in danger of becoming irrelevant in [Georgia] state politics." Boyd, "Suburban Story," On the difficulty Republicans had breaking into the Deep South between the 1960s and the 1980s, see Black and Black, *Rise of Southern Republicans*, particularly chaps. 4 and 5.

61. *Atlanta Constitution*, 4 February 1976.

62. *Atlanta Daily World*, 27 January 1976. *Journal of the House of Representatives of the State of Georgia at the Regular Session, Commenced at Atlanta, Monday, January 12, 1976, and Adjourned Friday, March 5, 1976* (2 vols.; Atlanta, 1976), 1:778–85; hereinafter cited as *Georgia House Journal*.

63. *Atlanta Constitution*, February 4, 1976. *Atlanta Daily World*, 5 February 1976; *Atlanta Constitution*, 5 February 1976.

64. *Atlanta Constitution*, 13 February 1976.

65. *Great Speckled Bird*, 1 April 1976.

66. *Atlanta Constitution*, 13 February 1976; *Great Speckled Bird*, 1 April 1976; *Georgia House Journal*, 1:1181–86.

67. *Atlanta Journal*, 6 March 1976.

68. Virginia Shapard, interviewed by Diane Fowlkes, 26 January 1988, P1988-01, Series C, Women in the Legislature, Georgia Government Documentation Project, Special Collections and Archives, Georgia State University Library, Atlanta. The negotiation of the Beckham bill and the eventual incorporation of the Beckham-Karrh amendment that changed the schedule from monthly to quarterly can be seen in *Georgia House Journal*, 1976, 1:829, 1180–82.

69. T. M. Jim Parham to Paul Broun, 17 February 1976, folder 17, box 53, Pauley papers; T. M. Jim Parham to Jack Watson, chair, and members of the Board of Human

Resources, 18 February 1976, folder 17, box 53, Pauley papers. The Senate revision passed on 26 February. *Atlanta Constitution*, 27 February 1976.

70. *Atlanta Constitution*, 28 February 1976.

71. *Atlanta Constitution*, 3 March 1976.

72. Untitled proposal clipped together with the note "March 4, 1976," RCB 19219, 1975–1983, Gov. George D. Busbee, Gov. Busbee's Work Files, Georgia Archives, Morrow, Ga.

73. *Atlanta Constitution*, 3 March 1976, 4 March 1976; untitled proposal clipped together with the note "March 4, 1976," Georgia Archives.

74. *Poor People's Newspaper*, April 1976. The newspaper points out that a coalition of activists made the victory possible. *Georgia House Journal*, 2:2775–80. The bill moved forward for the governor's signature. The final agreement included the provision that "the Department of Human Resources shall not increase beyond the February, 1976 level the percentage of need used in making the monthly benefit calculations, nor otherwise change the factors used in calculating monthly benefit payments so as to cause any increases thereof, other than mandatory changes resulting from federal or judicial mandates." Untitled proposal clipped together with the note "March 4, 1976," Georgia Archives; Pauley alerted GPRO members about the "win" in Frances Pauley to "Member", 15 March 1976, folder 11, box 37, Pauley papers.

75. *Atlanta Constitution*, 14 November 1979, 19 August 1982, 30 August 1982, 17 September 1983.

Conclusion

1. On Atlanta's Sunbelt profile, see, in particular, Tom Walker, "Late-Blooming City Still Has Its Share of Urban Problems, *Atlanta Constitution*, 15 April 1979. Also see *Atlanta Constitution*, 18 January 1970, 19 April 1974, 5 January 1975; *New York Times*, 9 January 1977; Southern Regional Council, *South's Economic Future*, chart 8.

2. This was consistent with efforts in other Sunbelt cities to curtail unionization, which many leaders felt would attract industry. On the anti-union campaign of another Sunbelt metropolis, Charlotte, North Carolina, see Gunn, "'Good Place to Make Money.'" On worker replacement, see McCartin, "'Fire the Hell out of Them.'"

3. Southern Regional Council, *South's Economic Future*, 20.

4. Cobb, *Selling of the South*, 259.

5. Hall and Williams, "Case Study," 92–95.

6. McKernan and Ratcliffe, "Events That Trigger Poverty Entries," 1146–69.

7. Of course, those efforts would sometimes fail due to internal or external stressors, as happened with NWRO and the Poor People's Campaign. But they also made measurable gains.

8. On Carter's comments regarding wage parity, see *Atlanta Constitution*, 19 August 1974. On the appointment of modern bureaucrat Jim Parham to head the DHR, see *Atlanta Constitution*, 2 December 1970. On Carter's presidency and its anti-poverty agenda, see Orleck, "Conclusion." On Carter's ill-fated attempts to implement welfare reform, see McAndrews, *Presidents and the Poor*, chap. 4. On Carter's urban policy, see Biles, *Fate of Cities*, chap. 7.

9. Various scholars and pundits have documented the late twentieth century's "war on welfare," including Chappell, *War on Welfare*, chap. 10; Katz, *In the Shadow*. On the election of Ronald Reagan as the turning point away from antipoverty policy innovation, see Orleck, "Conclusion."

10. Sam A. Williams is quoted in Tamar Hallerman, "1996 Olympics Energized Atlanta, but Uneven Legacy Lives On," *Atlanta Journal-Constitution*, 7 August 2021. On removing the homeless for the Olympics, see Associated Press, "Criminals, Homeless Targeted for Olympics," 21 March 1996.

11. Hallerman, "1996 Olympics Energized Atlanta."

12. On public housing loss as a result of the Olympics, see *New York Timex*, 19 July 1995.

13. The destruction of Atlanta's public housing was most closely documented by journalists at *Creative Loafing*. See, for example, Mara Shalhoup, "Where'd the Neighbors Go?" *Creative Loafing*, 24 February 2001, https://creativeloafing.com/content-184426-Cover-Story:-Where%27d-the-neighbors-go?.

14. U.S. Census Bureau, *Income and Poverty in the United States: 2019*, by Jessica Semega, Melissa Kollar, Emily A. Shrider, and John F. Creamer, P60–270, September 2020. In 2019, the South still had the highest poverty rate of U.S. regions, with 12.0 percent living in poverty.

15. Harrington, *Other America*.

16. *New York Times*, 14 February 1980.

17. *New York Times*, 17 April 2007.

18. *New York Times*, 17 April 2007.

19. *New York Times*, 14 February 1980.

20. *New York Times*, 2 September 1980.

21. The Poor People's Campaign intent to "change the moral narrative" is noted in "About the Poor People's Campaign: A National Call for Moral Revival," Poor People's Campaign, https://www.poorpeoplescampaign.org/about/. The launch dates of the Poor People's Campaign are noted in Shailly Gupta Barnes, "Waking the Sleeping Giant: Poor and Low-Income Voters in the 2020 Elections," Poor People's Campaign, October 2021, https://www.poorpeoplescampaign.org/waking-the-sleeping-giant-poor-and-low-income-voters-in-the-2020-elections/.

22. Jelani Cobb, "William Barber Takes on Poverty and Race in the Age of Trump," *New Yorker*, 7 May 2018.

23. Some see Moral Mondays as part of a larger countermovement to growing divisiveness and draconian conservative legislation. See Daniel Malloy, "North Carolina's Path to Battleground State Could Be Model for Georgia," *Atlanta Journal-Constitution*, 3 October 2016.

24. Heather Long, "Trump Touts His Economy," *Washington Post*, 4 February 2020.

25. Paul Krugman, "The G.O.P.'s War on the Poor, *New York Times*, 16 July 2018; William J. Barber II and Karen Dolan, "Trump's War on the Poor Has Just Begun," *Washington Post* 18 July 2018. Barber and Dolan's essay was in part a response to President Donald Trump's executive order 13828, which was revoked in February 2021 by President Joe Biden. On the successes and failures of the War on Poverty, see the essays contained in Bailey and Danziger, *Legacies of the War on Poverty*.

26. Barber and Dolan, "Trump's War on the Poor."

27. Jim Tankersley et al., "Trump's $4.8 Trillion Budget," *New York Times*, 10 February 2020.

28. David A. Super, "The Cruelty of Trump's Poverty Policy," *New York Times*, 24 July 2019.

29. *The Hill*, 21 January 2021; Katherine Schaeffer, "6 Facts about Economic Inequality in the U.S.," Pew Research Center, 7 February 2020.

30. Elena Delavega, "COVID-19: This Is How Many Americans Now Live below the Poverty Line," *World Economic Forum*, 21 September 2021; Brian Root and Lena Simet, "United States: Pandemic Impact on People in Poverty," Human Rights Watch, 2 March 2021, https://www.hrw.org/news/2021/03/02/united-states-pandemic-impact-people-poverty; Henry J. Aaron, "The Social Safety Net: The Gaps That COVID-19 Spotlights," 23 June 2020, Brookings Institute, https://www.brookings.edu/blog/up-front/2020/06/23/the-social-safety-net-the-gaps-that-covid-19-spotlights/.

31. Perry Bacon Jr, "How Georgia Turned Blue," *FiveThirtyEight*, 18 November 2020; Nate Cohn et al., "Detailed Turnout Data Shows How Georgia Turned Blue," *New York Times*, 17 November 2020.

32. Barnes, "Waking the Sleeping Giant."

33. The Biden administration proposals are outlined in Dylan Matthews, "Joe Biden Just Launched the Second War on Poverty," *Vox*, 10 March 2021; Ella Nilsen, "Georgia Went Blue," *Vox*, 15 January 2021.

34. On the demographic and voting shifts in the 2020 election, see James C. Cobb, "Why a Key Georgia County Flipped from Red to Blue—and What it Means for Democrats," *Fortune*, 17 December 2020.

35. *Poor People's Newspaper*, December 1972.

BIBLIOGRAPHY

Primary Sources
Manuscript collections
Department of Special Collections, Stanford University
Libraries, Stanford University, Calif.

Bob Fitch Photography Archive

Georgia Archives, Morrow, Ga.

Georgia League of Women Voters records
Georgia Board of Human Resources records
Georgia Secretary of State records
Governor George D. Busbee records

Ivan Allen [Jr.] Digital Archive, Georgia Institute of Technology, Atlanta

Kenan Research Center, Atlanta History Center, Atlanta
Atlanta Housing Authority Photographs
Atlanta Legal Aid Society papers
Bill Wilson Photograph Collection
Bedford-Pine Neighborhood Photograph Collection
Boyd Lewis Photographs
Living Atlanta Oral History Collection
Sanborn Fire Insurance maps

Library of Congress, Washington, D.C.

James Forman papers

National Archives at College Park, Md.

Community Services Administration records
Office of Economic Opportunity Records

Richard B. Russell Library for Political Research and Studies,
University of Georgia Libraries, Athens, Ga.

James F. (Jim) Martin papers

Robert W. Woodruff Library Archives, Atlanta University Center, Atlanta

Atlanta Urban League papers
Atlanta Community Relations Commission collection
Frankie V. Adams collection
Samuel W. Williams papers

Special Collections Department, Georgia State University Library, Atlanta

Atlanta City Planning Maps Collection
Atlanta Journal-Constitution Photograph Collection
Georgia Government Documentation Project
Voices of Labor Oral History Project

State Historical Society of Wisconsin, Madison

Cadmus Allen Samples papers
Mendy Samstein papers
Student Nonviolent Coordinating Committee Papers. Vine City Project (Atlanta)

Stuart A. Rose Manuscript, Archives, and Rare Book Library,
Emory University, Atlanta

Center for the Research in Social Change records
Community Council of the Atlanta Area records
Eliza K. Paschall papers
Emily and Ernest Woodruff Foundation records
Frances Pauley papers
Howard Moore papers
Southern Christian Leadership Conference papers

University of North Carolina–Chapel Hill

Southern Oral History Program

Microfilmed manuscript collections

Southern Regional Council papers, 1944–1968. Ann Arbor, Michigan: University Microfilms International
Student Nonviolent Coordinating Committee papers, 1959–1972. Sanford, N.C.: Microfilming Corp of America.

Interviews by the Author (available at the Peoplestown Project, https://thepeoplestownproject.com/oral-histories/, unless otherwise noted)

Mimi Bodell, 23 July 2009
J. Otis Cochran, 23 August 2012, 4 August 2016
Tom and Debbie Erdmanczyk, 31 August 2009
Gene Ferguson, 6 April 2009 (not on website, but in author's possession)
Austin Ford, 6 March 2009
Dennis Goldstein, 31 July 2009

James F. (Jim) Martin, 3 June 2014
David Morath, 10 August 2009
Patricia Royalty, 20 July 2009
Grace Stone, 2 March 2009
Susan W. Taylor, 9 June 2009
Deedie Weems, 30 March 2009

Interviews by other entities

Clemmons, Estelle. Interview by Bernard West. 27 September 1978. Living Atlanta
    Oral History Collection, AHC. Available at http://ohms.libs.uga.edu/viewer.php
    ?cachefile=dlg/livatl/ahc-637-032-001.xml.
Hill, Jesse. Interview by Carole Merritt. 11 August 2005. Voices across the Color Line
    Oral History Project. Kenan Research Center, AHC, https://album.atlantahistory
    center.com/digital/collection/VACL/id/52/rec/4.
Joye, Harlon. Interview by Philip LaPorte. 9 May 2006. Voices of Labor Oral His-
    tory Project. Special Collections and Archives, Georgia State University Library,
    Atlanta.
Lokey, Muriel. Interview by Carole Merritt. 4 January 2006. Voices across the Color
    Line Oral History Project. Kenan Research Center, AHC. https://album.atlanta
    historycenter.com/digital/collection/VACL/id/45/.
Shapard, Virginia. Interview by Diane Fowlkes. 26 January 1988. P1988-01, Series C.
    Women in the Legislature, Georgia Government Documentation Project. Special
    Collections and Archives, Georgia State University Library, Atlanta
Sweat, Dan. Interview by Clifford Kuhn and Shep Barbash. 22 November 1966. Geor-
    gia Government Documentation Project. Special Collections and Archives, Geor-
    gia State University Library, Atlanta

Newspapers and Magazines

Atlanta Constitution
Atlanta Daily World
Atlanta Inquirer
Atlanta Journal
Atlanta Journal and Constitution
Chicago Defender
Creative Loafing
Emmaus House News
Emory Magazine
Great Speckled Bird

Jet
Los Angeles Sentinel
N.C. Insight
New York Times
OAH Magazine of History
Poor People's Newspaper
Saturday Evening Post
Student Voice
Time
Vine City Voice

Government Documents

Atlanta Community Improvement Program. "A Model Neighborhood for Atlanta:
    Application to the Department of Housing and Urban Development for a Grant to
    Plan a Comprehensive City Demonstration Program." Atlanta: Atlanta Community
    Improvement Program, 1967.
Atlanta, Office of the Mayor. Atlanta Comprehensive Demonstration Program

[Model Cities Application], Application to the Department of Housing and Urban Development for Supplemental Funds. Atlanta: City Demonstration Agency, 1971.

Breslauer, Tamar B., and William R. Morton. "Social Security: Major Decisions in the House and Senate since 1935." Congressional Research Service. Updated 28 March 2019. https://fas.org/sgp/crs/misc/RL30920.pdf.

Carmichael v. *Allen*, 267 F. Supp. 985 (N.D. Ga. 1967).

Chief, Elizabeth. "Need Determination in AFDC Program." *Social Security Bulletin* 42, no. 9 (1979): 11–21.

DeWitt, Larry. "The Decision to Exclude Agricultural and Domestic Workers from the 1935 Society Security Act." *Social Security Bulletin* 70, no. 4 (2010): 49–68.

Fisher, Gordon M. "The Development and History of the Poverty Thresholds," *Social Security Bulletin* 55, no. 4 (1992): 3–14.

"Housing: Public Housing: Tenants' Bill of Rights." *National Clearinghouse for Legal Services Clearinghouse Review.* September 1968.

Journal of the House of Representatives of the State of Georgia at the Regular Session, Commenced at Atlanta, Monday, January 12, 1976, and Adjourned Friday, March 5, 1976. Atlanta, 1976.

Kaplan, Marshall, Sheldon P. Gans, and Howard M. Kahn. *The Model Cities Program: The Planning Process in Atlanta, Seattle, and Dayton.* U.S. Department of Housing and Urban Development. Washington, D.C.: USGPO, 1970.

National Advisory Commission on Civil Disorders. *Report of the National Advisory Commission on Civil Disorders.* Washington, D.C.: USGPO, 1968.

National Advisory Commission on Civil Disorders. *Report of the National Advisory Commission on Civil Disorders: Summary of Report.* Washington, D.C.: USGPO, 1968. http://www.eisenhowerfoundation.org/docs/kerner.pdf.

Research Atlanta. "Atlanta's Fight against Substandard Housing: Is it Working?" Atlanta: Research Atlanta, 1972.

State Library of Iowa. State Data Center Program. "Urban and Rural Population for the U.S. and All States: 1900–2000." https://www.iowadatacenter.org/datatables /I/urusstpop19002000.pdf.

"Techwood Homes." GA-2257, National Park Service, Historic American Building Survey, http://lcweb2.loc.gov/master/pnp/habshaer/ga/ga0600/ga0662/data /ga0662data.pdf.

U.S. Census Bureau. Census of Population, 1940. Vol. 2, *Characteristics of the Population.* Vol. 2. https://www.census.gov/library/publications/1943/dec/population -vol-2.html.

——. Census of Population, 1960. Vol. 1, *Characteristics of the Population, by Census Tracts.* Washington, D.C.: USGPO, 1963.

——. Census of Population, 1960: Supplementary Reports. *Poverty Areas in the 100 Largest Metropolitan Areas.* PC(S1)-54, 1960. https://www.census.gov/library /publications/1967/dec/population-pc-s1-54.html.

——. Census of Population, 1970: Supplementary Reports. *Poverty Status in 1969 and 1959 of Persons and Families, for States, SMSA's, Central Cities, and Counties.* PC(S1)-105, 1975. https://www.census.gov/library/publications/1975/dec/pc-s1-105 .html.

———. Census of Population, 1980: Subject Reports. *Poverty Areas in Large Cities.*
PC80-2-8D, 1980.

———. *Current Population Reports.* "The Extent of Poverty in the United States, 1959
to 1966." P-60, 1968.https://www2.census.gov/library/publications/1968
/demographics/p60-54.pdf.

———. *Characteristics of the Low-Income Population: 1971.* Elizabeth C. Shelburne,
Vivian M. Simmons, and Eldridgina A. Houston. P-60-86. Washington, D.C.:
USGPO, 1972. https://www.census.gov/library/publications/1972/demo/p60-86
.html.

———. Historical Poverty Tables: People and Families—1959 to 2020. https://www
.census.gov/data/tables/time-series/demo/income-poverty/historical-poverty
-people.html.

———. *Income and Poverty in the United States: 2019.* Jessica Semega, Melissa Kollar, Emily A. Shrider, and John F. Creamer. P60-270, 2020. https://www.census
.gov/library/publications/2020/demo/p60-270.html.

———. *Persons by Poverty Status in 1959, 1969, 1979, 1989, and 1999.* CPH-L-162.
https://www.census.gov/data/tables/time-series/dec/cph-series/cph-l/cph-l-162
.html.

U.S. Commission on Civil Rights. *Hearings before the U.S. Commission on Civil
Rights, Housing: New York, NY; Atlanta, GA; Chicago IL.* Washington, D.C.:
USGPO, 1959.

U.S. Commission on Civil Rights, Georgia State Advisory Committee to the United
States Commission on Civil Rights. *Toward Economic Opportunity in Housing in
Atlanta, Georgia.* Washington, D.C.: USGPO, May 1968.

U.S. Congress, Joint Committee on Housing. *Hearings before the Joint Committee on
Housing, Atlanta, GA.* Washington, D.C.: USGPO, 1947.

Secondary Sources

Allen, Frederick. *Atlanta Rising: The Invention of an International City, 1946–1996.*
Marietta, Ga.: Longstreet Press, 1996.

Allen, Ivan, and Paul Hemphill. *Mayor: Notes on the Sixties.* New York: Simon and
Schuster, 1971.

Ashmore, Susan Youngblood. *Carry It On: The War on Poverty and the Civil Rights
Movement in Alabama, 1964–1972.* Athens: University of Georgia Press, 2008.

Bacote, Clarence A. "The Negro in Atlanta Politics." *Phylon* 16, no. 4 (1955): 333–50.

Bailey, Martha J., and Sheldon Danziger, eds. *Legacies of the War on Poverty.* New
York: Russell Sage Foundation.

Baranski, John. *Housing the City by the Bay: Tenant Activism, Civil Rights, and
Class Politics in San Francisco.* Stanford, Calif.: Stanford University Press, 2019.

Bartley, Numan V. "1940 to the Present." In *A History of Georgia,* edited by Kenneth
Coleman, 339–407. Athens: University of Georgia Press, 1991.

Bass, Jack, and Walter De Vries. *The Transformation of Southern Politics: Social
Change and Political Consequences since 1945.* Athens: University of Georgia Press,
1995.

Bauman, Robert. *Race and the War on Poverty: From Watts to East La.* Norman: University of Oklahoma Press, 2008.

Bayor, Ronald H. *Race and the Shaping of Twentieth-Century Atlanta.* Chapel Hill: University of North Carolina Press, 1996.

Beck, Elizabeth. "National Domestic Workers Union and the War on Poverty." *Journal of Sociology and Social Welfare* 28, no. 4 (December 2001): 195–211.

Beltramini, Enrico. "S.C.L.C. Operation Breadbasket, from Economic Civil Rights to Black Economic Power." PhD diss., University of London, Royal Hollway College, 2013.

Berry, Jeffrey M. *Lobbying for the People.* Princeton, N.J.: Princeton University Press, 1977.

Bertram, Eva. *The Workfare State: Public Assistance Politics from the New Deal to the New Democrats.* Philadelphia: University of Pennsylvania Press, 2015.

Biles, Roger. *The Fate of Cities: Urban America and the Federal Government, 1945–2000.* Lawrence: University Press of Kansas, 2011.

———. *The South and the New Deal.* Lexington: University Press of Kentucky, 1994.

Birt, Charles J. "Family-Centered Project of St. Paul." *Social Work* 1, no. 4 (October 1956): 41–47.

Black, Earl, and Merle Black. *The Rise of Southern Republicans.* Cambridge, Mass.: Belknap Press of Harvard University Press, 2002.

Boyd, Tim. "The 1966 Election in Georgia and the Ambiguity of the White Backlash." *Journal of Southern History* 75, no. 2 (2009): 305–40.

———. "A Suburban Story: The Rise of Republicanism in Postwar Georgia, 1948–1980." In *Painting Dixie Red: When, Where, Why, and How the South Became Republican,* edited by Glenn Feldman, 79–97. New Perspectives on the History of the South. Gainesville: University Press of Florida, 2011.

Boyd, Tim S. R. *Georgia Democrats, the Civil Rights Movement, and the Shaping of the New South.* Gainesville: University Press of Florida, 2012.

Brown-Nagin, Tomiko. *Courage to Dissent: Atlanta and the Long History of the Civil Rights Movement.* New York: Oxford University Press, 2011.

Burke, Barlow, Jr. "Threat to Citizen Participation in Model Cities." *Cornell Law Review* 56, no. 5 (May 1971): 751–78.

Carroll, Tamar W. *Mobilizing New York: Aids, Antipoverty, and Feminist Activism.* Chapel Hill: University of North Carolina Press, 2015.

Carson, Clayborne. *In Struggle: SNCC and the Black Awakening of the 1960s.* Cambridge, Mass.: Harvard University Press, 1981.

Cha-Jua, Sundiata Keita, and Clarence Lang. "The 'Long Movement' as Vampire: Temporal and Spatial Fallacies in Recent Black Freedom Studies." *Journal of African American History* 92, no. 2 (Spring 2007): 265–88.

Chappell, Marisa. "Rethinking Women's Politics in the 1970s: The League of Women Voters and the National Organization for Women Confront Poverty." *Journal of Women's History* 13, no. 4 (Winter 2002): 155–79.

———. *The War on Welfare: Family, Poverty, and Politics in Modern America.* Politics and Culture in Modern America. Philadelphia: University of Pennsylvania Press, 2010.

"Citizen Participation in Urban Renewal." *Columbia Law Review* 66, no. 3 (March 1966): 485–607.

Clayson, William S. *Freedom Is Not Enough: The War on Poverty and the Civil Rights Movement in Texas*. Austin: University of Texas Press, 2010.

Clayton, Xernona, and Hal Gulliver. *I've Been Marching All the Time: An Autobiography*. Marietta, Ga.: Longstreet Press, 1991.

Cobb, James C. *The Selling of the South: The Southern Crusade for Industrial Development, 1936–1990*. 2nd ed. Urbana: University of Illinois Press, 1993.

———. *South and America since World War II*. New York: Oxford University Press, 2012.

Coleman, Kenneth. *A History of Georgia*. 2nd ed. Athens: University of Georgia Press, 1991.

Connerly, Charles E. *"The Most Segregated City in America": City Planning and Civil Rights in Birmingham, 1920–1980*. Charlottesville: University of Virginia Press, 2005.

Crawford, Fred R. *A Comprehensive and Systematic Evaluation of the Community Action Program and Related Programs Operating in Atlanta, Georgia*. Atlanta: Center for Research in Social Change, Emory University, 1969.

Dare, Robert. "Involvement of the Poor: A Study in the Maintenance of Organizational Values." Ph.D. diss., Emory University, 1967.

Davies, Gareth. *From Opportunity to Entitlement: The Transformation and Decline of Great Society Liberalism*. Lawrence: University Press of Kansas, 1996.

Davies, Tom Adam. *Mainstreaming Black Power*. Oakland: University of California Press, 2017.

Davis, Martha F. *Brutal Need: Lawyers and the Welfare Rights Movement, 1960–1973*. New Haven, Conn.: Yale University Press, 1993.

Davis, Murphy, ed. *Frances Pauley: Stories of Struggle and Triumph*. Atlanta: Open Door Community, 1990.

Deppe, Martin L. *Operation Breadbasket: An Untold Story of Civil Rights in Chicago, 1966–1971*. Athens: University of Georgia Press, 2017.

Dulles, Foster Rhea. *The Civil Rights Commission: 1957–1965*. East Lansing: Michigan State University Press, 1968.

Fairclough, Adam. *To Redeem the Soul of America: The Southern Christian Leadership Conference & Martin Luther King, Jr.* Athens: University of Georgia Press, 1987, 2001.

Feldman, Glenn. *Painting Dixie Red: When, Where, Why, and How the South Became Republican*. New Perspectives on the History of the South. Gainesville: University Press of Florida, 2011.

Ferguson, Karen. *Top Down: The Ford Foundation, Black Power, and the Reinvention of Racial Liberalism*. Politics and Culture in Modern America. Philadelphia: University of Pennsylvania Press, 2013.

Finley, Mary Lou. *The Chicago Freedom Movement: Martin Luther King Jr. and Civil Rights Activism in the North*. Louisville: University of Kentucky, 2016.

Foley, Michael S. *Front Porch Politics: The Forgotten Heyday of American Activism in the 1970s and 1980s*. New York: Hill & Wang, 2013.

Garrow, David J., ed. *Atlanta, Georgia, 1960–61: Sit-Ins and Student Activism.* Brooklyn, N.Y.: Carlson, 1989.

Germany, Kent B. *New Orleans after the Promises: Poverty, Citizenship, and the Search for the Great Society.* Athens: University of Georgia Press, 2007.

Gilens, Martin. *Why Americans Hate Welfare: Race, Media, and the Politics of Antipoverty Policy.* Studies in Communication, Media, and Public Opinion. Chicago: University of Chicago Press, 1999.

Gillette, Michael L. *Launching the War on Poverty: An Oral History.* Oxford Oral History Series. 2nd ed. New York: Oxford University Press, 2010.

Grady-Willis, Winston A. *Challenging U.S. Apartheid: Atlanta and Black Struggles for Human Rights, 1960–1977.* Durham, N.C.: Duke University Press, 2006.

Gunn, Jennifer Elizabeth. "'A Good Place to Make Money': Business, Labor, and Civil Rights in Twentieth-Century Charlotte." Ph.D. diss., University of Pennsylvania, 2014.

Haar, Charles M. *Between the Idea and the Reality: A Study in the Origin, Fate and Legacy of the Model Cities Program.* Boston: Little, Brown, 1975.

Hall, Bob, and Bob Williams. "Case Study: Who's Getting Rich in the New South." *Southern Exposure* 6 (Fall 1978): 92–95.

Hall, Jacquelyn Dowd. "Long Civil Rights Movement and the Political Uses of the Past." *Journal of American History* 91, no. 4 (2005): 1233–63.

Halpern, Robert. *Rebuilding the Inner City: A History of Neighborhood Initiatives to Address Poverty in the United States.* New York: Columbia University Press, 1995.

Harmon, David Andrew. *Beneath the Image of the Civil Rights Movement and Race Relations: Atlanta, Georgia, 1946–1981.* New York: Garland, 1996.

Harrington, Michael. *The Other America: Poverty in the United States.* New York: Touchstone, 1962.

Harris, Wade H., Jr. "Forcing Progress: The Struggle to Integrate Southern Episcopal Schools." Georgetown University, 2009.

Hawkins, Karen M. *Everybody's Problem: The War on Poverty in Eastern North Carolina.* Gainesville: University Press of Florida, 2017.

Hild, Matthew, and Keri Leigh Merritt. Introduction to *Reconsidering Southern Labor History: Race, Class, and Power,* edited by Matthew Hild and Keri Leigh Merritt. Gainesville: University of Florida, 2018.

Hobson, Maurice J. *Legend of the Black Mecca: Politics and Class in the Making of Modern Atlanta.* Chapel Hill: University of North Carolina Press, 2017.

Holliman, Irene V. "From Crackertown to Model City?" *Journal of Urban History* 35, no. 3 (March 1, 2009): 369–86.

———. "From "Crackertown" to the "ATL": Race, Urban Renewal, and the Re-making of Downtown Atlanta, 1945–2000." PhD diss., University of Georgia, 2010.

Holmes, Robert A. "Georgia Legislative Black Caucus: An Analysis of a Racial Legislative Subgroup." *Journal of Black Studies* 30, no. 6 (2000): 768–90.

Honey, Michael K. *Going Down Jericho Road: The Memphis Strike, Martin Luther King's Last Campaign.* New York: W. W. Norton, 2007.

———. *To the Promised Land: Martin Luther King and the Fight for Economic Justice.* New York: W. W. Norton, 2018.

Hornsby, Alton. *Black Power in Dixie: A Political History of African Americans in Atlanta*. Southern Dissent. Gainesville: University Press of Florida, 2009.

Horowitz, Daniel. "It Came from Somewhere and It Hasn't Gone Away: Black Women's Anti-Poverty Organizing in Atlanta, 1966–1996." MA thesis, Georgia State University, 2014.

Horwitt, Sanford D. *Let Them Call Me Rebel: Saul Alinsky—His Life and Legacy*. New York: Vintage, 1992.

Hower, Joseph E. "'A Threshold Moment': Public-Sector Organizing and Civil Rights Unionism in the Postwar South." In *Reconsidering Southern Labor History: Race, Class, and Power*, edited by Matthew Hil and Kerrie Leigh Merritt, 205–20. Gainesville: University of Florida Press, 2017.

Hunter, Floyd. *Community Power Structure: A Study of Decision Makers*. Chapel Hill: University of North Carolina Press, 1953.

Jackson, Mandi Isaacs. "Harlem's Rent Strike and Rat War: Representation, Housing Access and Tenant Resistance in New York, 1958–1964." *American Studies* 47, no. 1 (Spring 2006): 53–79.

Jackson, Thomas F. *From Civil Rights to Human Rights: Martin Luther King, Jr., and the Struggle for Economic Justice*. Philadelphia: University of Pennsylvania Press, 2007.

Jeffries, Hasan Kwame. *Bloody Lowndes: Civil Rights and Black Power in Alabama's Black Belt*. New York: New York University Press, 2009.

Jones, William Powell. "'Simple Truths of Democracy': African Americans and Organized Labor in the Post–World War II South." In *The Black Worker: Race, Labor, and Civil Rights since Emancipation*, edited by Eric Arnesen, 250–70. Chicago: University of Illinois Press, 2007.

Katz, Michael B. *In the Shadow of the Poorhouse: A Social History of Welfare in America*. New York: Basic Books, 1986.

Keating, Larry. *Atlanta: Race, Class, and Urban Expansion*. Comparative American Cities. Philadelphia: Temple University Press, 2001.

Keller, Frank Varist. "Spatial Patterns of Involuntary Moves: The Case of Atlanta's Model Neighborhood Area Residents." MA thesis, Georgia State University, 1974.

K'Meyer, Tracy Elaine. *Civil Rights in the Gateway to the South: Louisville, Kentucky, 1945–1980*. Lexington: University Press of Kentucky, 2009.

Kornbluh, Felicia Ann. *The Battle for Welfare Rights: Politics and Poverty in Modern America*. Philadelphia: University of Pennsylvania Press, 2007.

Korstad, Robert. *Civil Rights Unionism: Tobacco Workers and the Struggle for Democracy in the Mid-Twentieth-Century South*. Chapel Hill: University of North Carolina Press, 2003.

Korstad, Robert R., and James L. Leloudis. *To Right These Wrongs: The North Carolina Fund and the Battle to End Poverty and Inequality in 1960s America*. Chapel Hill: University of North Carolina Press, 2010.

Krueger, Brian S., and Paul D. Mueller. "Moderating Backlash: Racial Mobilization, Partisan Coalitions, and Public Policy in the American States." *State Politics & Policy Quarterly* 1, no. 2 (Summer 2001): 165–79.

Kruse, Kevin M. *White Flight: Atlanta and the Making of Modern Conservatism.* Princeton, N.J.: Princeton University Press, 2005.

Kruse, Kevin M., and Stephen Tuck, eds. *Fog of War: The Second World War and the Civil Rights Movement.* New York: Oxford University Press, 2012.

Lands, LeeAnn. *The Culture of Property: Race, Class, and Housing Landscapes in Atlanta, 1880–1950.* Politics and Culture in the Twentieth-Century South. Athens: University of Georgia Press, 2009.

Lang, Clarence. *Grassroots at the Gateway: Class Politics and Black Freedom Struggle in St. Louis, 1936–75.* Ann Arbor: University of Michigan Press, 2009.

LaShier, William Seth. "'To Secure Improvements in Their Material and Social Conditions': Atlanta's Civil Rights Movement, Middle-Class Reformers, and Workplace Protests, 1960–1977." Ph.D. diss., George Washington University, 2020.

Laurent, Sylvie. *King and the Other America: The Poor People's Campaign and the Quest for Economic Equality.* Oakland: University of California Press, 2018.

Lawson, Ronald, and Mark Naison. *The Tenant Movement in New York City, 1904–1984.* New Brunswick, N.J.: Rutgers University Press, 1986.

Lefever, Harry G. *Undaunted by the Fight: Spelman College and the Civil Rights Movement, 1957–1967.* Macon, Ga.: Mercer University Press, 2005.

Lerner, Gerda. *Black Women in White America: A Documentary History.* New York: Pantheon Books, 1972.

Levy, Peter B. *The Great Uprising: Race Riots in Urban American during the 1960s.* New York: Cambridge University Press, 2018.

Lewis, John, and Michael D'Orso. *Walking with the Wind: A Memoir of the Movement.* New York: Simon & Schuster, 1998.

Lieberman, Robbie, and Clarence Lang, eds. *Anticommunism and the African American Freedom Movement: "Another Side of the Story."* New York: Palgrave Macmillan, 2009.

Main, Eleanor C., and Gerard S. Gryski. "George Busbee and the Politics of Consensus." In *Georgia Governors in an Age of Change*, edited by Harold P. Henderson and Gary L. Roberts, 261–78. Athens: University of Goergia Press, 1988.

Mantler, Gordon. *Power to the Poor: Black-Brown Coalition and the Fight for Economic Justice, 1960–1974.* Chapel Hill: University of North Carolina Press, 2013.

Martin, Harold H. *William Berry Hartsfield: Mayor of Atlanta.* Athens: University of Georgia Press, 1978.

Matusow, Allen J. *The Unraveling of America: A History of Liberalism in the 1960s.* New York: Harper & Row, 1984.

McAndrews, Lawrence J. *The Presidents and the Poor: America Battles Poverty, 1964–2017.* Lawrence: University Press of Kansas, 2018.

McCartin, Joseph A. "'Fire the Hell out of Them': Sanitation Workers' Struggles and the Normalization of the Striker Replacement Strategy in the 1970s." *Labor: Studies in Working-Class History of the Americas* 2, no. 3 (2005): 67–92.

McKernan, Signe-Mary, and Caroline Ratcliffe. "Events That Trigger Poverty Entries and Exits." *Social Science Quarterly* 86 (December 2005): 1146–69.

McKnight, Gerald D. *The Last Crusade: Martin Luther King, Jr., the FBI, and the Poor People's Campaign.* Boulder, Colo.: Westview Press, 1998.

Miller, Zane L., and Bruce Tucker. *Changing Plans for America's Inner Cities: Cincinnati's Over-the-Rhine and Twentieth-Century Urbanism.* Columbus: Ohio State University Press, 1998.

Mittelstadt, Jennifer. *From Welfare to Workfare: The Unintended Consequences of Liberal Reform, 1945–1965.* Chapel Hill: University of North Carolina Press, 2005.

Mohl, Raymond A., ed. *Searching for the Sunbelt: Historical Perspectives on a Region.* Knoxville: University of Tennessee Press, 1990.

Nadasen, Premilla. *Rethinking the Welfare Rights Movement.* American Social and Political Movements of the Twentieth Century. New York: Routledge, 2012.

——— . *Welfare Warriors: The Welfare Rights Movement in the United States.* New York: Routledge, 2005.

Nasstrom, Kathryn L. *Everybody's Grandmother and Nobody's Fool: Frances Freeborn Pauley and the Struggle for Social Justice.* Ithaca, N.Y.: Cornell University Press, 2000.

——— . "'This Joint Effort': Women and Community Organizing in Vine City in the 1960s." *Atlanta History* 48, no. 1 (2006): 28–44.

Nickerson, Michelle, and Darren Dochuk, eds. *Sunbelt Rising: The Politics of Space, Place, and Region.* Philadelphia: University of Pennsylvania Press, 2014.

O'Connor, Alice. "Community Action, Urban Reform, and the Fight against Poverty: The Ford Foundation's Gray Areas Program." *Journal of Urban History* 22, no. 5 (July 1996): 586–625.

——— . *Poverty Knowledge: Social Science, Social Policy, and the Poor in Twentieth-Century U.S. History.* Princeton, N.J.: Princeton University Press, 2001.

Orleck, Annelise. "Conclusion: The War on the War on Poverty and American Politics since the 1960s." In *The War on Poverty: A New Grassroots History, 1964–1980,* edited by Annelise Orleck and Lisa Gayle Hazirjian, 463–66. Athens: University of Georgia Press, 2011.

——— . *Storming Caesars Palace: How Black Mothers Fought Their Own War on Poverty.* Boston: Beacon Press, 2005.

Orleck, Annelise, and Lisa Gayle Hazirjian, eds. *The War on Poverty: A New Grassroots History, 1964–1980.* Athens: University of Georgia Press, 2011.

Patton, Randall Lee. "Southern Liberals and the Emergence of a 'New South,' 1938–1950." Ph.D. diss., University of Georgia, 1990.

Perkins, Jason Micah. "The Atlanta Vine City Project, SNCC, and Black Power, 1965–1967." MA thesis, Ohio State University, 2008.

Peterson, Paul E., and Mark C. Rom. *Welfare Magnets: A New Case for a National Standard.* Washington, D.C.: Brookings Institution, 1990.

Phelps, Wesley G. *A People's War on Poverty: Urban Politics and Grassroots Activists in Houston.* Athens: University of Georgia Press, 2014.

Phillips, Kevin. *The Emerging Republican Majority.* New Rochelle, N.Y.: Arlington House, 1969.

Phillips-Fein, Kim. "Business Conservatism on the Shop Floor: Anti-Union Campaigns in the 1950s." *Labor: Studies in Working Class History of the Americas* 7, no. 2 (2010): 9–26.

Pingree, David H., and Rollin M. McCommons. "Organization of the Georgia General Assembly." In *Strengthening the Georgia General Assembly: Research Papers*, 3–27. Athens: Institute of Government, University of Georgia, 1970.

Piven, Frances Fox, and Richard Cloward. "The Weight of the Poor: A Strategy to End Poverty." *Nation*, May 2, 1966.

Piven, Frances Fox, and Richard A. Cloward. *Poor People's Movements: Why They Succeed, How They Fail*. New York: Pantheon Books, 1977.

——. *Regulating the Poor: The Functions of Public Welfare*. New York: Pantheon Books, 1971.

Pope, Andrew. "Living in the Struggle: Black Power, Gay Liberation, and Women's Liberation Movements in Atlanta, 1964–1996." PhD diss., Harvard University, 2018.

Porter, Michael Leroy. "Black Atlanta: An Interdisciplinary Study of Blacks on the East Side of Atlanta, 1890–1930." PhD thesis, Emory University, 1974.

Radcliff, Benjamin, and Martin Saiz. "Race, Turnout, and Public Policy in the American States." *Political Research Quarterly* 48, no. 4 (December 1995): 775–94.

Ralph, James R. *Northern Protest: Martin Luther King, Jr., Chicago, and the Civil Rights Movement*. Cambridge, Mass.: Harvard University Press, 1993.

Rodriguez, Akira Drake. *Diverging Space for Deviants: The Politics of Atlanta's Public Housing*. Athens: University of Georgia Press, 2021.

Rutheiser, Charles. *Imagineering Atlanta: The Poliics of Place in the City of Dreams*. New York: Verso, 1996.

Ryles, Tim C. "A Typology of Functions of the Georgia General Assembly." In *Strengthening the Georgia General Assembly: Research Papers*, 29–42. Athens: Institute of Government, University of Georgia, 1970.

Schank, Katie Marages. "Producing the Projects: Atlanta and the Cultural Creation of Public Housing, 1933–2011." PhD diss., George Washington University, 2016.

Self, Robert O. *All in the Family: The Realignment of American Democracy since the 1960s*. New York: Hill and Wang, 2012.

Shafer, Byron E., and Richard Johnston. *The End of Southern Exceptionalism: Class, Race, and Partisan Change in the Postwar South*. Cambridge, Mass.: Harvard University Press, 2006.

Shapiro, Thomas M. *The Hidden Cost of Being African American: How Wealth Perpetuates Inequality*. Oxford: Oxford University Press, 2004.

Shepard, Kris. *Rationing Justice: Poverty Lawyers and Poor People in the Deep South*. Baton Rouge: Louisiana State University Press, 2007.

Shrider, Robert E. "The Use of Indigenous Persons as Neighborhood Aides by Economic Opportunity Atlanta, Inc." MA thesis, Atlanta University, 1966.

Smith, Joseph. "A Study of the Relationship of Block Leadership to Citizen Participation in Harlem Park." MA thesis, Atlanta University, 1961.

Southern Regional Council. *The South's Economic Future: A Survey of State Development Board Members*. Atlanta: Southern Regional Council, 1978.

Spiers, John H. "'Planning with People': Urban Renewal in Boston's Washington Park, 1950–1970." *Journal of Planning History* 8, no. 3 (2009): 221–47.

Stone, Clarence N. *Economic Growth and Neighborhood Discontent: System Bias in* the Urban Renewal Program of Atlanta. Chapel Hill: University of North Carolina Press, 1976.

——. Regime Politics: Governing Atlanta, 1946–1988. Lawrence: University Press of Kansas, 1989.

Sugrue, Thomas J. Sweet Land of Liberty: The Forgotten Struggle for Civil Rights in the North. New York: Random House, 2008.

Sullivan, Patricia. Days of Hope: Race and Democracy in the New Deal Era. Chapel Hill: University of North Carolina Press, 1996.

Sundquist, James L. Politics and Policy: The Eisenhower, Kennedy, and Johnson Years. Washington, D.C.: Brookings Institution, 1968.

Theoharis, Jeanne, and Komozi Woodard, eds. Groundwork: Local Black Freedom Movements in America. New York: New York University Press, 2005.

Tuck, Stephen G. N. Beyond Atlanta: The Struggle for Racial Equality in Georgia, 1940–1980. Athens: University of Georgia Press, 2001.

Turner, Henry A. "How Pressure Groups Operate." ANNALS of the American Academy of Political and Social Science 319, no. 1 (September 1958): 63–72.

von Hoffman, Alexander. "The Lost History of Urban Renewal." Journal of Urbanism 1, no. 3 (2008): 281–301.

Walz, Thomas H. "Emergence of the Neighborhood Service Center." Public Welfare 27, no. 2 (April 1969): 147–56.

Wells, Rose Marie. "Samuel Woodrow Williams, Catalyst for Black Atlantans, 1946–1970." MA thesis, Atlanta University, 1975.

Wiese, Andrew. Places of Their Own: African American Suburbanization in the Twentieth Century. Historical Studies of Urban America. Chicago: University of Chicago Press, 2004.

Wilkerson, Isabel. The Warmth of Other Suns: The Epic Story of America's Great Migration. New York: Random House, 2010.

Wilkerson, Jessica. To Live Here, You Have to Fight: How Women Led Appalachian Movements for Social Justice. Chicago: University of Illinois Press, 2019.

Williams, Rhonda Y. The Politics of Public Housing: Black Women's Struggles against Urban Inequality. New York: Oxford University Press, 2004.

Windham, Lane. Knocking on Labor's Door: Union Organizing in the 1970s and the Roots of a New Economic Divide. Chapel Hill: University of North Carolina Press, 2017.

Woods, Randall Bennett. Prisoners of Hope: Lyndon B. Johnson, the Great Society, and the Limits of Liberalism. New York: Basic Books, 2016.

Wright, Gavin. Old South, New South: Revolutions in the Southern Economy since the Civil War. Baton Rouge: Louisiana State University Press, 1997.

——. Sharing the Prize: The Economics of the Civil Rights Revolution of the American South. Cambridge, Mass.: Harvard University Press, 2013.

Zeitz, Joshua. Building the Great Society: Inside Lyndon Johnson's White House. New York: Penguin Books, 2018.

Zelizer, Julian E. The Fierce Urgency of Now: Lyndon Johnson, Congress, and the Battle for the Great Society. New York: Penguin Books, 2015.

Butler Street, 31
Butler Street YMCA, 23, 27, 56, 223n78
Buttermilk Bottom, 17–18, 29, 31, 200

Cabbagetown, 17, 19
CACUR (Citizen Advisory Committee on Urban Renewal), 29, 30–31, 33–34, 41
Caldwell, Erskine, 76
Calhoun, John H., 59, 62–63, 64
Calloway, William L., 59, 95, 97–98
Capital Homes, 166
CAPs. *See* community action programs; Economic Opportunity Atlanta
Carmichael, Stokely: Atlanta Project closed by, 92; Dixie Hills unrest and, 116, 117; SCLC criticized by, 82; Summerhill unrest and, 110, 111, 112
Carter, Jimmy, 204
Carver Homes (Carver Community Apartments), 23, 24, 167, 247n83
Catholic Worker, 74–75
CCA. *See* Committee of Concerned Agencies
CCAA. *See* Community Council of the Atlanta Area
CCAC (Citizens Central Advisory Council), 101, 102, 104, 105
Cha-Jua, Sundiata Keita, 210n18
Children's Center of Metropolitan Atlanta, Inc., 47
"Christmas bonus" campaign, 143
Citizen Advisory Committee on Urban Renewal (CACUR), 29, 30–31, 33–34, 41
citizen participation: "maximum feasible participation" and, 11, 44, 52, 58, 61, 66, 92, 95, 96–101, 108, 215n59, 223n81, 225n99; of poor in EOA, 58, 60–62, 66, 96–101, 102, 103–5, 106, 107, 109, 117, 118, 215n59, 231n18, 232n25, 232n27, 233n46; in urban renewal, 16, 28, 29, 34, 41, 199, 200, 215n59, 217n84; in War on Poverty, 55–62, 215n56
Citizens Central Advisory Council (CCAC), 101, 102, 104, 105
citizens neighborhood advisory councils (CNACs), 101, 102, 104, 105
civic councils (civic leagues), 5, 11, 16, 21, 23–27, 214n32; EOA and, 105, 106, 109; Georgia Avenue/Pryor Street, 35, 106; Peoplestown, 113–14; Scott's Crossing, 63; SNCC and, 4, 35–41; South Atlanta, 16, 23–25, 37, 38, 39, 214n33; Summerhill, 111

Civil Rights Acts (1964), 67, 122, 129–30, 246n46
civil rights movement, 22, 32, 51, 55, 67, 211n19; disruption versus negotiation in, 36; economic focus of, 129; establishment leaders of, 6, 36, 41, 56, 59, 60, 93, 96, 102, 118, 160, 202; long, 4, 210–11n18; in shift toward local focus, 78; white resistance to, 40
civil rights unionism, 136, 138–39, 153, 229n75, 240n89
Civil War, 17
Clark University, 23, 27
Clayton, Xernona, 164
Clement, Rufus E., 22, 56, 58
Cloward, Richard, 4, 250n23
CNACs (citizens neighborhood advisory councils), 101, 102, 104, 105
Cobb, James, 203
Cochran, J. Otis, 106, 115–16, 227n30, 227n32; background of, 67; ESH created by, 69; playground creation and, 71; Summit criticized by, 102
Cochrane, W. R., 56, 59
Colbert, C. D., 35, 102, 106
Coleman, Clarence D., 56, 160
Collins, Marcus, 195
Columbians, 26
Commission on Civil Rights, U.S., 32
Committee of Concerned Agencies (CCA), 180–87; name change of, 187–90. *See also* Georgia Poverty Rights Organization
Common Cause, 183
communism, 115, 235n100
community action programs (CAPs), 5, 44, 52, 157; Republicans on, 115; state control of, 51. *See also* Economic Opportunity Atlanta
community centers. *See* neighborhood centers
Community Council of the Atlanta Area (CCAA), 45–49, 50, 51, 157, 200, 219n10, 220n21, 220–21nn31–32; budget of, 49; formation of, 44, 45–46, 65; legal aid and, 128; unusual structure of, 48; War on Poverty and, 51–52, 53, 54, 56, 57, 58
Community Improvement Program, 19
community organizing, 67, 69, 73, 74, 82, 92; materials lacking for, 70
Community Relations Commission (CRC), 113–14, 115, 116, 166, 236n116
Community Research Associates, 219n11
Concerned Citizens of East Lake, 169